FROM BEACHHEAD
TO BRITTANY

FROM BEACHHEAD TO BRITTANY

The 29th Infantry Division at Brest, August–September 1944

Joseph Balkoski

STACKPOLE BOOKS

Copyright © 2008 by Joseph Balkoski

Published by
STACKPOLE BOOKS
5067 Ritter Road
Mechanicsburg, PA 17055
www.stackpolebooks.com

All rights reserved, including the right to reproduce this book or portions thereof in any form or by any means, electronic or mechanical, including photocopying, recording, or by any information storage and retrieval system, without permission in writing from the publisher. All inquiries should be addressed to Stackpole Books, 5067 Ritter Road, Mechanicsburg, Pennsylvania 17055.

All photos courtesy of the 29th Division Archives, Maryland National Guard Joint Force Headquarters, Fifth Regiment Armory, 29th Division St., Baltimore, Maryland

Printed in the United States of America

10 9 8 7 6 5 4 3 2 1

FIRST EDITION

Library of Congress Cataloging-in-Publication Data

Balkoski, Joseph.
  From beachhead to Brittany : the 29th Infantry Division at Brest, August–September 1944 / Joseph Balkoski. — 1st ed.
      p. cm.
   Includes bibliographical references and index.
   ISBN-13: 978-0-8117-0325-3
   ISBN-10: 0-8117-0325-8
   1. Brest, Battle of, Brest, France, 1944. 2. United States. Army. Infantry Division, 29th—History. 3. World War, 1939–1945—Regimental histories—United States. 4. Brest (France)—History, Military. I. Title.

D762.B7B35 2008
940.54'214112—dc22

2007043199

For
Joseph H. Ewing
Company G, 175th Infantry, 29th Infantry Division
1944–1945

*A formidable soldier, eminent scholar, and devoted friend
who showed the way*

Contents

	List of Maps	ix
	Preface	xi
ONE	Brittany	1
TWO	Fortress Brest	33
THREE	The Key to the Whole Thing	63
FOUR	Holding Nothing Back	99
FIVE	Sergeant Hallman	139
SIX	They Also Served	187
SEVEN	Brestgrad	217
EIGHT	Giving Them the Works	251
NINE	The Tragedy Is Complete	279
TEN	Here Are Our Credentials	313
	Appendices	349
	References	363
	Bibliography	387
	Index	391

Maps

1.	Northwest Europe	4
2.	From Normandy to Brittany	10
3.	The Environs of Brest	21
4.	29th Division: August 25–27, 1944	36
5.	1/116 Infantry at Keriolet: August 27, 1944	46
6.	Task Force Sugar: August 25–30, 1944	55
7.	29th Division: Hill 103 and La Trinité, August 28–30, 1944	68
8.	115th Infantry: August 28–September 5, 1944	94
9.	175th Infantry: Hill 103, September 1–6, 1944	103
10.	116th Infantry and 5th Rangers: La Trinité and the Coastal Forts, September 1–6, 1944	117
11.	115th Infantry: September 6–9, 1944	141
12.	2/115th Infantry: Kerrognant, September 8, 1944	150
13.	29th Division: September 8–12, 1944	162
14.	115th and 175th Infantry: September 12–13, 1944	175
15.	Task Force Sugar: August 30–September 10, 1944	192
16.	29th Division and 5th Rangers: September 14, 1944	219

Maps continued

17.	The assault on Ft. Montbarey: September 14, 1944	229
18.	115th and 116th Infantry: September 15–16, 1944	243
19.	115th Infantry and 5th Rangers: September 15–17, 1944	259
20.	116th and 175th Infantry: September 15–17, 1944	271
21.	The Surrender: September 18, 1944	285
22.	29th Division Rest Areas: September 19–24, 1944	300
23.	European Theater of Operations Ports	324

Preface
29, Let's Go!

1. AN ESSENTIAL OBJECTIVE

It was a place the doughboys would never forget. Starting in 1917, they poured in by the hundreds of thousands, marching up the hill to Pontenazen Barracks and steeling themselves for the hazards of the trenches. In much more cheerful frames of mind, they flowed back to the same barracks in 1919 and waited for the blissful trip home to the States. Both going and coming, however, they endured interminable delays, during which the only antidote to boredom was to raise a little hell. In doing so, they discovered this curious foreign city with its hardy seafaring people who took special pride in their ancient Celtic roots and perhaps even greater pride in their nonconformity with traditional French culture. The Yanks came to know the city's dingy harborside, its steep hills, its stunning bluffs overlooking the sea, the impressively deep ravine of the Penfeld River, and above all its incessant rain and pervasive mud.

The doughboys would indeed remember this great French port city of Brest, but few of them would do so with affection. The soldier responsible for getting the troops home after the armistice, Lt. Gen. James Harbord, recalled, "The men were restless, which was quite understandable. They took it out on the rain and the mud, and sometimes on the poor MPs. They griped healthily—and they were a problem." During one of those depressing waits to get out of Brest, Gen. Smedley Butler, a legendary U.S. Marine with two Medals of Honor on his chest, strode down to the harbor with hordes of disheartened troops and—against all orders—snatched thousands of wooden planks, known as "duckboards," stored by U.S. Army quartermasters for eventual use in the trenches. As horrified MPs watched, the troops hauled the boards up Brest's hills and then, four miles inland, attempted to solve the mud problem in the AEF's inundated camp sites once and for all. "It lifted morale," Harbord recalled. "And [Butler] was known thereafter—but always beyond his hearing—as 'General Duckboard.'"

Brest was one of those places whose reputation swelled considerably during wartime. Centuries of intermittent conflict between France and Britain had instilled in both nations' sailors the military significance of Brest's mighty harbor. With a spacious anchorage that could hold countless warships, and a highly defensible rocky coast lining the harbor entrance, it was the perfect home port for the French Navy's Atlantic fleet. Generations of British sailors during the seventeenth, eighteenth, and nineteenth centuries experienced tedious blockade duty just outside Brest, striving to keep French men-of-war and privateers from escaping into the Atlantic. Meanwhile, corresponding generations of French sailors endeavored with equal fervor to break the blockade and wreak havoc on Britain's lifeblood, its merchant fleet.

However, shifting European alliances wholly transformed the perception of Brest in early twentieth-century military circles. With Britain and France newly united against the emerging ambitions of Germany, Brest was no longer a focal point in the struggle for European naval supremacy. Instead, in 1917 it assumed a much more pedestrian function as the major entry point into France during the Great War for Pershing's AEF, a purpose for which it was entirely suited since it is one of the closest ports in continental Europe to the United States.

Until World War II, Brest had never suffered extensive damage at the hands of a foreign power. Upon the Nazis' conquest of France in June 1940, however, that physical security vanished in an instant—and Brest would never be the same again. To the city's unhappy residents, it must have been supremely paradoxical that much of the carnage inflicted upon their homes over the next four years, which destroyed the city almost in its entirety, was carried out not by the hated Nazi conquerors, but by their would-be liberators, as Allied air power strove to devastate the harbor and dockside facilities so completely that deadly German U-boats could not use Brest as a safe haven. Despite the Allies' monumental effort to fulfill that task, German submarines continued to dock and replenish in Brest in comparative safety until just a few days before the Americans liberated the city in September 1944.

The act of liberation brought about a month-long frenzy of ruin so terrible that everything preceding it seemed puny in comparison. When it was over, and the Americans finally took the city, the distressed residents of Brest had no worldly possessions, no homes to which they could return, and no apparent means of sustenance. If this was liberation, it certainly was cruel; even so, the despicable Nazis were gone, and as difficult as it was to imagine, their departure signaled an infinitely brighter future.

The siege of Brest was just a small slice of the Allies' campaign to liberate western Europe, but regrettably, it is one that has been overshadowed by the much more exhilarating tale of the Anglo-American blitzkrieg across France, that mad dash from Normandy into Paris and then all the way to the frontiers of Germany. When the Germans finally surrendered Brest, the war had literally bypassed it, as the main battlefront was by then located 500 miles away. General Eisenhower eventually decided to disregard it completely, never putting its harbor and impressive port facilities to use. If the siege of Brest has permeated the history of World War II at all, it is primarily because of the tragic irony that the U.S. Army committed 75,000 men to its capture, of whom 10,000 became casualties. By the end of the war in Europe, Brest was a dead city—and not a single Allied troopship or supply vessel had docked there.

But the apparently purposeless campaign to capture Brest in September 1944 obscures a much more complex story, one that history has overlooked. Ultimately, Brest may not have contributed to Allied victory in Europe, but in truth, only days before its liberation, it was still high on Eisenhower's list of military priorities. To understand why, one must look back to the vital function Brest had provided for the AEF in World War I. In 1944 several generals in the highest reaches of the U.S. Army were especially keen to evict the German occupiers of Brest because they wanted to reinitiate the steady stream of men and materiel that had flowed so prodigiously from the United States directly to that city in 1917. If that goal could be achieved, a war-weary Germany could never hope to stand against the fresh hordes of GIs flooding northwest Europe, a force of millions of men who had been training incessantly in the States for a year or more, preparing to join the pivotal battle of the war.

Accordingly, those American and British military men who in 1943 planned the western Allies' paramount military undertaking of World War II, Operation Overlord, defined Brest from the start as an essential Allied objective. If Overlord's ultimate aim of liberating western Europe and bringing down the Nazi regime was to be achieved, its opening phase, the monumental June 1944 D-Day invasion of Normandy, must be quickly followed up with a buildup of men and materiel on an unprecedented scale. A logistical effort of such magnitude could occur only if the Anglo-American armies managed to secure ports that would be capable of handling the massive inflow. Such an impressive natural harbor as Brest was of course coveted by the Allied top brass, especially as it was situated little more than 200 miles from the Normandy invasion beaches. If Overlord developed according to plan, the Allies should capture Brest fewer than two months after D-Day.

However, the famous dictum that no military plan survives first contact with the enemy certainly held true in 1944, and even such a meticulously designed scheme as Overlord, with its field orders as thick as a Manhattan telephone book, crumbled the moment the Germans started shooting back. But even as Overlord fell more and more behind schedule, Ike and his top military chiefs never wavered: they still wanted Brest, right down to the moment it was finally liberated.

Then they decided they didn't want it anymore.

2. BLUE AND GRAY DIVISION, REDUX

This book tells the story of the liberation of Brest from the perspective of the 29th Infantry Division. The "Blue and Gray" Division originated in 1917, but its World War II incarnation dated from February 3, 1941, when President Roosevelt called its constituent units from the Maryland, Virginia, and District of Columbia National Guards into federal service for a period of one year. By the time the 29th Division reached Brest, that one-year period had swelled to more than three, and more than 12,000 men from its normal complement of 14,000 had became casualties.

Readers familiar with the tribulations and exploits of the 29th Infantry Division from England to Omaha Beach, followed by the advance deep into Normandy as far as St. Lô and Vire, will find an entirely different division in this volume than the one related in my earlier book, *Beyond the Beachhead: The 29th Infantry Division in Normandy*. The vast casualties suffered by the 29th Division from D-Day to the Normandy breakout had caused equal numbers of replacements to flow into the division like a torrent; by the time the 29th's role in the Normandy campaign mercifully came to an end after ten weeks of unceasing and brutal combat, each of its twenty-seven rifle companies had experienced a near-total turnover of personnel. Gone from the rolls of Blue and Gray infantry units were most of the savvy NCOs who had military experience dating to the National Guard's two-week summer camps before the war; most of the company-grade officers; and most of the privates and PFCs who had endured the impossibly tough training in England in preparation for the D-Day invasion.

One could hardly believe a military unit that had undergone such a rough initiation to combat could still function, but function it did. When the 29th Division set forth from Normandy to a new battleground in far-off Brittany, where a new mission awaited at Brest, there were many who thought the 29th was a better military unit than it had ever been before. True, the division was filled with new and untested men, but those soldiers who generated the plans and paperwork that made the division operate effectively—from rear-area division headquarters down to lowly battalion command posts at the front—had learned the hard lessons of war in Normandy and were much better soldiers for it. They had learned the patterns of the enemy's behavior; how to apply supporting weapons to the fight, particularly artillery, with deadly precision; how to care for their wounded; and above all that they could beat the skillful enemy with a style of warfare that was distinctively American.

The 29th Division's commanding general since July 1943, Maj. Gen. Charles Gerhardt, had ensured that a more subtle divisional trait acquired during the interminable training period in England would stick with the 29ers no matter how new they were to the division. This was the 29th Division's indomitable spirit, an unshakable brotherhood that had been the product of exceptionally rigorous training, practiced without letting up until that decisive moment when, for the first time in World War II, the division would enter combat on Omaha Beach on D-Day.

No matter how that battle turned out, no one could ever accuse 29th Division soldiers of being unready. For years they had practiced until there was nothing new to learn—and then they started practicing all over again: twenty-five mile hikes through the moors; amphibious training at the Assault Training Center; live-fire assault exercises at Slapton Sands; and anything else Gerhardt could concoct to prepare his beloved division for its moment in the sun.

From those tests of physical endurance emerged an attitude, almost wholly instilled by the commanding general, that the 29th Division was something special, something all 29ers should be proud of—not just while in uniform, but later as well, when they would slip off those uniforms and merge back into American society after the war. Gerhardt, a fiercely self-confident West Pointer and cavalryman of the old school, possessed the willpower of Napoleon, and like it or not, all 29ers had to live by his rules. Those who ignored them did so at their peril. The general's cardinal canon, which even cynical and lackadaisical soldiers soon followed, was that a 29th Division soldier must always look and act like a soldier. He must do this by displaying textbook military courtesy, taking care of his appearance and uniform, and observing all the Army's rules of hygiene. The 29ers soon observed that any GI with a growth of beard, a messy uniform, or who slouched with his hands in his pockets could not possibly be in the 29th Division.

On Omaha Beach, however, the 29ers learned that the enemy was just as ready to fight as they were, maybe even more so. That lesson was corroborated by ten weeks of frightful combat in Normandy. But somehow, the unique character of the 29th Division survived that turmoil, passed from veteran soldier to fresh replacement in a never-ending cycle of violence. In that kind of environment, a private with only a week or two in the line might suddenly find himself with three stripes on his sleeve—a new sergeant, to whom a handful of fresh rookies looked for guidance on a battlefield where one false move could lead to instant death. For better or worse, there was nothing to do in that situation except to teach the replacements what the new NCO himself had been taught a few weeks in the past, perhaps by a veteran of Omaha Beach: to do things the way 29th Division soldiers had always done them. Amid so much carnage, such trivialities seemed pointless and futile, but eventually no one could deny that the 29th Division was indeed special—and if those trivialities contributed to it specialness, they were worth it.

D-Day and the battle of the hedgerows in Normandy were over. The 29th Infantry Division was headed for Brest to capture the port so valued by Overlord planners.

This would be the 29th Division's second trip to Brest, for it had passed through there in July 1918 on its way to the trenches in the closing months of World War I. But there was a crucial difference between the Brest of 1918 and the Brest of 1944. The World War I version of the 29th Division had disembarked from its troopships and marched up Brest's precipitous harborside hills to Pontenazen Barracks as the happy Bretons sang in broken English, "Hail, hail, the gang's all here!"

If the 29ers hoped to reach Brest's harborside in 1944, they were going to have to fight a resolute enemy to get there.

ONE

Brittany

1. NEXT STOP: BERLIN?
The front line had ceased to exist, and every Allied fighting man in Normandy was presently fixated by one momentous contemplation: It won't take long to finish it now. Recently, one of Hitler's own insiders had endeavored to assassinate him, thereby hoping to avert the ruinous destiny toward which Germany was relentlessly being led by the führer. That effort had failed, but still those Allied soldiers who had observed the current condition of the German Army in Normandy could readily perceive that Germany's calamitous end was indeed imminent. General Eisenhower's top-secret intelligence summary for August 19, 1944, had stated that belief bluntly: "The enemy has lost the war."

German soldiers, whom in the recent past Allied troops had respected as formidable and highly motivated warriors, were streaming out of Normandy in a form that could only be described as a mob, ditching all their military paraphernalia and abandoning hundreds of burning tanks and trucks in a tableau that Ike noted "could only be described by Dante." If this was victory, it was undeniably sweet.

The GIs of the U.S. Army's 29th Infantry Division had been involved in the Normandy fighting from the beginning, and to prove it, they had more than 12,000 casualties—including 2,300 dead—in little more than two months in the line. If any outfit deserved to be in on the kill in

1

Normandy, it was the 29th Division, but that was an honor its exhausted members would gladly forego.

The date was August 21, 1944, and the 29ers had been out of the line for four glorious days. It was amazing how a soldier's state of mind could be healed by a few days out of earshot of German guns. A GI could never get used to the heart-stopping jolt triggered by the thunderous blast of a nearby enemy shell or the ripping burst of a machine gun, and he had seen the enemy kill so many comrades with those weapons that it was easy for him to draw the depressing conclusion that sooner or later he too would become a statistic. In a rear-area rest camp, however, decent food, hot showers, new uniforms, and USO shows with Hollywood stars again made life worth living. Letters from home could be read and reread with the attention they deserved and replied to with as much sentiment and detail as the censor's knife would allow. Above all, after perusing the clever division newsletter, *29 Let's Go*, with its blaring headlines depicting the steady decline of the Nazis in Normandy, not a single 29er could harbor any doubt that his side was going to win the war—and soon. The latest news proclaimed that in Paris the French Resistance had risen against the hated German occupiers and that Allied troops would arrive within a few days to complete the job. After four years of Nazi occupation, Paris's liberation would surely trigger a celebration the world would not forget. Would the Germans recover? Or would the Allies' next stop be Berlin?

Whatever the answer to those questions, the war was shifting to new locales far beyond Normandy and was about to drag the 29th Division with it. Regrettably, within the next week the exhilarating confidence of the Normandy triumph would vanish as the surprised 29ers discovered that the war was far from over. Evidently, those enemy soldiers who had avoided death or capture when the Allies' pincers snapped shut in Normandy were just as resolute as ever and were willing to die for their führer—as long as they took the lives of some good Americans with them. The 29ers were about to learn that there would be a hard fight ahead after all.

On August 21 the top U.S. Army field commander in Normandy, Lt. Gen. Omar Bradley, ordered the 29th Division to proceed with all possible speed to Brittany, that ancient Celtic land protruding into the Atlantic, pointing like an extended index finger toward the New World. The 29ers could not fail to notice that the journey to Brittany would carry them exactly in the opposite direction from Berlin, and even the greenest 29th Division replacement fresh from the States could comprehend that if there were German soldiers in Brittany, they were about to be cut off from their fatherland. They might nevertheless put up a stiff fight, but the inviolable principles of military operations would determine their fate. Sooner or later they would run out of food and bullets, and then they must submit. If the 29ers still had a role to fulfill in this war, it would surely be much more desirable to fight surrounded German soldiers in Brittany than those defending their homeland on the Rhine River or in Berlin.

But only time would tell whether the 29th Division's next job would be as tough as Normandy or the proverbial piece of cake that all 29ers yearned for.

2. TAKE BREST!

Military history proves that no general can succeed in war unless he wholly comprehends the intricate science of military logistics, for even the toughest soldiers will fail if they are not well armed and well fed. General Bradley adhered to that cardinal principle when he ordered the 29th Division to move into Brittany posthaste. At Brittany's far western tip lay the port of Brest, one of France's most impressive natural harbors, and if Bradley's soldiers needed to be armed and fed in the future, Brest would be a logical place for that war materiel to be delivered

According to General Eisenhower's Overlord plan for the invasion of northwest Europe, formulated in early 1944, Brest should have been under Allied control by August 1, 1944, fully operational and actively receiving thousands of troops and tons of supplies shipped directly to France from the United States—the identical purpose Brest had served in World War I for General Pershing's American Expeditionary Force. The fact that Brest was still under German control in late August 1944 had triggered alarm among Ike's staff, since without Brest many logisticians found it difficult to envision how they could provide the vast amount of supplies that would be required to support a forceful Allied offensive beyond Paris to the Rhine River and into the heart of Germany in the summer and fall of 1944. True, any military operation as immense as Overlord needed to be sufficiently flexible to adapt to shifting circumstances, but for the moment Ike and Bradley could not perceive any decent alternatives that would reduce or eliminate the Allies' need for Brest.

Bradley's intelligence officers had at first suggested that the job of taking Brest would not be too difficult. Reports indicated that not many Germans were deployed in Brittany, and those who were present were reportedly demoralized and poorly equipped and had been surprised by the abruptness of the American breakout from Normandy. There was solid evidence that the enemy had retained a first-class *Fallschirmjäger* (para-

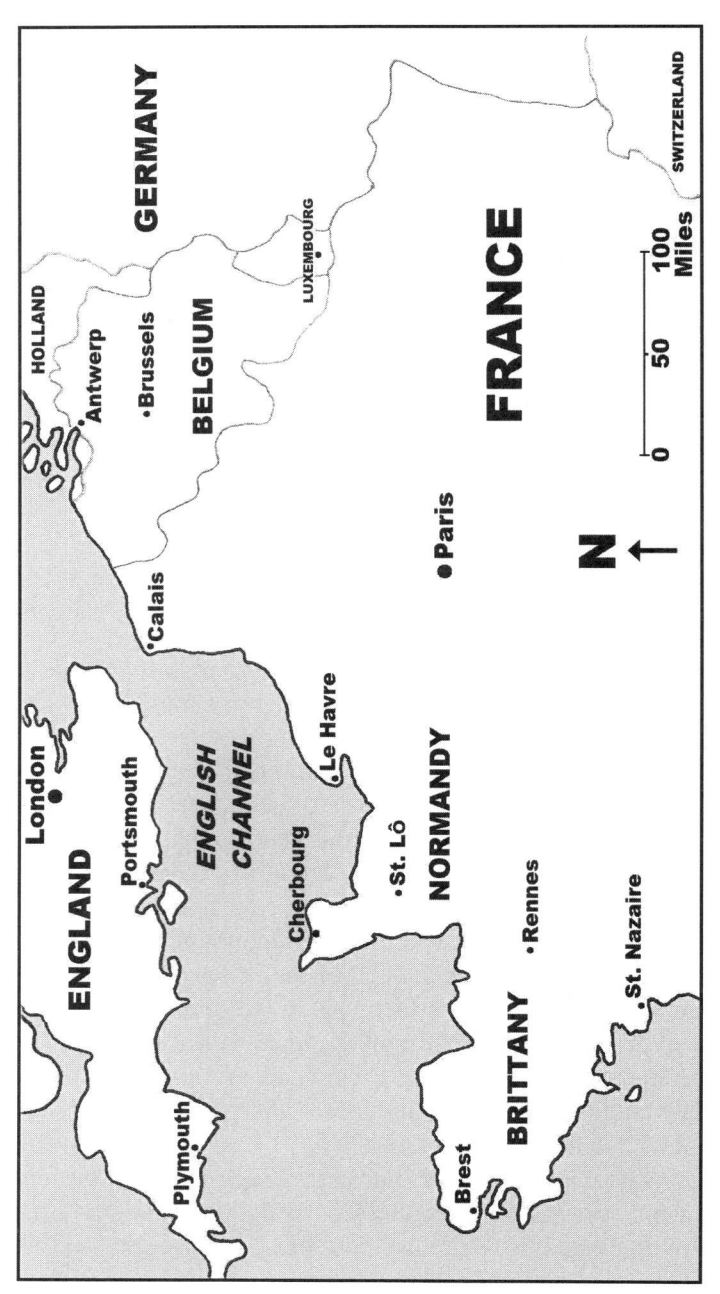

Northwest Europe

chute) division in Brittany, but it apparently was moving toward the Normandy front rather than retreating into the Brest fortifications.

Senior American generals had initially professed supreme confidence that Brest could be seized before the Germans could man its defenses adequately. On August 1 the audacious commander of the U.S. Third Army, Lt. Gen. George S. Patton, had issued a direct order to Maj. Gen. Robert Grow of the 6th Armored Division: "Take Brest." This was a daunting challenge, as Brest was more than 200 miles away through territory that not a single Allied soldier had so far entered during the campaign, and up until that time Allied movements of more than a few miles per day had been almost unheard of. Nevertheless, Grow's outfit was thoroughly trained to carry out lightning thrusts of this kind, and its commander—an ex-cavalryman, like Patton—was eager to demonstrate that his men were fully capable of turning the innovative method of warfare known as blitzkrieg upon its originators in an even more deadly form.

Patton had fully expected that the 6th Armored Division could do the job, and on August 1, displaying the characteristic bravado that habitually got him into trouble, he blurted to Grow that he had laid a wager of five British pounds with his insufferable rival, Gen. Sir Bernard Montgomery, that the 6th Armored could be in Brest by August 5, four days hence. Grow's men did not reach the Brest environs until August 7; much to Patton's chagrin, Monty would be five pounds wealthier. Even so, after the Germans had contained the Allies in Normandy for nearly eight weeks, the 6th Armored Division's lightning move gained countless headlines in the civilian and military press. But Grow's blitzkrieg would signify nothing unless he could push his men just a few more miles from the environs of the city, through the enemy's formidable defenses, directly into Brest proper—and this the enemy was resolved that he would not do.

The German commander in Brest, Col. Hans von der Mosel, had contemptuously rejected a surrender demand by Grow on August 8, so the 6th Armored had to attempt to take the city by storm. Unhappily for Grow, the Germans had far more defenders than he expected, and furthermore, the execution of a frontal assault against fixed enemy fortifications was unquestionably not the kind of mission for which a U.S. Army armored division was designed. It had less than one-third the infantry strength of a standard American infantry division, and against an unbroken cordon of German defenses, the armored division's prized mobility would be of no value. In a roughly analogous situation in June, when the Americans made a massive effort to seize the port of Cherbourg in Normandy, Bradley had to allocate three infantry divisions to do the job, and it took them a week of extremely hard fighting to do it. At Brest, the task had appeared just as arduous, and asking a single armored division to carry it out risked disaster.

Grow's predicament had been worsened by an erroneous intelligence report broadcast to Patton by a Third Army reconnaissance outfit on August 6: "Brest is ours." With all the positive news that had burst forth from the Allied armies lately, the report seemed entirely plausible, but it was of course untrue. Even worse, Grow had little chance of making it come true. That disheartening reality finally hit home on August 12 when Grow received orders to abandon his effort to take Brest and move east, leaving only a small containing force to keep an eye on the German garrison, which had swelled with the arrival of the first-class parachute division that Allied intelligence had identified in Brittany several weeks earlier.

If the Americans still wanted Brest, they were going to have to fight hard for it, and Bradley would have to find one or more outfits other than Grow's to take up that difficult job.

3. A QUESTION OF STRATEGY

Back in Normandy, the members of the 29th Division observed the developments in Brittany with indifference. After all, the lead headline in the *29 Let's Go* newsletter had recently proclaimed "Yanks in Brest!" and even if that detail turned out to be wholly incorrect, who cared? The war was obviously going to be decided on the main battle front, far from Brittany, and since the Allies were nearing Paris and the German Army in Normandy had been smashed, Brest was someone else's concern. The 29th Division had contributed manifestly to the destruction of that enemy army, and when the 29ers pulled into their rest camps on August 16 and 17, 1944, the only thing on their minds had been relaxation—a glorious period of tranquility, long overdue, for which the worn-out combat veterans had yearned for months. It was a shame that so many good 29ers had recently been buried deep in the Norman soil and had not lived to soak up this blissful serenity.

The first hint that something was amiss turned up when the 2nd Infantry Division, the 29th's long-time fighting partner at St. Lô and Vire, was suddenly pulled out of its nearby bivouac and packed into hundreds of U.S. Army trucks to begin a lengthy journey to Brittany. Soldiers' scuttlebutt spread the word that its destination would be Brest, where it would join Grow's covering force from the 6th Armored Division and Maj. Gen. Donald Stroh's 8th Infantry Division. With such a substantial body of troops, Bradley was obviously resolved to crush the resolute German defenders of Brest ruthlessly and with all possible speed. But the recent Cherbourg experience had ingrained in Bradley the need to apply crushing power when confronting German troops entrenched in sturdy static defenses, and in his view he needed at least three infantry divisions to complete the job—the same number he had committed at Cherbourg.

The final addition to that trio would be the 29th Division, which Bradley called back into the war after a rest of only five days. On August 21 the men of the Blue and Gray would head for Brest to join what promised to be a violent and swift campaign that could have only one end: the annihilation or capture of the entire German garrison. Lamentably, what the 29ers were about to endure would undeniably be violent—but certainly not swift—and ironically, hundreds of men who had just scrutinized the blaring "Yanks in Brest!" headline in the *29 Let's Go* newsletter would die in the struggle to ensure that that premature pronouncement came true.

The 29th Division would gain no momentous headlines of that kind in the Brest backwater because by then the most crucial events in the European theater would be occurring hundreds of miles away. Consequently, the effort to capture Brest would be almost forgotten by history, a hurtful oversight to the men who had stormed Omaha Beach on D-Day, taken St. Lô six weeks later, and would ultimately lose 3,000 comrades to death and wounds over the next month in Brittany. The GIs who would survive the Brest campaign, however, could never forget that campaign because it was among the toughest fighting that the 29th Division was subjected to throughout World War II.

To 29er veterans who witnessed the intensity of the struggle for Brest, it was disheartening to hear the inference by historians half a century after the event that Bradley's decision to commit three of the U.S Army's twenty-two available divisions in France to seize Brest—when the war in all likelihood would be decided elsewhere—was a critical mistake. In 1995 one prominent historian labeled the American effort in Brittany as "a huge military embarrassment to the Allies" and castigated Bradley for his "failure" of generalship and "lack of resolve" in challenging an "outdated" Overlord plan. That kind of second-guessing, however, entirely misses the point that the seizure of Brest was a fundamental pillar of the Overlord plan for the liberation of western Europe, a scheme that went far beyond Bradley's realm as commander of a single army group.

In a highly volatile military environment, Bradley had no crystal ball to foretell the military situation in France a week or month in the future.

The only factors on which he could base his decision to shift three infantry divisions to Brest with all possible speed were the operational situation in Normandy in mid-August 1944 and his responsibility to fulfill directives from his superior, General Eisenhower. Ike had provided not the slightest hint to Bradley that the liberation of Brest was no longer a priority according to the outlook of supreme headquarters. Indeed, on August 7 Eisenhower wrote to his boss, U.S. Army Chief of Staff George C. Marshall, detailing three major goals in the ongoing campaign in France, one of which was "to secure the Brittany ports quickly." The following day Marshall cabled Ike and was in complete agreement, pointing out that the swift seizure of Brest would allow the U.S. Army to speed up its movement of fresh divisions from the States to the European theater by conveying them directly to France rather than through English ports first. Ike concurred, an attitude he emphasized when he wrote to Montgomery on August 19: "We are promised greatly accelerated shipments of American divisions directly from the U.S., and it is mandatory that we capture and prepare ports and communications to receive them."

That notion certainly filtered down to Bradley, who largely had no choice in the matter: Brest must be taken as a matter of the highest priority. True, as Ike pointed out to Monty in his August 19 letter, the Allies' main concern was "the destruction of the remaining enemy forces on our front," but Bradley's decision to commit only three American divisions—less than one-seventh of his combat outfits present in the theater—to the Brest venture detracted very little from Eisenhower's main goal. In truth, two of those divisions—the 2nd and 29th—were in rest camps when Bradley ordered them to Brest in mid-August because by then they no longer could fit into the front lines in Normandy. Finally, Bradley well understood that speed was essential. In the grand scheme of Operation Overlord, the liberation of Brest was overdue. To correct that problem, Bradley intended to crush the German defenders of Brest with overwhelming force, just as he had done at Cherbourg. Given the mood of the time, Bradley's judgments with regard to Brest can by no stretch of the imagination be categorized as a "failure" of generalship, accompanied by a "lack of resolve." He did what he knew he had to do, and at the moment he did it, there was not a single voice of dissent.

4. GET STARTED NOW

And so it would be Brest. To reach that place, the 29th Division's commanding general, Maj. Gen. Charles Hunter Gerhardt Jr., would be obligated to move 14,000 men and all their heavy equipment more than 200 miles with little more than a day's lead time for his staff to make thorough arrangements. His division would have to move out on August 21 and be in position for a concerted attack on Brest along with the 2nd and 8th Divisions by the morning of August 23. To reach their objective on time, Gerhardt's truck convoys would have to navigate a complicated and meandering route over unfamiliar roads, none of which could be likened to an American highway, traversing territory that only recently had been occupied by the enemy and had not been totally secured. Further, there was always the danger of enemy air attack—a remote possibility, but one that defenseless truck units always feared.

This was unquestionably a thorny undertaking, one that only a highly competent and experienced staff could work out. The move was further complicated by the fact that the 29th was an infantry division whose soldiers normally had to march on foot to reach their destination. But there was certainly no time for that now: U.S. First Army would have to provide the 29th Division with six quartermaster truck companies straight away, increasing the division's inadequate complement of trucks by 300. Each of these celebrated General Motors "deuce and a half" trucks could carry twenty-five troops, and upon those trucks' arrival at the 29th Division's rest camps in Normandy, not a single 29er would have to walk to Brest. For this welcome support, the grateful infantrymen could thank America's vast vehicle production lines, which by the end of World War II would churn out 800,000 trucks of this type—a figure that surely filled the German architects of blitzkrieg with envy.

That the U.S. Army had by the summer of 1944 matured into a first-class military organization, far superior to its opponents in mobility, was proven by the 29th Division's arrival near Brest approximately thirty-six hours after its departure from Normandy, intact and ready to join in an advance against the German defenses the following day. Countless training maneuvers, both in the States and in England, had obviously yielded considerable dividends to the men who had made this relocation work smoothly.

As usual the 29th Division Reconnaissance Troop, commanded by Capt. Edward Jones, led the way. With its twenty-five jeeps and thirteen M-8 Greyhound armored cars, this 155-man outfit made good time. To avoid the Germans who 29th Division intelligence reports had indicated were still lingering along the north coast of Brittany, Jones's men followed an inland route, passing through remote villages with distinctive—and unpronounceable—Breton names such as Médréac, Plouguernevel, Huelgoat, and Landivisiau. Jones recalled, "Our maps were not the best; but we

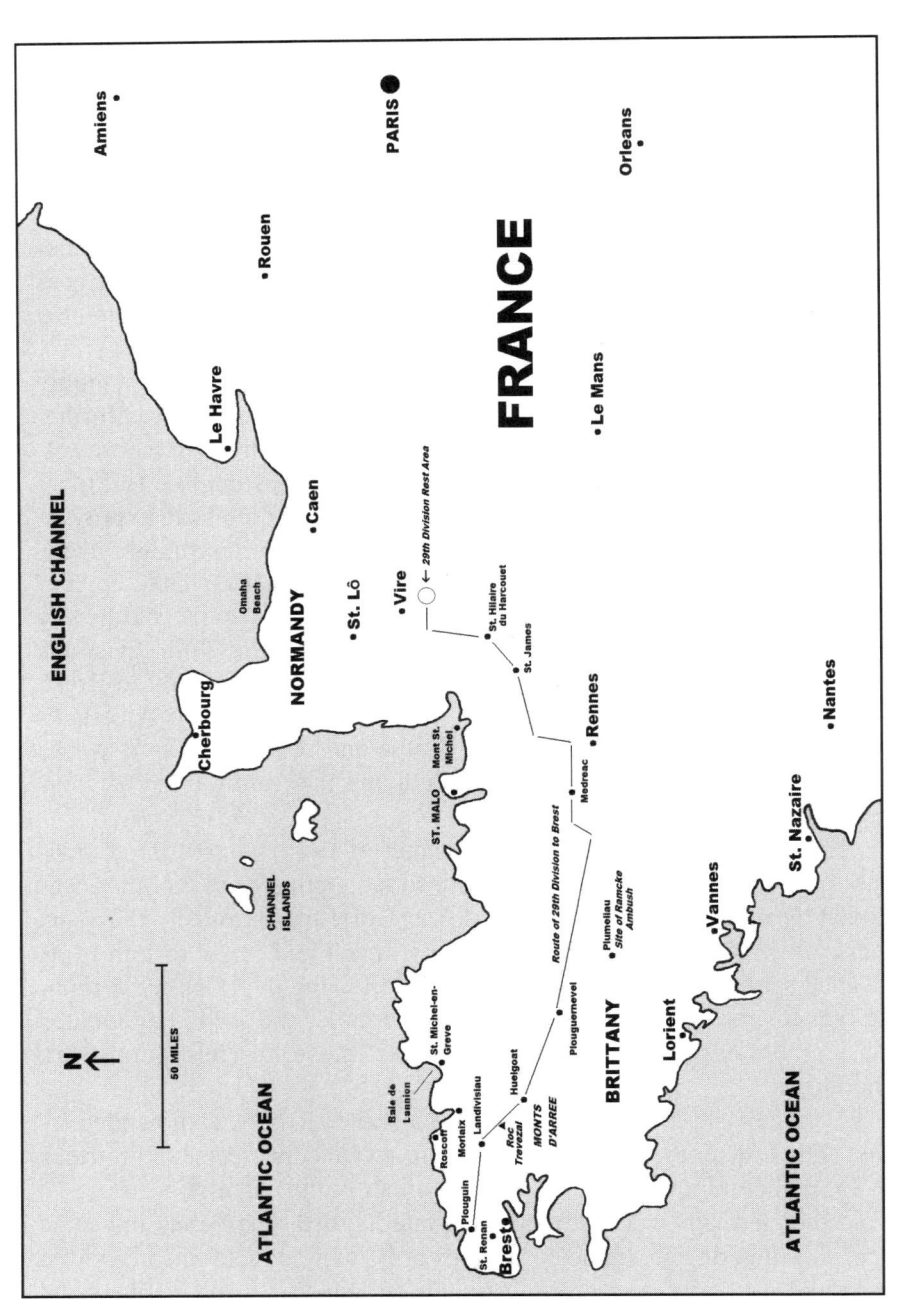

From Normandy to Brittany

managed." All the while he kept in constant communication with division headquarters with his special long-range AM radio set, notifying his demanding boss, "Uncle Charlie" Gerhardt, that the route was clear and that the divisional truck convoys back in Normandy could commence the long journey to Brest.

The pure scenic beauty of the Breton countryside was stunning, and to those men of the recon troop used to the ravages of war in Normandy, Brittany seemed a new and delightful world. About thirty miles east of Brest, in the Montagnes d'Arrée mountain range, Jones's column climbed a lonely road just north of Roc Trévezal, a 1,300-foot peak that is the highest in Brittany. The rocky mountainsides of this locale, swept by an incessant wind, were treeless, a peculiar feature to GIs who hailed from the east coast of the United States, but something the 29ers had gotten used to in their old training grounds on Dartmoor and Bodmin Moor back in England. From a military standpoint, Roc Trévezal was a perfect observation post, and the best part about it was that not a single German could be spotted anywhere in the vast vista of western Brittany that was visible from its summit.

Another notable feature of Brittany was its inhabitants, a sturdy race of seafarers and peasants, many of whom believed passionately that their unique culture set them apart from the rest of France. Indeed, the Breton language, known as Brezhoneg, resembles the Celtic family of languages, such as Welsh or Cornish, much more than it does French. During World War II, Brittany's isolation and its citizens' independent streak made it a rich breeding ground of resistance to the Nazi occupation, a detail that the 29ers immediately discerned as they pressed on toward Brest. In every Breton village through which the 29th Division would pass, local partisans who no longer felt any need to hide would offer valuable intelligence on the whereabouts of the enemy. Even better, Jones remembered that "people were out along the roads and greeted us like conquering heroes"—actions that for the most part the Normans had not demonstrated in the recently concluded campaign. "They gave us eggs, onions, tomatoes—just about anything. They were grand people," Jones observed.

Had the Germans in western Brittany had any intention other than fleeing into Brest, the 29th Recon Troop might have been in trouble. It was far out in front of the main body of the 29th Division, and as Jones recalled, "I had moved the troop fast—too fast—as our supply trains could not keep pace. We arrived in St. Renan [about seven miles northwest of Brest] almost out of food and fuel. By taking some fuel from here and there, we were able to keep mobile and retain the ability to fight if we had to, although if we had had a big fight and one that lasted some time, we would have been forced out of the vehicles to fight as infantry. It was the only time I was ever caught in such a situation."

Jones's men reached their destination about noon on August 21, just as the main body of the 29th Division, still back in Normandy, was about to set forth on the same momentous journey that the recon troop had just accomplished. A 210-mile motor march, however, was much more difficult for a group of 14,000 men than it was for 155. To facilitate the process, Gerhardt had sent out plentiful detachments of military policemen in Jones's wake with orders to man critical road intersections so that the 29th Division did not go astray—an event that the general must avoid at all costs, as he in all likelihood would be the one to shoulder the blame. Each battalion in the 29th Division, ranging in size from about 500 to 850 men, would move in its own convoy of approximately thirty-five trucks, most with accompanying one-ton cargo trailers stuffed with the trappings that all U.S. Army units needed to participate in modern warfare. Each of the division's three regimental combat teams—115th, 116th, and 175th—would be comprised of five such convoys: one for each of the regiment's three infantry battalions; one for its direct support artillery battalion; and one for headquarters, service, and attached medical and engineer personnel. A detachment of about 100 infantrymen in jeeps would scout well in front of each regimental convoy to ensure that the enemy did not lurk somewhere ahead, lying in wait to ambush the main column.

The movement appeared simple and neat on paper, but getting it started in the constricted and labyrinthine hedgerow country of Normandy required teamwork and timing seemingly as difficult as the Omaha Beach invasion. Gerhardt decreed that the 116th Infantry would lead the way, with a departure time of 8 P.M. on August 21, 1944. Division orders mandated that the convoys must keep going after dark, a requirement that any truck driver familiar with Normandy's narrow and winding roads must have received with skepticism. Just two hours before the 116th was set to start out, however, First Army headquarters signaled the 29th Division: "There will be no troop movements at night. You can move until 9 P.M. and then get off the roads until daylight. . . . The reason is because there are too many accidents at night."

It made sense for the division to postpone the 116th's departure until dawn of August 22, but the impetuous Gerhardt reacted to the First Army order by pronouncing: "We'll go ahead and get started now." Only about 100 trucks could get moving before dark on August 21, but to the general, at least it was a start. And if those trucks kept going a little past the 9 P.M.

deadline, who would notice? After all, it didn't actually get dark at this time of year in northern France until almost 10 P.M.

When the 29th Division finally got on the road in its entirety sometime before noon on August 22, its truck columns stretched more than 40 miles from head to tail—the equivalent of the distance between Washington, D.C., and Baltimore. The division's Piper L-4 "Grasshopper" aircraft—those diminutive and nimble "air observation post" scout planes in which Gerhardt himself habitually took joy rides—droned and swooped overhead; their pilots kept a sharp lookout on the snakelike progression of the convoys below, reporting any difficulties directly to Uncle Charlie by radio.

For a while, the trucks roared and jolted down the roads without difficulty. But when they reached what passed in Normandy for a main thoroughfare, the trucks' occupants could readily fathom that the 29th Division was in truth just a tiny cog in a giant military machine, one that was about to achieve a magnificent victory. It seemed as if the entire U.S. Army was on the move, and sharing the roads with all the diverse units and vehicles comprising that horde was anything but easy. The commander of the 110th Field Artillery Battalion, Lt. Col. John P. Cooper, observed: "Almost bumper to bumper, huge trailer trucks packed with rations, gasoline, and ammunition sped south while empty vehicles bowled along north to the beaches. So dense was the traffic that the division column found it almost impossible to cut into it, and delays resulted, which extended back to the initial point. About noon, when the 110th halted briefly for a roadside lunch, the unit got back in the stream of traffic only with great difficulty and delay."

About fifteen miles into the journey, when the procession of trucks reached the key crossroads village of St. Hilaire du Harcouet, there was one salient fact upon which all 29ers could agree: virtually all of the endless columns of U.S. Army vehicles were turning to the left, roaring to the east toward Paris, while the 29th Division was turning exactly in the opposite direction, headed for Brittany. Missing out on the City of Light was unfortunate, but on the whole, Brittany seemed the preferable option. Contacts in battalion and regimental intelligence sections had asserted that the Germans in Brest were not too numerous and were about ready to give up, and if those rumors were true, getting home in one piece seemed a reasonable possibility.

Furthermore, as the trucks turned west out of St. Hilaire, a sense of entering a fresh new world became increasingly palpable to the 29ers. So this was Brittany—not much different from Normandy so far, other than the fact that the observable signs of war were becoming fewer by the minute. The 29th Division was on its own now, a truth that dawned on the GIs as they peered out the backs of their deuce and a halfs and noticed that the traffic jams of Normandy had vanished. Presently, the trucks picked up speed, and conversation and sleep suddenly became almost impossible because of deafening engine noise, exhaust fumes, and the rutted roads. To make up time lost to traffic jams in Normandy, convoy commanders permitted their drivers to accelerate, sometimes up to 50 miles per hour—two and a half times the prescribed rate of daytime movement.

The first sizeable village beyond St. Hilaire was one with a thoroughly English name: St. James. From the high ground just east of that village, the 29ers could see the ancient Benedictine abbey of Mont St. Michel, whose lofty steeple emerged from the coastal flatlands nearly fifteen miles in the distance like the Emerald City in the Land of Oz. Just south of the D30 road followed by the 29th Division truck convoys, the municipality had recently donated pasture land for a U.S. Army cemetery, and only in the past week or so had those fields been cleared and partially filled with the graves of those members of the 8th Infantry Division who had recently died in combat. What fate had in store for the 29th Division was anybody's guess, but no one could possibly have realized then that nearly 350 of those thousands of 29ers now roaring by that cemetery in Army trucks would die in combat over the next month at Brest and would eventually find a final resting place in those same fields just outside St. James.

Such disheartening thoughts, however, were far from the 29ers' minds. At the moment, the most noticeable detail of the long journey to Brittany was that the Bretons were elated to see the 29th Division. The executive officer of Cooper's 110th Field Artillery Battalion, Maj. Donovan Yeuell, observed:

> The roads were lined with happy, smiling people: grateful old men and women, cigarette-starved and chocolate-hungry young farmers, pretty blond Breton girls, and laughing children, all greeting us as the beneficent liberators and offering us all they could in wines, eggs, and poultry as tokens of their sincere appreciation. I am sure that nobody, not even the Parisians, was more grateful than these warm-hearted, freedom-loving people of Brittany. It somehow made the coming battle for Brest seem easier to face.

Cooper added: "Everyone enjoyed the ride hugely. . . . The universal greeting was the 'V-for-Victory' sign, made with outstretched fingers."

Further evidence of the inhabitants' exhilaration was a sign stretched across the main street of one Breton village proclaiming "Welcome To Our Liberators"—in English. As the 1945 official history of one of the 29th Division's regiments declared, "Tuesday, August 22, was one of the most glorious days in the history of the 115th Infantry."

It was long overdue.

5. SUMMER SOLDIERS

In its three and a half years of active service, the 29th Division had endured seemingly endless periods of rigorous training and achieved several military successes that contributed profoundly to the Allies' effort to trounce the abhorrent Nazi regime. The June 6, 1944, assault on Omaha Beach and the St. Lô and Vire offensives in July and August were missions that only an expert military unit could carry out, and the division's fulfillment of those tasks had revealed to Ike and Bradley just how effective the 29th Division's training had been.

Nothing, however, could adequately prepare the division for its imminent assault on Fortress Brest for the simple reason that the 29th Division of Omaha Beach had ceased to exist. Virtually every regimental, battalion, and company commander of Blue and Gray infantry units had turned over—in some cases a half-dozen times. That turnover was even more severe for the GIs at the sharp end of the 29th Division spear—those in rifle platoons who had engaged the enemy for countless weeks in what was euphemistically referred to as "close" combat. If there were any riflemen left in the 29th Division's Brest procession who were veterans of Omaha Beach, in all likelihood they had already been wounded and subsequently returned to their platoons from a rear-area hospital upon recuperation. Everyone else was a replacement. Even the 29th Division's beloved assistant division commander, Brig. Gen. "Dutch" Cota, was gone. Cota had been an inspiration to every 29er since the training days in England and had stood at the front with the fighting men on the sands of Omaha Beach and in the rubble of St. Lô and Vire, but now he was in charge of the 28th Infantry Division and was about to lead his new outfit through the streets of Paris in the liberation parade.

General Gerhardt would greatly miss him and all the other absent combat veterans. All the tough training back in Cornwall and Devon meant nothing anymore if no one who had benefited from it remained in the division. Could the new men and their leaders measure up? They had had almost no time to learn Gerhardt's peculiar ways—and in truth had barely gotten a chance to know their comrades' names. The potency of the

Blue and Gray Division had always derived from its unshakable brotherhood, and the new men would be walking in the footsteps of some formidable soldiers.

The crucial issue was whether the U.S. Army was training infantry recruits back in the States effectively enough so that they could pass out of a forgettable and gloomy replacement depot directly into the front lines and perform as proficiently in combat as men who had been together for months or even years. Given the enemy's formidable fighting tenacity, many hardened combat veterans professed skepticism about the replacements' reliability. But Gerhardt had no reservations: To him, as soon as a new man sewed the divisional blue and gray ying-yang patch on his left shoulder, it would not take him long to realize that he was part of a winning team. The Normandy campaign, however, had established that many new arrivals did not live long enough at the front to grasp that concept. In the end, only the inevitable assault on Fortress Brest would prove whether the new 29ers were just as good at war as their predecessors.

Much more important to Gerhardt would be the aptitude of new officers to lead men capably in the chaos of battle. The general had always been much tougher on company commanders and field-grade officers than he was on privates, and so many new infantry leaders had assumed commands within the division lately that some old-timers wondered how the newcomers could adhere to Gerhardt's impossibly high standards.

Brest would prove there was little reason to fret. The majority of the fresh leaders—replacement officers and men who had been promoted to new commands from within the 29th Division—were competent commanders and ultimately would contribute markedly to the division's luster rather than detract from it. Perhaps Gerhardt was right after all: there was something about that blue and gray patch that made a soldier into a better warrior.

It had taken more than a year, but Gerhardt had finally cast off his old mindset that officers with National Guard backgrounds could not rise above the command of an infantry battalion, an organization of about 800 men. In the interwar period, the Regular Army had habitually viewed the National Guard with skepticism, and as Gerhardt was a West Pointer and traditional cavalryman of the old school, for most of his prewar career, he had held to the standard conviction of his peers that "summer soldiers" who had learned the rudiments of soldiering one night per week and for two weeks during annual training could not possibly lead sizeable units in battle against the expert enemy practitioners of blitzkrieg. But even Gerhardt had to admit that a man's performance under fire was a much better indicator of his leadership proficiency than his military origins, and for the first time in years, those few surviving National Guard officers in the 29th Division who had proved themselves in battle could speak of their soldierly backgrounds with dignity.

When the Blue and Gray Division set out for Brest, two of its three regimental commanders were men who had distinguished themselves in long careers in the Maryland National Guard. Lieutenant Colonel Louis Smith of the 115th Infantry was a 1920 graduate of Johns Hopkins University in Baltimore who joined the 5th Maryland Infantry in 1921. He had been an English major in college, but Smith abandoned the world of great literature and instead absorbed himself in the much more intricate science of electrical and mechanical engineering. In a long career with the Baltimore Gas and Electric Company, Smith became one of the country's most respected members of that field. The forty-seven-year-old Smith was short and somewhat chubby, but Gerhardt eventually gathered that he was just as talented at military skills as he was at his civilian job.

Another member of the National Guard whom Gerhardt had grudgingly come to respect was Lt. Col. William Purnell, commander of the 175th Infantry. A prewar fixture in the Maryland National Guard, Purnell had joined the "Dandy 5th of Maryland"—the same regiment he now commanded—in 1924. Purnell had the looks of Clark Gable, an exceptional mind sharpened by a law degree from Harvard University, and all the trappings of a good soldier. Those who saw Purnell in combat remembered him as one of the bravest soldiers they had ever seen. On June 7, 1944, the day following the D-Day invasion, Purnell had grabbed an M-1 rifle and stalked German snipers in houses beyond Omaha Beach. (He recalled with amusement, however, that the first time he attempted to fire that rifle, it jammed.) With traits such as those, the forty-year-old Purnell seemed destined to gain an exalted position in the Blue and Gray Division, but in the recent past, Gerhardt had twice passed him over when filling a vacancy in the 175th's top command slot. Only on July 30, when regimental commander Col. Ollie Reed had been killed at Villebaudon, did Purnell get his chance. According to Gerhardt, the looming battle at Brest would determine whether or not Purnell and Smith could perform up to the standards he expected of West Pointers.

There was a world of difference in status between a regimental CO and the much less exalted job of battalion commander, but to Gerhardt, the effectiveness of the 29th Division depended on the quality of the men who led his battalions, particularly the commanders of the division's nine infantry battalions. Those outfits bore the brunt of the division's combat load, and one of the general's customary proverbs declared, "This war is won at battalion level." In truth, his proclivity to relieve battalion COs who did not meet his rigorous standards instilled in the officers who currently held those commands a persistent fear of losing their jobs in disgrace—and in some cases an abiding dislike of their commanding general. However, one new man who came to the division shortly before the journey to Brest, Maj. Randolph Millholland, quickly became one of Gerhardt's favorites and in fact developed into one of the most effective and admired battalion commanders in the 29th Division in World War II.

Millholland was yet another old-timer from the Maryland National Guard who had served for more than ten years as a noncommissioned officer in the 1st Maryland Infantry, the designation by which the 115th had been known in the interwar years. That he possessed an exceptional ability to inspire men to fight well had clearly been established by his dynamic leadership of the 29th Ranger Battalion, a special unit of volunteers drawn from the 29th Division in early 1943 that Millholland had successfully led through the impossibly tough British commando school in Scotland. That unit had been disbanded in late 1943, after which Millholland was assigned to a Ninth Air Force unit that was analyzing how fighter-bombers could best support infantrymen—techniques that would prove invaluable in the Brest campaign. The thirty-seven-year-old Millholland had spent most of his military career with the 29th Division but ironically had missed its notable accomplishments at Omaha Beach, St. Lô, and Vire. Now he was back, and the Blue and Gray Division was a much better fighting organization because of it.

General Cota's departure for the 28th Division had left an opening in the 29th's assistant division commander slot, but all 29ers agreed that no human being could ever adequately replace Dutch Cota. Nevertheless, General Bradley had to try. If his recent record in Normandy was a valid indicator of his leadership skills, the man selected for the job, Col. Leroy Watson, was a peculiar choice. A member of the same 1915 West Point class as Bradley and Ike, Watson had been a major general just a few weeks previously and had held the exalted job of commanding general of the 3rd Armored Division during the Normandy breakthrough near St. Lô in late July. However, he had run afoul of his demanding corps commander, Maj. Gen. Joseph Lawton Collins, who relieved Watson of command—an event that had caused Watson's rank to be reduced by two grades.

Normally, such an indignity would cause the slighted officer to seek passage on the next freighter heading back to the States, but Watson had gamely asked Bradley for permission to remain in the theater and ultimately to regain a combat command in any role Bradley deemed appropriate. His classmate Bradley was impressed and granted Watson's wish. A call in late August from Twelfth Army Group headquarters to Gerhardt in the 29th Division war room settled the matter. Watson, who only recently had been senior to Gerhardt, would now have to accept much lesser command authority, and as a colonel, his role as "assistant" division commander was blurred by the fact that the 29th Division's artillery chief, Brig. Gen. William Sands, outranked him. Above all, Watson did not seem the type who could match Dutch Cota's vitality; in all fairness, not a single person in the U.S. Army in 1944 could.

Since his arrival in Europe in July 1943, Gerhardt had been fortunate to serve superior officers who were more forgiving than General Collins. That situation could change in Brittany, however, as Gerhardt would now have to take orders from two men who had never before worked with the 29th Division and were unfamiliar with Gerhardt's unusual personality.

One of these was the commander of the U.S. Third Army, the fearsome Gen. George S. Patton, a man who had habitually made the lives of mere division commanders decidedly stressful. Patton held responsibility under the Overlord plan for taking Brest, and therefore, Gerhardt would apparently have to prove himself all over again to this most demanding of generals. But Patton had mellowed in recent months because of the distinct possibility that the supreme commander would send him home at reduced rank if, as Ike noted, he did not learn "to keep his mouth shut." Furthermore, Patton and Gerhardt—both old cavalrymen—shared a passion for horsemanship and would have much common ground when recalling the old days of the Regular Army, before the rush to mechanization had forced horses out of the U.S. Army for good. In truth, some might describe Gerhardt as a younger and smaller version of Patton.

In the end, however, Patton's relationship with Gerhardt and the 29th Division would be distant because the Third Army commander's mind was elsewhere. Brest was still important, but as the 29th Division truck convoys were racing into Brittany, Patton's leading armored spearheads were racing in precisely the opposite direction, 350 miles to the east, and had already reached the Seine River southeast of Paris. In that exhilarating rush, it seemed as if virtually no enemy troops stood between the Third Army and Germany. If Patton sought glory, he would not find it at Brest. Obviously, he would not have much time to spare for the 29th Division in the upcoming weeks—which, as far as the 29ers were concerned, was probably a good thing.

The immediate boss to whom Gerhardt would have to answer on a daily basis during the assault on Fortress Brest would be Maj. Gen. Troy Middleton. Bradley had designated Middleton's VIII Corps as the responsible command for the liberation of Brittany, and by August 23, 1944, with the arrival outside Brest of the 2nd, 8th, and 29th Divisions—as well as two elite ranger battalions—Middleton seemingly had the force necessary to capture that key objective within the next week.

Unlike Gerhardt, the fifty-four-year old Middleton was an unassuming man, hobbled by arthritis—an infantryman to the core who had once rejected an offer to join the cavalry with a declaration that would have made Uncle Charlie's blood run cold: "I just don't like a horse." Over his military career, Middleton had forged a deep bond with frontline soldiers, a sentiment that derived from his service as a U.S. Army enlisted man prior to World War I, when it took him more than two years to rise from private to corporal; from his experience in the trenches on the Western Front, in which he was speedily promoted and became the youngest regimental commander in the American Expeditionary Force; and from his time as commanding general of the 45th Infantry Division from October 1942 to December 1943, a period that included the arduous and costly Sicily and Salerno invasions. The most famous 45th Division enlisted man of them all, the soldier-cartoonist Bill Mauldin, once inscribed one of his legendary "Willie and Joe" cartoons for Middleton with the dedication: "With love and respect from a pair of his senior dogfaces"—a message that one suspects would have been far more subdued had it been offered to Gerhardt.

It would take some time for Gerhardt and his staff to get used to their new commander, but that was of no consequence. Under Middleton's direction, the 29th Division and all the other units assembled outside Brest had a job to do, and now the time had come to start doing it.

6. A LOUSY PLACE FOR WAR

Middleton could have simply tried to starve the Germans out. Within seven or eight weeks, the Germans in Brest would—in theory—begin to run out of the items they needed to live and fight, and Middleton's plentiful artillery could have accentuated their mounting discomfort by keeping up a steady barrage on every fighting position and rear-area installation within enemy lines. Such a tactic could save considerable American lives, but supreme headquarters had made it plain that there was no time for that.

On August 23, 1944, the day the 29th Division truck convoys arrived in the Brest environs, the only functional French port of substantive size under Allied control was Cherbourg, and given the swelling number

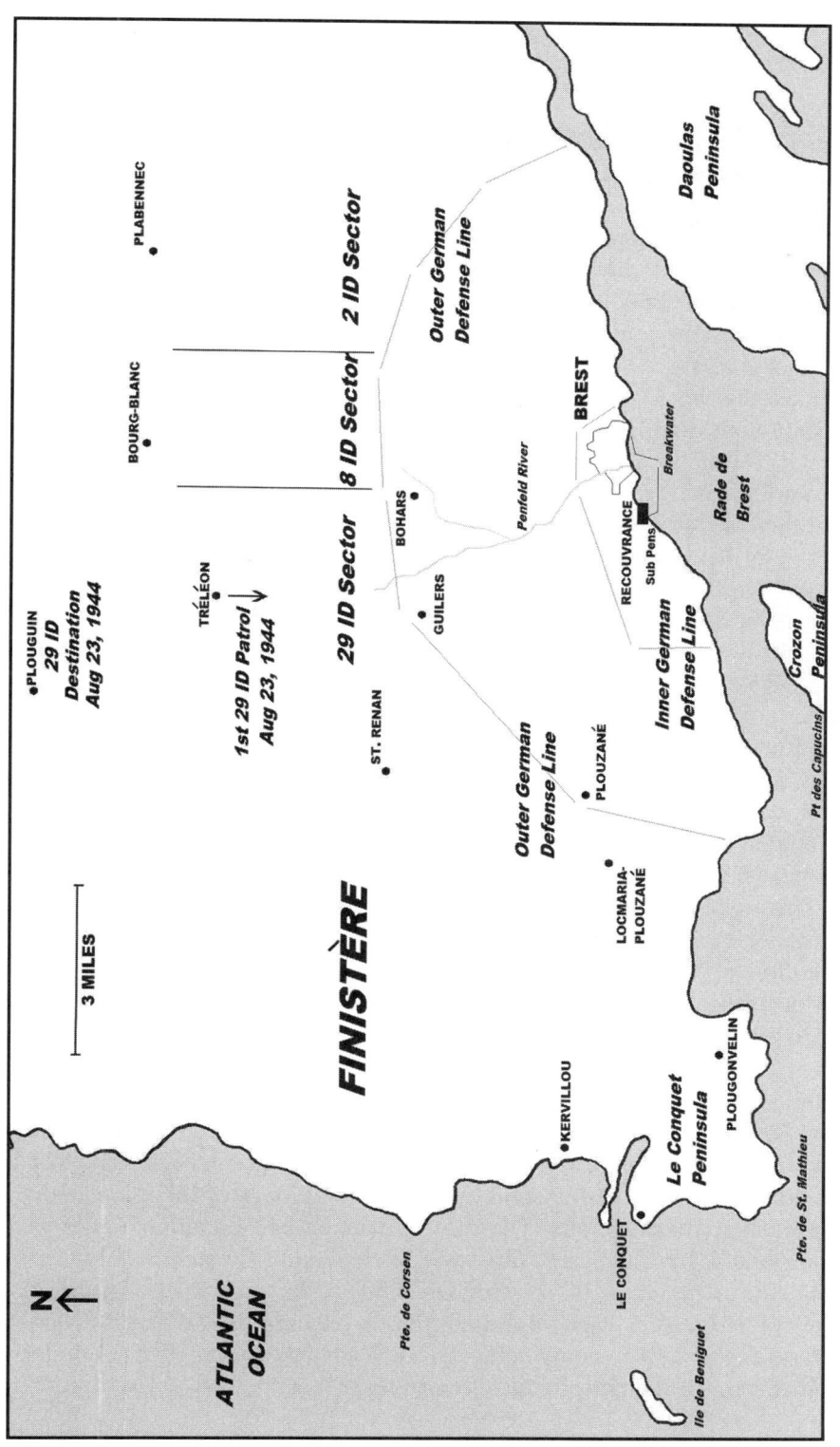

The Environs of Brest

of Allied troops on the continent, that place was woefully inadequate to handle the massive influx of men and supplies the Allies would need to maintain the initiative. True, the Allied armies were advancing rapidly, and several substantial French harbors seemed on the verge of liberation. None of them, however, offered as immediate a solution to the Allied logistical nightmare as Brest—assuming Middleton could seize it quickly. Ike needed Brest now, and Middleton would have to attack aggressively to fulfill that goal. Besides, had Middleton attempted to starve the Germans out, the enemy would have been free to thoroughly wreck Brest's harbor installations, and in that unfortunate event, the Allies might never get to use it. From the American perspective, therefore, every GI hoped the upcoming task would not evolve into a siege, for that sort of methodical military operation would take time and would not offer Ike immediate relief for his mounting supply problems. If Middleton attacked aggressively, Brest should be in American hands by September 1, 1944—or so the top brass thought.

Brest was a city of about 100,000 souls, many of whom had long since departed their homes to avoid what was about to occur. Brest is situated on high ground on the north side of a natural harbor, known locally as the Rade de Brest (Brest Roads), seemingly vast enough to hold the entire U.S. and Royal Navies combined. The German scheme for the defense of this crucial place was straightforward. In a semicircle whose radius extended about four miles from the city center, the Germans had established fighting positions that would cover any conceivable land approach to Brest from north, east, or west. Should the Americans penetrate those lines, the enemy had established stronger fallback positions much closer to the city, in part tied into sturdy French forts dating back in some cases to the seventeenth century. Although those ancient fortifications had been designed in a wholly different military era, they would nonetheless severely challenge the GIs who would shortly be ordered to capture them.

For the 29th Division, the Brest campaign officially began on the evening of August 23, 1944, as the last of the truck convoys from Normandy pulled into their destination at the little village of Plouguin, about ten miles north of the city. The 115th Infantry's 2nd Battalion, under the command of Lt. Col. Tony Miller, was the first outfit to enter the front line, relieving a battalion of the 8th Division at the crossroads hamlet of Tréléon at 6 P.M. Miller wasted no time in pushing patrols south toward Brest to feel out the enemy defenses. They advanced more than two miles and encountered only sporadic German resistance.

Back at Plouguin, the new site of the Blue and Gray war room, Gerhardt and his staff were categorically optimistic, and the report from Miller's patrols helped to fuel that optimism. Middleton had ordered fifteen corps-level artillery units to support VIII Corps' impending offensive against Brest. Some of these units were armed with super-heavy 8-inch and 240mm howitzers, and when that firepower was combined with the abundant Eighth and Ninth Air Force fighters and bombers scheduled to join in the attack, the 29th Division would have some impressive support. Even the aged Royal Navy battleship, HMS *Warspite*—a veteran of the 1916 Battle of Jutland and the much more recent D-Day invasion— would assist the Yanks with its massive 15-inch guns. How could the enemy expect to stand against such an extraordinary display of firepower? On August 23, an observer from Bradley's headquarters attached to the 29th Division stated what every 29er wanted to hear: "This job at Brest should not be too hard for all the troops we are getting here."

Such positive sentiments were apparently corroborated by a drunken enemy paratrooper captured by the 115th Infantry, who reported that a senior German officer had recently been dismissed from Fortress Brest by the garrison commander because he "didn't believe Brest could be defended and wanted to surrender." Gerhardt was of course delighted by that news. The 29th Division would surely be entering Brest soon, and to prepare for that moment, the general ordered his infantry commanders to start training their men in street-fighting tactics.

But the 29th Division would not be doing any street fighting for nearly one month, and in that interval, it would lose more than 3,000 men. In retrospect, that kind of ferocious enemy resistance would amaze the 29ers, particularly because the Germans at Brest had no realistic chance of winning. Middleton, however, grasped from the beginning that the enemy certainly would not be a pushover, a conclusion he had reached as a consequence of the fighting that had only just recently ended at St. Malo, a minor harbor on the north coast of Brittany just west of the abbey of Mont St. Michel. In the aftermath of the Normandy breakout in early August, Bradley had ordered Middleton to seize St. Malo, even though it did not possess much strategic importance for either side. It took the VIII Corps' 83rd Infantry Division two weeks and much heavy fighting to do the job; even as Middleton was preparing for his assault on Fortress Brest on August 23, the tenacious Germans still held on to a key island immediately adjacent to the St. Malo harbor entrance, thereby preventing Allied cargo ships from discharging their loads. In response to an American surrender demand, the German garrison commander at St. Malo had offered a reply that should have foreshadowed the enemy's attitude at Brest: "[I am] a German soldier, and a German soldier does not surrender."

To Allied fighting men, such illogical talk was mere bluster. Plenty of dedicated German soldiers had surrendered in this war, and if they didn't, they would soon die. Still, to Gerhardt, whose men were about to initiate the attack on Brest, the contemplation of the enemy's fierce resistance at St. Malo must have been disconcerting. If the Germans had fought so resolutely for a comparatively minor objective, what would they do to defend Brest, a site of much more critical importance? Furthermore, the German defenders of St. Malo had been caught up in the Allies' Normandy breakout and could prepare only modest defenses because of time constraints. But at Brest the enemy had been permitted more than three weeks to gather all their outlying units throughout western Brittany and prepare for the task ahead. One of them was a fresh parachute division, and from their experiences in Normandy, the 29ers knew how hard those exceptional enemy paratroopers would fight. How many Germans had made it into the Brest enclave before Middleton had effectively sealed them off from the outside world was anyone's guess, but that number was unquestionably large.

In the end, the only way to ascertain the Germans' strength and resolve at Brest was to seek out and attack them, and the 29th Division was about to do just that. One of the prime factors that could contribute to that attack's success was intimate knowledge of the terrain, but clearly, the 29ers had not been on the ground long enough to gain a decent level of familiarity. The best company commanders, platoon leaders, and their senior NCOs could do was to scrutinize the newly issued maps of the Brest area with as much care as time would allow—and then hope for the best.

Hasty briefings by regimental and battalion COs had at least revealed with a fair degree of clarity the 29th Division's role in the upcoming campaign. Middleton's plan of attack was simple. (How could it be otherwise when there was no reasonable alternative to a frontal attack on the enemy's defensive lines enclosing Brest?) The VIII Corps' first step was to trap the enemy in Brest by sealing off any possible avenue of escape. As that cordon tightened, the Americans' grip on the enemy would sooner or later amount to a stranglehold. Middleton had three infantry divisions at his disposal—the 2nd, 8th, and 29th—and on his situation maps, his staff divided the American perimeter into three arcs, each of which would become a divisional sector. The 8th Infantry Division held the center; the 2nd Division, on the left, held the eastern arc; and the 29th Division, on the right, the western arc.

When all was ready, the offensive would jump off with a concerted attack by all three divisions, backed by the might of the air force—

weather permitting. The obvious object was to punch through the enemy's outer defenses and head straight for that part of Brest that Ike's logisticians wanted most, its harbor side. But even if the Americans could not penetrate into the city proper by a lightning stroke, Middleton hoped that the intensity of the attack would demoralize the German defenders and swiftly shatter their ability to resist.

All the outfits scheduled to join in the Brest offensive had traveled a long way in a short time to reach western Brittany. That accomplishment had been impressive, but there was one vital factor that all agreed had not yet been adequately addressed: supply. The only materiel that units would have available in the next few days to support the upcoming assault would be those items they had carried with them on their trucks. Supply lines back to rear-area depots were not yet functioning smoothly, and G-4 (supply) officers on the staffs of Middleton's three infantry divisions would need time to get matters in order. Accordingly, Middleton put off the main attack until Friday, August 25, at 1 P.M. Even with that slight delay, it would not be easy for infantry and artillery units to gather the ammunition stocks they would need—a situation that might become even more difficult should the enemy offer fierce resistance, thereby forcing the Americans to use up all the ammunition they had on hand.

In the meantime, the 29ers had a chance to examine their new surroundings, and what they saw could be described only as disheartening. True, the Bretons on the whole were much more delighted than the Normans to see the Americans convene in their neighborhood. But in the Brest environs, the land itself bore a remarkable similarity to the places in Normandy the 29th Division had just fought over for eleven consecutive weeks, and that was a type of terrain the 29ers wished never to see again. The Norman locals referred to it as *bocage*, but the American fighting men simply called it "hedgerow country"—as well as many cruder names that only a bitter and exhausted GI, who knew that kind of land intimately, could concoct. There was virtually no better defensive terrain in France, and the unfortunate truth was that for almost that entire eleven-week period in Normandy, the Germans defended while the Americans attacked. Now the Blue and Gray Division would again be forced to push through this wretched countryside, with its diminutive farm fields laid out in inscrutable jigsaw patterns, all enclosed by stout earthen banks topped by thick hedges and shrubs. Even worse, much of the land was crisscrossed by narrow country lanes seemingly leading nowhere, all of which were cloaked by a verdant foliage so dense that they appeared gloomy and sinister even in broad daylight.

On the whole, it was a lousy place to fight a war.

7. A PILE OF RUINS

The German defenders of Brest could not help contemplating their dismal prospects. Just a few weeks ago, they had considered themselves fortunate to have been held back from the Normandy cataclysm, for every German Army unit that had been sucked into that vortex had been decimated. Now the U.S. Army had entirely cut off the Brest garrison from the fatherland, but at least the German defenders were still living and not as of yet in Allied POW camps. Perhaps the American propaganda leaflets that had routinely fluttered down from the sky over the past several days were right. Those leaflets had proclaimed, "BREST IS LOST . . . BUT YOU ARE NOT! It is only a question of time until Brest falls before the power of Allied material superiority. Neither General Ramcke [the German commander of Fortress Brest] nor your own bravery can change this decision. Nevertheless, American troops have been ordered to spare the life of every German soldier who surrenders. You still have the opportunity to get home to your families."

Meanwhile, a wholly different kind of message had been communicated to the German garrison from its new leader, Gen. Hermann-Bernhard Ramcke, who had slipped into Brest with the 2nd *Fallschirmjäger* (Parachute) Division on August 9 and superseded von der Mosel two days later as commander of Fortress Brest: "Faithful to the oath we have sworn to the führer, the people, and the fatherland, and safeguarding the traditional honor of the German soldier, we are going to defend the Fortress Brest to the last grenade, committing our very lives; and shall cede this important military port to the enemy only as a pile of ruins." These were subjects of profound consequence to German soldiers, who had been implanted with the notion of faithful duty to their homeland since their first days in uniform and even before; their ears surely pricked up when they heard Ramcke employ the powerful expression "traditional honor of the German soldier." The American leaflets made some valid points, but duty unquestionably superseded them. Consequently, the defenders eventually had to come to terms with the brutal fact that their fates were apparently limited to one of two possibilities, death or a prisoner of war camp, and to many fanatical Nazis, the latter was not much better than the former.

In an army populated by generals with dynamic leadership skills and extraordinary military capabilities, Generalleutnant (Major General) Ramcke was conspicuous within the Wehrmacht for his aptitude to get tough jobs done. Unlike most of those generals, the fifty-five-year-old Ramcke had nothing to do with the German Army's legendary panzer corps. In fact, he had enlisted in the German Navy in 1905 and remained in that service until he transferred to the army in 1919. In 1940, while the panzer generals were basking in the glow of their great blitzkrieg victory over the Anglo-French armies in France, Ramcke had been learning the art of parachuting out of airplanes—at the age of fifty-one. Soon he was a qualified *Fallschirmjäger*, and since those elite airborne fighters were considered part of the Luftwaffe, Ramcke thereby had gained the distinction of serving in all three branches of the German armed services in a military career that had so far spanned thirty-five years.

Ramcke had come to Adolf Hitler's attention in May 1941 when, as the colonel of a parachute regiment, he played a decisive role in the German airborne assault on Crete, which resulted in the seizure of that vital Greek island in the Mediterranean and the capture or expulsion of its entire Commonwealth garrison. In this monumental airborne operation, Ramcke and his comrades had demonstrated to the world that airborne forces could accomplish what conventional units could not. Hitler had considered Crete a remarkable—but exceedingly costly—success. A few more airborne operations as costly as Crete would practically wipe out the vaunted German paratroop force, and it would not be easy for Hitler to replace those highly trained warriors. For that reason, Ramcke correctly surmised that he would not jump into battle again. Over the next three years, however, he would lead his elite paratroopers into combat as conventional ground troops in every major theater in Europe during World War II: North Africa, Italy, Russia, and eventually France, where he commanded his beloved 2nd *Fallschirmjäger* Division.

A fellow German general by the name of Wilhelm Ritter von Thoma—once the commander of the famed Afrika Korps—characterized Ramcke as "a fervent Nazi [who] boasted loudly about his division and his activities. Above all, he didn't let anyone forget that he was the only one who could work something out, and he was the one who had the experience required." A somewhat sarcastic von Thoma concluded, "[Ramcke] is a good soldier—and a courageous NCO!"

At Brest, there was hardly a better German soldier Hitler could have picked to inspire troops in what amounted to a hopeless cause. He would harbor no pessimism: Even though he and his men could only end up dead or captives, he could still "win" by making the Americans pay a high price in lives and time, just as Hitler had proclaimed. But defending static positions was hardly the ideal use of elite German airborne troops. Duty to the fatherland was of course paramount, but even Ramcke had to admit that this assignment was an unlucky break that would in all likelihood bring his career to an abrupt end. "However bad things looked," Ramcke later observed, "I was a soldier and had to fight. There was nothing for me to do but by all means defend the town of Brest until the last shot had been fired and only to surrender it to the Americans after it had been reduced to ruins. That is a fortress commander's duty."

The Bretons were also about to introduce Ramcke to a type of combat he had not yet experienced firsthand in World War II. That abrupt introduction would be made in June 1944, shortly after the transfer of Ramcke and his 2nd *Fallschirmjäger* Division from Germany to western Brittany. Driving in an open staff car hundreds of miles behind the front, accompanied by several bodyguards in a trailing vehicle, hardly seemed a hazardous activity for a general like Ramcke, who had routinely stayed close to his men on the battleline. The French peasants absorbed in their work in the nearby pastures as Ramcke's car roared by seemed harmless enough, but even if they weren't, how could they know that one of the German occupants of the passing automobiles was the commander of the newly arrived 2nd *Fallschirmjäger* Division?

But this was Brittany in the immediate aftermath of D-Day, and the countryside was crawling with clandestine partisans of the FFI (*Forces Françaises de l'Intérieur*), the renowned French Resistance. On the afternoon of June 15, 1944, several FFI members, hidden in a cleverly camouflaged ambush position on a hill just west of the village of Pluméliau, waited patiently for a lucrative enemy target. The FFI team was led by a daring and experienced fighter named Bénoni Lamour, a veteran of the renowned International Brigades in the Spanish Civil War. Lamour knew a good target when he saw it, and when Ramcke's vehicle approached the hill, he ordered his men to open fire at point-blank range with their submachine guns. In the blast of close-range gunfire, Ramcke was lucky to avoid death, but the passenger sitting next to him in the rear seat, his chief of staff, Maj. Herbert Schmidt, was killed and toppled into the general's lap.

To Ramcke, acts such as these were "terror," not war; he resolved that if he was to carry out his mission of defending Brest against the imminent American assault, he must respond to FFI attacks forcefully. He did so and, after World War II, would pay a high price for it when a French military court sentenced him to five years of hard labor for the "war crimes" his *Fallschirmjäger* had allegedly perpetrated as they retreated toward Fortress Brest in July 1944 through dozens of Breton villages whose unfortunate inhabitants included several FFI members or those who provided them safe havens. Ramcke would not return to Germany as a free man until June 1951, but for years, he insisted that his behavior toward the Bretons had been correct. "At Brest itself, three death sentences, signed by me, were carried out—on German soldiers, not the local inhabitants," he declared in captivity. "I evacuated [the inhabitants of] Brest. If I had not done so, the population would have suffered enormous losses."

Ramcke somewhat naively assumed that a frank lecture to the local Breton authorities would alleviate the problem of "terrorist" attacks by the FFI. He recalled how he

> summoned all the parish priests, teachers, and mayors, and through a clever interpreter made the following speech: "Gentlemen, I have asked you to come here in order to say a few important words in the interests of your country's safety. Grave outrages against the military power are taking place everywhere, usually on the part of either young people or those who have come in from elsewhere. . . . You know as well as we that the American and British secret services are behind these people and are smuggling arms to them. . . . There is, however, a French government in Vichy that is the only existing one for the country, and the only one recognized by the French people, and we [the Germans] are the de facto power. Just imagine what it means to intrigue in this way against these two authorities; it isn't honest, open warfare—it's treachery. You put yourself in the worst possible light and make yourselves accessories to the crime if you harbor such people in your parishes. Therefore you will observe the instructions that have been given: On the door of each house shall be written the number of people living there; and beware of harboring in your parishes persons who are suspicious in any way . . ." [I] made such an impression that all the priests preached the gist of my talk from the pulpit the next Sunday. The fact that I did that will go to my credit.

As for most Bretons, however, the "impression" made by Ramcke was decidedly negative, and despite everything Ramcke said to reduce local support for the FFI, the Resistance flourished, significantly hampering German military activities as Middleton's VIII Corps rushed into Brittany following the Normandy breakout. Indeed, from Middleton's perspective, it was good that the FFI was fighting on his side. The Breton Resistance fighters were undeniably tough men and women who made the Americans' job easier by incessantly harassing the enemy, providing valuable intelligence on Ramcke's order of battle, acting as local guides, and performing security duties behind American lines once Middleton had pocketed the Germans inside Brest. But even Gerhardt had to admit that the FFI carried out warfare unconventionally. "They take few prisoners," he commented starkly in his monthly report in August 1944. Indeed, one could even detect in Middleton a twinge of sympathy for the plight of his opposite number in Brest. Although Middleton would later characterize Ramcke as "ruthless," he added, "He is nevertheless a soldier [and] a pretty decent sort."

One thing the FFI apparently did much better than Middleton's own intelligence staff was to judge the number of German troops encircled in Fortress Brest and their resolve to fight. An August 21 29th Division intelligence report noted:

> An estimate of 16,500–20,000 troops has been made by VIII Corps; 8,500 army and the remainder naval and marine. . . . A prisoner captured from the 7th Parachute Regiment states that food and water are critical and morale is very low. . . . A question exists as to whether or not the will to resist will continue when a show of strength is made by us and when the natural inclination of the naval and marine garrison not to fight a ground battle penetrates the command.

The French Resistance asserted from the beginning that the estimated German garrison of Brest was between 40,000 and 50,000—a figure based on a thorough familiarity with the many diverse German Army, Navy, and Luftwaffe units, as well as paramilitary labor and construction groups that were trapped in Brest upon the U.S. Army's arrival. That the FFI's figure was much more accurate than the Americans' original estimate of Ramcke's strength at Brest became plain to Middleton's staff within a few days. In the end, when the Americans finally tallied up the German dead and prisoners at the close of the battle, it turned out that the Resistance fighters had been correct from the beginning. Many members of the garrison were unenthusiastic labor troops, many of whom were not even German, but the core of the garrison was composed of tough paratroopers with whom the FFI had been clashing for weeks, and for them to give up without much of a fight was inconceivable—especially with Ramcke at the helm.

Given the comparative manpower strengths of the opposing forces at Brest, the Americans certainly did not possess the numerical superiority U.S. Army field manuals recommended for a set-piece attack against a fortified position occupied by well-prepared enemy troops, many of whom the GIs would soon learn were fanatical fighters. In truth, Middleton had little better than a one-to-one advantage. However, he had one crucial thing that Ramcke lacked: an operative route to rear-area supply depots. American troops could therefore conduct themselves at Brest safe in the knowledge that their quartermasters would strive to provide fresh supplies of food, bullets, and shells, whereas the Germans would have to cope with the rations and ammunition stockpiled in Brest when the Americans encircled the city. To Ramcke, it was a vast disadvantage that would eventually determine his fate.

Later, Middleton loudly complained that Ike's logisticians conferred only low priority to the task of supplying his corps because of pressing developments on the main battlefront beyond Paris, but his predicament was nothing compared to Ramcke's. Once the Americans launched their attack on Brest and the combat swiftly swelled in intensity, it was as if a man who had merely missed a single meal was fighting against another who had not eaten for a week. Sooner or later, the starving man would weaken first. Nevertheless, Ramcke had a large number of determined fighters inside his lines—far more than the Americans realized when they initiated their attack on August 25. As John Cooper of the 29th Division's 110th Field Artillery Battalion later concluded, "The unexpectedly large number of Germans inside Brest explained the long and bitter fight we had to wage to capture that place."

Shortly after the 29th Division's arrival at Brest, Gerhardt dispatched a liaison officer, Maj. Charles Custer, to VIII Corps headquarters. Over the next several weeks, Custer's new job at Middleton's command post gave him a remarkable perspective on the Brest operation. One of the first scenes he witnessed, the arrival of a German medical officer in American lines under a flag of truce, he promptly related to Gerhardt by telephone. "He was taken to the corps command post blindfolded and complained to General Middleton about the treatment of German prisoners by the FFI [since] the FFI shot any and all POWs on sight," Custer observed. "The German told General Middleton he was sorry he could not see [Middleton's] face because he was blindfolded. . . . General Middleton told him that he would probably see it sometime in the near future."

TWO

Fortress Brest

1. TOUGH GOING
General Gerhardt had hoped that August 25, 1944, would be a date that would stand out forever in the annals of the 29th Infantry Division. Compared to what the division had just achieved in Normandy, however, the opening day of Middleton's great offensive against Brest turned out to be somewhat anticlimactic and mostly forgettable.

It all began on a note of disappointment. A coordinated attack by the 2nd, 8th, and 29th Infantry Divisions was set to commence at 1 P.M. on August 25, but only an hour before jumpoff, Middleton phoned his three division commanders with bad news: the ground attack missions that the Ninth Air Force had promised in support of the attack had been cancelled. No explanation for this distressing development was provided. The weather could not have been the problem, for flying conditions—although far from perfect—were evidently stable enough for pilots to take off, observe enemy targets below, and safely return to base. Middleton ominously appended his message, "We will go ahead anyhow." From the infantrymen's perspective, it was not an auspicious way to begin a major offensive.

The immediate problem, as always, was the Germans. Where were they? The 29th Division had not been in the line long enough to figure out the answer to that question, and the division's August 25 attack would be analogous to a blindfolded boxer advancing out of his corner of the ring to confront his opponent. Before the 29ers could inflict punishment on the Germans, they would have to feel for the enemy, pushing ahead until they encountered resistance and then smashing that resistance with the devastating infantry and artillery one-two punch that had worked so effectively in Normandy.

Gerhardt's plan for the August 25 attack was straightforward simply because there was no alternative. The basic assault plan called for all three 29th Division regiments—115th Infantry on the left (east), 116th in the center, 175th on the right (west)—to advance steadily southward on a broad front until the enemy's line of resistance was ultimately pinpointed. When that event occurred, and the division's momentum inevitably slowed down, the general ordered units farther back in the attacking columns to slip around the enemy's western flank in a classic enveloping maneuver. The overall effect of Gerhardt's design would bring about a divisional battle line that swung like a door, pivoting at the hinge on the left and smashing forward in a wide arc on the right. If the 29th Division could swiftly slam that door shut, Gerhardt hoped the enemy's outer defensive lines at Brest could be effectively outflanked, forcing the Germans to pull back to their last-ditch inner positions just outside the city. At that point, one determined frontal attack could finish off the enemy. Only time would tell whether or not that strategy was realistic. If it was not, the 29th Division could be in for a battle of attrition little different than Normandy.

Anxious 29th Division riflemen soon discovered that Breton terrain wholly favored the Germans, who typically camouflaged their resistance nests so cleverly in the hedgerow country that they were virtually imperceptible until the GIs approached at point-blank range. At that instant, the Germans would suddenly open fire with a few ripping bursts from their deadly MG42 machine guns and kill or wound a few American riflemen unlucky enough to be caught in that fusillade. Those 29ers who survived those bursts had no choice but to dive for cover and determine the source of the enemy fire, but by the time they did, and then cautiously moved against it, the Germans had already shifted to another equally well-hidden position.

From Gerhardt's perspective, it was at first difficult to discern whether the many points of German resistance encountered on August 25 were parts of the enemy's main battle line or just outposts designed to impede the American advance temporarily. As the day wore on, however, the enemy's intention became clear. Each time the 29ers prepared to initiate a set-piece attack with infantry and artillery on a newly located German strongpoint, by then the enemy had moved someplace else—exactly where, no one could tell. Ultimately, Gerhardt figured out that the Germans were waging a skillful delaying action, yielding plenty of time for their main line of resistance to get ready while inflicting as many casualties as possible on the Americans, who became more and more wary of the Germans' ghostly presence. Whatever it was the Germans were doing demonstrated how skilled they were at this type of fighting.

Still, the 29th Division's accomplishments on August 25 were considerable. Although the enemy had fought skillfully, the 29ers nevertheless managed to make gains of two to three miles—a pace that would have been considered remarkable in Normandy. Furthermore, the 29th Division's August 25 casualty count of approximately seventy was modest when compared to the dreadful daily toll of the brutal hedgerow fighting outside St. Lô and Vire. In the end, the division's August 25 experience was aptly summarized by Gerhardt in an 8:27 P.M. telephone call to General Middleton: "We made quite good progress, considering. It's been pretty tough going."

At nightfall on August 25, the feeling of puzzlement and frustration among staff officers in the 29th Division command post at Tréléon was palpable. The division had advanced at a steady pace since 1 P.M., but for those staff members armed with grease pencils whose job was to continuously update frontline positions on divisional map overlays, it was virtually impossible to mark with certainty the places where the Germans ultimately intended to stand and fight this battle, as sooner or later they must do. If decisive results had been expected on August 25, those results had definitely not been achieved. After August 25, the 29th Division was physically closer to the heart of Brest, but it was obviously no closer to breaking the enemy's will to resist. To accomplish that essential goal, much hard fighting remained. By Middleton's order, that fighting would resume at 8 A.M. on August 26, when the 29th Division would press on yet again toward Brest.

An attack on Brest by 334 RAF heavy bombers on the night of August 25 was supposed to weaken the enemy's will to resist, yet like almost all attempts to use strategic bombers in support of ground troops in World War II, it did not accomplish much. In this case, the RAF adhered to its standard procedure of attacking during the hours of darkness, and consequently, its bombardiers could not possibly pinpoint German strongpoints on the 29th Division front without accidentally hitting American troops. The air attack was therefore limited to targets well behind the front, mainly in Brest's harbor district. To many, this tactic made little sense, as Middleton's overriding mission was to capture Brest's port facilities—

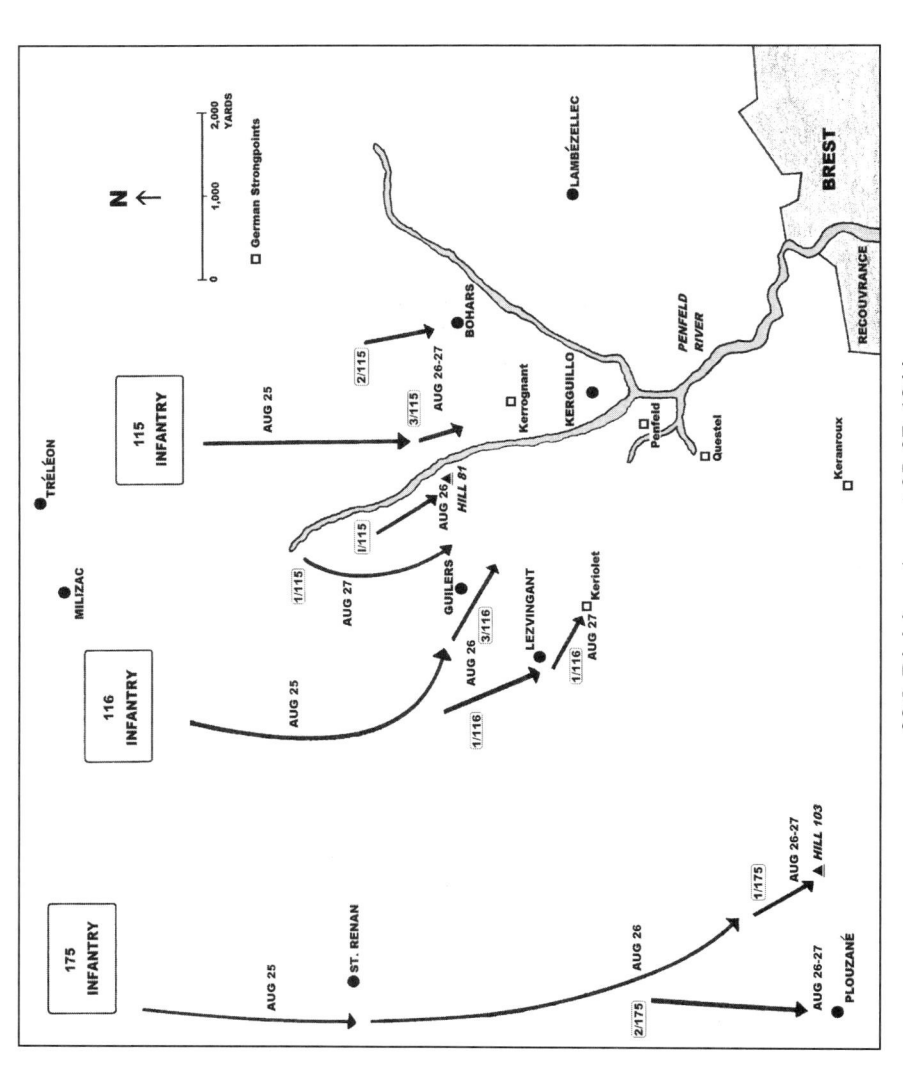

29th Division: August 25–27, 1944

intact if possible—so that American troops and supplies could pour into that city directly from the United States just as they had in the last war. If Allied heavy bombers were going to wreck the harborside, the upcoming task faced by American repair crews would seemingly be that much more difficult once Middleton captured the city.

The RAF bombers reportedly sank two German destroyers and generated huge smoke clouds that billowed to astonishing heights in the harbor for most of the following day, but those were not results that would make the 29ers' upcoming task any easier. In fact, the U.S. Army Air Force's official history of its World War II operations concluded starkly that all the heavy bomber attacks throughout the Brest siege "did no material damage to modern concrete structures . . . and involved a considerable waste of effort."

Cynical 29ers had learned in Normandy that the job of rooting the stubborn enemy out of foxholes and field fortifications always fell to the men with rifles and hand grenades, regardless of Allied air supremacy. Would Brest be any different? General Bradley was determined that it would indeed be different, and he therefore ordered the U.S. Ninth Air Force to do everything in its power to ease the infantrymen's burden.

In a few more weeks, the 29ers would not be so cynical anymore.

2. NOTHING SHORT OF SENSATIONAL

Twenty-ninth Division veterans of the Brest campaign would long remember Saturday, August 26, 1944, as the day they realized that the struggle that lay ahead would not be the pushover they had hoped for. Sunrise on August 26 exposed a pervasive ground fog accentuating the ambiguity of the previous day, when the 29ers had not been able to fathom the enemy's strategy. But by early afternoon, that uncertainty, along with the fog, had vanished. The 29th Division was about to discover exactly where the enemy would make its stand in the battle for Brest, and with that discovery came the obvious but disheartening conclusion that the surrounded Germans, rather than suffering from demoralization as a consequence of heavy air attacks and the apparent hopelessness of their situation, were highly motivated for the upcoming struggle. Indeed, the 29th Division battle line that developed by sunset on August 26 would in large measure remain stagnant for about ten days, an interval during which the division would lose more than 1,300 men.

All 29th Division action reports detailing the struggle on August 26 agreed on two salient points: first, compared to the previous day, the fighting was much more intense; and second, there was no longer any doubt about the location of the enemy's main line of resistance, for by dusk the enemy was disputing every foot of ground and had slowed the 29ers' forward progress to a pace that was even slower than the worst of the Normandy fighting.

Those GIs who had survived Normandy understood the enemy's skill at defensive warfare, but their first close-up look at the German lines outside Brest surely was discouraging. An observer with the 116th Infantry on August 26 understated the case when he noted: "It was not known that the ground embraced in the 1st Battalion's sector [just south of Guilers] had exceptional fortifications." Those defensive works, scattered at intervals across the front, included concrete pillboxes encircled by thick coils of barbed wire, zig-zag trenches with numerous machine-gun pits, lengthy antitank ditches, and bombproof shelters. Such defenses were just as sturdy as the ones the 29th Division had faced on D-Day at Omaha Beach, and when the Germans sited them amid the omnipresent hedgerows with their usual ingenuity, the defenses would probably be even more difficult and costly to overcome. For those 29ers who had expected the fighting in Brittany to be short and comparatively easy, the strength of the enemy's defenses was a shock. Even worse, there seemed to be no way to bypass them, and accordingly, frontal attacks would be Gerhardt's only option if VIII Corps was to fulfill its mission and have Brest in American control within the week.

Yet again there was no subtlety in the August 26 scheme of attack. Gerhardt ordered Col. Lou Smith's 115th Infantry to press straight south on a broad front toward Brest, just four miles distant—Lt. Col. Tony Miller's 2nd Battalion would be situated on the left; Maj. Randolph Millholland's 3rd Battalion on the right. Miller's immediate objective was the village of Bohars, and to get there, his men would have to cross open ground adjacent to a railroad track and push forward about 500 yards—a seemingly trivial distance on a map, but in reality, it turned out to be much more than the 2nd Battalion could handle. The Germans had every field south of the tracks zeroed in with machine guns and mortars, and no matter how Miller's men endeavored to maneuver, they could not get around this formidable resistance. In the hedgerow country north of Brest, it was the Germans and not the Americans who held that coveted advantage known in military field manuals as "fire superiority."

To the 29ers, it seemed as if the enemy was observing anything that moved south of the railroad tracks, and they were probably right. The enemy had posted observers in the lofty steeple of the Bohars church, and to help solve their tactical dilemma, the Americans resolved to knock that steeple down. It was one of those unfortunate episodes in war that Blue and Gray soldiers had experienced before and would certainly face again, but when the lives of good men were at stake, there was no choice. An M-10 tank destroyer, probably from Company A, 644th Tank Destroyer Battalion, was picked for the job; its high-velocity and highly accurate 3-inch gun took less than an hour to demolish what had taken skilled craftsmen years to construct. That success, however, seemed to have no impact on the Germans, who managed to hold on to Bohars for nearly two more weeks.

About a mile to the west of Bohars, Millholland's 3rd Battalion endured the same type of difficulties as Miller's outfit. As Company L, commanded by Capt. Earl Tweed, plunged southward through the baffling hedgerow country, a platoon under the command of T/Sgt. Ralph Snyder scrambled over a hedge into a field that was covered by an unseen enemy machine gun no more than twenty-five yards away. When that machine gun opened up, ten of Snyder's men were killed or seriously wounded in a matter of seconds. According to the 1945 official regimental history, "Sergeant Snyder took off his equipment, discarded his weapon, donned a Red Cross armband, and attempted to reach his wounded men. He was killed. The situation was hopeless for the wounded men and apparently some of them realized it. Corporal George (Tommy) Clayton, one of the wounded, killed himself with his own weapon to forestall any other attempts to come to his aid." It did not take long for the other badly wounded men to expire, leaving eleven American corpses—including Snyder's—in no-man's-land, grotesquely sprawled in a pasture so exposed to enemy fire that their comrades could not recover the bodies for a week.

Company L had learned an essential lesson the hard way: the closer the 29th Division approached Brest, the fiercer the Germans would fight to retain it. Another 3rd Battalion outfit, Company I, also discovered that truth as it warily pushed south parallel to the unfortunate Company L on the west side of a creek, lined by steep, wooded banks. Led by 1st Lt. Dwight Gentry, Company I was striving to seize a piece of terrain that had been noted by Gerhardt as a crucial objective after a thorough examination of his 1:25,000-scale U.S. Army map. Actually, any time contour lines came together on a map in a tight little circle, indicating a commanding hill, American generals always took notice, for these were the perfect observation points they needed in order to identify enemy strongpoints and accurately direct the U.S. Army's legendary firepower.

Lieutenant Gentry was moving his men toward one of those elevations—designated Hill 81 on the map—when the enemy intervened. The fight that erupted quickly swelled in intensity, and amid all the sound and fury, Company I's forward progress was brought to an abrupt halt. Many 29ers were hit, among them Gentry, but according to the Silver Star citation that the U.S. Army would later award him for this action, "[s]eeing that the company was in a precarious situation, he refused to be evacuated and remained to direct operations until given a direct order to submit to medical treatment."

Normally, a U.S. Army rifle company contained six officers, but by the time of Gentry's departure, Company I was down to none. Soon, that outfit's senior NCO, T/Sgt. Walter Hedlund, had to shoulder a job that would normally be the responsibility of a captain. A native of Lowell, Massachusetts, Hedlund was highly respected within the company because of the rigorous combat training he had received in 1943 at the legendary British commando school in Scotland as a member of the 29th Ranger Battalion, a short-lived unit composed of 29th Division volunteers that had been led by Hedlund's current battalion commander, Major Millholland. Despite his unfamiliarity with the current tactical situation, Hedlund's ensuing leadership of the company was remarkable. At the close of its monthly action report for August 1944—usually a dry recitation of facts and figures—the 115th Infantry made a highly unusual reference to Hedlund's actions on August 26 in a postscript labeled "Special Mention of Outstanding Incident." This report noted:

> Tech Sergeant Hedlund was at this time pinned down in a position in advance of the rest of the company, but he made his way back to inquire as to the advisability of attempting to unite them with the rest of the company. Finding that the company commander [Gentry] was unable to lead, he immediately assumed command and in the midst of fierce enemy fire and resultant confusion he reorganized the company, arranged for the withdrawal of the leading platoon [by calling upon the 110th Field Artillery for a smoke barrage], and established a defensive line that withstood a very powerful German thrust. His leadership and bravery on this occasion were nothing short of sensational—more confused circumstances would be difficult to conceive. So outstanding was his leadership that he was left in command of the company until wounded in action two days later.

In a hospital somewhere in England, Hedlund would soon be granted a battlefield commission as a lieutenant and subsequently return to the 29th Division, which by then was fighting in western Germany. After the war,

Millholland remembered that he had put Hedlund in for a Medal of Honor, but the paperwork never got past Gerhardt, who was notoriously stingy in matters related to military decorations. Ultimately, the 29th Division would grant Hedlund the Silver Star for the action at Hill 81, just as it had done for Gentry.

When sunset brought the ferocious fighting to a close, the obstinate Germans continued to control Hill 81. Colonel Smith, the 115th's commander, spoke to Gerhardt by telephone that evening, and he remarked, "Sorry I can't report success for Blue [the 3rd Battalion]. The resistance was much stiffer than was expected. We had a lot of machine guns backed up with high-velocity fire, and then we got some fire from over there in the Lemon [116th Infantry] area too." Gerhardt recommended "folding up for the night" and waiting for morning to try a new line of attack.

Smith indeed tried a new line of attack on August 27, but yet again it failed to work, and that day turned out to be the regiment's toughest day of fighting in the 29th Division's campaign to take Brest, costing the 115th Infantry the excruciating total of 124 casualties. Smith attempted to send Maj. Glover Johns's 1st Battalion, formerly in regimental reserve, on an end run around the obstinate German defenders at Hill 81, but on the east side of Guilers, that outfit ran straight into another redoubtable enemy strongpoint and had to cope with the same sort of fierce resistance that had impeded Smith's other two battalions the previous day. The 1st Battalion suffered heavily and made little progress. The official regimental history noted: "Not only were the forward elements constantly harassed by roving SP [self-propelled] guns, but for the most part the troops had reached the enemy's MLR [main line of resistance], and the advance met concentrated machine-gun and rifle fire from the chain of connected emplacements and strongpoints." The 2nd and 3rd Battalions did no better. The enemy had the 115th Infantry's front thoroughly covered.

Colonel Smith's unfortunate regiment had run straight into the proverbial wall, one that would apparently take weeks and cost the regiment hundreds of casualties to breach. Even if Smith could ultimately smash his way through the enemy's impressive defenses, would the effort and casualties be worth it? And could he do it fast enough so that Ike could soon open up Brest as a supply base? Only Generals Gerhardt and Middleton could answer those questions.

3. SUICIDE ATTACK
If Gerhardt wished to slam the door shut on the German garrison of Brest, he visualized the 115th Infantry as the hinge while the other two pillars of the 29th Division, the 116th and 175th Infantry, represented the swinging

door. Both of those regiments therefore had to push southward on August 26 and eventually effect a difficult and risky sharp turn to their left (or east)—a change of direction executed for the most part while in contact with the enemy. The 116th Infantry, under the command of Col. Philip Dwyer, would thrust into and through the town of Guilers, sweeping forward along the tight inner arc while hanging on to the hinge represented by the 115th Infantry at Hill 81 and Bohars. Meanwhile, the 175th Infantry, led by Lt. Col. William Purnell, would move out of St. Renan and follow the much more lengthy outer arc toward another one of those alluring series of concentric circles on 29th Division maps that had caught Gerhardt's eye. This one, Hill 103, sat near the village of Plouzané—and in a few days it would go down in the history of the 175th Infantry as one of the toughest battles of World War II.

It was a good plan, but as usual, the enemy had an effective response. As a consequence, rather than the slamming forward movement Gerhardt had envisioned, Uncle Charlie's swinging door would smash into unforeseen and decidedly robust enemy strongpoints and would come to a crashing standstill. It would take more than a week to get Gerhardt's swinging door moving again, and by then, the only way to do it was to put all of the 29th Division's weight behind it and shove forward steadily against ferocious and unyielding enemy resistance. By the close of August 26, the distressed 29ers knew that they could never achieve a quick and decisive triumph at Brest. Even worse, ultimate victory—if indeed it could be achieved at all—was going to cost many men. Unhappily, the time had come for 29th Division graves registration personnel to pick a suitable spot for another temporary division cemetery.

The 116th Infantry had participated in more than its share of grueling combats so far in World War II, so nothing the enemy would throw in its way in August 1944 could surprise its veterans anymore. Nevertheless, the battle that was about to erupt around a seemingly inconsequential hamlet with a characteristically Breton name, Keriolet, would be among the Stonewall Brigade's most intense fights of the war. The hard part was that it was so unexpected. When Maj. James Morris, commander of the 1st Battalion, received his orders from Dwyer on the morning of August 26, he later noted it as "a routine assignment." With the 3rd Battalion on the left and the 2nd in reserve, Morris's outfit would push forward to seize its initial objective, the hamlet of Lezvingant; then it would move toward Keriolet, an intersection on some of the highest ground in that locale, where six important roads came together less than a mile south of Guilers.

Not many Germans got in Morris's way at Lezvingant, but beyond that little town, enemy resistance became progressively more stubborn. By evening, 1st Battalion patrols had advanced 500 yards southeast of Lezvingant, stopping for the night about an equal distance west of Keriolet. So far, so good, but that night, Morris's men suspected that the following day, August 27, 1944, would be anything but routine. The reason for that deduction was evident to all, for once darkness fell, such a cacophony of enemy fire, mostly of the antiaircraft variety, erupted beyond the 29ers' frontline hedgerows from the high ground around Keriolet that the GIs realized they had stumbled into a hornet's nest. Something big was just ahead of the 1st Battalion, and the enemy was sure to fight hard to retain it.

The events of August 27 would prove that assumption correct. Morris ordered his outfit to jump off at 9 A.M. with Company A on the left, B on the right, and C in reserve. At first progress was steady, but the advance slowed as it pushed farther east toward Keriolet. A U.S. Army historical officer who interviewed Morris three weeks later noted in his report: "The skirmishing took the usual form. The enemy resisted with a machine gun and five or six riflemen covering each hedgerow. The battalion advanced by fire and movement—mainly along the ditches running parallel to the perpendicular hedgerows. In this way the battalion worked into the outer edge of the prepared defenses of Keriolet, losing quite a few men as it proceeded."

Shortly after noon, Morris moved up to Company A's frontline hedgerow, and what he saw there jolted him. The Germans had cleared wide-open fields of fire of at least 100 yards in depth in front of the Americans, dotted here and there with wooden stakes designed to frustrate the landing of Allied gliders. The enemy had also cut lengthy gaps in the pervasive hedgerows near Keriolet so that the 29ers could not seek refuge behind them. Beyond the scarred hedgerows and wide-open pastures was a formidable antitank ditch backed by profuse bands of barbed wire. All of these impressive defenses enclosed several heavy antiaircraft gun positions and a few concrete pillboxes and underground shelters. These were undeniably the strongest German defenses the 116th Infantry had encountered since Omaha Beach, a place that Morris himself had seen firsthand on D-Day.

Morris did everything in his power to circumvent a deadly frontal attack by trying to maneuver his battalion around Keriolet, but the wily enemy fully expected that tactic and was ready for it. Morris committed his reserve, Company C, on his left and tried to flank the German strongpoint from the north, but the mystifying labyrinth of hedgerows and the enemy's well-hidden resistance nests thwarted that scheme and eventually it came to nothing. Company B had better luck on the right and managed to swing around the strongpoint's southern side before it ran into an eruption of enemy fire and came to an abrupt standstill. In just a few moments, that fusillade inflicted several casualties, one of whom was an enterprising Company B squad leader, wounded by a burst of fire as he tried to covertly approach a German machine-gun nest. Lamentably, that 29er's name went unnoticed by history and even now he cannot be identified, but what history did in fact notice was how he was rescued by the valiant actions of his assistant squad leader, Sgt. Samuel Baker. Baker was described by a fellow squad member as "a man's man from South Carolina" and "a great soldier," who used to amuse his comrades in bivouac by quietly crooning the old 1922 Gus Kahn tune, made famous by Al Jolson, "Carolina in the Morning."

According to a witness, the desperate squad leader lay in an open pasture, "bleeding from his legs, his face ashen, eyes glazed, shouting, 'Help me! Somebody, please! Help me! I'm going blind!' . . . Sergeant Baker jumped up and went into the field, crawling in plain view of the enemy toward him. He removed his cartridge belt and used it as a tourniquet on the squad leader's leg. He then struggled to drag him back to the hedge, where we were able to help get both men back to safety."

Remarkably, Baker went back into the field to get the squad leader's discarded helmet, and this time he was not so lucky. As remembered by that same witness, "A shot rang out. Baker seemed to bounce off the ground. A single bullet had ricocheted off his leg, arm, and face, but he kept crawling with the helmet. When he reached safety, he calmly examined his miraculously superficial wounds, gave himself first aid, and pronounced himself fit for action."

Back at the battalion command post, the sickening realization hit Morris that Company A would have to attack Keriolet by the seemingly impossible method of a frontal attack. This was an affecting choice, for Company A had been decimated in the opening minutes of the D-Day invasion when it executed a direct amphibious assault on German defenses in front of the Vierville Draw on Omaha Beach. Those defenses were little different from those the company now faced at Keriolet. But to the outfit's current members, now under the command of 1st Lt. Wilbur McCormack, Omaha Beach was entirely unfamiliar history because hardly a man who had survived that maelstrom still remained with the unit.

The thirty-six-year-old Maj. Jim Morris was a veteran soldier who, as a college student at the University of Maryland, had enlisted as a private in the 1st Maryland (later 115th Infantry) of the Maryland National Guard in

1926. He had come ashore on D-Day with the 115th Infantry, but had been withdrawn from the front a few weeks later after suffering foot troubles that almost crippled him. Gerhardt respected his command ability, and when a recovered Morris returned to the 29th Division in late July, the general transferred him to the 116th Infantry as an executive officer of one of its three infantry battalions. Such a reassignment was unusual because the 116th was a Virginia National Guard unit while Morris had spent fifteen years of his career in the Maryland National Guard. But after the dreadful casualties of Normandy, such distinctions were now meaningless, and Morris was accepted into the Stonewall Brigade regardless of his origins simply because he was a skilled military leader. He had proved that when the 3rd Battalion of the 116th under his command captured the key city of Vire in a daring evening assault on August 6, 1944.

What Jim Morris had to order Company A to do must have been one of the toughest commands of his life. There was only one way to get at the Germans inside the Keriolet strongpoint—and that was for the members of Company A to charge as swiftly as possible straight across the foreboding open ground bordering the antitank ditch. If they could make it to the ditch, they could take cover in it and work forward from there. To suppress the enemy defenders, Morris strived to arrange for artillery support, and even an air strike by Ninth Air Force fighter-bombers, moments before McCormack's men would jump off, but as he later noted to the U.S. Army historical officer who interviewed him about this affair: "It looked like a suicide attack." Despite the fact that Company A had been reduced to about 60 men from its normal complement of 200, Lieutenant McCormack's terse reply to Morris's order—"I'll try it"—displayed at least some hope. McCormack was a recent replacement officer and new to combat, and it was difficult to imagine a rougher initiation to the front lines.

Although the 29th Division had taken several steps since Normandy to improve its means of communication with the Army Air Force, the process of calling in an air strike against a stubborn enemy strongpoint like Keriolet was still not easy. Colonel Dwyer first requested air support at Keriolet at about 3:30 P.M., but McCormack's men had to wait nearly three hours for it to materialize for reasons the frustrated riflemen could not fathom. Company A was situated no more than 500 yards from the enemy strongpoint, but to the Ninth Air Force, that distance was too close for comfort if the 29ers wished to avoid friendly casualties. An experienced air force liaison officer at 29th Division headquarters telephoned the 116th Infantry command post: "I think that's very close—but if you want it, OK. Have the men display [colored] panels when aircraft come over."

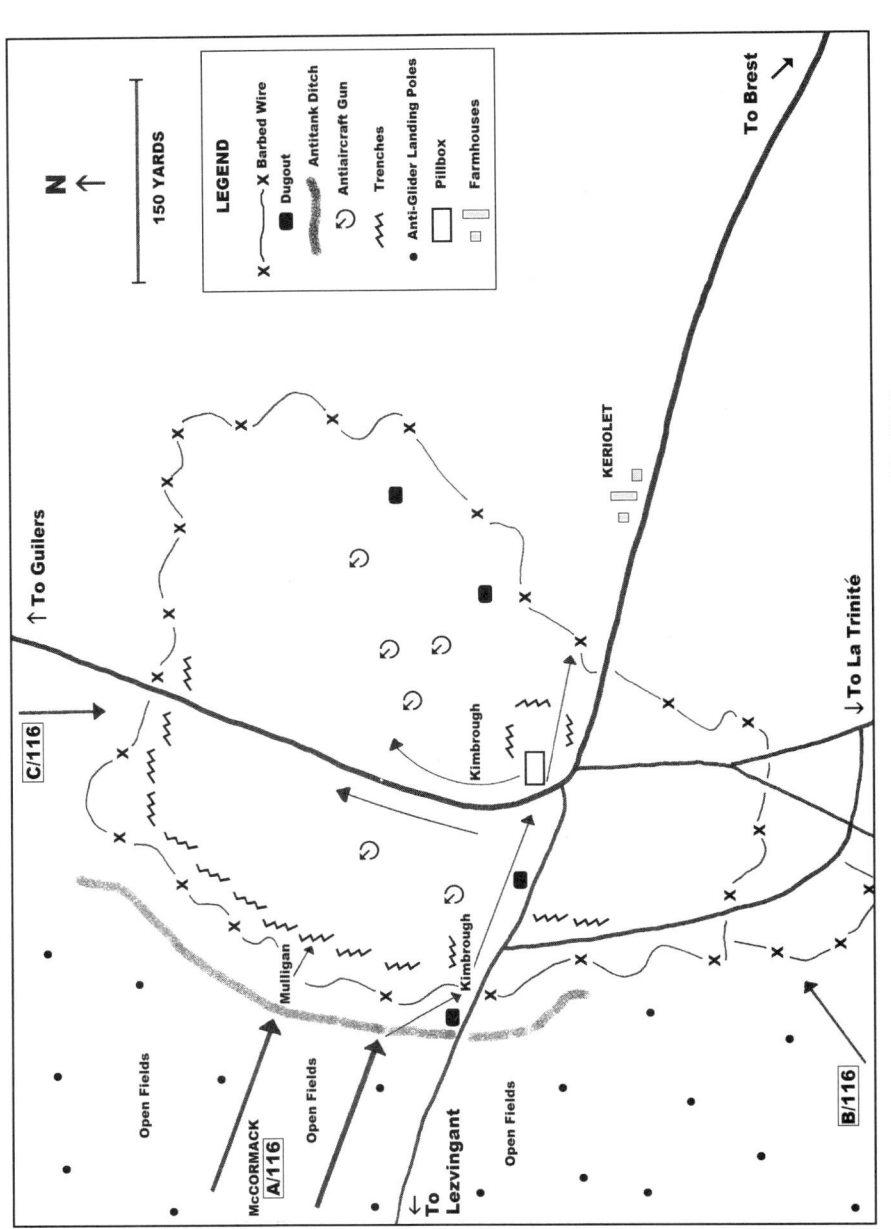

1/116 Infantry at Keriolet: August 27, 1944

Overhead, four P-47 Thunderbolt fighter-bombers circled like vultures, waiting for the right mission, but when Dwyer discovered that they were armed with the Army Air Force's new incendiary bombs stuffed with jellied gasoline, he suspended the strike: those weapons, he mistakenly surmised, would have little impact on the enemy's concrete fortifications and dugouts. However, he declared a willingness to wait for Thunderbolts equipped with conventional ordnance, and at about 6:25 P.M., he got his wish. Four P-47s armed with 500-pound bombs arrived, and when their pilots spotted Keriolet, they banked and descended toward it with the screeching dive German soldiers had come to dread since D-Day, a maneuver they knew would presently be followed by bomb blasts of immense proportions. From the air force's perspective, however, the results at Keriolet were disappointing. According to the Ninth Air Force liaison officer, "The [lead] pilot said he was afraid he didn't do us much good. . . . Most of the bombs went over."

But results that failed to impress American observers in all likelihood had just the opposite effect on the Germans. Proof of this fact derived from McCormack's astonishing success in moving Company A over the deadly open fields west of Keriolet and into the protective cover of the antitank ditch, an attack that at first glance had promised to rank with the Charge of the Light Brigade in the annals of military futility. McCormack's men rose up and moved forward from their frontline positions at 6:30 P.M., just a few minutes after the Thunderbolts had departed, rushing into what seemed like certain death. Morris noted that it looked "like an old-fashioned charge, the men firing their rifles from hip and shoulder as they advanced." Amazingly, they made it into the enemy's antitank ditch—only twenty-five yards short of the German defenders—with only three casualties: one killed and two wounded. It could have been worse—much worse—but in all probability, the Germans had been stunned by the Thunderbolt attack and their attention diverted by Morris's attempt to flank the strongpoint from north and south with Companies B and C. Still, the mission was far from over because McCormack's men had not yet pierced the barbed wire barrier and therefore could not directly assault the enemy's pillboxes and entrenchments.

Coming to close grips with such a resolute enemy would obviously be even tougher than crossing the open ground, but Company A had already come this far, and there was no turning back. To do the job, audacity would be required, and that trait was promptly supplied by Sgt. Daniel Mulligan, who grabbed a pair of wire cutters, bounded out of the antitank ditch, dashed across a small belt of open ground, and flopped down next to the wire. His intentions were clear to friend and foe alike, and as he frantically clipped at the wire to establish a gap, a burst of enemy fire caught him and inflicted a mortal wound. What he had set out to do, however, he had accomplished—at the cost of his life. Such "bold determination, aggressiveness, and unselfish devotion to duty" would eventually earn Sergeant Mulligan a posthumous Silver Star.

McCormack was also fortunate that the alert leader of his 1st Platoon, Lt. Orman Kimbrough, discovered an unguarded enemy communication trench leading off the antitank ditch. The Germans paid a high price for that negligence, for along that trench Kimbrough successfully infiltrated about twenty men under the wire and straight into the enemy's main network of defenses. McCormack and the rest of Company A followed shortly thereafter, sticking to Kimbrough's covert route or passing through the gap cut by Mulligan.

It hardly seemed possible, but this small group of 29ers had penetrated inside the heart of the Germans' Keriolet defenses. For them to hold it, however, they would have to kill, capture, or drive away the enemy defenders, whose numbers obviously exceeded their own and who demonstrated no desire to yield or flee. Those Germans were paratroopers of the elite 7th Company, 2nd *Fallschirmjäger* Regiment—the same kind of ferocious fighters the 29ers had clashed with repeatedly outside St. Lô and who could not be pushed out of their positions by anything short of a supreme effort.

According to the U.S. Army historian who later interviewed Company A survivors of the Keriolet battle, "The fight inside the position became a personal, hand-to-hand action," fought for the most part with rifles and grenades inside buildings, along zig-zag trench lines, and in underground dugouts. Despite the odds against them, the 29ers fought ferociously, and Kimbrough's men soon found themselves in custody of forty-three dazed prisoners.

McCormack, however, was still in a desperate situation. The Germans were dropping a deadly artillery barrage on their own positions, even though they stood just as much chance of killing their own men as the Americans. Kimbrough was wounded—twice—and McCormack sprained his knee so badly that he soon would be forced to crawl if he wished to move. Eventually, as indicated by an action report, "Those of the enemy who had remained under cover came to see that they were opposed by very small numbers. . . . McCormack, looking about him, could count only twelve of his men. He figured it was time to get out."

Getting out, however, would be almost as difficult as getting in. The 29ers were fighting in small groups, scattered over the enemy strongpoint, and McCormack found it impossible to contact anyone except those within range of his voice. He ordered his little cluster of men to depart by means of the same German communications trench they had used to get in. Meanwhile, he would cover them from the rear. The escape route remained open, but because of his injury, McCormack faced the excruciating prospect of crawling on his hands and knees all the way back to American lines. He and his men made it, and Major Morris later noted that the only reason the outnumbered 29ers had made it into Keriolet in the first place "was because of the impetuosity of the two leaders—McCormack and Kimbrough."

A paratrooper by the name of Rudolf Müller who participated in the defense of Keriolet summed up the somewhat more simplistic German version of the battle: "The position changed hands two or three times. The Americans, however, could not hold on for more than an hour since our counterattacks dislodged them each time."

As for Kimbrough, he and seven other Company A members failed to make it out on time and were captured, but he and two comrades escaped as the Germans marched them to the rear. A compassionate French family tucked them away into a corner of their farm and cared for them until the Americans finally took Keriolet—nearly two weeks later.

Keriolet typified the 29th Division's experience in Brittany so far, and unfortunately also forecast what Gerhardt's depleted infantry outfits would endure over the next three weeks. In that interval, the appalling aftermath of the Keriolet battle, with its palpable residue of human and environmental debris, left an indelible impression in the minds of both sides' combatants, who could now grasp the realities of the brutal brand of positional warfare their fathers had endured in the last war. Paratrooper Müller recalled one of the most distasteful of those realities: "An odor of decaying flesh spread rapidly because the days were very hot—and we could not bury the dead as the slightest noise provoked American fire."

Instead of the mop-up campaign some optimistic 29ers had hoped for, to reach Brest, the Blue and Gray Division would be forced to cope with terrain just as taxing as Normandy, a seemingly endless series of daunting German strongpoints and abundant enemy fighters who were thoroughly primed to fight to the last round.

So much for the backwater of the European theater.

4. RUBBED RIGHT OFF THE MAP

If there was one piece of terrain on the 29th Division front that was truly significant, it was Hill 103. Situated five miles west of Brest, this key height had a value that Gerhardt could not fail to grasp simply because it towered over much of the open terrain west of the city by forty or fifty yards. If American artillery observers could occupy its summit, they would be capable of calling in devastating howitzer fire on any German military activity they could directly observe with the speed and precision the enemy acutely feared. There was almost no major military action the Germans could carry out west of Brest that the Americans could not observe in daylight from the top of Hill 103.

In the fighting to come, Hill 103, known locally as Colline de Cocastel, would unquestionably yield to the 29th Division all the many vital advantages of the coveted "high ground" described in detail in U.S. Army field manuals; that is why on August 26 Gerhardt assigned the 175th Infantry the essential mission of seizing it without delay. As part of the division's sweeping movement around the enemy's defenses northwest of Brest that day, the 175th jumped off from St. Renan in the morning and made good progress, advancing steadily southward for four miles and heading straight for Hill 103 and the village of Plouzané, one mile to the west.

For once it seemed as if the Yanks had caught the Germans by surprise. Colonel Purnell's scheme of maneuver called for the 1st Battalion to capture Hill 103, while the 2nd Battalion seized nearby Plouzané. The 1st Battalion was commanded by Lt. Col. Roger Whiteford, who had only recently recovered from a severe wound to return to the outfit he had led since the training days in England and the D-Day invasion—and had served with almost without interruption since 1924. Whiteford had suffered his wound on June 17, 1944, on a hill north of St. Lô that was almost the exact height as the Colline de Cocastel. That earlier battle in Normandy on Hill 108—known forever in regimental lore as "Purple Heart Hill"—had brutally tested the 1st Battalion's military proficiency and triggered hundreds of casualties, but in the opinion of the U.S. Army, Whiteford's men had passed that test so staunchly that it would soon award his outfit the Distinguished Unit Citation, a highly prestigious and rare military honor that survivors of the battle would treasure for the rest of their lives. Regrettably, however, little more than two months later, military exigencies in Brittany had forced Whiteford's outfit to establish yet again that it was still proficient. The top brass had decreed that the 1st Battalion must seize Hill 103 by sunset on August 26, but for those few GIs still with the battalion who had fought on Normandy's Purple Heart Hill, the upcoming task threatened to trigger a battle that could be a repeat of that terrible struggle in June. The Germans, too, held strong attachments to high ground, and if they lived up to their reputation as expert fighters they would never give up Hill 103 without a fight.

For a while those worries seemed unfounded. Whiteford's men trudged up Hill 103 from the northwest, moving warily up the slopes from hedgerow to hedgerow toward the crest: so far, not a single German. By late afternoon they were only a few hundred yards from the summit, so close to that key objective that Gerhardt had gained the impression from Purnell's sanguine reports by telephone that the hill was under the control of the 29th Division.

It seemed almost too good to be true—and it was. The Germans were certainly there, and they were ready. They opened up with a fusillade of machine-gun and small-arms fire that stopped the 29ers in their tracks. Purnell decided to halt Whiteford's men where they stood and reorganize for a much more deliberate attack at 9:30 A.M. the next morning, August 27, an effort that would be supported by Sherman tanks from Company A, 709th Tank Battalion. Such concentrated force would surely finish the Germans off. But the determined enemy repelled that fresh assault and yielded not a foot of ground the entire day, inflicting appalling casualties on the 1st Battalion. Among those killed in action was Capt. Walter Rowan, the commander of Company A.

The 175th's battle for Hill 103 would continue: for how much longer was anyone's guess. In a telephone exchange that evening with his old friend from the Maryland National Guard, divisional operations officer Lt. Col. William Witte, Purnell summarized his predicament by stating a fact that everyone already knew: "Hill 103 is a very important place—I think that is why the Germans are fighting for it so hard."

While Whiteford's 1st Battalion struggled on the slopes of Hill 103, the 2nd Battalion, led by Maj. Claude Melancon, endeavored to liberate the vital crossroads village of Plouzané. Melancon, a Cajun from the Louisiana bayou country west of Baton Rouge, was described by his radio operator, T/4 Jack Montrose, as a man who, "at the blink of an eye, could change from a docile, quiet individual to the most threatening and meanest battalion commander ever encountered." Still, Montrose admired his commander greatly, and noted: "Melancon never desired any glory, recognition, awards and such for himself . . . [and he] applied logic, a commodity lacking in many commanders, who simply followed orders and directed troops as though everything was a training exercise"—a trait Montrose concluded "saved many lives." Seven months later, Melancon would suddenly depart the 29th Division for special leave in the States when he learned the shocking news that his wife and daughter had been killed in a car crash back in Louisiana.

The German paratroopers defending Plouzané at first exhibited a firm desire to hold it, a goal that seemed entirely practicable because skilled enemy artillery observers atop Hill 103, less than a mile to the east, could easily discern the 2nd Battalion's approach routes. For that reason Melancon's troops were subject to a ferocious and accurate artillery and mortar barrage from which it was almost impossible to hide. A Company E medic, T/5 Don McKee, remembered,

> We were right beside a rather high hill [Hill 103], and the Germans were up on the hill. We had just pulled into the area, so we didn't know the terrain at all. . . . I was standing in a group of three, in a farmyard, which was the headquarters for Company E, and I think three of us were standing there talking, and a mortar shell came in and landed so close that it killed two of the guys and hit me. All I can remember is being propelled through the air several feet—and then I was out of it.

But Purnell had at his disposal some highly impressive means of delivering heavy firepower of the American variety, including a type the Germans could not match: airplanes. In late afternoon on August 26, he remarked that American artillery and fighter-bombers might "rub the town right off the map." When that kind of devastating shower of American shells and bombs was ultimately delivered, it did almost exactly that to the unfortunate town of Plouzané, and that pounding helped Melancon's men to wrest control of it from the Germans by the morning of August 27.

It was a victory of sorts, but for the citizens of that devastated town, the price of liberation was perhaps higher than they had foreseen.

5. ENTER TASK FORCE SUGAR

General Gerhardt's plan of operations at Brest had created a predicament for the 29th Division that he needed to solve in a hurry. By swinging his troops around the west side of Brest and thereby fencing the enemy garrison inside that city, he would cut off large bodies of German troops behind the 29th Division's lines, all of whom occupied fortified positions scattered in the region between Brest and the western extremity of the Brittany peninsula. This was a vast area, stretching thirteen miles from Brest to the ancient lighthouse at Pointe de St. Mathieu, a striking headland of rocky cliffs pounded incessantly by the surging Atlantic surf. Unless Gerhardt figured out a way to deal with the numerous enemy soldiers and sailors who would shortly be pocketed behind his front, they were certain to raise havoc behind American lines and could paralyze the 29th Division's efforts to capture Brest.

In truth, on August 25, the day the 29th Division opened its attack on Brest, no one could tell for sure how many enemy troops were located on the western tip of Brittany and where they were deployed. To find out that crucial information, Gerhardt created a special 1,300-man task force, including about 150 29ers from the 175th Infantry (consisting mostly of the regimental cannon company), as well as three troops (companies) of mechanized cavalry, a tank company, a self-propelled tank destroyer company, an engineer platoon, and even a small British signal detachment.

One unique outfit placed at Gerhardt's disposal was Lt. Col. James Earl Rudder's legendary 2nd Ranger Battalion, parts of which had executed the remarkable ascent of the Pointe du Hoc cliffs on D-Day, while the remainder had landed alongside the 29th Division on Omaha Beach. The task force would swell considerably in size in the days ahead, but for the moment the majority of its troops were not 29ers, but members of corps- or army-level units attached to Middleton's VIII Corps. The fact that most of those soldiers had never before served under Gerhardt and did not understand his quirky character would soon lead to personality conflicts, particularly between Gerhardt and Rudder.

Since the 175th was the 29th Division's westernmost regiment, the sector in which the task force would operate nominally fell within the 175th's zone of operations. Gerhardt therefore ordered Lt. Col. Arthur Sheppe, the 175th's executive officer, to take charge of the task force under the supervision of his commanding officer, Colonel Purnell. Sheppe's first order of business was to push west toward the Atlantic coast as soon as he got his extemporized command in order.

The thirty-nine-year-old Sheppe, who had enlisted as a private in the Virginia National Guard in 1920 at the age of sixteen, was already unique in divisional history because he had served in field grade–level command positions within all three infantry regiments in the 29th Division: 115th, 116th, and 175th. Since D-Day, he had cultivated a reputation as Gerhardt's primary pinch hitter, taking command of outfits that needed shaking up and standing ready to fulfill any special task his commanding general concocted. For Sheppe, therefore, the conglomeration of units designed to clean up western Brittany, designated "Task Force S" ("S" standing for the first letter of Sheppe's name), was a natural. Within a few days, however, the GIs comprising the task force—most of whom had never served under Sheppe—would commonly refer to their curious new outfit as "Task Force Sugar."

Sheppe needed to examine the terrain where his task force must soon operate, and accompanied by Purnell, he set out to do that at 2 P.M. on August 25—at almost precisely the same moment when, 350 miles eastward, American and French troops were dashing down the Champs-Elysées to liberate Paris. Sheppe's much more mundane task was to ascend Hill 145, a summit three miles west of St. Renan from where the vast panorama of western Brittany's Finistère region, all the way to the Atlantic, was visible in a single, spectacular glance. Not a German was in sight, but appearances were deceiving.

To find out for sure where the Germans were lurking and precisely how many enemy troops he would have to overcome, Sheppe ordered Troops A and C of the 86th Cavalry Reconnaissance Squadron, an element of the 6th Armored Division, to initiate the task force's vital mission. U.S. Army cavalrymen had been employing horses expertly for 165 years, but in the rush to mechanization in the early 1940s, the horse soldiers' beloved mounts had been unceremoniously replaced by armored cars and jeeps. Nevertheless, their primary mission, dating back to George Washington's day, had not changed: They must scout beyond friendly lines and provide accurate intelligence of enemy whereabouts to their commanders. Over the next two days those progressive cavalrymen did just that, probing aggressively westward between Hill 145 and the ocean. According to their official report, "little opposition was met," except in one important sector. The most essential detail the cavalrymen learned about the enemy was that somewhere between 1,500 and 1,800 German sailors and ground troops were concentrated in the peninsula known locally as Le Conquet, about twelve miles due west of Brest. Named after the picturesque fishing village on the Atlantic coast two miles north of the St. Mathieu lighthouse, that peninsula was a highly defensible piece of terrain of about ten square miles.

The enemy had erected an impressive strongpoint about a mile and a half southeast of Le Conquet village, designated the Graf Spee Battery after the notable German admiral of World War I who had given the Royal Navy fits for a few months in 1914. Had Gerhardt realized that this battery was one of the Atlantic Wall's toughest fortifications, featuring four 280mm (11-inch) naval guns housed in giant concrete casemates surrounded by trenches, minefields, and barbed wire, he might have allocated Sheppe many more men and much heavier firepower. However, he would grasp that reality as soon as the Graf Spee Battery's guns, normally

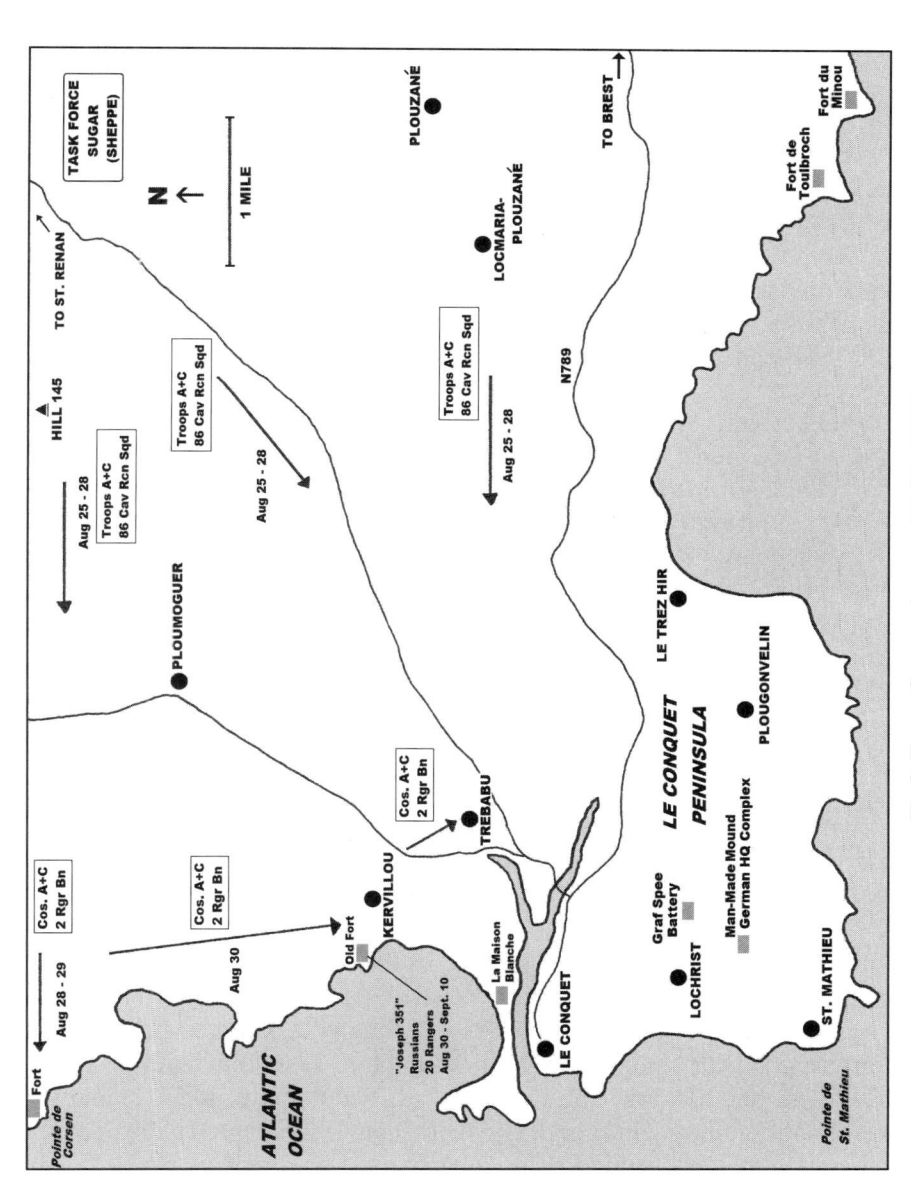

Task Force Sugar: August 25–30, 1944

oriented to fire seaward, periodically rotated 180 degrees to hurl their massive shells inland, directly into the rear of the 29th Division's lines seven or eight miles away as Gerhardt maneuvered his division to encircle Brest. One unfortunate member of the 115th Infantry who had the dreadful experience of coming under fire from one of those huge shells noted that it "came in with a noise like a rushing wind," with an enormous blast effect far more deadly than anything the 29ers had been subjected to so far in World War II.

Capt. Robert Walker, the 116th's intelligence officer, had always endeavored to maintain an air of nonchalance when he was subjected to an enemy artillery barrage, but the impact of one of those large-caliber shells, which he recalled "made the earth tremble," was not so easy to ignore. "A sergeant came by and handed me an object about the size of a bowling ball, but heavier," Walker observed. "As I held it I could feel a sharp point in the surface pierce my fingertip because I had to grip it that hard to keep from dropping it. He had dug the fragment out of two feet of earth near his foxhole, and it was covered with mud. . . . It was the only time anything from the enemy drew blood from me—but it wasn't good enough for a Purple Heart."

To Sheppe, it was imperative that he swiftly reveal to the enemy garrison of Le Conquet that they were completely cut off from Brest and would soon face a simple choice: surrender or die. On August 25, the thirty-one-year-old Royal Navy battleship HMS *Warspite*—known as "The Old Lady" by her adoring crew—thoroughly pummeled the Graf Spee Battery with salvos from its 15-inch guns from the remarkable range of sixteen miles, called in with great accuracy by a British forward observer team. Later, Ninth Air Force aircraft accentuated the Germans' loneliness by pounding Graf Spee and other nearby positions with a cascade of bombs. By the morning of August 28, Sheppe's men had sealed off all the roads leading out of the peninsula, and the enemy's isolation was indeed complete. Sheppe, however, knew that if the Germans resolved to fight on, as they almost always did, his skimpy task force—which the enemy appreciably outnumbered—would not possess sufficient punch to finish them off. In that event, Gerhardt and Middleton would eventually have to substantially reinforce Task Force Sugar if it harbored any hope of overcoming the formidable Le Conquet defenses by direct attack.

The 86th Cavalry Squadron's rapid advance managed to isolate a few minor enemy pockets outside of the Germans' main enclave at Le Conquet, and those were small enough for Sheppe to deal with straight away with no outside help. One German fort at Pointe de Corsen, a rocky promontory five miles north of the Graf Spee Battery that is one of the westernmost points on the French mainland, was garrisoned by a force defined by an American intelligence report as "50 in number, thirty to fifty years old, mostly coast guardsmen . . . supplied by fishing boats from Brest."

On the evening of August 28 a task force comprised of Companies A and C of Rudder's 2nd Ranger Battalion moved up and prepared to assault that position. It looked like a tough mission, but the task force commander, Capt. Edgar Arnold, was a veteran of the early-morning Omaha Beach assault on D-Day, and compared to that cataclysm, this job would in all likelihood be easy because the enemy garrison apparently did not have its heart in such a hopeless cause. In fact, part of the garrison attempted to escape during the night, and French partisans killed ten of them. Near midnight, the enemy force actually offered to surrender, but that procedure, according to Sheppe's report, was "interrupted by their own artillery coming from La Maison Blanche" [another German fort about three miles to the south].

The following morning, August 29, Colonel Rudder took over from Arnold and announced, "I am attempting to have the garrison surrender." The rangers, assisted by a platoon of M-10 tank destroyers from the 644th Tank Destroyer Battalion, stood poised to storm Corsen, but it turned out to be unnecessary. At 10 A.M., Rudder radioed to the 29th Division war room: "Fifty-six Germans have surrendered. There are also four dead."

If the German defenders at Corsen had been such easy pushovers, then all of the Le Conquet peninsula—and perhaps Brest as well—could soon be in American hands. Rudder's rangers pushed on confidently, moving three miles southward. The next day, August 30, they encountered a much more formidable enemy strongpoint on another lofty headland just west of the village of Kervillou, labeled on U.S. Army maps simply as the "Old Fort." According to Rudder, "Patrols indicated that this position was held by fifty Germans [with] a machine-gun pillbox, consisting of four guns, which enabled them to fire north, south, east, and west. Stone and concrete emplacements housing a 20mm [antiaircraft] gun and mortars were located at the base of the cliff. . . . The approach to this position was in plain view of the fortifications at La Maison Blanche [about one mile to the southwest], which gave artillery support." Rudder's force of about 120 men was too small to make a frontal assault against such a strong position, which was surrounded by minefields, trenches, and barbed wire. The high-velocity 3-inch guns of the 644th's tank destroyers tried to penetrate the enemy pillboxes, but Captain Arnold reported to Rudder that their effect was "doubtful."

Expending American lives on such an isolated enemy outpost was hardly sensible, and therefore Rudder ordered Arnold to leave twenty rangers behind to contain the "Old Fort" at Kervillou and move the remainder of his men south to join the main body of Task Force Sugar in its effort to cut off and ultimately neutralize the large German enclave on the Le Conquet peninsula. Arnold obliged, but much to his amazement, he unexpectedly was the beneficiary of reinforcements enabling him to leave behind more than one hundred men at Kervillou instead of the twenty specified by Rudder. These reinforcements were not rangers, nor even Americans for that matter. Rather, they were Russians, ex-prisoners of war captured by the Germans on the Eastern Front, who until recently had been serving as unenthusiastic laborers and paramilitary troops for the German occupiers of Brittany. The arrival of the 29th Division in the Brest environs, however, had presented the Russians with an opportunity to turn on their masters, and under the leadership of a shadowy character known to history only by the inexplicable appellation of "Joseph 351," they offered their services to Arnold. He accepted, and now, armed with weapons provided by the French Resistance, the mysterious Joseph 351 and his Russians joined with the twenty rangers left behind by Rudder to contain the German garrison at the Old Fort. The rangers were glad to have some help, but those scruffy and ferocious Russians, who angrily vowed that they would give the hated enemy no quarter, were a startling sight.

The rangers would have to deal with the Old Fort at Kervillou later, and in the meantime, it was fortunate that Russia was an American ally. It was much more important right now that Task Force Sugar capture the enemy's heavy naval guns at the Graf Spee Battery, and this Rudder immediately set out to do.

5. MARCELLE

With the exception of Brest, Le Conquet, and a few scattered enemy strongpoints, western Brittany was free of its German occupiers for the first time in more than four years. That was certainly agreeable to the Bretons, who for the most part had joyously welcomed the 29th Division and looked forward to resuming their lives that had been so harshly interrupted by war. But when would normality return? Colonel Cooper of the 110th Field Artillery Battalion noted: "When we first got to Brest, thousands of civilians had voluntarily gotten out of the city and crowded the countryside, particularly back where the 29th Division's service units were. They needed food badly, but we had only limited 'overs.' In spite of orders, the drain of generosity to these people, including many children, caused me to move my Service Battery forward to the area where there weren't so many civilians. This solution at least stopped the clash of emotions within us: obey orders—or give them food?"

The lives of 29th Division soldiers and the local Breton populace intertwined for just a few short weeks in the late summer of 1944, but the results were from time to time poignant. On Sunday, August 27, Cooper's 110th Field Artillery conducted its first religious services in Brittany in a field behind a farmhouse north of Bohars. "Father Pat" O'Grady, the beloved 115th Infantry chaplain from Baltimore who had been with the 29th Division since its February 1941 mobilization, conducted the service. The natives' religious persuasion was mostly Roman Catholic, so O'Grady's mass attracted several local farmers and their families, who Cooper noted were "dressed in their pathetic best." Typically, the barriers of language and culture conspired to make the initial face-to-face contacts between GIs and French civilians somewhat awkward, but O'Grady's austere service in a simple pasture brought the young American warriors and the hardy Breton peasants together, wordlessly, in their shared deference to God.

In the line of duty, however, the 29ers encountered entirely different sorts of Frenchmen. These were the members of the FFI, the famed French Resistance, whose men—and in some cases women—had been shouldering the hazardous burden of defying the German occupiers of Brittany long before the 29th Division came upon the scene. But the Americans' arrival had suddenly transformed a partisan war into a conventional one, and the members of the FFI soon found themselves fulfilling much more pedestrian tasks than they were used to. Serving as local guides for the Americans and maintaining order in areas behind the front lines were of course not roles that embraced the drama of sabotaging a railroad line or ambushing a German staff car. From the partisans' viewpoint, however, this makeover was entirely positive because it suggested that their mission of more than four years' duration was nearly fulfilled. When the last of the hated German occupiers departed western Brittany, the natives would at last regain their freedom, a victory in which the FFI members could take enormous pride because they had contributed markedly to it.

But the Americans still had a hard fight ahead at Brest, and in the meantime FFI leaders made it clear to their liberators that they would support that effort. General Gerhardt accepted that offer gladly, issuing an order that declared, "Regiments will maintain direct liaison with the FFI units operating in their respective sectors." The 29ers, however, were skeptical, and Gerhardt directed his chief intelligence officer, Lt. Col. Paul Krznarich, to prepare a document explaining the FFI's value. "Since this will be our first encounter with the FFI, it is desired that all personnel of this command be acquainted with their existence and description," Krznarich wrote. "The FFI are dressed partly in ramshackle uniforms, partly in civilian clothes. They wear armbands of red, white, and blue with 'FFI' written on them. They are organized and operate under a commandant with whom liaison is effected by higher headquarters. The most important point to caution troops about is that the FFI are armed with German weapons.... The work of the FFI has been and continues to be excellent. Not only has their enthusiasm for rounding up and killing Germans been of extreme value, but they can be used for security [and] as guides."

In truth, most 29ers at first could not perceive the value of such a seemingly disordered group of foreign fighters in the difficult task the division faced in the days ahead at Brest. Holbrook Bradley, a *Baltimore Sun* reporter who had been with the division since D-Day, noted that the Resistance fighters were "dressed in an array of equipment ranging from the picturesque clothes of Breton fishermen to the French uniform . . . [giving] the impression of a rabble or comic opera army." But Gerhardt noted in his monthly report for August 1944 that the FFI "was well commanded and quite efficient—with good spirits," a sentiment later echoed by Bradley, who reported to his readers in September that the FFI was "one of the most important elements engaged in the task of clearing the remaining Nazis from this area." The Resistance fighters had quickly proved that point to the 29ers, particularly in the fluid and sometimes bewildering situation faced by Colonel Sheppe as he rushed Task Force Sugar westward toward the Le Conquet peninsula to deal with scattered pockets of the enemy—about which the FFI knew much more than he did.

The commandant of the FFI fighters in the Brest *arrondissement* was a diminutive fifty-six-year-old French Army professional named Baptiste Faucher, known to the 29ers throughout the campaign only by his *nom de guerre* "Commandant [Major] Louis." Members of the 29th Division had never before seen a major at such an advanced age, but one could not fail to be impressed at Louis's dedication to his country's eventual liberation. He had been stationed in Africa in 1940 when the Germans invaded France and arrived back in his homeland only in time to witness the humiliation of his government's capitulation to the enemy.

It was a humiliation that Louis, like thousands of others, would not allow himself to forget. Bradley interviewed him in early September 1944 and related the commandant's story in a *Baltimore Sun* article:

As senior commander of the ten cantons of Brest, he took charge of organized sabotage and anti-Nazi efforts throughout the area. Then, as invasion grew imminent, he left Brest and went into hiding with the Maquis. . . . As the tide of Allied advance pushed toward Brest, Louis's FFI command came out into the open and began active opposition to the enemy as an army unit. Many towns on the peninsula and much hinterland were cleaned up by this force, which has achieved the name of one of the toughest outfits in operation here. Today this well-organized element is fighting side by side with our regiment [the 175th Infantry].

Gerhardt thought so highly of the Resistance fighters that he decorated Commandant Louis with a U.S. Army Bronze Star at the close of the campaign.

Of all the members of the FFI affiliated with the 29th Division at Brest, certainly the most memorable was Marcelle Bouyer, a fifteen-year-old Breton girl who had attached herself to the 115th Infantry as a medic. Despite her youth and lack of formal training, this was a task with which she was entirely familiar. In the secretive FFI community, she had nursed Resistance fighters who had been wounded in the uprising in western Brittany following D-Day; later, upon the arrival of the U.S. Army's 6th Armored Division in the Brest environs in the aftermath of the Normandy breakout, she cared for wounded GIs from that outfit. When the 29th Division showed up at Brest in late August, the members of the 115th Infantry's Company G were greeted by the astonishing sight of a petite and attractive French girl, wearing a GI helmet and dressed in a U.S. Army tanker's uniform with Red Cross armbands. A large black hunting dog seemed to be her constant companion. Once, when Company G was marching down a road toward the front, it passed its neighbor, Company F, and a member of that outfit, Pvt. Ray Moon, could not help noticing the peculiar "aid man," who he remembered "was the smallest soldier I had ever seen—no more than five feet tall and perhaps one hundred pounds." The locks of hair protruding from the rear of Marcelle's helmet finally convinced Moon that this was no soldier.

The 29ers gratefully accepted Marcelle's offer to assist in the care of the wounded, and for the next several weeks, she carried out those duties with great compassion and bravery, gaining the admiration of all 29ers who watched her in action. She spoke virtually no English, but according to Moon, she was capable of belting out the lyrics of popular American songs, first among them "Pistol Packin' Mama," recorded in 1943 by Bing

Crosby and the Andrews Sisters with its bouncy chorus: "Lay that pistol down, babe, lay that pistol down!" War is an endeavor that tends to make those involved appear older than they really are, and Marcelle was no exception. When she attached herself to a 29th Division combat unit, she perhaps did not realize what she was getting herself into, for most 29ers who glimpsed her for the first time certainly did not perceive an adolescent girl, but rather a striking figure in womanhood's full bloom.

Had only a single soldier behaved toward Marcelle imprudently, it could have cast negative aspersions on the 29th Division for weeks. But every night, the commander of Company G, 1st Lt. Robert Rideout, placed a sentry outside Marcelle's tent, and according to a member of that company, PFC Henry Green, Rideout himself dug a foxhole just for her. Private Moon observed: "The entire company did what it could to respect her privacy." That privacy was also upheld because Marcelle invariably kept by her side her beloved dog, which was noticeably protective of its owner.

It was all highly irregular, of course, but as long as no sticklers who routinely quoted U.S. Army regulations grumbled to the top brass, Marcelle could remain with her boys from the 115th Infantry and perform the work she knew made a real difference in their lives. Those 29ers who understood her dedication to that work deeply respected her for it. In fact, several months passed before someone finally complained about her presence with the regiment. By then, Marcelle had departed Brittany for Holland and was helping to care for the many members of the 115th who had been wounded in the 29th Division's fall offensive into western Germany. But regulations finally caught up with her, and sometime prior to Christmas, her comrades woke up to find her gone. Private Moon spoke for dozens when he remarked, "Life for me in the infantry was never the same."

THREE

The Key to the Whole Thing

1. LA TRINITÉ

For the 29th Division, the three-day period from August 25 through August 27, 1944, had amounted to a costly setback that might be more properly defined as a defeat—had General Gerhardt permitted such an odious word to be used in the war room. In truth, nothing the general tried had worked. With their usual doggedness, the Germans had stopped the 29ers cold at Bohars, Keriolet, and Hills 81 and 103. Even worse, the 29th Division's initiation into combat in Brittany had shrunk its manpower rolls by more than 500 men, a toll that matched some of the costliest periods of fighting in Normandy. High hopes for a swift and decisive victory at Brest had vanished, a major disappointment that forced the weary fighting men to conclude bitterly that the top brass was not about to grant a meaningful rest period to the 29th Division anytime soon. By the time that respite would be allowed, if ever, all infantryman who grasped the harsh realities of a World War II battlefield surely wondered whether they would still be living and breathing men. The forlorn GIs had to accept the undeniable truth that Brittany was going to be no different from Normandy—and might even be worse. As the 29th Division's chief intelligence officer later noted somewhat plaintively, "The name 'Fortress Brest' meant exactly what that name implied."

If Brest had to be taken, there had to be a better way to do it than battering through the enemy's prepared defenses in a series of frontal attacks. Therefore, for the fourth day of the Battle of Brest, August 28, Gerhardt resolved not to abandon his "end-run" strategy, a series of sweeping flanking maneuvers that had probed for weak spots in the German lines. That scheme had not detected any vulnerable points in the first three days of battle, but there was still more room between Hill 103 and the coastline west of Brest to keep trying. If the Germans were stretched as thin as VIII Corps intelligence reports had first indicated, a lucky 29th Division unit could indeed discover such a weak point, and then the road to Brest might not be so difficult after all.

However, if Gerhardt wished to persist in that line of reasoning, he would have to radically alter his methodology for the simple reason that he had run out of men who were still free to maneuver. The only logical course of action at this point would be to pull an entire infantry regiment out of the line and order a neighboring regiment to extend its front to cover the resulting gap. On the evening of August 27, that is precisely what Gerhardt decided to do.

The general opted to withdraw the 116th Infantry from the 29th Division's center and shift it far to the south, a movement that promised to be awkward because the Stonewall Brigade was at that moment heavily engaged in relentless fighting in and near the enemy's Keriolet strongpoint. Gerhardt phoned the 116th's command post at 8:20 P.M. on August 27 and informed Colonel Dwyer, "Pull out and go around Purnell [CO, 175th Infantry, currently engaged at Plouzané and Hill 103]. You will have all three battalions and go down in column." The astonished Dwyer would have plenty of work ahead of him if that difficult maneuver were to work, and consequently, he and his staff would have no time for sleep that night.

Too, someone would have to plug the gap created by Dwyer's withdrawal, and to fulfill that role, Gerhardt contacted Col. Lou Smith at the 115th Infantry's command post and issued a straightforward order: "Take over the full front of both your regiment and Dwyer's." Smith's men had faced tough fighting for the past three days, and the regiment was already stretched thin on a front of over two miles holding down the 29th's left flank from its link-up point with the neighboring 8th Division all the way to the town of Guilers. Extending Smith's lines would be just as tricky as Dwyer's imminent maneuver, as the 115th would have to extend its right flank by more than a mile while in direct contact with the enemy—at night. Once this extension of the line was complete, however, Smith could at least look forward to some relief because, as the 115th's official history later observed, "The tremendous frontage of the regiment and the lack of any reserve force made an attack with anything larger than a combat patrol out of the question."

U.S. Army field manuals provided precise details on how to carry out maneuvers such as those Colonels Smith and Dwyer would have to initiate, but against an enemy as alert as the Germans, reality would differ appreciably from warfare as described in a book. Unlike Smith, Dwyer was a professional soldier who had entered the U.S. Military Academy in 1919 after serving as an enlisted man during World War I. Upon his graduation as a member of the class of 1923, he had spent the bulk of his career in the infantry. This included a spell from 1927 to 1930 in Tientsin, China, as part of the renowned 15th Infantry, which had been commanded during part of that time by a brilliant lieutenant colonel named George C. Marshall. During the current war, Dwyer had spent eighteen months in the Aleutian Islands as commander of the 153rd Infantry, an Arkansas National Guard outfit that had been called up in 1940 just a few months before his current command, Virginia's 116th Infantry. Described by a subordinate as "portly, taciturn, and stern—with a dead-serious demeanor," Colonel Dwyer seemed older than his forty-four years. He was, however, a dependable soldier whom Gerhardt had come to appreciate since he had joined the 116th just before the fall of St. Lô.

Dwyer's essential goal was to swing the 116th Infantry in an arc twelve miles to the southeast and cut the road known locally as the N789, the main thoroughfare leading westward out of Brest toward the Le Conquet peninsula. Like all of Gerhardt's previous end runs, the 116th would begin this move by pulling out of the line, heading west and then south, finally turning 90 degrees to the east at a point specified in orders—directly toward the city of Brest. For the most part, those maneuvers must be carried out in darkness and, as the regimental action report for August 1944 lamented, through "strange territory, with no knowledge as to the presence of friendly or enemy troops [and] very little prior reconnaissance and no flank protection." One of Dwyer's customary maxims was "Estimate the situation," and that is just what his harried staff now would be forced to do.

Maj. Charles Cawthon's 2nd Battalion was the logical unit to lead Dwyer's maneuver because on August 27 it was in regimental reserve and had not yet been heavily engaged in the Brest fighting. The 3rd Battalion would follow, and the 1st, which had been badly mauled in the attempt to capture Fort Keriolet, would bring up the rear. The first objective, about seven miles from the front, would be the village of Locmaria-Plouzané.

One mile beyond that place, the 116th would aim for the vital N789 road, at which point the Stonewallers would turn east, follow that thoroughfare, and head straight for La Trinité, an important crossroads town just four miles west of Brest's medieval city walls.

At least that was the way Gerhardt intended his scheme to work, and unlike most complex military operations, that was indeed the way it did work. The first objective at Locmaria-Plouzané could have been difficult, for as little as Dwyer's staff knew of the enemy's whereabouts, that town might have contained an entire German panzer division. Fortunately, however, it turned out to be under the control of French Resistance forces under the command of "Commandant Louis," and except for those Germans who were dead or prisoners, not an enemy soldier was in sight. The 116th's subsequent turn to the east, too, was comparatively simple. By nightfall on August 28, Cawthon's 2nd Battalion was only about a mile short of La Trinité, ready to launch a coordinated attack with the 3rd Battalion the following day.

For the 116th Infantry, the repositioning was an impressive success. A report by the regiment's intelligence officer, Capt. Robert Walker, noted: "The shifting of the whole regiment in a night, immediately following its disengagement from contact with the enemy . . . required split-second timing and superior control by all troop leaders, not to mention precise staff coordination. The endurance and alertness shown by the men was inspiring."

But wars cannot be won solely by maneuvers, no matter how efficiently they are carried out. Sooner or later, American and German troops would have to engage in combat somewhere outside the walls of Brest—a truth that was convincingly established by the ferocious combat that erupted between the 116th Infantry and the enemy west of La Trinité on August 29 and 30. Major Cawthon recalled, "The 2nd Battalion had the lead and began to bleed. . . . It was the bloody type of hedgerow fighting that we had hoped had been left behind in Normandy." Every soldier who came to Brittany with the 29th Division had harbored that same hope, but that hope would vanish in an instant at La Trinité.

At 7 A.M. on August 29, the 116th commenced its attack with Cawthon's battalion in the lead. As the day wore on and enemy resistance stiffened, Dwyer threw Maj. William Puntenney's 3rd Battalion in on Cawthon's left, but that ploy did no good. La Trinité was only about 2,500 yards beyond the American line, but as the Stonewall Brigade's August 1944 action report declared, "The resistance put up by the enemy was bitter." Major Puntenney corroborated that point when he observed: "The

German paratroopers were as good as any enemy troops we had fought since the Normandy landings and were carrying out Hitler's orders to fight to the last man and last bullet."

As the 3rd Battalion joined the fray, a disaster befell Company I when a German shell landed in the middle of a crowded briefing, killing nine men—including five officers. As soon as he heard of this calamity, Capt. Archibald Sproul immediately set out from the 3rd Battalion command post to the front lines to help salvage the fortunes of the unfortunate Company I. A twenty-eight-year-old Virginian with a degree from Washington and Lee University, Sproul had experienced a meteoric military career during which, in less than four years, he had risen to second-in-command of the 800-man 3rd Battalion after enlisting as a private in the Virginia National Guard in November 1940. That rise would continue after World War II, when Sproul would assume command of the 29th Division in 1965. His fellow Stonewallers regarded Sproul highly, and the award of a Distinguished Service Cross for his heroics on Omaha Beach did much to reinforce that admiration.

Captain Sproul had recently returned to the 3rd Battalion after suffering a wound at St. Lô in July, and at Brest on August 29, 1944, he was about to receive an Oak Leaf Cluster to his first Purple Heart. Major Puntenney recalled, "Shortly after Sproul arrived at the [Company I] CP, he was wounded by more artillery fire. It was nearly midnight when the stretcher-bearers brought him back to the battalion CP. He had been hit in the leg, a serious wound, but not life-threatening. I kidded with Archie a little bit and told him it was a hell of a way to end his duty with us by having to go off to the hospital again."

At 5:30 P.M., by which time the 116th had only managed to push ahead about 500 yards, Gerhardt phoned Dwyer with the observation: "I think you better fold up for the evening." Dwyer protested that his men could still make progress before dark, but the general brushed him off with the abrupt declaration: "We'll jump off at 0700 in the morning [of August 30]." Before August 29, Cawthon's 2nd Battalion had been spared the worst of the Brest fighting, but that day's battle west of La Trinité had yielded casualties that company clerks could scarcely keep pace with. Furthermore, Dwyer was still far short of his objective at La Trinité, a place that Cawthon remarked "seemed impervious to our guns."

Gerhardt's latest attempt at a wide flanking maneuver to get into Brest had yet again failed to locate a soft spot in the German lines. Dwyer tried to push his regiment straight ahead again on the morning of August 30 toward La Trinité, but the outcome was hardly an improvement on the

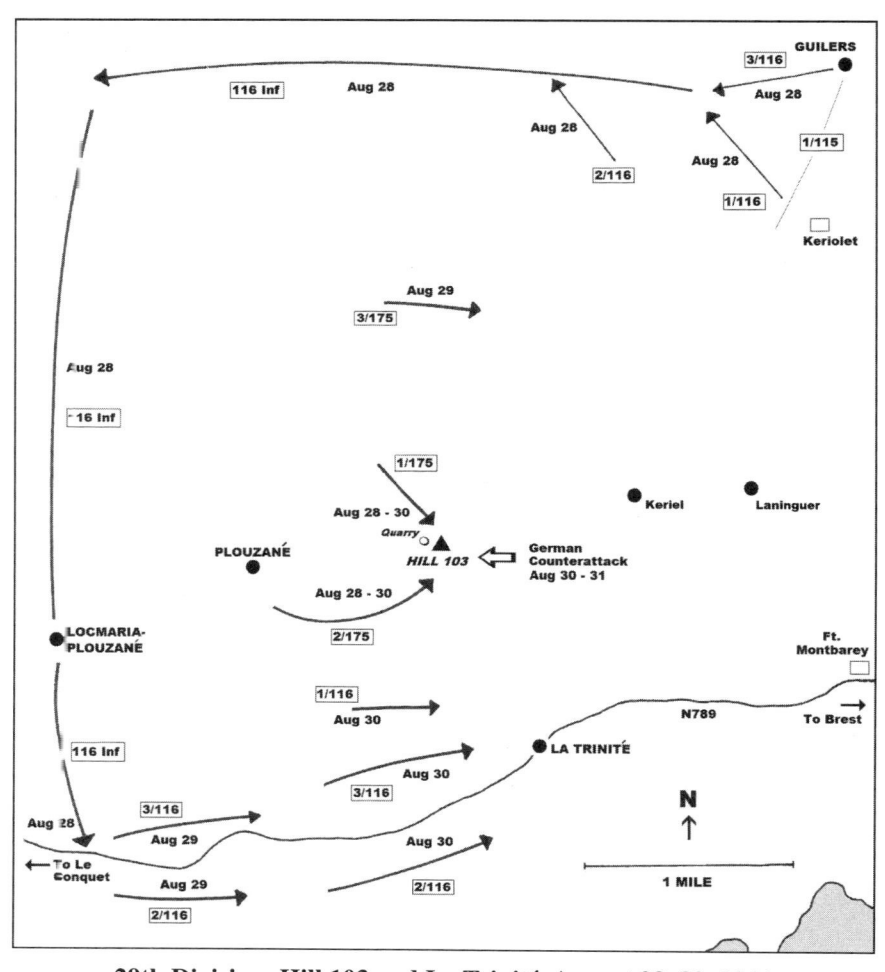

29th Division: Hill 103 and La Trinité, August 28–30, 1944

previous day and resulted in nearly 100 more casualties. After two days of ruthless fighting the 116th was still about a quarter of a mile short of La Trinité, and the regiment's offensive power was so drained that it could not carry on the next day, August 31. Even the commitment of Dwyer's reserve 1st Battalion could not re-energize the attack, for that outfit had been badly mauled during the battle at Keriolet on August 27 and was hardly ready to resume major offensive operations.

Dwyer's men—and all 29ers for that matter—needed a rest, and Gerhardt knew it. Nearly a week of bitter fighting had revealed one salient fact to all members of the 29th Division: the Germans were not beaten. Perhaps a division-wide stand-down on August 31 would be a good idea.

2. HILL 103

The 116th may have been in a dreadful blind alley at La Trinité, but for Colonel Purnell's 175th Infantry, the predicament was even worse. Late on August 26, the 175th had come heartbreakingly close to seizing that vital height known as Hill 103, about a mile and a half north of La Trinité, but the Germans had thrown in considerable numbers of reinforcements with strict orders not to budge from the summit—a mission they had carried out impeccably on August 27 in the face of a frontal assault by the 1st Battalion, under the command of Lt. Col. Roger Whiteford.

On August 28, Gerhardt, whose exasperation was mounting by the hour, ordered Purnell to renew with much greater fury his assault on Hill 103, which the general insisted was the key to the enemy's defenses at Brest. The Germans evidently agreed with that hypothesis, for they had fortified the hill with a diligence reminiscent of the trench lines and redoubts on the Western Front in World War I.

Gerhardt and Purnell, however, could not at first grasp the thoroughness of the enemy's defenses on Hill 103; the warren of trenches, tunnels, dugouts, pillboxes, and caves into which the Germans had transformed the hillcrest were so cleverly constructed that the first time the 29ers discerned them was when they walked straight into them, an event that invariably triggered plentiful casualties. Minefields and thick bands of barbed wire surrounded the entire position, which Whiteford's men had failed to breach on August 26 and 27, even when assisted by tanks.

Still, even had the 29ers been able to penetrate the wire into the enemy enclosure, much more effort would have been required to expel the Germans from the hill. Three sturdy pillboxes stood squarely in the 1st Battalion's path, each of which was assembled with massive stone blocks two feet thick—resistant to almost every weapon at Whiteford's disposal, including the Sherman tanks. The pillboxes were linked by deep trenches, from which several tunnels emanated. The tunnels led to a few underground dugouts, including a command post, radio room, hospital, and living quarters. Even a direct hit by a 1,000-pound bomb would in all likelihood fail to drive the Germans out of such ingeniously designed defenses.

Immediately behind this maze of fortifications, on the hill's southeast slope, lay an old Breton stone quarry, oval-shaped, about 150 feet long and 50 feet deep, a vast pit that provided the enemy with an effective refuge from the American bombardment that was bound to increase in intensity the longer the Germans held on to the hill. An even more effective hideout was a large cave that could be accessed through a tiny entrance at the base of the quarry on its southwestern wall. The cave extended for more than 100 yards to a point underneath a nearby farmhouse, well beyond the barbed wire perimeter surrounding the hill's summit. As Purnell was about to discover, with defenses as robust as those, the Germans would be capable of holding out against great odds for a considerable period, even in the face of the heavy air and artillery bombardments the Americans habitually applied when their infantry attacks stalled.

Purnell would try again at noon on August 28, and this time he thought he had a more creative plan. First, he would add more attackers to the equation by bringing up Maj. Claude Melancon's 2nd Battalion from Plouzané, the village one mile west of Hill 103 seized by the 175th Infantry the previous day. Second, he would change the axis of his attack by using Whiteford's 1st Battalion to tie down the enemy on the northwest face of the hill—seemingly the side with the toughest defenses, which the Americans had not dented for the past two days. Meanwhile, Melancon's 2nd Battalion would maneuver around the hill's south face to get around those robust fighting positions. As Purnell informed Colonel Witte at the 29th Division's war room early on August 28, "We're [going] in on the south side, and believe this may be the key to the whole thing."

Sadly, it was not. As Melancon soon realized, the Germans were there, and they were keen to fight. The 175th's regimental intelligence officer commented, "Enemy positions were well dug in, cleverly concealed, and [their occupants] resisted our advance with typical paratroop fanaticism." Still, the 29ers pressed home their attack with resolve for the simple reason that it seemed the only way to get this awful battle over with. The combination of the Americans' tenacity and the Germans' determination not to be moved produced a combat of remarkable intensity, fought for three straight days at extraordinarily close range, during which, as a 175th action report noted, "much hand-to-hand combat and exchange of grenades took place."

Gerhardt's impatience began to show early on. He phoned Purnell at 5 P.M. on August 28 and demanded heatedly: "When are you going to take that hill?" Purnell expressed confidence that the job could be done soon—how else could one reply to an angry Uncle Charlie?—and the following morning, just as the 175th was about to make yet another attempt to reach the summit, Gerhardt phoned again to rekindle Purnell's resolve. "Let's get after it and drive this thing!" the general barked.

For the August 29 assault, Purnell had yet another idea. During the first three days of the Hill 103 fight, Gerhardt had not allowed him to employ Lt. Col. William Blandford's 3rd Battalion since that outfit was the 29th Division's only substantive infantry reserve. However, as the division staff had come to recognize Hill 103 as the essential objective in the 29th's drive to take Brest, Gerhardt had agreed to release the 3rd Battalion for Purnell's use. For Purnell this was a profound relief, as the events of the past three days had clearly demonstrated that securing a target as tough as Hill 103 with only two-thirds of his command was grueling, costly—and perhaps impossible.

Purnell's scheme was to throw the 3rd Battalion into the battle a mile north of Hill 103, thereby drawing enemy attention and resources away from the main fight. As Purnell explained to Witte, "There's a good deal of organized [enemy] troops in back of that Hill 103. What I want to do is make Blandford's attack very conspicuous, and I think when we pull it off, it might have the effect to cause those babies to pull out."

Purnell ordered Blandford to push ahead aggressively and search for a vulnerable seam in the enemy's defenses. If such a seam could be uncovered, the 3rd Battalion would get behind the hill and surround it. In that event Purnell expected the German defenders at Hill 103 to wilt and die like a forlorn weed in a drought.

But there was more to it than that. If the Germans had so far not yielded to the 175th's efforts, Purnell yearned to hammer the enemy all across the regiment's front with a furious preparatory bombardment. As the 29ers and Germans were so closely engaged near the peak of Hill 103, air strikes by Ninth Air Force fighter-bombers would pose just as much risk to friendly troops as the enemy. It would therefore have to be artillery. Purnell noted to Witte, "I've talked it over with [Maj. Sherwood] Collins [executive officer, 224th Field Artillery Battalion], and I want to fire a preparation in back of that hill with all I've got. That's where the [enemy] stuff is. . . . After that the 3rd Battalion should go right through."

Threatened on both flanks of the hill as well as directly on the crest, the German defenses were undeniably stretched thin on August 29. All three of Purnell's battalions attacked forcefully throughout the day, and the prevailing thought among 29ers was how much more can the Germans take? Reporter Holbrook Bradley of the *Baltimore Sun* observed: "Our men hung on to their precarious perch while our artillery pounded one side of the ridge and Jerry pounded the other. And during this time it was almost impossible to see the enemy because any movement brought on a fusillade of small-arms fire." But in a situation such as this, the 29ers were at a vast disadvantage because their only source of cover from enemy artillery was provided by entirely inadequate and hastily dug foxholes, whereas the Germans could hole up in their nearly invulnerable pillboxes, trenches, caves, and the quarry pit. Indeed, that evening Purnell had to admit, "I don't think the artillery is doing any good [even though] we saw some places our artillery concentrated on, and it looked like machine-gun fire."

Measured by the progress of the assault, the 175th's attack could hardly be categorized as blitzkrieg. But by sunset on August 29, the Germans on top of Hill 103 were nearly surrounded. That was not good enough for Gerhardt, who displayed his notorious temper in a phone call to Purnell: "We've been fooling with this hill for two days, and we've got to get somewhere! We're going to knock it off now. . . . Don't wait for anything!"

The 29ers were close, but they had still failed to penetrate the barbed wire perimeter surrounding the enemy strongpoint on the hilltop and the adjacent quarry on the southeast slope. Purnell knew that Gerhardt's anger would steadily mount the longer Hill 103 remained in German hands, and to rectify that situation, he ordered something that the 175th Infantry had done only rarely so far in World War II: a night attack. The unit closest to the summit, Company A, would use bangalore torpedoes—the same weapons that had proved so effective in neutralizing enemy fortifications and barbed wire on Omaha Beach—to sneak forward in the darkness and blow gaps in the wire, through which the 29ers would immediately scurry to deal directly with the enemy defenders in the trenches and pillboxes beyond.

It was not easy, but it worked. The enemy fired flares, creating macabre illumination that evoked a titanic struggle in no-man's-land during the last war. A 175th action report noted how deadly the Germans had made the top of Hill 103: "Fields of fire were cleared on all sides, and numerous antipersonnel mines were strewn over the approaches." The bitter fighting continued at daybreak on August 30, but by afternoon the job was done: the Yanks were finally in control of the crest. Holbrook Bradley later reported:

> We could smell the sour odor of decaying flesh we'd become accustomed to back in Normandy, but had almost forgotten during the past few weeks. Hill 103 was the most desolate waste we've seen yet. As we looked over the area there was hardly a square yard that hadn't been hit by shells from ours or the enemy's guns. . . . Dead German paratroopers and equipment lay about us on the ledges and on the floor of the quarry below.

The 175th Infantry had gained a notable victory, but at great human cost. Close to 200 members of the regiment had become casualties on August 29 and 30 alone, and a cheerless Purnell reported to Witte that "The 2nd Battalion rifle company total is about 175 men; 1st Battalion rifle company total, about 140 men." Normally those figures would have been about 550 soldiers each, clear evidence that only five days of fighting outside Brest had so seriously depleted Purnell's regiment that he had to wonder if it could carry on without significant infusion of replacements. Unfortunately, given the enemy's unexpectedly stubborn resistance at Brest, rumors emanating from VIII Corps headquarters indicated that the number of replacements available to all commands would, at least for the moment, be entirely inadequate.

Purnell had learned the hard truth that the Germans were down—but not out. Col. Paul Krznarich, the 29th Division's intelligence officer known affectionately to one and all as "Murphy" because his surname was so difficult to pronounce, reported to Middleton at 1:35 P.M. on August 30: "We're on it [Hill 103]—but so are the Jerries." The Dandy Fifth had driven the enemy off the hilltop and inflicted grievous casualties, but apparently the German paratroopers had retreated only a few fields down Hill 103's eastern slope and were preparing to do what they routinely did when they had been driven from a key position: counterattack. At about 10 P.M. on August 30, the Germans came swarming back up the hill, into and beyond the quarry, determined to take it back from the Americans. This time it was the 29ers' turn to hold on to a piece of terrain that their generals had declared indispensible.

If there were two words that Gerhardt detested, they were "counterattack" and "retreat"—so much so, in fact, that he prohibited their use in the 29th Division war room. His staff officers still whispered among themselves of the shocking incident in Normandy when he had summarily relieved a field grade officer from the G-2 section when that pitiable soul had innocently declared that a 29th Division outfit was "retreating." Therefore, when reports filtered back from Hill 103 that that position, secured at great cost less than twenty-four hours previously, was suddenly being subjected to a furious enemy assault, Gerhardt's staff was understandably fretful about how to communicate that alarming development to their boss. Ultimately, an apprehensive officer approached Gerhardt to report that the enemy was "advancing with enthusiasm"—Uncle Charlie's preferred expression. In this event, that phrase was wholly appropriate because it precisely defined the Germans' attitude.

By this stage of the war, Purnell knew Gerhardt well enough that there must be no "retreat" from the hill, and thus—assuming the Americans could hold—there would be no need to employ that offending word when communicating with the war room. Even so, the enemy displayed such protracted "enthusiasm" on Hill 103 that a concerned Purnell surely wondered whether or not his men could hang on. That concern was accentuated by freshly captured German paratroopers, who revealed to their interrogators how desperate the enemy was to get back Hill 103.

During the frenzied and confused fighting on and around the hill, Sgt. Steven Melnikoff, a squad leader in Company C, surprised four Germans riding down a narrow sunken road in a captured U.S. Army jeep—apparently lost. He promptly took the disoriented Germans prisoner and observed that one of them, clothed in a dress uniform including immaculate gloves and armed with only a pistol cased in a shiny holster, was evidently a valuable catch. Sergeant Melnikoff was later awarded the Bronze Star for this accomplishment because the testimony and documents obtained from those four enemy captives—and dozens of others like them—revealed that the Germans' counterattack orders had dictated that "they must get the hill at all costs," a directive that allegedly originated from General Ramcke himself. One prisoner, a paratrooper by the name of Siegfried Ehlert, noted to his captors that the enthusiastic German troops were drawn from a company of the 2nd *Fallschirmjäger* Regiment—described by a 29th Division intelligence report as the "toughest" enemy unit at Brest. According to that same report, "Ehlert added that the Nazis had abandoned their positions on the hill [on the afternoon of August 30] only through a misinterpretation of orders."

At 1 P.M. on August 31, a grim Purnell declared to Gerhardt, "We fought hard for the hill, and I don't want to pull anyone out and let [the Germans] come back." For the moment the general could offer nothing except the declaration, "Well—hang on tight!" Hanging on, however, would not be easy, as the Germans were firing virtually all of their available artillery within range at Hill 103, including some large-caliber coastal guns, in a seemingly endless barrage. A 175th Infantry action report noted, "Supply of food, ammunition, and water to the frontline companies was very difficult due to enemy artillery fire," an obvious indicator that the isolated 29ers on the summit would not be able to hold on forever against such enemy zeal.

In his newspaper column, Bradley noted, "The battle at this point turned into a hand-grenade duel." During this appalling struggle, the leadership of 1st Lt. Grant Darby, the commander of Company C, was noteworthy, and Purnell would see to it that the young lieutenant from Colorado would soon receive the Silver Star. According to the citation, Darby was "a constant inspiration to his men," as he led them from the front, personally performed several arduous patrols, and marked safe paths through enemy minefields. "On numerous occasions Lieutenant Darby led parties of litter bearers to the wounded," the award pronounced. "Many times during this highly contested engagement, Lieutenant Darby, under devastating enemy fire, crawled to the wounded and personally administered first aid."

This time it was the Americans who could take advantage of fixed defenses on the hilltop, and with the vital assistance of supporting artillery and heavy mortar outfits in the rear, Purnell's men managed to stand fast. Indeed, for every shell the Germans fired into Hill 103 on August 31, the Americans in all likelihood fired back two or more, a response that generated at least some solace among the worn-out 29ers because they knew that however disagreeable were their lives presently, the Germans were definitely worse off.

Of particular value to the 175th at the height of the Hill 103 battle was Company A, 86th Chemical Mortar Battalion, an VIII Corps outfit that, at Witte's insistence, was transferred to Purnell's control because of a shortage of howitzer ammunition in 29th Division field artillery units. The 86th's crews promptly began to saturate the far side of the hill with highly accurate high-angle fire from their twelve heavy 4.2-inch mortars, and this the enemy could not stand for long. When some dazed German paratroopers later fell into American hands, they acknowledged the mortar barrage's effectiveness: in their words, it was "whispering death" because the 86th's shells made virtually no sound as they descended to earth to fulfill their deadly work. A week after the fall of Brest, Witte saluted the mortarmen with the simple observation: "They did a superb job." In a written message

Purnell added: "Those 4.2 mortars are really effective. They can really lay it down. I'll take all I can get of those in preference to artillery." To this message, however, a disturbed Gerhardt appended a hastily scribbled note: "They [the mortars] are OK in close—but they are not to take the place of artillery."

Gerhardt had intended August 31 to be a day of recuperation for the entire 29th Division. So it had been for both the 115th and 116th Infantry, but the enemy had not afforded the unfortunate members of the 175th a moment of relaxation at a place defined by Holbrook Bradley as "one of the heaviest battlegrounds of the war." Nevertheless, the vital summit of Hill 103 was finally in American hands for good, and even if the quarry was still disputed ground and considerable numbers of resolute German troops lurked just beyond the crest, Gerhardt knew that the enemy was beaten.

He hoped that it was only a matter of time now.

3. FEAST OR FAMINE

More than a year and a half of nearly continuous combat against the renowned German Army had taught the Americans many hard lessons about the nature of modern conflict. In both this war and the last, the Germans had revolutionized military tactics and reaped enormous successes when their innovative combat methods had been practiced against more conformist opponents. When the German Army marched into Paris in June 1940, only four years prior to the 29th Division's assault on Omaha Beach, the U.S. Army had totaled a mere 180,000 men, including Air Corps personnel, and possessed neither the weapons nor the doctrine it would need to defeat a much larger and far more progressive enemy. In the intervening four years, the Americans had had to make up for much lost time and occasionally paid a severe price for such deplorable unpreparedness, but from those difficult experiences emerged a distinctively American method of waging modern war, one that focused principally on those qualities of the burgeoning U.S. Army that the enemy could not hope to match. Charlie Gerhardt's 29th Infantry Division was just one of ninety U.S. Army divisions that had been thoroughly primed to practice that method, and the defeat of the German foe in Normandy had proved that that approach to modern warfare was working.

The essence of the American way of war was to overwhelm the enemy: with manpower, with production, with firepower. In the American Civil War, Generals Grant and Sherman had established that such a strategy was highly effective, and although warfare had of course changed profoundly since the mid-nineteenth century, it was plain that Germany could not equal the Allies in any of those three essential categories that defined a nation's ability to fight. Therefore, according to the American way of thinking, if the Allies could hold the strategic initiative and maintain continuous offensive pressure on the enemy, the Germans must eventually yield on the battlefield, and Hitler's downfall must soon follow.

That such an approach to war was imperfect, however, was obvious to any Allied soldier in the European theater. As the 29th Division and many other outfits had learned since D-Day, against an enemy as formidable as the Germans it could take a long time before substantive results were achieved by a strategy of bludgeoning the foe to death; the cost of those results in terms of dead and wounded comrades could strain even the best U.S. Army units to the breaking point. Furthermore, the concentrated application of American military might was a staggering logistical challenge, and not surprisingly, the U.S. Army occasionally experienced severe breakdowns that would temporarily cripple its combat units and yield to the enemy a much-needed respite.

In the European theater of operations, Brest was an acknowledged backwater, and those U.S. Army units fighting there, including the 29th Division, would eventually suffer such a breakdown, one that could only be described as a monumental snafu. As the 29ers were about to learn, crushing the enemy with overwhelming force was impossible when the tools to fulfill the job were lacking.

The United States—the renowned "arsenal of democracy"—had been churning out war materiel at a prodigious rate for years, but American soldiers in all combat theaters around the world had learned the hard lesson that production, even on a mammoth scale, was meaningless unless their senior commanders could convey that materiel to the front expeditiously. That point was driven home in the late summer of 1944, when the U.S. Army became a victim of its own stunning success. The immediate consequence of the Allies' Normandy breakout in late July was an exhilarating and long-awaited period of mobile warfare, during which the Anglo-American armies raced across France, liberated Paris, and surged forward like a tidal wave all the way to Belgium, Holland, and the German frontier—all in a matter of weeks.

Apparently, the western Allies could carry out lightning warfare even better than its German inventors. But the Americans and their allies had moved so far and so fast across France that they had outrun their supply lines, generating acute shortages of vital supplies they would need to press into Germany and on to Berlin. That category of military resources known somewhat inscrutably in the U.S. Army as "Class III"—gasoline and oil—had not been the primary concern of Allied logisticians for nearly two months after D-Day for the obvious reason that the Normandy campaign was more evocative of the stagnant trench lines of the last war than it was of the new type of mobile operations known as blitzkrieg. When modern mechanized armies fulfilled their intended purpose, however, they subsisted in large measure on Class III supply, and at the beginning of September 1944, Allied supply officers speedily discerned that there was not enough of it to sustain all of Eisenhower's divisions if they were to maintain their astonishing momentum. Available gas and oil had to enter France at only a few ports currently under Allied control, the combined capacity of which was inadequate to handle the vast quantities Ike required. Furthermore, the Allies had to transport those vital supplies hundreds of miles from Normandy to the front. The dilemma facing Eisenhower after the euphoria of the liberation of France triggered logistical crises that filtered all the way down to division level and below, and from which it took the U.S. Army months to recover.

Ike's predicament emphasized why Middleton's VIII Corps was currently fighting so hard to seize the port of Brest. At Brest, however, the distressed Middleton soon grasped a supreme paradox: To alleviate the Allies' logistical difficulties, he had orders to secure Brest with all possible speed, but to secure Brest against the kind of ferocious resistance the enemy was offering, he himself needed an abundant stock of materiel—particularly ammunition. Unfortunately, those needs were not adequately addressed by Middleton's boss at Third Army, the formidable General Patton. As VIII Corps' initial attack against Brest stalled in late August, Middleton realized that his stockpile of ammunition—known as "Class V" supply in Army field manuals—would not be sufficient for him to persevere in the kind of sustained and vigorous offensive he knew would be required to take Brest.

In truth Middleton's quandary was desperate: His corps was conducting what amounted to an entirely independent operation, hundreds of miles away from the main front. Before the attack on Brest had begun, VIII Corps' senior supply and ordnance officers had driven to Patton's headquarters to meet their Third Army counterparts and inform them of Middleton's logistical requirements. Patton's senior staff officers, however, had been frosty and unreceptive. They had turned down Middleton's initial ammunition requisition because they believed that VIII Corps had exaggerated the enemy's strength at Brest. Middleton's corps, they said, should be capable of seizing Brest in about a week—on or about September 1,

1944—with a grand total of about 5,000 tons of ammunition, which amounted only to about 25 percent of what Middleton had requested. Later, one senior U.S. Army ordnance officer even described VIII Corps supply demands as "hysterical." As events developed, however, Third Army was dead wrong: actually, Middleton had vastly *underestimated* German strength at Brest, and after just a few days of combat in the environs of that city, even those senior American leaders who under normal circumstances were cheery optimists could not imagine that Brest could be captured by September 1.

They were right. For the most part, the vast physical distance separating Middleton from Patton triggered that unfortunate crisis, for Patton had his eyes on the Rhine and, beyond that, Berlin. Brest was undeniably important, but by late August it was a sideshow to Patton. Middleton would have to cope with less ammunition than he had asked for simply because Third Army troops racing across France into Lorraine needed it more. Looking back to the capture of Cherbourg and St. Malo and the heavy Class V supply requirements of those endeavors, however, Middleton could not accept that answer if his superiors expected him to take Brest.

A quick glance at a map by even a fresh second lieutenant in a lowly supply outfit indicated the necessity of an immediate change in VIII Corps' affiliation with Third Army. Patton was just too far away—and had his mind on other matters. Let him go; Old Blood and Guts just might win the war on his own. Actually, Omar Bradley at Twelfth Army Group was focused on Brest much more keenly than Patton because he understood how much Generals Eisenhower and Marshall valued that place, and Bradley's future depended on how well he carried out those two generals' wishes. Therefore, immediately before Middleton's assault on Brest was ready to jump off, Bradley permitted him to bypass Third Army in terms of supply and deal instead directly with the "Communications Zone," the lofty logistics command responsible for all U.S. Army supply on the continent. Known to all by its acronym, COM-Z, this command was controlled with an iron hand by Lt. Gen. John Lee, who answered not to Bradley, but to Eisenhower at supreme headquarters.

Fortunately for Middleton, his shift from Third Army to COM-Z, coupled with Bradley's powerful influence, resulted in a near-total endorsement by General Lee of VIII Corps' lengthy supply wish list. It did not hurt that Middleton and Lee had known each other well in the pre–World War I Regular Army. Unfortunately for Middleton, however, receiving Lee's approval had only served to trigger another, much more severe, problem. The top brass may eventually have guaranteed Middleton the ammunition stocks he needed to take Brest, but in the chaotic conditions in which COM-Z was currently operating, conveying those stocks to Brest proved an almost insurmountable challenge. Roland Ruppenthal, the U.S. Army's official COM-Z historian, noted in his 1953 book *Logistical Support of the Armies* that Middleton's dilemma "simply evidenced the overextension of the entire logistical structure, which had accompanied the sudden success of August. The difficulties in filling VIII Corps' requirements centered largely on the by-now chronic lack of transportation. Competition for overland transport was at its height at the time, the ammunition shortage occurring in precisely the same period as the gasoline shortage."

Clear proof of that overextension within the 29th Division was provided by Capt. Frank Hines, commander of the 29th Quartermaster Company, in his after-action report detailing the operations of his fifty-one deuce-and-a-half trucks during the Brest campaign. He observed, "During this period it was necessary for the company vehicles to frequently go as far as Omaha Beach and Cherbourg for Class II [clothing and tools] and Class IV [construction materials] supplies for the division." As a one-way journey to those places from Brest was greater than 200 miles, over roads that were hardly adequate to handle incessant heavy truck traffic, the severe strain on supply personnel and their vehicles involved in the Brest operation surfaced early in the campaign.

COM-Z resolved to send Middleton what he needed both from stockpiles on hand in France, by means of trains and trucks, as well as from stores in England, transported directly to Brittany in eleven U.S. Navy LSTs. But of the 8,000 tons of ammunition COM-Z had promised Middleton, only 5,300 tons had been received by VIII Corps as of August 30, nearly a week after the assault on Brest had commenced. That failure was a devastating blow to Middleton, for unless COM-Z satisfied his Class V supply requirements, he would be forced to reconfigure his timetable for the liberation of Brest and perhaps even shut down the offensive altogether. Indeed, the official VIII Corps after-action report on the Brest siege later noted: "The supply problem had been a constant source of apprehension to the Corps since the beginning of the siege, and by September 1 became a primary factor in the operation."

What had gone wrong? Plenty, according to Middleton. Brittany's rail network, in Allied hands for less than a month, was not fully operational; 500 U.S. Army deuce-and-a-half trucks, whose drivers had been issued orders to pull out of their "Red Ball Express" supply runs between Normandy and the main battle front on the German frontier, did not show up in Brittany for several days; and most of the LSTs arrived at their discharge point on Brittany's north coast far from fully loaded with ammunition. In truth, much to the disappointment of VIII Corps supply officers, some vessels showed up stocked only at about 25 percent of their normal capacity.

The seaborne supply route offered Middleton his most promising chance of obtaining ammunition because the vessels' skippers held orders to sail straight to Brittany from England—and in a few cases later on, directly from the United States. Each ship's precious cargo was intended specifically for VIII Corps and therefore could not be snatched from Middleton's grasp by generals more senior to him, such as Patton, who claimed a more pressing need for it.

Even so, the conveyance of large quantities of supplies to Brittany by sea was far from smooth. Not a single port that was both operable and of sufficient size for Middleton's needs existed within reasonable driving distance of VIII Corps lines at Brest. Accordingly, the Navy was at first obliged to sail its vessels into the Baie de Lannion, a protected body of water on Brittany's north coast fifty miles northeast of Brest. The bay encompassed a tiny port named St. Michel-en-Grève, but it was much too small to handle a supply effort of that magnitude. The LST skippers therefore had no choice but to glide up onto a nearby beach, wait for low tide, and open their massive bow doors to unload their cargoes directly onto the sands—a time-consuming procedure so strenuous that the U.S. Army had to hire French civilians, who were paid in food, to transfer the shipboard materiel into trucks for the long journey to Brest. Shortly thereafter, the supply logjam was partially relieved when the Navy opened up the nearby ports of Morlaix and Roscoff, both of which were closer to Brest than St. Michel.

The impromptu effort to supply Middleton was a nightmare for those men responsible for providing the fighting men at the front with the items they needed to take Brest. True, as a result of Middleton's demands, many articles became available to VIII Corps in abundance, but ammunition—particularly artillery ammunition—was not one of them. Middleton became so concerned that on August 29 he took the unusual step of writing directly to Bradley, noting: "Our ammunition situation is critical due to failure to meet our initial request [8,700 tons of ammunition, plus a 12,000-ton allowance to restock expended stores]. If something is not done immediately, I will have to stop offensive action."

Only once before in its short but violent combat history had the 29th Division experienced an ammunition shortage, and that deficiency had paralyzed offensive operations for weeks. That unfortunate situation had occurred in the aftermath of the great English Channel storm from June 19 to 22, 1944, which had destroyed the artificial Mulberry harbor off Omaha Beach and virtually shut down the discharge of U.S. Army supplies into Normandy for a few days. As a result, the 29th Division had been obligated to call off its attempt to liberate St. Lô while its supply officers hoarded what limited ammunition stocks remained on hand.

In many respects, however, the ammunition shortage endured by the 29th Division at Brest was even more challenging than the one in Normandy. The enemy's Brest defenses were formidable, featuring concrete and steel pillboxes, minefields, and barbed wire—elements that the 29th had almost never encountered in abundance in Normandy after D-Day. The 29ers promptly grasped that to overcome such tough defenses, manned for the most part by fanatical paratroopers, they would need lots of firepower—a requirement that obviously could not be met without plentiful ammunition. Ike had said that Brest must be taken, and if that ammunition was not forthcoming, the 29th Division somehow or other would have to make do with whatever meager resources were on hand.

Furthermore, when the ammunition shortage had set in in Normandy in June, the top brass had thankfully decreed that the front line occupied by the 29th Division should remain passive for a while, and therefore Gerhardt had faced little or no pressure from his superiors during that period to conduct an offensive and achieve significant military objectives. In contrast, Middleton was under relentless pressure from above to capture Brest, and if COM-Z did not provide him with the ammunition he needed to do the job, it was hardly likely that he would be allowed the same luxurious and lengthy period of passivity that Gerhardt's 29th Division had been granted in Normandy while supplies on the invasion beaches swelled to acceptable levels. What was the point of sending three top-notch infantry divisions hundreds of miles away from the main battle front to accomplish an important mission if they were merely going to remain inert, observing rather than destroying the enemy? Such a strategy would make no military sense, and even if Middleton on August 29 would threaten to suspend his assault on Brest due to an ammunition deficiency, Eisenhower and Bradley, although sympathetic with Middleton's plight, expected prompt results. There could be short breaks in the offensive, but the effort to capture Brest's vital harbor must persevere even under imperfect logistical conditions. As Ike once noted, his generals were "expected to meet emergency situations with ingenuity and increased intensity of effort."

Since its training days in England, the 29th Division had been trained to practice warfare relentlessly, some might say even brutally, employing all its resources in a concerted effort to pound the enemy into submission. As the Germans were defending ground they had occupied for years, the burden of attack was overwhelmingly on the 29ers, and history had confirmed that against modern weaponry attacks stood little chance of success unless the enemy was inundated by a crushing maelstrom of fire, ranging from hand grenades to heavy howitzers. In the first week of the Brest campaign, however, the 29th Division—particularly its artillery—simply did not possess enough ammunition on hand to achieve that purpose, and even worse, because of Middleton's supply difficulties, the limited amounts of expended ammunition could not be replaced in a timely manner.

If Ike and Bradley expected the 29th Division to assault a heavily defended position, that was hardly the way to do it, and as many 29ers noted, if this was one of those proverbial cases of fighting with one hand behind one's back, the job ahead would be slow, costly, and exhausting— and from August 25 through August 31, 1944, those adjectives precisely described the division's effort to take Brest. After the first few days of the assault, when it dawned on Middleton and Gerhardt that the Germans would not be pushovers, the Blue and Gray Division's ammunition deficiency became progressively worse, reaching a low point on August 31 when Gerhardt announced with some alarm to Middleton: "[We have a] restriction on artillery ammunition today. We're cut down to three-tenths of a unit of fire."

In the U.S. Army a "unit of fire" was simply a measurement of ammunition supply, expressed in a number of rounds per weapon. For 105mm howitzers it was 160 high-explosive rounds; for 155mm howitzers it was 125. Therefore, a "three-tenths" unit of fire indicated that the division's three 105mm artillery battalions each had fewer than 50 rounds per howitzer available to fire that day, while the 227th Field Artillery Battalion's twelve 155mm howitzers were each down to fewer than 40. Gerhardt's unease concerning this deficiency must have been acute, given that the U.S. Army's *Staff Officers' Field Manual* (FM 101-10) specified that an attack against permanent fortifications would require howitzers to expend *two* units of fire on an offensive's first day alone (320 high-explosive rounds for a 105mm howitzer), plus one unit of fire each day thereafter. Furthermore, FM 101-10 also stipulated that in the first two hours of any prepared assault, 105mm howitzers would be expected to expend fifty rounds—an undertaking that by August 31 would have completely depleted the 29th Division's artillery of its ammunition supply. Colonel Witte announced later on August 31 that "[we] upped our artillery ammunition from three-tenths to five-tenths—and we may get more," but that was not much of an improvement.

Reducing artillerymen in a cutting-edge military unit to dispensing their meager supplies of shells in such a miserly fashion was hardly representative of the mighty U.S. Army. But the adaptable 29th Division gunners resorted to extraordinary measures to ensure that when their infantry comrades launched an attack, fire support of some kind would always be available. Without that support, the infantrymen's progress—if any—would surely be sluggish and costly. Consequently, each artillery battalion's service battery, which was responsible for providing the gunners with ammunition, ran its two-and-a-half ton supply trucks nearly continuously from Brest to the nearest ammo dumps and back again, an exhausting round trip of nearly 200 miles over poor roads. According to Cooper of the 110th Field Artillery, "For our service battery, this was one of the hardest jobs of the war."

If Gerhardt had to maintain the initiative at Brest, as Middleton's orders insisted, the 29ers must swiftly adjust to this highly abnormal logistical situation. Fortunately, as the U.S. Army had proven since D-Day, adaptability was an American military hallmark. If artillery ammunition was scarce, the U.S. Army offered an impressive array of alternatives.

Army Air Force fighter-bombers could make up for whatever limits the artillery had to endure—assuming that pilots and infantrymen could learn to work together. This was of course a questionable assumption given the record of tactical air power in Normandy, but the 29ers could at least try. To make up for artillery ammunition shortages at Brest, therefore, the Ninth Air Force doubled fighter-bomber support for the 29th Division starting on September 3, and further boosted that aid the following day. Still engrossed by capturing Brest and putting its harbor to immediate use, on September 4 Eisenhower directed Ninth Air Force's commander, Maj. Gen. Hoyt Vandenberg, to "utilize maximum number of aircraft which can be effectively employed in support of this operation." By September 5, more than two-thirds of Vandenberg's fighter-bomber groups were operating in Brittany.

Furthermore, Middleton had provided Gerhardt with so many diverse corps-level ground units, such as chemical mortar, tank destroyer, antiaircraft, tank, and heavy artillery battalions, that the 29th Division clearly had several fire support options above and beyond its organic howitzers and the Ninth Air Force. However, many of those VIII Corps outfits, particularly the heavy artillery battalions, could provide little relief since they too were severely restricted by ammunition shortages—in some cases worse than divisional units.

One weapon that helped mitigate Gerhardt's dilemma was the heavy 4.2-inch mortar, forty-eight of which were provided to each corps-level chemical mortar battalion. Originally designed as a deliverer of gas and smoke shells on the battlefield, the 4.2-inch was a formidable weapon that since D-Day had evolved into surrogate and very effective short-range artillery. Witte noted the significant contribution tendered by the mortarmen at Brest: "The 29th Division leaned heavily on heavy mortars, whose supply of ammunition was not restricted. We had only one company of the 91st Chemical Mortar Battalion at first [it was actually Company A, 86th Chemical Mortar Battalion], but after the 8th Division was pinched out [around September 12], we got another [Company B]."

Twelve, and ultimately twenty-four, heavy mortars were helpful, but they would obviously not cure the 29th Division's ammunition shortage by themselves. Furthermore, their short range limited their use to enemy targets two miles distant or less. However, another potent American weapon, the 3-inch antitank gun, was available in plentiful numbers at Brest in both towed and self-propelled varieties as the primary arm of U.S. Army tank destroyer battalions, several of which operated with VIII Corps. Since intelligence had deduced that Ramcke's German garrison was practically devoid of tanks, and the Americans therefore need not worry about them, the 29ers had the luxury of using the 3-inch antitank guns as substitute artillery.

One highly effective tank destroyer battalion, the 821st, had been closely affiliated with the 29th Division since Normandy. Raised at Camp Carson, Colorado in July 1942 and commanded in Brittany by Lt. Col. Howard Arbury, the 821st was an experienced outfit that had endured much tough fighting alongside the 29ers at St. Lô and Vire. The 821st added significantly to the 29th Division's firepower, for it possessed thirty-six towed 3-inch guns—a number equal to the entire complement of M2 105mm howitzers in Gerhardt's inventory. True, since the 821st was formed to destroy enemy tanks, about one-quarter of its ammunition stocks consisted of armor-piercing rounds, which were not very useful as high-explosive shells in long-range fire missions against enemy troops in the open. Still, the 3-inch gun's eight-mile range actually surpassed the range of a 105mm howitzer by more than a mile, and its high-explosive shell, although considerably smaller and lighter than a 105mm, was almost as lethal. Furthermore, the crews of the 3-inch guns cherished their weapons' renowned accuracy. Consequently, at Brest the 821st in effect acted as an ad hoc light artillery unit, a role for which it was entirely suited since many of its officers, including Colonel Arbury, had been trained as artillerymen and were decidedly enthusiastic about lending a hand as much as possible to their artillery comrades when enemy tanks were nowhere to be seen.

Gerhardt assigned one tank destroyer company to each of his three 105mm field artillery battalions, a supplement of twelve 3-inch guns per battalion, which in effect doubled the number of tubes 29th Division artillerymen would have available for fire missions. The 821st's Company A, under the command of Capt. Edward Burke, was attached to Cooper's 110th Field Artillery Battalion, and later Cooper noted how much that attachment had ameliorated his potentially crippling ammunition problem: "Linesmen installed telephone communication to the company, and 110th observers conducted daily registrations for the unit to insure accurate results in map firing. Undertaking a large share of the harassing and interdictory missions, the company materially increased the volume of such fire, particularly at night. The arrangement made good use of the automatic supply of ammunition which a tank destroyer unit received, thus enabling the 110th to conserve its heavier ammunition for use in attacks and on targets of the moment. Company A continued in this role until the capture of Brest."

In the U.S. Army's table of organization for its 1944 infantry division, one oddity that provided Cooper and other 29th Division artillery commanders an added opportunity to enhance their firepower was the allocation of six M3 105mm howitzers to each of the division's three infantry regiments in a unit known as the regimental cannon company. Training infantrymen in the rudiments of gunnery had always seemed peculiar, but according to the prevailing tactical doctrine of the interwar years, M3 "infantry howitzers" were supposed to deploy near the front lines, under the regimental commander's control, and pound enemy strongpoints with close-range direct fire. In actuality that doctrine proved unsound and was almost never practiced, and accordingly, in combat the nearest field artillery battalion generally adopted the cannon company and employed it as an extra firing battery.

In comparison with a standard 105mm howitzer, an M3 was small and light, and consequently, its range was limited to little more than half that of the much more impressive field artillery version. Nevertheless, both types used identical shells, and therefore as long as an enemy target was within range of the M3 model, the enemy could not tell the difference. Hence, when German strongpoints were situated inside a radius of about three and one-half miles from an American artillery position—the effective range of an M3—artillerymen could engage those targets with the infantry howitzers and preserve their precious ammunition for targets at longer range.

Clever improvisations such as those enabled the 29th Division to maintain decent fire support for its frontline infantrymen for a while, but they only postponed the inevitable. Middleton's ammunition deficiency was serious—and getting worse by the day. In early September the situation deteriorated to a level that was later categorized by a corps report as "critical." That report concluded: "Ammunition reached such low levels that much of the operation was suspended." This deplorable situation triggered an angry message from a SHAEF observer at Middleton's headquarters to a senior supply officer at COM-Z. "Getting ammunition out here is a vital matter, which your office does not seem to understand," he wrote. "We must have not only ammunition but also information relative thereto. . . . What in the name of Pete is wrong with Com Zone?"

With many 29th Division artillery units down to half a unit of fire or less as of August 31, a swift answer to that question was required if Ike still yearned for Brest as a major entry point into France for American men and materiel. From that date through September 7, Gerhardt had to suspend major offensive operations on three separate days (August 31, September 4, and September 7), pauses that not only threw the American timetable for the liberation of Brest off schedule, but also gave the enemy an unexpected chance to recover and reorganize. The Germans would make every effort to ensure that those providential breaks would reinvigorate their effort to retain Brest for as long as possible.

In military planning an emphasis on logistics is a hallmark of a good general, and Middleton certainly was a good general. Even before the 29th Division's arrival in Brittany, he had been issuing blatant warnings to his superiors about his looming supply difficulties. More than two weeks into his campaign to take Brest, those difficulties had not been solved, and even worse, he had to wonder whether or not they ever would be. The impasse became so serious that on September 6 a 29th Division liaison officer attached to VIII Corps headquarters, Maj. Charles Custer, reported Middleton's pessimistic attitude to Gerhardt: "Our Brest operation will not continue until we have a sufficient supply of artillery ammunition. . . . General Middleton has sent a letter to higher headquarters telling them to give him sufficient supplies to carry this operation through or relieve him of command." With or without Middleton, if those supplies were not forthcoming, could Brest still be captured?

On August 31, Patton had paid a visit to VIII Corps headquarters outside Brest, where he had attempted to answer that question in a critical meeting with Bradley and Middleton. Although Bradley had released Patton's Third Army from the responsibility of supplying VIII Corps, Patton was still nominally Middleton's immediate superior. According to Patton, Middleton "was not sanguine about the capture of Brest and was full of complaints about the lack of daring on the part of the infantry. Also COM-Z had failed to bring up the amount of ammunition they had promised. I told him the explanation concerning the infantry was that they were tired out from having fought so long. On the way back I told Bradley that I could not fight on four fronts indefinitely and would like VIII Corps turned over to someone else. Bradley, as usual, had been thinking the same thing."

On September 5, VIII Corps underwent a profound change that would finally help to reverse Middleton's fortune. Starting on that date Patton would not have to concern himself with VIII Corps anymore. Instead, Middleton would now answer directly to the new U.S. Ninth Army, under the command of Lt. Gen. William H. Simpson. The fifty-six-year-old Simpson was one of the youngest graduates in the U.S. Military Academy's class of 1909—the same class as Patton. Although he had graduated almost at the bottom of his class, he was one of the most esteemed general officers in the U.S. Army in 1944—an expert trainer of troops and very much Patton's opposite, a man to whom logic and humility, rather than bravado and egotism, came entirely naturally. When Simpson recalled his uncomplicated command philosophy at Brest, he proved that point: "What I did was just let General Middleton run the show down there," he declared. As Middleton had been the commander on the scene for weeks prior to Simpson's arrival, that kind of thinking was wholly correct, but it was surely not the attitude of a man like Patton.

Simpson could not immediately rectify Middleton's supply dilemma, but since an army commander carried a good deal more weight than a mere corps commander in the highest reaches of the Allied command, Ninth Army's activation could only serve to help Middleton rather than hurt him. Even better, an army headquarters was much more capable of handling complex logistical issues than a corps staff, which was oriented for the most part to straightforward combat operations. Finally, unlike Patton, Simpson would be focused entirely on securing Brittany. All other considerations were secondary, an outlook that from Middleton's perspective must have been extraordinarily refreshing.

By September 8, Middleton's supply situation began to improve dramatically, and just a few days after that, VIII Corps was actually overflowing with ammunition. That happy development would allow the 2nd, 8th, and 29th Divisions to carry out the kind of forceful warfare they had gotten used to and succeeded at in Normandy. Starting on September 8 and continuing until the fall of Brest ten days later, the entire 29th Division, or at least a major portion of it, would carry out vigorous attacks daily, giving the enemy virtually no chance for recuperation. Pressure of that kind over the course of several consecutive days would eventually be too much for the enemy to stand.

Patience is a military virtue, and at Brest the VIII Corps staff had to follow that trait while the logistical mess that thwarted Middleton's purpose sorted itself out. That mess would finally be solved, as U.S. Navy LSTs spilling over with ammunition jammed into the tiny north Breton ports of St. Michel-en-Grève, Morlaix, and Roscoff; lengthy supply trains and mud-spattered Red Ball Express trucks at long last made their appearance in VIII Corps' zone; and every idle U.S. Army vehicle anywhere near Brest was pressed into emergency service. By the time Brest fell on September 18, VIII Corps had accumulated 25,000 tons of ammunition—a sufficient quantity for about ten days of intense combat.

For Middleton it had been one of those proverbial cases of famine followed by feast. Taking Brest would have been much easier had it been the other way around.

4. SCHNITZELWERFER BATTERY

By September 1, 1944, no commanding officer of a 29th Division infantry unit, by any stretch of his imagination, could assess his first week in the line at Brest as easy. Seven days of bitter fighting, even tougher than Normandy, had cost the division 1,200 casualties—with many more sure to follow as a consequence of the enemy's apparent willingness to fight to the last man and last bullet, as Ramcke had avowed. Judged by comparative levels of hardship, however, some 29th Division outfits had fared better than others. Col. Lou Smith's 115th Infantry had joined in the division's opening attack on Brest on August 25 and had vainly struggled to push ahead for two more days, but starting on August 28, Gerhardt had called off Smith's attack, indicating that his regiment's role for the foreseeable future would be defensive. That piece of delightful news slowly filtered through the regiment from top to bottom, and when it was absorbed by the fighting men, they could at last breathe deeply and take in the happy thought that they would in all likelihood live to see at least a few more sunrises.

Gerhardt, however, had always insisted that within his division a defensive posture must positively not be passive. True, members of the 115th Infantry would not be ordered to make any major assaults for several days, but the general still expected them to patrol aggressively, snatch enemy prisoners, and in general make life as unnerving as possible for their opposite numbers across no-man's-land. The 115th men at the front who shouldered the heaviest combat burden, however, had learned long ago that the best way to stay alive in the current war was to stay put and dig in—and those rational acts were what they yearned to do.

Gerhardt intended to deploy his two other regiments, the 116th and 175th, on narrow frontages so that their attacks could be concentrated on a few key objectives. To fulfill that goal, the 115th Infantry had been obligated to extend its front considerably, and by the morning of August 28, Smith's regiment was undeniably stretched to its limit. Even more troubling, the following day the 115th's line became appreciably thinner when Gerhardt pulled Maj. Randolph Millholland's 3rd Battalion from the front and placed it in that status so treasured by fighting men, "division reserve." Smith would thereupon have to cover a front of more than four miles with two understrength infantry battalions, a risky posture that under normal circumstances would have invited German attack. But the Germans were hard-pressed by the Americans at many other points on the Brest front, and Gerhardt considered it highly unlikely they would display their customary "enthusiasm" toward the 115th any time soon. Fortunately for Smith, it turned out Gerhardt was right.

Meanwhile, Millholland's 3rd Battalion, in its enviable reserve role, would stay busy. In fact no 29th Division outfit that was out of the line could ever relax without Uncle Charlie's unambiguous consent, and this he was far from willing to do as long as Brest remained under German occupation. At Gerhardt's insistence, reserve units had to train nearly incessantly to sharpen their combat skills, a task that could hardly appeal to men in desperate need of rest—but which was obviously preferable to actual combat. Millholland's 3rd Battalion, however, had a special role to fulfill because it would be the first 29th Division unit to carry out a major new policy recently formulated by Gerhardt, one that was designed to address the severe problems the division had experienced in Normandy with replacements. In truth, the infusion of replacements into all U.S. Army divisions was never a smooth process, but within the 29th it was particularly trying because virtually no American division had lost more men since D-Day—in excess of 12,000 as of the most recent count. All of those fighters had to be replaced, and to do that, hordes of new men, none of whom had had any relationship with the 29th Division in the past, had to be acclimatized to their brutal new lifestyle and learn the ways of their new outfit. It was a cold and sometimes inhumane practice that could try the souls of even the toughest soldiers, a detail that Gerhardt could not fail to notice because it relentlessly impacted the competence of his division.

A U.S. Army general could absorb the intricate details of running a division from staff college courses and field manuals, but those guides could not teach him how to exert effective leadership on and off the battlefield during active combat operations. That intricate art required him to display the entirely contrary attitudes of insensitivity and compassion as the military situation demanded. Most soldiers viewed Gerhardt as the type of general who would exhibit far more insensitivity than compassion, but that appraisal was unfair. By August 1944, he certainly understood better than anyone in his division that for the 29th to retain its richly deserved reputation for combat proficiency, replacements needed to be nurtured much more capably than they had in the past. "Our first replacements right after D-Day had to be put right into units, and many a man joined the division at night—and if his unit was heavily engaged, he was dead before anyone had really known him," Gerhardt observed. "As soon as we could, we adjusted so that depleted battalions, when in reserve, were given three days to absorb, train, and equip all replacements. Such men had an opportunity to throw a live grenade and fire a full clip of live ammunition from their rifles."

In a memorandum composed by Gerhardt in early September 1944, he referred to this new practice as a "get-acquainted period [in which] each leader learns his individuals, topped off by platoon and company tactical exercises. . . . Replacements should not go into battle without such a three-day period." On August 29 Gerhardt emphasized that point to the 115th's executive officer, Maj. Harold Perkins: "We needn't send men into battle unless they know what it's all about," he growled.

In its bivouac area near the town of Le Drévez, Millholland's battalion would for the next few days test those ideas. Gerhardt's directions to Millholland were specific:

> NCOs and officers must be capable and energetic in conducting recruit training. The officer will supervise training in three prescribed battle drills, and one NCO will conduct each battle drill. One NCO will conduct training in bazookas and hand grenades, one NCO will conduct firing of rifle grenades, and one NCO will conduct firing of M-1 rifle and BAR [Browning Automatic Rifle]. Training will be for three days. The battalion will continue to train in hedgerow tactics and assault section organization and tactics.

In truth, only combat could confirm whether or not that training made any difference. As for Gerhardt, he required no confirmation, and that autumn he would refine his concepts further by establishing an official "29th Division Training Center," one of the most innovative and effective solutions to the U.S. Army replacement crisis in the European theater. He made it plain that one of the first actions a replacement must undertake upon arrival at his new outfit was to sew the 29th Division's blue-and-gray patch onto the upper left sleeve of his uniform. Only then, according to the general, would the soldier know that he had a genuine home.

The 29ers had seen enough German soldiers so far in World War II to appreciate that their enemies relished the opportunity to make the lives of American fighting men hell. Regardless of the strategic situation, the front line was never a safe place, and the Germans, with seemingly infinite cunning, repeatedly demonstrated to their opponents that death could strike at any time by means of nearly invisible snipers, uncannily accurate and abrupt mortar barrages, booby traps, mines, and many other insidious killing techniques.

After Normandy the 29ers were thoroughly accustomed to the acute paradox of warfare in hedgerow country. The Germans were always close, incredibly close, but they only rarely showed themselves. Only a small field and a hedgerow or two typically separated the antagonists, and any GI in the front line who became careless, even for just a second, risked a bullet through his head courtesy of a well-hidden enemy sharpshooter. Generally, the Germans achieved no appreciable military benefits from those kinds of brutal acts other than to momentarily terrorize and infuriate their opponents, but by this stage of the war, the 29ers had long ago discarded the idea that modern infantry combat could be a gentleman's pastime and had themselves become highly adept practitioners of that kind of unorthodox warfare. Starting on August 28 in the lines north of Brest, Smith's 115th Infantry had the opportunity to prove it. Three days of hard fighting beginning on August 25 against fanatical German paratroopers had supplied Smith's men with plenty of incentive for payback, and when Gerhardt directed the 115th to stay put for a few days, to many members of the regiment the chance for settling a few scores with an enemy they heartily despised was compelling.

Every forty-one-man rifle platoon in the 29th Division was supposed to include a single well-trained sharpshooter, armed with the ancient but legendary M1903 Springfield rifle and attached sniper scope. Since D-Day, however, nearly continuous combat had triggered such a high rate of turnover within the platoons that leaders found it virtually impossible to retain snipers. Accordingly, most of the Springfields vanished, and sniping skills were for the most part overlooked.

Along the 115th Infantry's stagnant battle line at Brest, however, GIs who possessed those skills abruptly found themselves especially busy, even though the last few days of August 1944 would supposedly be "quiet." That many members of the 115th were obviously expert in the use of firearms was noted by the 1945 regimental history:

> One ingenious G Company rifleman rigged up a dummy using a discarded raincoat and helmet, and placed the decoy by an open gate where the enemy in the next field could not help seeing it. The bait worked, and a German fired at the figure. Unfortunately for him, he poked his head up over the hedgerow to see the results of his shot, and was promptly shot by the G Company man. [This incident took place at 6 P.M. on August 30.] Several times alert snipers picked off Germans who were heedlessly picking cabbages or relieving themselves in the wrong places.

German snipers also took a toll of 29ers, of course, but late on Saturday, September 2, the regimental journal featured an entry that seemed like a report of the outcome of a football game: "The [sniper] score stands 23-6 in our favor."

If the 115th's object was to inflict plentiful casualties upon the enemy, there had to be a more efficient means to do it than sniping with mere rifles. The commander of the 115th's 2nd Battalion, Lt. Col. Tony Miller, gave some thought to the matter and eventually came up with an innovative method that just might accomplish the goal. The thirty-one-year-old Miller was a Baltimorean who had joined the Maryland National Guard's 5th Regiment in 1931 as a private. Commissioned as a second lieutenant in 1938, Miller had thrived during the 29th Division's lengthy training in England and combat period in Normandy to become one of Gerhardt's preferred combat leaders. The division newspaper, *29 Let's Go*, described him as "a tall, burly guy with all the flavor of a real commander. There's no padded stuff about him. He looks like just what he is—a damn good fighting soldier."

Miller's scheme called for up to eight two-man bazooka teams to operate as an integral unit, popularly known later as the "Schnitzelwerfer Battery," which, starting late at night on August 30, would creep forward undetected to various frontline positions at intervals the Germans could not predict. Directed by Miller's operations officer, Capt. Robert Boyd of Minneapolis, Minnesota, the teams would load their bazooka tubes with white phosphorus rockets and fire them all at once, lobbing them at high angles into the enemy lines. Boyd's Schnitzelwerfer Battery would then beat a hasty retreat to avoid the inevitable enemy response. Each rocket

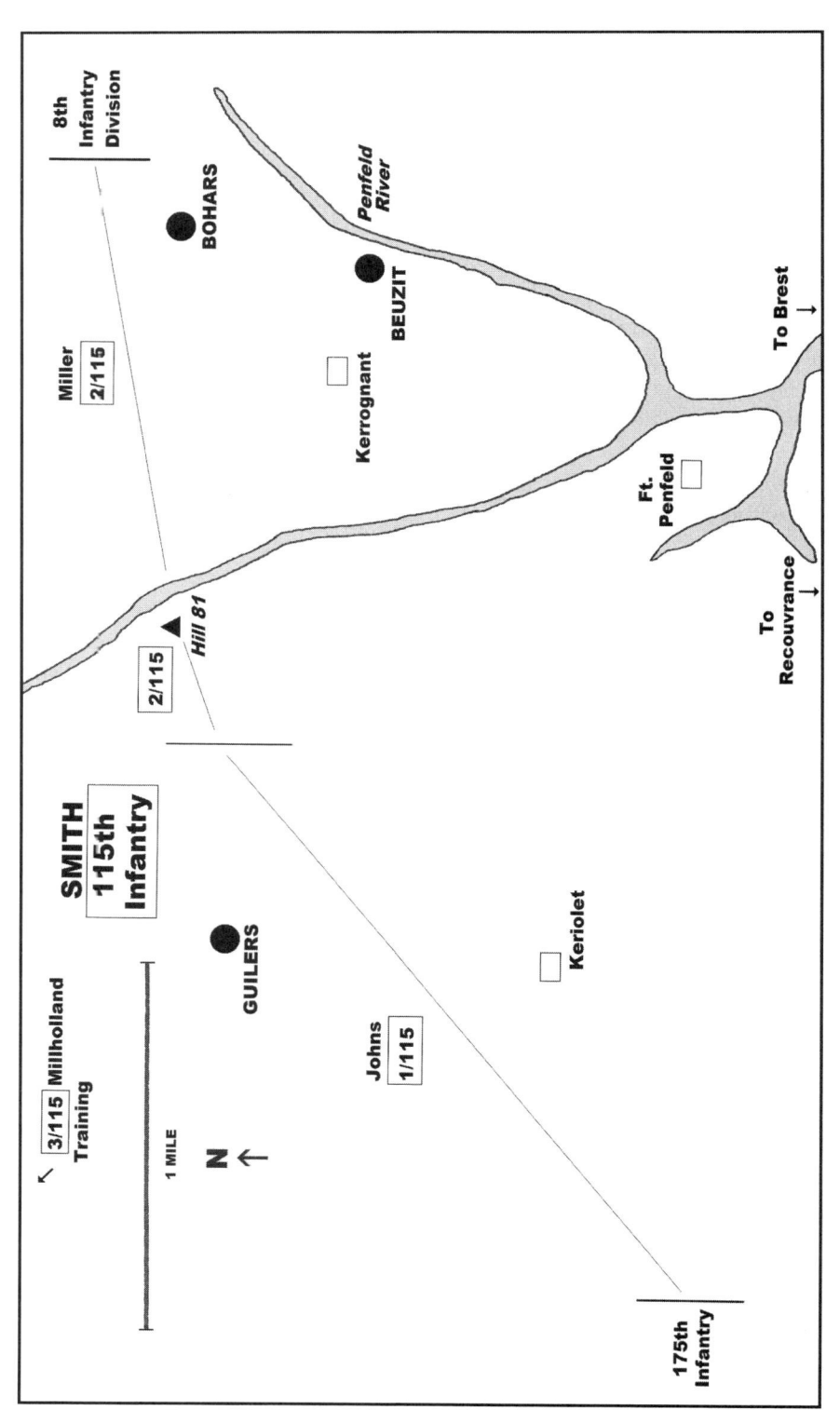

115th Infantry: August 28–September 5, 1944

contained a pound of white phosphorus, which would scatter upon impact in a circle with a diameter of nearly forty yards. The near-simultaneous blast of eight white phosphorus rounds was impressive, generating clouds of thick white smoke and hundreds of white-hot particles that would inflict ghastly wounds or death on anyone unfortunate enough to be hit by one. In the words of a *29 Let's Go* article, "The ensuing noise and confusion [in the German lines] indicated that Jerry was not altogether happy about what took place."

One German weapon the 29ers had always wanted the U.S. Army to imitate was the *Nebelwerfer*, the infamous six-barreled rocket projector of several different varieties, whose missiles were popularly known to the GIs as "screaming meemies." The division had been introduced to this weapon on Omaha Beach, and it did not take long for the men to grasp how effectively it could saturate a sizeable area in a matter of seconds with large pieces of flying shrapnel that easily could cut an unprotected soldier in two. The *Nebelwerfer* was remarkably simple in design, and by August 1944 the U.S. Army had just come up with its own 4.5-inch version, so fresh that it would take some time for its untrained users to figure out the most effective means of employing it.

At Brest, the U.S. Army Ordnance Department loaned three of those experimental rocket launchers to the 29th Division, which Gerhardt allocated to his three regiments, one apiece. The projectors were mounted on trucks, and once the rockets were loaded on the firing rails, the operators carried out their decidedly inexact aiming procedure, which consisted simply of maneuvering the trucks until the angle of fire looked right, and adjusting the elevation of the rails to account for range. That range, at most, was only 1,000 yards. The rockets were fired electronically by means of toggle switches in a control box, and when those switches were flipped the result was an abrupt and highly impressive display of the thriving new science of rocketry. In rapid succession, the rockets blasted off with thunderous roars, yielding exhaust trails that arched gracefully into the sky like the water jets of a majestic ceremonial fountain.

In theory the rocket launchers could deliver firepower at a level that would make Miller's improvised Schnitzelwerfers, or even a conventional 105mm howitzer battery, appear puny in comparison. The 29th Division rocketeers, however, learned within a matter of days that in actual combat their new weapons had some serious drawbacks. Above all, the operators found it almost impossible to hit a target at which they were aiming, and since the rockets emitted telltale smoke trails that advertised a launcher's position more plainly than a large billboard inviting the enemy to retaliate posthaste, it was obviously not a good idea to fire more than one or at most two barrages from the same position. Furthermore, several flaws in the rockets and their launching mechanisms had not yet been worked out, and as the 115th Infantry's history noted, "The weapon had to be sent to Ordnance almost as often as it fired."

Nevertheless, within the 29th Division's area of operations in late August, the rockets turned out to be a reasonably effective means of aggravating the enemy and an irrefutable signal to the German soldiers trapped in Brest that if they did not surrender soon, that aggravation soon was going to get appreciably worse. In September the 29th Division's ordnance officer, Lt. Col. Philip Root, concluded in his official report, "The rocket launcher, T-27, provides a splendid close-support weapon to the infantry capable of a large volume of fire. The explosive of the 4.5-inch rocket is similar to that of a 105mm high explosive artillery shell." Ultimately, the Ordnance Department greatly improved the launchers, and the U.S. Army created five nondivisional rocket field artillery battalions armed with jeep-mounted launchers. Only two of those deployed overseas, both to the Pacific theater.

The rockets offered compelling evidence that both sides' array of weapons would continue their deadly advancement for as long as the war would endure. How far this progression would go was anybody's guess, but it did not take a military genius to calculate that an infantryman's chances of surviving on a modern battlefield were getting smaller by the day. Even so, in the 115th Infantry's lines at Brest, the war at times exhibited the brutal simplicity of the pre-gunpowder era. At one point some members of the regiment concocted an ingenious but primitive sling-shot mechanism that flung rocks into the German lines. In comparison to some of the sophisticated weapons the GIs had become used to, such a contraption seemed somewhat ludicrous, but even if it did not injure any Germans, the enemy was surely surprised at the remarkable measures the 29ers were willing to take to retain the initiative.

For the 115th Infantry, the supposed "quiet" period was anything but. Despite the fact that, starting on August 28, the regiment received no attack orders from Gerhardt for a week and had only two of its three battalions in the front lines, it still suffered more than 100 casualties, the majority of whom came from only two rifle companies, E and G. Most of this harm was inflicted by cleverly sited German artillery, a source against which the 29ers could not readily respond because of the serious ammunition shortage. Furthermore, American air assets were for the moment tied up supporting attacks by the 116th and 175th Infantry.

Reporter Holbrook Bradley visited the frontline positions occupied by Miller's battalion and immediately noticed how busy the 29ers had been with their GI shovels. "The outfit was well dug in, and each man used his own ideas as to the construction of trenches," he observed. "The main effort, of course, was to dig one which offered the most protection and at the same time achieved a certain amount of comfort. So they ranged all the way from a large log-roofed underground hut to a shallow slit trench with a straw roof."

Incessant patrol activity, which Gerhardt insisted upon, also took a toll on members of the 115th, both physically and psychologically. The purpose of those patrols, according to a 2nd Battalion report, was "combat reconnaissance—to learn if the enemy was still present, to engage him if found in small numbers, then to return." The patrols were much more hazardous than that report implied, mostly because the Germans, too, were very aggressive patrollers. In the hedgerow country, especially at night, there was a good chance that opposing patrols would stumble into one another with violent consequences. Miller notified members of his 2nd Battalion of this danger on August 29, when he "cautioned all companies to be on the alert during the night for possible infiltration of our lines by small groups of the enemy seeking to harass our rear installations."

Just a few weeks after this phase, a U.S. Army historical officer interviewed members of the 2nd Battalion and noted how intense that patrol activity had been. "The action was frequently too close even for a satisfactory use of grenades," he reported. "Lieutenant Robert Rideout [CO of Company G] was walking about in his own lines one day, and he shot a German officer at a range of twenty feet. One sergeant of Company E was knocked down when a hand grenade landed on his helmet. A noncom in Company G, while walking along a hedgerow, felled a German scout on the other side with his rifle, using it as a club."

Irregular combat of this type over several days was extraordinarily stressful because the 29ers could never let down their guard. The front lines were so treacherous that it was even difficult for company commanders to get food to the men in the forward hedgerows. As Bradley observed in a *Baltimore Sun* article, "The boys have been living on iron rations [4-ounce D-Ration chocolate bars] supplemented by anything they can forage from the surrounding farms. However, there is one item in the life of a soldier that is brought up through hell or high water—hot coffee—and there is always plenty on hand."

Late on September 3, General Middleton issued VIII Corps realignment orders that greatly relieved the strain on the 115th Infantry. The following morning, in the zone covered by Miller's 2nd Battalion on the regiment's left flank, the 28th Infantry of the 8th Division took over a substantial portion of the front near the village of Bohars. At the same time, on the 115th's opposite (right) flank, the 175th Infantry relieved Maj. Glover Johns's 1st Battalion along a lengthy sector of its battle line south of Guilers. As a result of Middleton's directive, the 115th's sector of more than four miles was cut in half, but a transformation of that kind could mean only one thing: The 115th Infantry Regiment would soon be launching a major attack. When that happened, its members would surely yearn for the days when the front was, at least in theory, "quiet."

Once in a while, the members of the 115th got lucky. A soldier from Company E was digging a foxhole behind a hedgerow one day when he exhumed what turned out to be a French farmer's hidden cache of cognac. In truth, he discovered so many bottles that the 115th's regimental history observed, "The original one-man foxhole assumed the dimensions of a CP installation." Sadly, a few days later, Company E's improvised liquor warehouse met its end. According to Sgt. Edwin Sweeney, "The low point of the battle occurred when [a German] artillery shell landed in the cognac warehouse and set it ablaze before our eyes."

FOUR

Holding Nothing Back

1. A FINE DAY FOR THE DIVISION

By September 1, 1944, the only truly significant terrain objective on the 29th Division's front outside of Brest—Hill 103—had been transformed by several days of intense attacks by the 175th Infantry into what reporter Holbrook Bradley categorized as a "desolate waste." The hill's devastated appearance did not diminish its value, however, for it was the kind of ground U.S. Army artillery observers often fantasized about but had only rarely seen in actual combat since D-Day. The tough enemy paratroopers defending the hill had been shoved back by the 175th's relentless assault, but much to General Gerhardt's surprise, the Germans refused to accept defeat. By the first day of September, the 29ers certainly controlled the crucial hilltop, but Gerhardt could not yet rejoice over that accomplishment since the enemy's front line was so close to the crest—only twenty-five yards in some places according to Bradley—that it was virtually unusable as an observation post. One 175th officer remembered, "We could sometimes hear German conversation and hear the horse-drawn wagons moving up from their rear to bring up food." As a consequence of the enemy's close proximity, any 29th Division soldier on the summit had to spend most of his time in a foxhole if he hoped to survive.

If Colonel Purnell wished to avoid Gerhardt's wrath and remain in command of the 175th Infantry, he would have to satisfy the general's unshakable desire to secure this piece of real estate as soon as possible. Purnell, however, grasped that the achievement of that aim would be a terrible ordeal, for the 175th was worn out by a week of continuous maneuver and battle. The regiment had suffered more than 350 casualties since the commencement of the attack on Brest and had so far received no replacements to make up for that loss. The last three days of August, when the battle for Hill 103 had surged in intensity, had been particularly grueling. Furthermore, given the 29th Division's rapidly dwindling ammunition supply, it did not appear likely that Purnell could offset his paucity of riflemen with the standard display of awesome firepower that was the American army's hallmark. In truth, the only reason why Lt. Col. Clinton Thurston, commander of the 224th Field Artillery Battalion, was able to offer Purnell any fire support at all at Hill 103 was because most of the limited quantities of artillery ammunition that had been delivered to the 29th Division in the past several days had been forwarded directly to Thurston's outfit. Even so, the 224th was missing one of its three firing batteries, since Battery B was serving in support of Task Force Sugar in the Le Conquet peninsula.

On September 1, Purnell hoped that cunning could accomplish what brute strength could not. If his new scheme of attack worked, the resolute enemy defenders of Hill 103 would be pocketed by a finely coordinated enveloping attack. The pincers would be formed by Maj. Claude Melancon's 2nd Battalion south of the hill and Lt. Col. William Blandford's 3rd Battalion to the north, and when they joined somewhere beyond Hill 103, the enemy troops on that vital elevation would have no escape route.

It was a good plan, but for two consecutive days it failed to work. The September 1 assault opened at 7 A.M., but the Germans, as usual, were ready. Melancon's outfit managed to push ahead a few hundred yards on the southwest slope of the hill before running into resistance that the division's G-3 journal probably understated when it defined the enemy as "very stubborn." Meanwhile, the German paratroopers stopped Blandford's battalion cold at two farm hamlets with distinctive Breton names, Mézer Braz and Kersquivit, about a mile northeast of Hill 103.

For the 175th Infantry, the physical and mental strains of nearly a week of fierce combat were becoming increasingly evident. Given the regiment's severely depleted condition, Gerhardt suspected that Purnell's men were in no state to maintain the effort to finally secure Hill 103. At 8:27 A.M. on September 2, he spoke directly with Purnell and declared: "I wouldn't be too serious about this thing today. . . . You just develop your present position. Push your patrols and get moving. If things are easy—

hop to it!" But things were not easy for the 175th that day, despite the help offered to Blandford's 3rd Battalion by several Sherman tanks from Company A, 709th Tank Battalion, under the command of Capt. Thomas Perry. According to Purnell, the tanks "got bogged down in the mud," after which Blandford made little effort to push his worn-out infantrymen further against the enemy's seemingly unbreakable front. As for Melancon's outfit, Purnell observed: "The 2nd Battalion is up against some pretty stiff resistance and has not made any ground." In the end, the 175th's comparatively modest casualty count of eighteen on September 2 verified that Purnell in fact had prudently heeded Gerhardt's morning directive.

Apparently the pincers Purnell had hoped would surround the German defenders of Hill 103 had been shattered by the enemy before they could snap shut. At 11:08 A.M. on September 2, Middleton at VIII Corps headquarters complained to Gerhardt about the 175th's supposed lack of progress: "Can't they get around that thing?" he grumbled. "That's what they wanted to do, but they haven't got the strength," Gerhardt responded. "The 175th just doesn't have the people to do anything offensively. They have some replacements, but they have to brush them up on what's necessary. We'll be all set for tomorrow, though."

If the 175th was to carry on, Gerhardt needed to infuse it immediately with fresh manpower, so late on September 2, he took the unusual step of detaching the 115th Infantry's 3rd Battalion from its normal chain of command and placing it directly under Purnell's control. That outfit, under the command of the highly regarded Maj. Randy Millholland, was a good choice to help re-energize the 175th's assault, for it had just spent several comparatively restful days behind the front integrating a large body of replacements into its three rifle companies. As of September 2, it was the only infantry battalion in the 29th Division at anywhere near its full complement of riflemen, and as such was probably equal in combat strength to any two of Purnell's battalions combined.

When Millholland's battalion attacked at 8 A.M. on September 3, with I and K Companies leading, it immediately made good progress. By orienting its attack directly to the south, the battalion managed to find a seam in the enemy's defenses, and even better, as the regimental history noted, "The speed of the attack caught some of the German security detachments on the hill by surprise." By noon, the 29ers were just short of the farm complex of Penhoat, about one-quarter mile southeast of Hill 103. When they reached that vital objective, the last remaining escape route for the German defenders on the hill would be cut off. The enemy grasped that reality, too, and when several prisoners were brought in for interrogation to the 175th's S-2 (intelligence) section that morning, they freely admitted that their side had at last abandoned that vital elevation. At 3:33 P.M., Purnell made the announcement Gerhardt had been anticipating for a week: "Hill 103 is clear of Jerries and available for artillery observers." As an afterthought, he observed, "There are piles of dead Jerries."

Millholland's outfit had finally broken the stalemate in this key sector of the Blue and Gray front, a significant success that Gerhardt noted when he spoke to regimental commander Col. Lou Smith of the 115th Infantry that afternoon. "Your 3rd Battalion really did swell today!" he crowed. Later, the general got Millholland himself on the phone and declared, "I think you did a marvelous job today. Keep on this way and you'll get promoted before you know it!" Millholland modestly replied, "Thank you, sir.... It was Colonel Purnell's work." Gerhardt concluded, "You're new, and it's new people [we need]. This has been a fine day for the division, and you carried the load!" (Gerhardt was actually mistaken that Millholland was "new" to the 29th Division, as the major had spent nineteen years of his career as a part-time guardsman and full-time soldier with the division before leaving to take command of the short-lived 29th Ranger Battalion in Britain in 1943. He returned to the 29th Division after the end of the Normandy campaign.)

Considering its source, praise of that kind could cause the spirit of any 29th Division combat leader to surge. Gerhardt kept his word and would soon reward Millholland for his feat of arms by granting him the Bronze Star and promoting him from major to lieutenant colonel—a rare admission by a very demanding general that at least some officers with National Guard origins were indeed top-notch warriors.

Gerhardt promptly ordered his staff to set up a special observation post on the crest of Hill 103 just for his use. The division newsletter, *29 Let's Go*, reported:

> From here the general can keep his eye on a vast stretch of our front lines: more than an entire infantry regiment is in clear view. The general visits the post frequently during the course of a day.... A line-up of the optical instruments at the OP are: a B.C. [battery commander] telescope; a 20-power single lens observation telescope; and a captured Jerry B.C. scope. These, plus all varieties of field glasses. [Also] Sgt. Albert Rogers of the G-2 section has drawn a panoramic sketch for the general.

On September 4, Purnell pulled his exhausted 1st and 2nd Battalions out of the line so they could undergo the same three-day infusion of

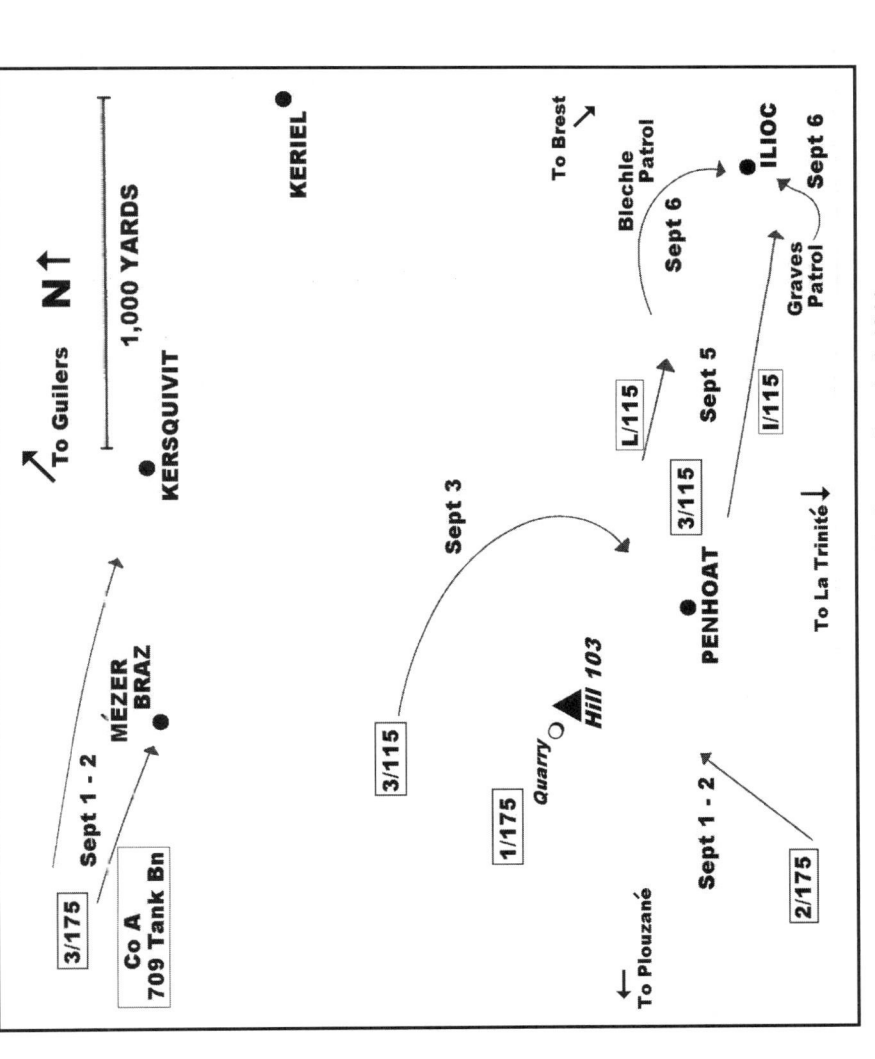

175th Infantry: Hill 103, September 1–6, 1944

replacements and fresh training that Millholland's outfit had just received with such beneficial results. The 175th would thereupon be forced to cover a front of more than three miles with only two battalions: Blandford's 3rd on the left, or north, flank; plus Millholland's battalion on the right, or south, flank. It would be several days before Gerhardt would transfer Millholland's men from Purnell's control back to their rightful commander, Colonel Smith.

The Germans on Purnell's front were beaten, but the 175th's worn-out condition and its extended front suggested that there would be no continuation of the attack on September 4, and probably for a few days thereafter. Even Gerhardt admitted to Middleton, "It's about gotten to the point now that all [the 175th] can do is just contain them." In truth, the worsening ammunition shortage throughout VIII Corps virtually compelled a halt in American offensive operations throughout Brittany for a few days. Middleton issued an order to that effect on the 4th and notified Gerhardt verbally at 4 P.M. that day: "We'll mark time again tomorrow [September 5]."

Despite Gerhardt's reply—"Got you. . . . I understand the order"—he could not "mark time" if the enemy was obviously pulling back and vulnerable to another American push. In the event the Germans were retreating, the general had a plan in mind for the 175th on September 5, but when Purnell got wind of it, he had the temerity to blurt to Gerhardt: "I don't believe an attempt to advance would be desirable . . . except minor adjustments, until we are ready to make a general advance."

But fresh reports from Lt. Col. "Murphy" Krznarich's intelligence team at the 29th Division war room indicated that the enemy on Purnell's front had disappeared, and if that detail was correct, Gerhardt needed to know precisely how far the Germans had withdrawn and where they would stand and fight. Brest was literally within sight now, and the general could smell blood. I'm thinking about making a night attack," Gerhardt told the doubtful Purnell. "We might do it tonight—I'll be thinking it over."

He didn't have to think very long. If the Germans had pulled back, Gerhardt reasoned, in all likelihood there would not be any severe fighting until their positions had been pinpointed. He therefore issued orders for an unusual nocturnal advance on September 5 shortly after midnight. His directive applied only to Millholland's outfit—still on loan from the 115th Infantry—and two battalions of the 116th Infantry occupying the division's southernmost front near the village of La Trinité.

Millholland's objective would be an intersection about one mile east of Hill 103, a vital locale where five roads came together near an assortment of sturdy Breton farm buildings known collectively as Ilioc. Whether or not the Germans would make a stand at Ilioc farm, Gerhardt had no idea, but he was determined to find out immediately. If they did, the general had no intention of allowing them the luxury of thoroughly preparing their defenses for the Americans' inevitable attack. To disrupt that preparation, Gerhardt was determined to maintain continuous pressure on the enemy—a tactic he had repeatedly urged his subordinates to practice since D-Day, even if their outfits were worn out and understrength. Unfortunately, as Millholland's 29ers were about to find out, the Germans had already prepared their defenses at Ilioc thoroughly, and the 29th Division would ultimately suffer heavy casualties breaking the enemy's resistance at that formidable strongpoint in bitter fighting that would endure for a week.

Gerhardt's night attack on September 5 was intended to catch the enemy by surprise, but it ended up surprising the Americans more than the Germans. Advancing even a short distance in the baffling hedgerow country at night against a known enemy position was difficult enough, but pushing forward in the pitch-black gloom through that completely unfamiliar and labyrinthine farmland, toward an objective nearly 1,000 yards distant, especially when no one seemed to know precisely where the Germans were located, was nearly impossible.

Millholland's battalion jumped off at about midnight, with Company L on the left, Company I on the right. Almost immediately, the two companies lost contact with one another, and in the words of the regimental history, "Both became confused and lost direction." Fortunately, the enemy did not at first offer stout resistance, prompting Purnell's veteran operations officer, Capt. Henry Reed, who had joined the Maryland National Guard as a private in 1931, to inform the 29th Division war room at 3:30 A.M.: "Our boys are just running into some small stuff; it doesn't seem to be organized." Regrettably, reports of that kind helped to trigger positive assumptions at division headquarters that turned out to be groundless. At 3:47 A.M., Witte contacted VIII Corps' command post and announced that Millholland's battalion had reached Ilioc, and a few hours later, Gerhardt corroborated that detail by proclaiming to Middleton: "We did it. We jumped at midnight and moved about 1,000 meters. They [the enemy] evidently pulled back."

Unfortunately, the September 5 affair was a classic instance of the wholly dissimilar viewpoints held by frontline troops and division headquarters amid the proverbial fog of war. When the situation at Ilioc finally crystallized around noon, it was clear to all that Millholland's 29ers had not advanced nearly as far as Gerhardt had claimed to Middleton. At daylight, the American riflemen had needed several hours to orient themselves, and when they did, it turned out that Company L had advanced a mere 350 yards, while Company I had gained about 800. As for the report that the 3rd Battalion had seized Ilioc farm: If Millholland's men had failed to figure out precisely where they were during their nocturnal advance across the inscrutable hedgerow country, how could they have known whether or not they had gained that important objective? Even Gerhardt later had to admit that Ilioc was still in German hands. Worse, it would remain so for a week.

On the positive side, Millholland's casualty count on September 5, amounting to about twenty men, was comparatively light compared to what had transpired at Hill 103 in the past week. A blind nighttime attack against unidentified enemy positions could have been worse—much worse. Furthermore, thanks to the aggressive patrolling initiated by Millholland in the afternoon of September 5 and later, Gerhardt would eventually figure out precisely where the enemy had shifted its main line of resistance after the fall of Hill 103 and could therefore prepare a methodical assault against that new line. He fervently hoped that that assault would be the decisive and final one the 29th Division would have to undertake at Brest.

Several patrols conducted by Millholland's men toward the German position at Ilioc actually achieved some notable successes. In fact, Gerhardt awarded the Silver Star to one member of Company L, S/Sgt. Francis Blechle, for leading three daring scouting missions over a twenty-four-hour period starting on the evening of September 5. According to a 5:45 P.M. message on September 6 from Millholland's command post to the division war room, one of Blechle's patrols "is reported to have taken an entire platoon [actually about twenty men] of the 11th Company, 2nd Parachute Regiment in the vicinity of 884993 [a map coordinate, indicating Ilioc farm]." Given the fighting prowess of German paratroopers, this was a remarkable achievement, especially as Blechle's patrol contained only five men. Another patrol was conducted by S/Sgt. Edd Graves of Company I, described by the *29 Let's Go* newsletter as "a tall, wiry, daring man from Tennessee . . . a big bear-hunter from the Smoky Mountain country." Graves grasped the élan of his current *Fallschirmjäger* opponents because he himself had been trained as a U.S. Army paratrooper. Near Ilioc, he and his comrades netted fourteen more prisoners—clear evidence that Gerhardt's insistence on maintaining the initiative whenever possible was paying dividends.

Late on September 7, Gerhardt pulled Millholland's outfit out of the line—with the exception of Company K—and placed it in reserve for a few days of rest. Gerhardt visited the battalion on September 9, and aside from his obvious annoyance that many members of Company I were not wearing their helmet chin straps hooked underneath their chins as per U.S. Army uniform regulations, he was delighted by what he saw. According to the battalion journal, "[Gerhardt] congratulated the battalion for marvelous work [and] credited Blue-6 for it" ["Blue-6" was Millholland's call-name in 29th Division radio and telephone transmissions].

Gerhardt filled Millholland's place in the front lines with the somewhat rejuvenated 2nd Battalion, 175th Infantry, whose original commander as of D-Day, Lt. Col. Millard Bowen, had returned on September 6 to reassume command after recovery from wounds he had suffered in Normandy. Bowen replaced the highly respected Maj. Claude Melancon, who had performed splendidly in Bowen's absence and in fact would stay on as Bowen's executive officer and play a vital role in the upcoming fighting. Bowen was an experienced soldier who had joined the National Guard as a private in the 1st Maryland Infantry in 1935 after having gained a law degree from Southeastern University in Washington, D.C., at the age of twenty-one. His Normandy wounds, however, still troubled him greatly, and he would lead the battalion for only three weeks before departing and yielding command to Melancon again.

When the dust settled in the 29th Division war room following the confused fighting around Ilioc, Colonel Witte was finally able to depict on his situation map the military situation in that sector of the front with a reasonable degree of accuracy. Gerhardt's immediate conclusion upon scrutinizing that map was that there was no longer any room for subtlety. If he was to fulfill the 29th Division's mission at Brest, Purnell's 175th Infantry—and every other infantry unit in the division for that matter—must initiate unremitting frontal attacks and smash the enemy back into Brest, now less than four miles distant. The general, however, comprehended that two vital prerequisites must be met before he could launch those brutal assaults: first, his tired and depleted infantry battalions must be rested and suffused with replacements; second, he must obtain much more ammunition. Gerhardt could to some extent deal with the first requirement himself. The second, however, he could not control, and if the ammunition problem was not solved soon, the 29th Division's offensive would be seriously impaired, perhaps even to the point of paralysis.

Fortunately, reports from VIII Corps headquarters indicated that adequate ammunition stocks were on the way and would arrive shortly. Still better, the top brass at U.S. Twelfth Army Group had indicated to Middleton that ammunition would flow into Brittany in profusion for as long as it took him to finish the job and capture Brest. Finally, Ninth Air Force fighter-bombers were by now poised for an extraordinary effort in support of the upcoming offensive, and with the enemy encircled in a shrinking enclave, German troops would find it increasingly difficult to shield themselves from that concentrated aerial assault. In short, if the upcoming battle developed as Gerhardt expected, the enemy would be shattered within the next few days, and then, instead of striving to outwit German generals on the battlefield, he could be receiving Ramcke's sword in Brest when the enemy finally gave up.

Uncle Charlie could only dream of what a glorious page in 29th Division history that would be.

2. VICTORIES MONITORED BY DEATH

The 29th Division's effort to capture Brest in the first days of September was by no means limited to Purnell's 175th Infantry. While Purnell's men were waging their bitter struggles for Hill 103 and Ilioc, Gerhardt had ordered Col. Philip Dwyer's 116th Infantry to plunge ahead on the 175th's right, or southern, flank toward the vital crossroads village of La Trinité, which the Stonewall Brigade had been striving to capture since August 29. According to Gerhardt, La Trinité was almost as important as Hill 103. That village straddled the main east-west N789 road connecting Brest and the Le Conquet peninsula and was situated only three miles west of the German Navy's infamous submarine pens on Brest's harborside. According to Gerhardt, one determined thrust could carry the 116th Infantry forward directly to that objective.

Anyone who had witnessed the events at Hill 103 in early September 1944 could hardly imagine that infantry combat could be any more intense than that violent struggle. But in fact the 116th's effort to capture La Trinité was even worse, an assertion that is confirmed by the division's official casualty figures. For the six-day period of combat ending on September 3, the 116th Infantry's casualty total of 469 exceeded that of the 175th by more than 50 percent.

Both regiments' efforts were characterized by blunt and costly frontal attacks, supported by miserly artillery fire because of VIII Corps' severe ammunition shortage. Unlike the 175th, however, the 116th Infantry occupied a remarkably awkward position, with a wide-open right flank that was entirely vulnerable to enemy counterattack. Amazingly, while his men smashed ahead toward La Trinité, an astonished Dwyer also had to contend with German troops in his rear, some of whom were posted only two miles behind his lines in a chain of five ancient French forts situated along the rocky Brittany coastline west of Brest. For the moment Dwyer had no choice but to ignore those enemy strongpoints if he wished to focus all his energies on La Trinité, as Gerhardt's directive had stipulated. He hoped that they would prove no worse than a minor annoyance, but unfortunately, they were in fact much worse than that.

All three of the 116th Infantry's battalions jumped off toward La Trinité shortly after 7 A.M. on September 1. At this point in the campaign, no one was surprised that the enemy was ready and that forward progress was almost imperceptible. Three hours later Dwyer delivered the perplexing news to Gerhardt that the 116th was "getting artillery fire from all directions." Gerhardt demanded to know, "Are you going to get anywhere today?" Dwyer's blunt response—"Not very fast"—served to indicate to the general that a breakthrough on the La Trinité front would not occur anytime soon.

Gerhardt would eventually have to solve the predicament posed by the enemy's vexing artillery fire, but in the meantime, Dwyer must press on with his effort to seize La Trinité. The 116th jumped off at 10:30 A.M. on September 2, again with all three battalions in line. In the words of the regiment's monthly action report, the units "doggedly pushed forward against heavy enemy resistance in the form of SPs [self-propelled guns], machine guns, small arms, and artillery fire . . . but little ground [actually about 250 yards] was gained throughout the day."

At one point Dwyer complained to Gerhardt, "We're getting lower in strength everyday—both in officers and men." The general, with his habitual bluntness, replied: "That's expected." The 116th managed to push ahead only about 500 yards in the first two days of September; at that rate of advance, it would take weeks to seize Brest. On the evening of September 2, at Gerhardt's insistence, Dwyer withdrew his exhausted 3rd Battalion from the front line for a short rest period, during which its depleted manpower would be restored by the infusion of plentiful replacements—a procedure that was regrettably becoming the norm in the 29th Division during the unexpectedly tough fighting in Brittany. But if fresh infantrymen were needed to reinvigorate the 29th Division's attack on Brest, that is what the general had to do.

On September 1 Gerhardt implored his boss, Middleton, to send him reinforcements so that he could solve the dilemma Dwyer had to deal with on his wide-open right flank. Middleton consented and issued immediate orders to deploy four companies from the 5th Ranger Battalion, currently attached to the 2nd Infantry Division, to the problem area. Ranger companies were much smaller than their rifle company counterparts in the

29th Division, and those ranger reinforcements amounted only to about 250 men. But the 5th Rangers were superb fighters, a fact that Gerhardt readily grasped because that outfit had landed alongside his 29ers on D-Day at Omaha Beach, and it had carried out its mission on that dreadful shoreline with impressive determination.

The twenty-six-year-old Maj. Richard Sullivan, the 5th Ranger Battalion's commander, was a proven combat leader who had recently been awarded the highly prestigious Distinguished Service Cross for his heroism on Omaha Beach. He had enlisted in the historic 101st Infantry of the Massachusetts National Guard at Boston as a private in 1936 and had later been commissioned as a second lieutenant when President Roosevelt inducted the 26th "Yankee" Division into federal service in January 1941. Along with many other members of the 26th Division, Sullivan, by then a captain, had joined the newly organized 5th Ranger Battalion at Camp Forrest, Tennessee, in the summer of 1943 as its first executive officer. As Capt. John Raaen, CO of the 5th Rangers' Headquarters Company on D-Day and at Brest, recalled those training days: "'Sully' was a stickler for discipline and precision—such a strong leader that he actually ran the battalion." Raaen remembered that after Sullivan broke his foot while on a field exercise in Florida, "He would not allow the doctor, or anyone else for that matter, to take his boot off. As far as I know, he kept that boot on his foot until he shipped out to England. It healed in his 'boot' cast."

Upon receiving his orders from Middleton to reinforce Dwyer's 116th Infantry, Sullivan immediately borrowed some trucks and moved his men in late afternoon on September 1 to an assembly point at the village of Locmaria-Plouzané, about three miles behind the 116th's frontline hedgerows at La Trinité. But when he arrived there and learned the details of the mission Gerhardt expected his unit to execute, even a bold combat leader like Sullivan must have allowed himself a moment of doubt as to whether or not such a daunting job could be fulfilled. Sullivan gathered that the offending enemy howitzers firing into the 116th Infantry's rear were located in the chain of five small forts still occupied by German troops behind Dwyer's lines on the rocky headlands west of Brest. It would be Sullivan's duty to assault due east along that coastline, capturing or neutralizing each of those forts in succession. If he could accomplish that mission swiftly, Dwyer's burden would be considerably alleviated.

The forts, however, were separated from each other by intervals of about a mile, and the many deep ravines cutting through the omnipresent coastal cliffs in those intervals represented some of the toughest terrain in the Brest area. Furthermore, the Germans had considerably augmented each fort's defensive potential with their customary thoroughness, employing barbed wire, minefields, antitank ditches, concrete gun emplacements, and more. Intelligence reports indicated that each strongpoint was occupied by a garrison numbering in the hundreds, and if those occupants fought obstinately, the sequence of attacks required to take each fort in turn would in all probability be tough and protracted. Even worse, Sullivan would be obligated to attack with little more than half of his battalion because Middleton had directed him to leave behind three of his seven companies (A, C, and E) with the 2nd Division when he departed for Locmaria-Plouzané. Sullivan's force must therefore accomplish its mission against an entrenched enemy that outnumbered it considerably—a tactic that U.S. Army field manuals would have categorized as highly imprudent.

On the other hand, French military engineers had designed those forts decades ago, when the primary threat to Brest would in all likelihood have come from the sea; they were built chiefly as coastal defense positions. By attacking them from the landward side, Sullivan was in effect striking them at their most vulnerable points. Even better, when on the afternoon of September 2 Sullivan initiated his force's movement toward his first objective, Fort Toulbroch, the rangers promptly captured ten German troops. When Sullivan reported that fact to Gerhardt, he added a significant detail: "[Enemy] morale poor. Troops reported to be willing to surrender if given a chance." The Germans defending the forts were not paratroopers, and if the rumor about their low self-confidence were true, maybe Sullivan's task would be much easier than he had first imagined.

That rumor turned out to be valid. A probe by a Company B platoon led by 1st Lt. Louis Gombosi at dusk on September 2 revealed that at least some of the enemy would fight, but just how vigorously no one could yet tell. The following day, Sullivan brought up two companies (B and D) to make a set-piece attack. As the rangers had no intrinsic artillery save for their light mortars, Sullivan requested air strikes on Toulbroch by the Ninth Air Force. When the fighter-bombers arrived around noon, their bombing accuracy was poor, so at 1:15 P.M. Sullivan appealed for yet another try. This time the pilots wanted the target marked with colored smoke fired by 29th Division howitzers, but at 2:22 Sullivan reported that the smoke shells had apparently been duds: the pilots could detect no signs of smoke anywhere. The artillerymen promptly substituted more reliable white phosphorus rounds instead, and the pilots soon had Toulbroch directly in their bomb sights.

At 2:31 eight P-47 Thunderbolts roared in and smashed the fort with several direct hits with 1,000-pound bombs. Just to make life for the enemy garrison even more unpleasant, the fighter-bombers returned for low passes over Toulbroch to strafe anything that moved—even though, according to the 5th Rangers' official history, "Lt. Gombosi and his platoon were less than 100 yards from the fort." It was a stunning success, later remembered by Colonel Cooper of the 29th Division's 110th Field Artillery as "a perfect example of cooperation between infantrymen, artillerymen, and fighter-bomber pilots."

According to the 5th Rangers' action report, only six minutes elapsed between the departure of the P-47s and the enemy's collapse at Fort Toulbroch. Emerging from their casemates with shell-shocked expressions and their hands over their heads, 247 German prisoners fell into the rangers' hands. Given that Sullivan had boldly launched the attack with fewer than 100 rangers, Gerhardt recognized this as a spectacular achievement. At 2:39 Sullivan radioed the war room that his men were in Fort Toulbroch, and when Gerhardt later read the typewritten transcript of that message, he penciled in a single word next to it: "Excellent."

Captain Raaen observed,

> In combat, Sully didn't stay in the CP. He was out with the troops. I remember learning that on his first such journey [at Brest], he went to one of the companies and lay down beside each ranger, asking such questions as, "What is your assigned field of fire?" "What is the range to the woods over there?" "Who is on your right?" "How far is he?" "Where is your section leader located?" And the men appreciated it because he brought sharply to mind the things that would save their lives—if not that night, then in future nights.

But with success came difficulties. Sullivan feared that when the Germans realized how few Americans had bested them, they might reassess their decision to surrender and suddenly become defiant. If the 5th Rangers were to press on eastward to the next enemy strongpoint, Fort Minou, somebody was going to have to take the prisoners off his hands immediately. At 3:20 P.M. he radioed Witte: "We are having a little trouble down here," followed by some strong words about what would happen to the captives if the "trouble" got any worse. Witte jumped on the problem, and at 4:10 Maj. Bob Minor from the 29th Division's G-2 shop phoned Sullivan to say, "If you can march the prisoners to the Lemon [116th Infantry] command post, we can take care of them for you." There would surely be a wealth of valuable intelligence those prisoners could offer, and

Minor wanted to extract that information as soon as possible. Later, Gerhardt himself contacted Sullivan to reassure him about the prisoner issue. "We are going to send you some FFI [French Resistance fighters] to take over in back of you," Gerhardt declared.

At 9 A.M. on the following day, September 4, an animated Gerhardt announced to Sullivan: "We have a POW report that they've evacuated the next fort in front of you [Fort Minou]. Rush that thing!" Sullivan promptly complied and committed Company D to the task. Fort Minou was situated at the neck of a narrow promontory featuring a picturesque old lighthouse at its southern tip, just five miles due west of Brest harbor. The fort's garrison of more than 300 men should have been able to hold out for a considerable time against a much smaller attacking force, but the Germans obviously did not have their hearts in the task. By late afternoon, Minou and its entire garrison were in American hands, at a cost to Company D of fifteen casualties.

Sullivan had achieved two noteworthy victories with only a portion of his command, but he knew he could accomplish even more impressive results if Middleton would only release the rest of the 5th Ranger Battalion from the 2nd Division's control. He got his wish at 5 P.M. on September 4, when Middleton finally allowed the 200 rangers of Companies A, C, and E to join their comrades in the struggle that would shortly become known as "The Battle of the Forts." That was decidedly good news for Sullivan, who would soon need those reinforcements badly.

Two forts down and three to go. But already that partial fulfillment of the 5th Rangers' mission had considerably alleviated the problem created by enemy artillery fire originating from behind the 116th Infantry's lines. Gerhardt was so happy with Sullivan's accomplishments that he radioed the 5th Ranger Battalion's adjutant, Capt. Edmund Butler, "Congratulations! Get me info on Sullivan and send it up here so I can call him up and pin a medal [a Silver Star] on him." Later, Gerhardt had Sullivan promoted from major to lieutenant colonel.

Gerhardt clearly marveled at the rangers' aggressiveness, and on September 5 he noted to Middleton, "That kid Sullivan and his gang are super!" According to Captain Raaen, after the close of the Brest campaign he offered Sullivan and several other ranger officers the opportunity to command battalions within the 29th Division. "Some of my battalion commanders just haven't had enough experience in command," Gerhardt observed to Raaen. "You rangers are superbly trained and could handle one of my battalions easily." However, a disappointed Gerhardt noted that none of the rangers would accept his offer.

Dwyer's 116th could now press on toward its elusive objective at La Trinité, secure in the knowledge that the problem of enemy troops behind the regiment had been addressed. At 8 A.M. on September 3, with Maj. Jim Morris's 1st Battalion on the left and Maj. Charles Cawthon's 2nd Battalion on the right, the worn-out men of the Stonewall Brigade yet again leaped over their frontline hedgerows on the word of their leaders, to come face-to-face with their opponents, those fanatical German paratroopers who had been making the 29ers' lives hell since Normandy. It was the third straight morning Gerhardt had ordered the 116th forward, but this time, minus his habitual buoyancy, he concluded, "This thing will either be successful by 10 A.M. or we aren't going to do it."

In fact the enemy paratroopers made sure that the 116th Infantry could not "do it." According to the 29th Division's monthly after-action report for September 1944, "The plan was to have artillery concentrations just ahead of the advancing troops, and for the troops to take immediate advantage of this fire . . . [but] the concentrations failed to dislodge the enemy from his well dug-in positions. The enemy offered stubborn resistance for every inch of ground it yielded to our troops." When Gerhardt granted permission for Dwyer's 29ers to "button up" for the remaining hours of September 3, the evidence was clear that his coveted breakthrough had not occurred: the 2nd Battalion had moved forward only about 300 yards; the 1st Battalion about half that distance. Such "progress" amounted to a gain of just a few hedgerows—and left the regiment still a considerable distance short of La Trinité.

The 116th Infantry was relearning the hard lesson of Normandy: The German Army's best fighters could not be overcome in a single, decisive stroke. Rather, they must be pulverized, day after day, relentlessly—until so few of them were left alive that their resistance finally broke. A platoon leader in Company G, 2nd Lt. William Arendt, recalled that in the fighting at La Trinité, "We took a dozen or more prisoners, but they weren't paratroopers. Paratroopers, we learned, we mostly had to kill to get past."

Regrettably, to reach that point the 29ers, too, would lose many good men. In that type of drawn-out and brutal combat, the salient concern among 29th Division leaders was that the Americans might snap before the enemy did. Fortunately for Gerhardt, they almost never did, a testament to the overwhelming preponderance of men and materiel the United States was applying to the conflict, as well as the spiritual and physical resilience of those lucky 29ers who managed to survive the ordeal in one piece. The 116th Infantry had endured Omaha Beach, St. Lô, and Vire—and now there was La Trinité, a terrible place that had by this time cost most of the regiment's rifle companies nearly half their men. According to Cawthon, the battle for La Trinité "was a microcosm of war at all times and levels. It encompassed misconception, chance, rashness, violence, courage, despair, victory, and defeat—all monitored by death."

Capt. Robert Garcia, an experienced D-Day veteran who by now commanded Company E, observed how abruptly death could strike in the brutal combat at Brest:

> There was a devastating shell burst among a group of men, killing [T/Sgt. Willard] Ashlock and Newcomb. [There is no "Newcomb" in the 116th Infantry's roll of killed in action; Garcia presumably meant T/Sgt. Alva Newton, a veteran of Omaha Beach and one of the 29th Division's most renowned athletes during the training period in England.] Sergeant Graham Pearce was wounded by the burst. I had just moments before left that group, admonishing them to "break it up," for groups were always vulnerable. Sure enough—in came a German shell to do its damage. Pearce came stumbling over to me for help. He was in bad shape . . . I patched him up as best I could. I took a morphine syrette out of its wrapping, broke off the tip, and plunged it into Pearce. . . . When I went to write a note about what I'd done, I found that I had lost my pencil. I still had my notebook, so I took a twig, and using blood running from Pearce's wound, scribbled a note about giving him morphine, stuck it in his shirt, and left.

A frustrated Gerhardt ordered the 116th to stand fast on September 4, but that short rest would end at the stroke of midnight. The war room was beginning to receive astonishing reports from 29th Division scouts that the German line seemed to be giving way all across the front, and if those stories were true, Gerhardt meant to hasten that dissolution. The general therefore directed Dwyer's 1st and 2nd Battalions, along with Major Millholland's 3rd Battalion, 115th Infantry, at Hill 103 to initiate a rare nighttime assault, an awkward procedure even for seasoned troops. When Witte radioed Dwyer, "What do you think about this thing?" Dwyer replied, "If we get as much [enemy] artillery as we have been getting at night, this night attack is going to be pretty difficult."

To lessen that difficulty, the attack would be made in platoon columns, whose members would be strung out one behind the other in long files led by an officer or senior NCO following a precise compass heading. Scouts laid out white tape, delineating platoon boundaries, so that the GIs would not wander off course—an easy mistake at night in hedgerow country. To enhance visibility of friendly troops in the dark, the 29ers tied pieces of white cloth around their arms or pinned them to the backs of their uniforms, but somewhat incongruously, several men also blackened their faces so that the enemy would have a harder time seeing them. "I can still see [1st Lt. George] Herrick [CO, Company G] with those long Ichabod-scarecrow legs and flapping arms heading into the night," recalled Lieutenant Arendt. "His company followed, like dutiful schoolboys out for a disciplinary hike. We were well inside German lines by this time, but there was no hesitation."

Somehow it worked. In the words of a 1st Battalion report of the affair, "The attack was made without artillery preparation [and in some cases with orders not to fire rifles save in an emergency]. The enemy was apparently caught off guard. Wire entanglements were quickly negotiated and [objectives] occupied." Dwyer's men pushed ahead 600 yards in just a few hours, a noticeably brisk rate of advance compared to the progress of the past week. Even better, darkness provided a highly protective shield for the attackers, and enemy resistance was therefore so ineffective that American casualties were amazingly light. (Among those casualties, however, were Lieutenants Herrick and Arendt of Company G, both of whom were badly wounded.) The key crossroads at La Trinité was finally in American hands for good.

The Americans readily understood that when they seized a piece of terrain the Germans valued, the enemy invariably counterattacked—promptly and ferociously. At about 6 P.M. on September 5 the Germans did exactly that at La Trinité, falling suddenly upon the unfortunate Company G, which occupied the extreme right of the 29th Division's front line. The enemy force consisted of about 100 men, paratroopers for the most part, but reinforced by sailors snatched from Brest's harborside to make up for the paratroopers' heavy losses. The Germans, displaying the attitude that Gerhardt euphemistically referred to as "enthusiasm," threatened to undo everything the 116th Infantry had accomplished in the last twenty-four hours.

Company G had landed in the first wave on Omaha Beach on June 6, 1944, but hardly any men who had survived that calamitous event and the subsequent struggle in Normandy still remained with the outfit. Fortunately, one who did was T/Sgt. Wilson Carr, a Virginian, who by this time was one of the most skilled and respected soldiers in the 2nd Battalion. One among many of Carr's traits that triggered that respect was vigilance, and that quality paid off handsomely during the late afternoon of Sept-

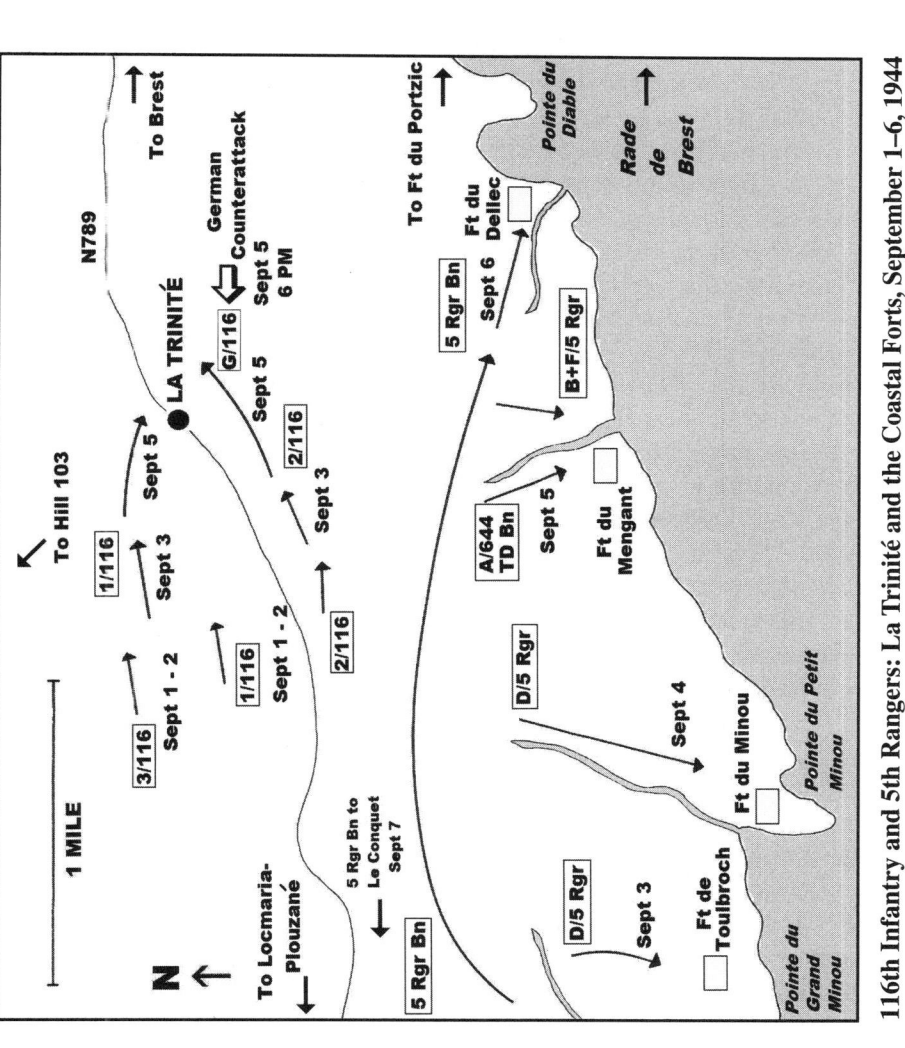

116th Infantry and 5th Rangers: La Trinité and the Coastal Forts, September 1–6, 1944

ember 5. When the Germans laid down a heavy barrage on Company G's frontline hedgerow, Carr suspected that as soon as that barrage closed they would follow up with an infantry attack. He was right: A quick peek over the hedgerow revealed the amazing spectacle of the onrushing enemy in a German version of a *banzai* charge. The 2nd Battalion's commander, Major Cawthon, spoke with Carr afterward and remarked,

> [Carr] had begun picking them off with his rifle—he was credited with fifteen—and shouting to his platoon to get up and fight or be killed. Enough joined him to wipe out the attackers. . . . The field in front of the right G Company platoon was littered with bodies in paratrooper smocks and others in [sailor] uniform. It was a profusion of death I had not seen in so small a place since the first day at St. Lô.

By a general order issued at Ninth Army headquarters in early 1945, Sergeant Carr was awarded the highly prized Distinguished Service Cross.

When a concerned staff officer from the 29th Division's war room phoned the 116th's command post and inquired about the outcome of the enemy's assault on Company G, Maj. Maurice Clift, the 116th's operations officer, calmly replied: "They took care of it." Taking care of it, however, had cost many lives—among them Capt. Elmer Faircloth, one of the most respected officers in the 2nd Battalion. Faircloth had only recently served as Cawthon's executive officer, but on September 1 had moved to the front to take command of Company F, which had become leaderless because of the devastating casualties suffered at La Trinité. He was killed amid the chaos of the enemy's September 5 counterattack, and Cawthon remembered him fondly as "the type of soldier who inspires trust by his example of common sense, steadiness, and cheer."

Gerhardt knew the 116th Infantry was thoroughly spent. Furthermore, the VIII Corps ammunition shortage was not getting any better, and until that problem was solved, it hardly made sense for the regiment to continue its attack. Capturing La Trinité had cost the 116th almost 600 men, but in the heartless statistical game of modern war, Dwyer actually had more men on his rolls at the close of the battle than he did when he started due to the reception of 750 replacements in the 116th Infantry from September 2 to September 5. Amazingly, thirty-six of those replacements were officers, fresh and with no battle experience, most of whom had the unenviable task of marching from a replacement depot straight into the ranks of a rifle company and then leading its hard-edged soldiers into a battle that all historical evidence indicated would be ruthless.

Gerhardt would finally pull the 116th's 1st Battalion out of the line for a rest on September 8, and the 2nd Battalion two days later. In the meantime, if the regiment was too drained to attack, it must still conduct that military function the general always insisted upon: "aggressive patrolling." For five straight days after the capture of La Trinité, therefore, the 116th Infantry—minus its 3rd Battalion, currently in the Le Conquet peninsula with "Task Force Sugar"—did exactly that. The division's operations journal, however, noted remorsefully that this patrolling "was conducted with the intention of discovering evidence of enemy withdrawal, which was not found to be extensive."

While the 116th Infantry was securing La Trinité, Sullivan's 5th Ranger Battalion was resuming its dynamic drive eastward on September 5 along the Brittany coastline toward Brest. Sullivan's next stop, less than four miles west of Brest, was Fort du Mengant, whose array of pillboxes, trenches, barbed wire, and minefields reflected the enemy's typical defensive ingenuity. One thorny problem for Sullivan was that a seemingly impassable ravine separated Mengant's two separate bastions, each of which was situated in terrain entirely favorable to the defender. With such a geographical advantage, the fort—which reportedly contained more than 150 German troops—should have been able to resist Sullivan's attack easily. The huge difference in the morale of the opposing forces, however, yet again turned out to be a much more important factor than geography. In this case, Napoleon's famous dictum that, in war, "morale is to the physical as three is to one" was entirely applicable.

In truth, Sullivan had several sources of help. Gerhardt provided him with Company A, 644th Tank Destroyer Battalion, possessing twelve self-propelled M-10 tracked vehicles armed with deadly 3-inch guns. According to Sullivan's after-action report, those weapons' long-range, high-velocity fire "greatly aided" the 5th Ranger Battalion when they "took the [four] pillboxes in the fort opposite under a heavy direct fire as F Company began its assault."

And then there was the U.S. Army Air Force, which again supplied Sullivan with close air support. This time, however, the air support was too close even for Sullivan. He had opened the attack on Fort du Mengant from the north at 3 P.M. on September 5 with Company B, and later, when no appreciable progress was being made, he threw in Company F from the west. By late afternoon, however, the situation as defined by the 5th Rangers' after-action report had become "critical." Ranger casualties were mounting, and apparently, only desperate measures could break the stalemate. According to Sullivan's account, Company F provided that desperate act when at about 6:30 P.M. it "immediately attacked across the ravine and took the fort at 877958 [a map coordinate—the fort's eastern bastion] with a bayonet charge." Yet again the rangers' aggressive spirit had carried the day.

But at 7:16 P.M. an alarmed Major Sullivan radioed the 29th Division war room, "These planes are bombing right where my men are— four-motor jobs [B-17s or B-24s] and P-38s [Lightnings]. They are over too far to the west. . . . The P-38s started dropping bombs in the fort where we are." Sullivan later reported that due to the bombs' blast, "Several men got thrown up in the air, and it reduced the effective strength of the company [F] from 62 to 47. . . . [However], nobody was evacuated." Somehow the normally meticulous procedures followed by air support officers to report friendly troops' locations to the fighter-bomber pilots had broken down. Even worse, the heavy bombers had intended to target Fort du Portzic, nearly three miles to the east, but some errant bombs had actually landed within Sullivan's zone.

Fortunately, no one had been killed by the mishap, but it had been a close call. By nightfall, both halves of Fort du Mengant were under the control of the 5th Rangers, and seventy-two more German prisoners were handed over temporarily to the FFI. Several dozen German corpses littered the enclosure that had only recently been a formidable enemy strongpoint.

Early the next morning, September 6, the 5th Rangers and their comrades from the 644th moved a mile to the east to seize the next enemy strongpoint in the coastal chain, Fort du Dellec. This time the Germans offered virtually no resistance, as the majority of the fort's inhabitants had already fled. Even so, thirty-nine more prisoners were taken at a cost of one wounded ranger. By now Sullivan's troops were even with Dwyer's 116th Infantry on their left flank at La Trinité, but for the moment Gerhardt did not consider it prudent for the 5th Rangers to push ahead to their final objective, Fort du Portzic. While Sullivan had methodically been seizing the coastal forts, Gerhardt had become greatly annoyed by the failure of his "Task Force Sugar" to clear the Le Conquet peninsula; to help solve that problem, he decided to convey most of Sullivan's battalion to that sector in late afternoon on September 7. There, the rangers would soon learn that their locale may have changed but not their mission.

Gerhardt's satisfaction with the rangers prompted him to write to Sullivan:

> I desire to commend you and the members of your battalion for superior participation in active combat while attached to this division. . . . Without exception, your battalion has taken all of its

objectives quickly and with minimum losses. Throughout, your cooperation and enthusiasm has been of the highest class. The outstanding examples of prompt and aggressive action were the capture of Forts Minou and Mengant.

The general ordered his staff to file the paperwork required for the award of the exalted U.S. Army Distinguished Unit Citation to the 5th Rangers, but in the fall the U.S. Ninth Army would turn that request down. Had it been granted, it would have added an Oak Leaf Cluster to the Distinguished Unit Citation the battalion had already been awarded for the D-Day assault.

Dwyer's 116th Infantry, too, had done well, but unfortunately its accomplishments were not the kind that generated headlines. For more than a week, the regiment had fought and won a battle of attrition, but the wrecked town of La Trinité, finally in American hands, hardly seemed a prize worthy of such sacrifice. The Stonewallers had battled a much higher class of German fighters than those who had clashed with the rangers in the coastal forts, and Dwyer had an exceptionally lengthy casualty list to prove it.

During the 116th Infantry's glorious rest period that followed the fall of La Trinité, two men paid visits to the regiment's bivouacs, both of whom would leave lasting impressions on the GIs. The first was Maj. Nigel Ryle of the British Army, the twenty-nine-year-old commander of B Squadron, 141st Regiment, Royal Armoured Corps. (In the British Army, an armored squadron was the equivalent of a U.S. Army tank company. Unlike the Americans, who placed a captain in command at that level, the British employed a major.) To the captivated 116th Infantry staff, who had worked with many British officers during the regiment's lengthy training period in England, Ryle at first emerged as a formulaic model of the upper-crust British Army officer corps. That impression, however, was entirely misleading. His squadron's World War II history noted: "[He was] proud of his trim moustache, proud of his military figure, and was one of the very few people capable of still looking like a soldier even in battle dress. He occasionally took time off to worry about his two gray hairs." But combat in Normandy starting in late June had established his reputation as an expert combat leader, and that expertise would shortly help the Yanks overcome one of the enemy's toughest strongpoints at Brest, a place no American or British soldier who fought there would ever forget—Fort Montbarey.

Major Ryle's armored outfit came with highly unusual tanks known as "Crocodiles," which the 29ers had never seen. At a meeting with U.S.

Army officers at Middleton's VIII Corps headquarters, Ryle described his beloved "Crocs" to the curious Yanks: "We have fifteen tanks on the way down here from north of St. Lô. These are specially equipped tanks with a flamethrower in addition to the 75mm gun. The [flamethrower] has a range of over 100 yards. We have used them in combat very successfully. They should work fine on the Brest job if we can get in close enough to these pillboxes and emplacements." Flamethrowers were undeniably brutal weapons, but already at Brest far too many good 29ers had died storming the enemy's fixed fortifications. To the members of the 116th Infantry, who had learned that it could take days and many American lives to overcome a single pillbox, the contemplation of incinerating the tough German paratroopers who occupied those pillboxes was heartening.

A few years in the past, B Squadron had been an ordinary infantry company, a part of a unit designated the 7th Battalion, Royal East Kent Regiment—a historic British Army outfit that held the nickname "The Buffs" for more than 200 years. However, in the rush to match the enemy's impressive capability to carry out blitzkrieg, the battalion was converted to a tank unit in 1941 and thereupon gained its much more pedestrian title of 141st Regiment, Royal Armoured Corps—although the proud new tankers did continue to wear The Buffs' regimental insignia on their berets. Like the 29ers, the British tankers had expected a decent rest period after their prolonged campaign in Normandy had come to an end with the near-total defeat of the German Army at Falaise. But that idyllic respite was cut short by U.S. Ninth Army's urgent summons to embark their Crocs on huge American tank transporters and head for Brest posthaste. Futile assaults against the enemy's fixed fortifications at Brest had indicated to Middleton the urgent need for those Crocodiles, and there was no time to lose.

By this stage of World War II, the U.S. and British armies had intertwined about as closely as two such diverse military organizations ever could. Consequently, the initial attempts at cooperation between the 29ers and the British tankers were effortless, and given their common goal of eradicating the hated Nazi regime, that smooth collaboration was perhaps not much of a surprise. A British officer recalled, "The 29th Division was for B Squadron a superb impression of the American Army. The 'Let's Go!' boys were the sort of guys with whom you were proud to scrap." That remarkable mix of informality and devotion to American military tradition that defined the U.S. Army in 1944 made a lasting impression on the British, one of whom noted with amazement that a 29th Division enlisted man, when asked by Ryle to identify himself, blurted: "Why, major, just call me Tony!" And yet that same observer recalled that later, in actual combat, "as the recce [reconnaissance] parties crawled past the forward slit [trenches], without exception the [Americans] manning them would stand up and salute: 'Mornin', Cap,' or 'Mornin', Major.'"

While the 116th Infantry was resting behind the lines, Major Ryle introduced them to his remarkable Crocodiles. Ryle's second-in-command, Capt. Harry Cobden, observed:

> Crocodiles were unknown to them, and we spent some time demonstrating the capabilities of the tank itself and the flame gun. We invited them to advance through the flame in order to take full advantage of its effectiveness. To persuade them that it was feasible and relatively painless, we demonstrated advancing on foot behind a flaming Crocodile, then running forward through the flame in the final assault. The joke was that most of us had never done this before and were probably more apprehensive than the doughboys!

The practical details imparted by the British concerning how to best utilize the Crocodiles were useful, but far more noteworthy to the GIs was the tankers' overall promise: If you run into trouble, we'll be there to help. It was a promise that was much appreciated—and never forgotten by those Yanks who would later witness its fulfillment by Ryle's veterans at Fort Montbarey.

The second special visitor to the 116th Infantry's rest camps was about as opposite from Ryle as a human being could be. He was a portly, forty-four-year-old U.S. Army lieutenant colonel named Samuel Lyman Atwood Marshall, popularly known by his initials: "SLAM." During the interwar years Marshall had gained a reputation as a hard-hitting Detroit newspaperman and eventually specialized in a subject in which isolationist America then had little interest: military affairs. He was an early believer in army mechanization, and he corresponded regularly with the renowned British advocates of that cutting-edge military philosophy, Basil Liddell Hart and J. F. C. Fuller. Like his British role models, Marshall was an innovative thinker whose forceful and sometimes unconventional military opinions infuriated some, but inspired many more. One of his future subordinates, the celebrated World War II historian and biographer Forrest Pogue, remembered Marshall as "cocky," and added: "Equally ready with a good story or a quick decision, he was the type who attracted or angered people quickly. His characterizations of individuals who crossed his path could be withering, and he could upbraid people who failed to carry out his orders in a most caustic manner."

In the fall of 1942, Marshall returned to the Army in which he had served as a young man during World War I. One year later, as a major and a new member of the U.S. Army's Historical Branch, he joined the 27th Infantry Division for the invasion of Makin Island, a part of the Gilbert Islands chain in the Pacific. A few months later, he participated in the 7th Infantry Division's assault on Kwajalein atoll. In the aftermath of both invasions, Marshall gathered the American participants and interviewed them by taking an approach he would later refer to as the "group critique method." Marshall's interviews yielded an immediate and fairly accurate insight into the details of those battles, and his 1944 book on Kwajalein, *Island Victory*, launched his career as the U.S. Army's most celebrated historian of World War II. As Marshall described his method: "Battle is never a maelstrom into which all are drawn equally, but is rather a continuing line of small eddies which are sometimes tactically related and sometimes not. The thing to do is to find the starting point . . . and then develop that episode and all subsequent episodes in chronological order and relation to one another."

SLAM traveled to Europe in the spring of 1944, determined to play a role in what promised to be one of the war's defining moments—D-Day. In the aftermath of that momentous invasion, Marshall spent weeks interviewing veterans of the 82nd and 101st Airborne Divisions and scrutinizing the terrain where those outfits had descended into Normandy on June 6, 1944. After generating hundreds of pages of notes on that subject, which would later be pieced together in his book *Night Drop*, he turned his attention to Omaha Beach and the 29th Division.

If SLAM's intention was to learn the precise details of what had occurred on that deadly coastline by traveling to Brittany and conducting his "group critique" interviews with the 116th Infantry's D-Day survivors, he was almost too late. According to Marshall, "When I got to the command post of the 116th Regiment, the commander [Col. Philip Dwyer] was anything but receptive. . . . He thought my mission was a sheer waste of time. He said to me: 'Don't you realize that the regiment which fought at Omaha no longer exists?'" Dwyer was exaggerating—but only a little. By the time Marshall arrived in Brittany, the 116th Infantry had been bled so severely by more than two months of nearly continuous combat that in each rifle company of roughly 200 men, typically less than ten men who had experienced the invasion remained on the company rolls. When he learned that detail, even Marshall had to admit that "too much time had passed."

But ten men were better than none, and to those war-weary few, Marshall described his aim as a simple and direct plea for truth: "What you did is considered of sufficient importance that the Army believes it should be a part of recorded history. We are here today to determine the facts. It is your duty to relate what you know of them to the best of your ability, holding nothing back and exaggerating nothing. . . . What is learned here today may help save the lives of other American soldiers or add to your own company's efficiency."

The end result of Marshall's interviews with the 116th Infantry was a remarkable document titled *Group Critique Notes*, roughly sixty pages of single-space typewritten prose on flimsy onion-skin paper that amounted to one of the first reliable accounts of the Omaha invasion. Despite the noticeably skimpy number of participants in Marshall's interviews, *Group Critique Notes* remains a seminal document in D-Day historiography more than sixty years after its creation.

However, in the aftermath of World War II, the conclusions reached by SLAM Marshall as a consequence of those combat interviews would appall many 29ers. First among those perplexing deductions was Marshall's later claim that a military catastrophe was averted on Omaha Beach by the heroic behavior of only 47 soldiers of the 35,000 who landed on D-Day. In a meeting with General Eisenhower, Marshall observed: "If fate had eliminated that same 47 in the first few minutes, Omaha Beach could not have been held. . . . In the clutch of desperation, we had been pulled through by a smattering of heroes."

To the members of the 116th Infantry who had been lucky enough to survive Omaha Beach, this was an astonishing and completely false assertion. Since Marshall never indicated how he arrived at forty-seven as the "smattering" number of key Omaha Beach players or who exactly those forty-seven were, his theory was harshly rejected by many D-Day veterans. By the time Marshall arrived at Brest to study the 116th Infantry, only 5 percent of the regiment's D-Day personnel remained. The 116th's commander on June 6, Col. Charles Canham, had been transferred to the 8th Infantry Division, and its operations officer, the legendary Maj. Tom Howie, had been killed at St. Lô. None of the 116th's three battalion commanders on D-Day were still with the regiment at Brest, and virtually all the company commanders were gone. In analytical conditions such as those, how could Marshall learn the truth by spending just a few days with the 116th at Brest?

One of the most respected leaders in the 116th Infantry on D-Day, the 2nd Battalion's Maj. Sidney Bingham, later articulated an argument entirely antithetical to Marshall's, which expressed much more truthfully the 116th Infantry's view of Omaha Beach. "Everything that was done was done by small groups led by the real heroes of any war," Bingham declared. "Most of them were killed, and very, very few were decorated chiefly because no one was left to tell about what they did. The minefields behind the beach were strewn with these guys. They were lying around the hedgerows on top of the bluffs and, of course, they were piled—literally—on the beach proper."

On Omaha Beach, Bingham was an eyewitness—and Marshall was not. Bingham would gain the Distinguished Service Cross for his D-Day heroics. In fact the U.S. Army would ultimately grant more than 150 Medals of Honor and DSCs for valor on Omaha Beach—fifty-six to members of the 1st Infantry Division alone. Therefore, Marshall's supposition that the actions of only forty-seven men turned the tide on Omaha Beach could make no sense to those who grasped that the U.S. Army's procedure for handing out its two highest decorations for battlefield bravery was anything but casual. Marshall's aide would later categorize his boss as an "intuitive thinker," but in this case the theories concocted by Marshall as a result of his interviews of the 116th Infantry at Brest in September 1944 revealed that his intuition was obviously wrong.

One of the 116th Infantry's most expressive witnesses among those interviewed by Marshall on September 12, 1944, was twenty-one-year-old T/Sgt. Theodore Fettinger of Company G, a native of Maplewood, New Jersey, who had landed in the very first wave of the invasion. Characterized by his commander as "the best platoon sergeant I have ever seen," Fettinger's short tenure at the University of Maine had been interrupted by his entry into the Army, in which he quickly excelled as a highly dependable and motivating noncommissioned officer. His ability to speak German had come in handy on the battlefield more than once.

No matter how hard one tried, it was not easy to eradicate the appalling sights of Omaha Beach from one's psyche, and in Sergeant Fettinger's keenly observant mind, those sights had remained in sharp focus. For such a young man, Fettinger had a maturity and eloquence beyond his years, and his way of relating Company G's role on Omaha Beach provided Marshall with an indispensable insight into the common soldier's perspective on the invasion. Fettinger's story epitomized the experiences of every member of the 116th Infantry on D-Day—an amazing tale of chaos, death, and fear in which the meticulously planned invasion fell apart the moment the 29ers first set foot on French soil. Marshall, who described Fettinger as "a D-Day hero," noted that "Fettinger's method of command was elementary. He kept yelling: 'Get your ass on up there!' and that was enough to get [the men] going forward again."

In July, while recovering from a wound he had suffered at St. Lô, Sergeant Fettinger had described his combat experiences to his family somewhat more emotionally than he later would to Marshall.

> I make no claims for bravery, but from the time we learned the actual hour [of D-Day] until now, I have done many things I would never before have believed myself capable of doing; and I have seen things and experienced thrills which before I would never have been able to stand. Men of the last war are loath to talk of their war experiences. I never knew why. I do now. [Fettinger's father, who died in 1942, was a World War I veteran.] To talk war to someone who has never seen war is like telling fairy tales to grown-ups.... There is a veil of mystery, which makes men incapable of comprehending what it is all about. There is something sacred about the finality of it all. Many times, when a veteran is asked to speak about his experiences, he won't say anything because he can't. War is incapable of description.

Sooner or later, however, someone must describe World War II in all its enormity, and that task would eventually devolve upon historians. But who precisely those historians would be depended on which side won the war, and as of September 1944, that issue had not yet been decided. Consequently, as the dreadful summer of 1944 drew to a close, the most pressing concern of American soldiers like Fettinger was to ensure that historians like Forrest Pogue, and not those in the mold of Josef Goebbels, would ultimately write that history. But before that virtuous goal could be fulfilled, Fettinger's 116th Infantry would have to fight many more battles, and the first of those was what the Americans hoped would be the final attack on Brest.

On September 14, 1944, the 116th trudged from its rest camps back to the front lines, where its members would soon make an all-out effort to crack the enemy's Brest defenses once and for all. How long that would take was anybody's guess.

Three days later, Sgt. Ted Fettinger was dead.

3. BRING ON THE PLANES
By the end of the first week of September 1944, the American VIII Corps offensive to secure Brest had been sustained for two weeks, a period that General Bradley had originally envisioned as more than sufficient for Middleton to capture that crucial port city. Bradley's assumption, however, was based on an intelligence estimate that 10,000 Germans defended

Brest, a number that turned out to be less than 25 percent of the actual figure. The 29th Division and its attached units had suffered close to 2,000 casualties during those fourteen dreadful days, and although the 29ers had gained considerable ground, they had succeeded only in cracking the enemy's outer defense line. The Germans' inner—and final—lines promised to be an even tougher position to overcome.

The Americans did not at first have many clues hinting at how Ramcke and his German garrison had been affected by the VIII Corps onslaught. Late on August 28, however, an 8th Infantry Division captain in the Medical Corps by the name of Markle, who had been captured and held for a few days in Brest, was returned by the enemy to American lines in company with ten other U.S. Army medical personnel. Captain Markle carried with him a message from Ramcke to Middleton concerning the location of German military hospitals in Brest with a request that they be neither bombed nor shelled. Included in that message was the somewhat sardonic comment, "I assume you will need your [medical] personnel in the present situation." Middleton, however, suspected that some of Ramcke's "hospitals" were actually ammunition dumps, and he eventually replied, "I note that the hospital installations are so widely dispersed that I feel it would be an impossibility to prevent endangering some of them with unobserved artillery fire and by bombing from aircraft, both day and night. If such should happen, it would be entirely unintentional."

To Middleton, however, much more important than Ramcke's message was Captain Markle's impression of how the Germans were so far coping with the rigors of the siege. According to Markle, German soldiers in Brest were restricted to a breakfast of black bread, accompanied by atrocious butter and coffee substitutes, the former prepared from whale oil and the latter from a substance Markle could not figure out. For lunch, the Germans were each issued one slice of bologna and, for dinner, some soup—both supplemented by the same bread they had been issued that morning at breakfast. Markle emphasized that the Germans "had no water to speak of; and the majority of the garrison are drinking wine and calvados and are all in a semi-drunken condition." Under culinary conditions such as those, Middleton wondered how long the Germans could keep up their formidable resolve.

But much more important than the enemy's diet was the issue of American military action: was it impacting the Germans' ability to resist? According to Markle, "The effect of our bombing and artillery fire is tremendous. Our strafing and bombing were very effective on Sunday [August 27]." To Middleton and Gerhardt that was indeed good news, but even more encouraging was the captain's observation that the Germans had apparently resigned themselves to ultimate defeat. German guards repeatedly asked Markle if they would be taken to POW camps in the United States when the Americans entered the city. When the senior German noncommissioned officer at the prisoner of war compound in Brest learned by radio of the recent seizure of Paris by the Allies, he proclaimed this event as "good news" to the astonished American POWs.

If that outlook was typical of the entire German garrison, Brest would be in American hands soon. But there was an acute difference between the attitudes of dispirited German rear-echelon troops and highly motivated paratroopers on the front lines, a difference that many senior American officers could hardly believe, but which was obvious to 29th Division infantrymen who were in the process of trying to kill those enemy paratroopers in brutal close-range combat. From the 29ers' perspective many of the enemy fighters seemed entirely willing to die for the fatherland, a trait that made the American effort to capture Brest infinitely more challenging than Markle's comments had suggested. Indeed, in addition to their fearsome array of weapons and superior fighting skills, the German paratroopers were characterized by an astonishing self-confidence that had convinced some of them that they just might be able to hold back the Americans and avoid the calamity that had been shaping up at Brest since the Normandy breakout. One paratrooper NCO later remarked: "We were not overly impressed at the time by our American opponents. They struck us as extremely cautious, unwilling to venture forward without thorough reconnaissance and artillery bombardment."

That German NCO might also have appropriately noted his opponents' reliance on air power, for American and British medium and heavy bombers had reduced Brest to a level of devastation that rivaled cities such as Berlin, Cologne, or Hamburg. The commander of the 29th Division's 110th Field Artillery Battalion, Lt. Col. John Cooper, witnessed the drama of one of those devastating air attacks and recalled: "I was at an observation post on high ground north of Brest, watching one air raid through a powerful battery commander's telescope. I could see individual buildings blossom out and collapse as bombs hit them. It was strange to watch an enemy-held city bombed directly to our front and still be completely safe. Some fighter planes were escorting the bombers, and one darted through the formation, cutting a B-17 Fortress in two—and down they came."

After the fall of Brest, however, the 29ers discovered to their dismay that the massive Allied air bombardment of the city, which had seemed so crushing to those GIs who could observe it directly, did not in actuality have much impact on the German defenders. According to a study titled "The Effects of Air Power on Military Operations in Western Europe," published by the U.S. Twelfth Army Group in 1945, "For months before the beginning of our operation on the continent, Brest had been subjected to heavy bombing raids designed to interfere with its use by the Germans as a base for submarine warfare and other military purposes. In consequence there existed an adequate system of air raid shelters and air warnings within the built-up part of the city. Civilians stated that though much of the town was destroyed long before the invasion, very few casualties to personnel occurred as the shelters were sufficiently strong to withstand the attacks."

If German soldiers had to live underground to avoid the Allies' deluge of bombs, there was no better place to do it than Brest. The city's three-mile-long harborside and the lower reaches of the Penfeld River, which emptied directly into that harbor, were lined with lofty cliffs and bluffs, into which the locals had excavated several sizeable tunnels and dugouts. Those dark and grim subterranean dungeons, one of which contained an enormous German hospital, provided near-perfect protection from Allied shelling and bombing.

Even more remarkable were the German Navy's renowned submarine pens, those massive sets of protected docks built by Organization Todt in 1941 on the harbor's western periphery to accommodate up to eighteen U-boats. Those edifices, altogether one-fifth of a mile long, fifty-five feet high, with a solid concrete roof nearly twenty-five feet thick, had for years stoutly resisted all efforts by Allied warplanes to penetrate them with bombs. Just before the 29th Division's arrival at Brest, however, Royal Air Force Lancaster bombers managed to pierce the roof in a few places with their new and phenomenally powerful six-ton "Tallboy" bombs. Even so, the pens were so immense that it would take hundreds of Tallboys to destroy them completely. In truth, the Allies had no time for that, and more to the point, near-misses from the Tallboys could devastate the harbor that the Allies themselves hoped to be using in a matter of weeks.

German military personnel would find a safe haven from Allied bombs inside the pens throughout the siege, a major benefit for Ramcke since those massive structures were seemingly large enough to house his entire garrison. After the fall of Brest a German prisoner revealed that the Allied bombardment "was nerve-wracking, but it did no damage to us in bunkers." The U.S. Twelfth Army Group "Air Power" survey went one step further when it concluded, "The protection afforded by the shelters . . . undoubtedly enabled the enemy to hold forth in the face of our ground attack longer than he would otherwise have been able."

Nevertheless, the deluge of Allied ordnance on Brest was so intense that one German paratrooper recalled, "There was always something gurgling or whistling through the air—bombs from above, or shells from the countryside. No matter where you were in Brest, in the front lines or in a downtown street, it was never safe to be more than a few yards from cover." Even if that bombardment was not killing or incapacitating many German soldiers, it had a deleterious and lasting impact on enemy morale, especially as it quickly became obvious to the entire Brest garrison that there was no hope of rescue by the Luftwaffe. An even more bitter pill for the surrounded German troops to swallow, however, was their absolute inability to replenish expended supplies. Putting up with that sort of one-sided battle for more than a few weeks eventually had to strain the resilience of even the toughest German fighters—or so Middleton and Gerhardt hoped.

In retrospect, even top American and British air commanders had to admit that B-17, B-24, and Lancaster heavy bombers had been asked to fulfill missions at Brest that were, in the words of the Twelfth Army Group "Air Power" study, "beyond their capabilities." When employing Allied strategic air assets in direct support of ground operations, that same conclusion, unfortunately, had been reached many times before and would be reached again. In contrast, U.S. Army Air Force tactical aircraft, such as P-47 Thunderbolt, P-38 Lightning, and P-51 Mustang fighter-bombers, were assigned to ground-attack missions at Brest for which they were entirely suited, and consequently, their efforts were greatly valued by the 29th Division infantrymen whom the pilots resolved to support. In fact the level of cooperation between American ground troops and pilots at Brest was higher than it had ever been before in World War II in any theater, and would eventually serve as a model for how U.S. Army airmen could genuinely help their ground brethren overcome seemingly insurmountable enemy resistance.

The Americans had to admit that in terms of projecting air power in Brittany, conditions were just about perfect. Not a single German fighter plane that could contest the skies was based anywhere near Brest. Furthermore, the late summer weather for the most part was highly suitable for flying. Even so, however, effective air-ground cooperation at Brest would be a supreme challenge, a detail that the Normandy campaign had proven time and again to the frustrated infantrymen who held the thankless burden of fighting through the deadly hedgerows beyond Omaha Beach. As a bitter Gerhardt once remarked, the system of air-ground coordination as it then existed was "insupportable, and we did not try to use this aid."

According to the old system used in Normandy, an infantry unit that ran into stubborn enemy resistance could request air support, but its request had to be forwarded to a distant U.S. Army Air Force headquarters that was not in touch with the ground soldiers' immediate needs. The fighter-bombers would arrive, but only after the passage of a considerable time period—sometimes twenty-four hours or more. As Gerhardt pointed out, "Due to changes in the situation . . . often missions that are scheduled cannot be flown."

Just in case anyone had forgotten, the air forces were still an integral part of the U.S. Army. In Brittany, senior Army commanders would finally correct the flaws in close support operations by implementing a solution so simple that those whose jobs were significantly eased by it, from the corps commander all the way down to riflemen, could only wonder why it had not been put into practice before. That solution, worked out by the Ninth Air Force and Bradley's headquarters, was designated the "air alert" system, the foundation of which, as a Twelfth Army Group action report noted, "was the mutual exchange of staff personnel with the authority and training to act in an operational capacity." That somewhat arcane U.S. Army phraseology boiled down to one essential detail: air and ground units must achieve an exceptionally high level of cooperation if the infantrymen's burdens were to be lessened.

The secret to tactical air power success would be staff officers at divisional level who entirely devoted themselves to the task of effective air-ground coordination. Sarcastic infantrymen on the front line probably wondered how a command post already top-heavy with staff officers needed any more. But this was different: If those staff personnel could do their jobs well and bring down a deluge of bombs on the heads of enemy troops in a timely manner, the grateful American infantrymen would probably offer to pay the staff officers' salaries out of their own pockets.

Now and then the U.S. Army did the right thing, and in the instance of tactical air power it eventually did. The first and probably most essential requirement of the new air alert system was to provide a permanent slot within the headquarters of each U.S. Army division for an airman, preferably a senior and experienced pilot who fully grasped how Army Air Force fighter-bombers conducted operations. By the time the 29th Division had moved to Brittany in late August 1944, the person holding that position, known officially as the divisional "air support officer," had become an integral figure in the 29th Division war room and would play a vital role in the upcoming campaign by telling the ground soldiers what fighter-bombers could or could not do.

Something more than that, however, was required, since the air support officer's job would be meaningless if he was not provided with timely and reliable intelligence about the situation on the front lines. Thankfully, the air alert system guaranteed that two field-grade staff officers at division headquarters, with official job titles of "assistant operations officer (air)" and "assistant intelligence officer (air)," would focus relentlessly on pinpointing the location of known friendly and enemy troops and disseminating that information to the air support officer. Equally important, however, would be an astute ability to judge the places at the front most in need of air support, such as enemy strongpoints impervious to conventional artillery or locales where the Germans were massing for counterattacks. All infantrymen under enemy fire obviously desired air support, but it would be the information gathered and shared in the divisional command post that would determine the lucky few who would actually receive it.

As the air alert scheme was practiced by the 29th Division at Brest, at least one four-plane flight of fighter-bombers, typically armed with 500- or preferably 1,000-pound bombs, would fly more or less continuously in daylight over the divisional front. On some particularly critical days, that number was doubled to eight. Subject to the limits of their fuel supply, the aircraft patrolled back and forth across the battle zone, waiting for a call from the ground to drop their ordnance on a particularly stubborn enemy resistance nest. That flexible arrangement allowed 29th Division battlefield leaders as far down the chain of command as company commanders to request immediate air support when their men ran into trouble, a benefit that had been almost unheard of in Normandy. The cutting-edge radio and telephone equipment that was a hallmark of the U.S. Army ensured that those requests were transmitted and answered quickly.

It was of course true that not every infantryman who received air support would be satisfied by the results. Still, as Gerhardt noted, the presence of friendly warplanes in the sky over the front "tends to increase aggressiveness on the part of infantry soldiers. It bolsters their confidence and decreases the enemy's effectiveness." One 29th Division battalion commander at Brest pointed out: "Would you like to be in Jerry's boots at such a time?" The faster the pilots could respond to the needs of the ground troops, the greater the morale boost. In the 29th Division, Gerhardt observed that "the average time lapse between request for and receipt of air support by frontline companies was 30 to 45 minutes. In one instance only 10 minutes were required."

The pilots' jobs suddenly turned remarkably difficult and dangerous the moment they received approval to attack an enemy strongpoint. From their lofty perspective, the American flyers could not discern the front lines with certainty without the help of ground controllers, and even a momentary lapse in judgment or a trivial error in map-reading could cause a pilot to inflict more destruction on American troops than on the Germans. In Normandy the 29th Division had endured such appalling mistakes more than once.

Efficient control of the deadly fighter-bombers was therefore a categorically weighty and stressful undertaking, but on the 29th Division's front at Brest, it was handled with consummate skill by soldiers and airmen who had only meager experience in that kind of work at the start of the campaign. Gerhardt reported, "During the entire operation against the city of Brest, no casualties among our ground personnel were caused by our friendly planes." Given the recent history of air-ground cooperation in the U.S. Army, that was a fantastic accomplishment, made possible only by strict rules of engagement that had markedly intensified since Normandy.

To mark the front lines, 29th Division infantry units as small as rifle squads carried with them rectangular panels about three square feet in size, colored for easy recognition from the air. Despite Gerhardt's remark, "The closer the air strikes, the better [an infantryman] likes it," the 29th Division air-ground team was hesitant to call in a fighter-bomber attack if those recognition panels were 500 yards or less from the proposed target. Even half that distance seemed perfectly prudent from the perspective of a frontline hedgerow, but dive-bombing was an exceptionally difficult skill to master, and even an apparently insignificant error in judgment by a pilot at the moment of bomb release would cause that bomb to miss its target by several hundred yards with potentially disastrous results.

For the 29th Division's air-ground team, it was tempting to agree to an air strike on a stubborn German strongpoint, but safety dictated that many calls for air support from beleaguered infantrymen would have to be rejected. That policy caused one American observer to complain, "[An air strike] normally had no immediate effect on enemy troops in the front lines except to weaken morale. The value of air support was felt by our small units only after they had progressed to the target area [behind the front] and saw the extent to which enemy supporting weapons and strongpoints had been reduced." That statement, however, would have been promptly contradicted by Major Sullivan of the 5th Rangers, who witnessed firsthand the hugely beneficial results of air bombing and strafing against Fort Toulbroch on September 3, when many of his troops were closer than 200 yards from the target.

To help the pilots do their jobs, an order came down from Middleton to the 29th Division on the afternoon of September 3: "Effective 4 September 1944 and for the duration of the Brest campaign, front lines of ground troops will be marked during daylight by cerise-colored fluorescent panels." The Germans of course were not so accommodating. The wily enemy did everything it could to thwart the American "Jabos" (*Jagdbomber*—literally "hunter-bombers"), for the Germans had learned that when those American warplanes were roaming overhead in daylight, it was unwise to move in the open, conduct artillery fire, or move supply columns up to the front. As a matter of necessity the enemy practiced camouflage techniques expertly, and consequently, the American pilots repeatedly found it exceptionally difficult to perceive their targets.

But while the Germans were frantically striving to hide, the 29ers were toiling with equal fervor to identify the enemy's positions so the fighter-bomber pilots could clearly distinguish what they were about to attack. The 29th Division's air support officer noted, "We plot the target on an aerial photograph of the area, and then describe it over the radio in terms that the pilot will be able to see coming in over the target." But for a fighter-bomber pilot to pinpoint that target in the baffling hedgerow country was tricky. One clever method the 29ers came up with to aid the aviators was for a nearby artillery battalion to fire several colored smoke shells on the target. The billowing smoke produced by this barrage would typically linger over the target for a minute or so, and when the pilots arrived over that locale, the air support officer would instruct them by radio to search for the colored smoke used by the artillery in that mission. Eventually, the pilots and cannoneers agreed that red smoke was best because from the pilots' perspective it was the easiest color to detect. Cooper of the 110th Field Artillery observed, "Within the 29th Division, this practice became SOP [standard operating procedure] for all close-in air support."

Ground support missions were undeniably helpful, but they were also risky. Brest had been the target of Allied air attacks for years, and accordingly, the German garrison possessed a plentiful supply of potent antiaircraft weapons. Moreover, air-ground cooperation demanded that the American pilots fly at comparatively low altitudes, well within the range of small-caliber enemy antiaircraft guns and even light automatic weapons. To counter the enemy's flak, 29th Division artillerymen became adept at immediate retaliation. The moment American warplanes appeared overhead, alert artillery observers grabbed their binoculars and scanned the German lines, striving to detect nearby sources of enemy antiaircraft fire. If a German flak gun could indeed be observed, the artillerymen promptly called down upon it a furious barrage of howitzer shells, usually with uncanny accuracy. Such an impressive performance typically caused the enemy to think twice before opening fire with abandon on American aircraft, a development deeply appreciated by the pilots.

Still, the Germans managed to shoot down plenty of American aircraft at Brest, and when they did, 29th Division soldiers who witnessed those distressing events invariably peered into the sky, hoping to catch the reassuring sight of a billowing parachute slowly descending to earth—evidence that the pilot had survived.

One such incident on September 4, 1944, became one of the most celebrated episodes in 29th Division history. That day a 354th Fighter Group Mustang piloted by Capt. Edward Whitman was hit by a German 20mm shell, wrecking its cooling system and filling the cockpit with smoke. Whitman had been shot down once before in the Pacific, so he knew what he must do. He aimed his Mustang at the American lines, unbuckled his harness, and at 3,000 feet flipped the plane over and plummeted out. He pulled the cord on his chute and descended into a pasture near a small village—where exactly, he did not know, but he hoped it was within American lines.

A few French farmers approached, and as reporter Holbrook Bradley recounted in a *Baltimore Sun* article, "[Whitman] had a slight scalp laceration and a strained leg; then set about convincing the French that he was an Allied flyer—and learned he was a mile behind his own lines. A telephone call brought doctors, an ambulance, and an invitation from the troops near whom he had landed to drop in for supper." It turned out that the troops offering that thoughtful invitation to Whitman were from Cooper's 110th Field Artillery—the same Maryland National Guard unit in which Whitman had enlisted as a private in Battery D at Pikesville on July 10, 1939. (Whitman's father, a captain, was at that time also a 110th member.) The twenty-two-year-old Whitman had been commissioned as a second lieutenant in the 110th in November 1940, the rank he held when President Roosevelt had called the entire 29th Division into federal service on February 3, 1941. That summer he departed the 110th to join the 29th Division's 104th Air Observation Squadron, an outfit that would soon be separated from the division and would become the core unit of the new Maryland Air National Guard following World War II.

In early 1942 Whitman graduated from flying school in Texas. At Brest, more than two years later, he unexpectedly returned to his old comrades in the 110th Field Artillery in a most unusual way. As the 29th Division newspaper, *29 Let's Go*, noted: "Fate had planted him right in our lap—just as he liked it." Whitman was brought to the 29th Division war room, where he chatted with Gerhardt and signed the general's guest book. After signing, he added one sentence: "It's wonderful to see the 29th again!"

As a U.S. Army report noted in the aftermath of the Brittany campaign, "Fighter-bombers probably never before had worked so closely with attacking ground forces." The level of air-ground cooperation at Brest represented a pioneering moment in the history of the American Army, and the 29th Division had materially participated in it—a distinctly ironic detail given the recent Normandy experience. True, fighter-bombers were not a solution to every tactical dilemma faced by ground soldiers, and they certainly were of no value at night and in poor weather. But when the 29ers witnessed the striking benefits of American air power in the brutal frontal attacks characterizing the Brest campaign, they quickly became converts and did everything in their power to smooth the linkage between pilots and infantrymen. At a corps-level air power conference on September 26, 1944, Colonel Witte remarked, "It can be said that the major part of knocking out strongpoints . . . may be credited to the Air Force. Air also had a very great psychological effect in destroying the morale of the enemy."

Positive proof that the 29ers devoted themselves fully to the new air alert system is provided by an examination of the 29th Division's official "war room journal," a transcript of incoming and outgoing radio and telephone communications at division headquarters that had been established by Gerhardt's edict when his first command post had been set up in a quarry just beyond Omaha Beach on D-Day. In Normandy the verbal exchanges recorded in that transcript almost never mentioned tactical air support. In contrast, when the 29th Division shifted to Brittany in late August 1944 and the ground fighting at Brest suddenly surged in intensity, the journal's tone changed entirely—a detail that Gerhardt could not fail to notice because he read and initialed each page every evening. At Brest several new officers regularly appear in the historical record, most of whom were dedicated to the task of ensuring that the vast power represented by the Ninth Air Force would no longer be untapped. The most prominent of those were the division's air support officer, Maj. Horace ("Hank") Wetherell, and its assistant operations officer, Maj. James Porter, whose words appear in the transcript during this period with an even greater frequency than Gerhardt himself.

When tactical stalemates at the front threatened to paralyze offensive operations, Wetherell and Porter consistently offered air power solutions to ground commanders that only a few weeks in the past had not been a part of the 29th Division's repertoire. Wetherell was described by a September 10 *29 Let's Go* article as "the head of the fabulous network which sends a thousand bombs crashing down upon Blue and Gray enemy targets. When you hear a P-38, or P-47, or P-51 humming overhead, winging out toward the Jerry lines, the chances are the pilot at the controls has received his instructions from this Ninth Air Force officer." On September 10, Gerhardt decorated Wetherell with the Bronze Star "for his outstanding work against the enemy."

As a direct consequence of all the meaningful reforms comprising the new air alert system, the Blue and Gray Division—already a mighty and highly experienced military organization—abruptly became much more formidable, a change that all 29ers at the front deeply appreciated. Near the close of the Brest campaign, the commander of the 115th Infantry's 1st Battalion, Maj. Glover Johns, spoke for all when he noted, "I feel that [we] couldn't have done what [we] did without the planes."

But could there be too much of a good thing? Gerhardt thought so. A few days after Johns's observation, he warned: "We have gotten to a point in which we feel that we have to have air support to move. From now on we are going to have to move on our own. . . . I don't want to hold up for air strikes." In the air-ground team, according to the general, airmen were a big help, but on the battlefield the ground soldier would always be the final determinant of victory. That detail would probably never change.

FIVE

Sergeant Hallman

1. KERROGNANT

In the unfathomable hedgerow country outside Brest, the activity defined by General Gerhardt as "active patrolling" was a deadly cat-and-mouse game that could quickly undermine the physical and spiritual health of even the most experienced 29ers. The general relentlessly pressured his three regimental commanders to carry out such pursuits even during periods when the front was comparatively tranquil, a requirement that filtered down the chain of command to the forlorn infantrymen with M-1s and BARs, who naturally did not always react to this obligation with enthusiasm. To many of the 29ers who had to carry out those tense missions, the benefits—if any—were habitually outweighed by the risks, and the steady and disheartening toll of daily casualties even for units in so-called "quiet" sectors seemed to validate that sentiment.

The members of Lt. Col. Lou Smith's 115th Infantry, however, were about to learn why the U.S. Army had made Charlie Gerhardt a general, and by the end of the first week of September 1944, the 115th's proficiency at patrolling had reaped intelligence so valuable that it would soon yield immense battlefield benefits. At Gerhardt's direction, the 115th's 1st and 2nd Battalions had been holding their positions north of Brest, between the villages of Bohars and Guilers, since August 28, and had contributed to the offensive operations of their comrades in the 175th and 116th Infantry at Hill 103 and La Trinité only with diversionary fires and other forms of minor harassment of the enemy. But of course Gerhardt had no intention of retaining the 115th in passive status forever; in fact, by the morning of September 5, the tactical situation in other sectors of the 29th Division's front had progressed to the point at which Smith knew that he would soon have to throw his men back into the fight with a vengeance.

Gerhardt's usual vigor, however, was restrained by a factor beyond his control: the severe ammunition shortage plaguing Middleton's VIII Corps. Until that dilemma was solved, the 29th Division simply did not possess adequate artillery shells to support a major assault by the 115th Infantry. Happily, Gerhardt's dialogues with Middleton hinted that improved logistical circumstances were imminent, and when that moment finally arrived, Gerhardt would be able to throw the entire 29th Division into the battle for Brest just as he had been trained, with a ferocity for which the U.S. Army was renowned.

To prepare for that instant, Gerhardt would intensify his demands for energetic patrolling by Smith's 1st and 2nd Battalions. By September 5 the tactical situation was so volatile that Gerhardt deduced a major enemy pullback was about to occur; if it did, he needed to know the details as soon as possible. To catch the Germans as they withdrew and organized their new lines, or at least to figure out where the enemy's seams and weak points were located, would offer significant advantages in the upcoming battle. That kind of vigorous patrol activity could of course be hazardous against an enemy as alert as German paratroopers, but lacking it Gerhardt could not know where the enemy's vulnerable points were. If the 115th Infantry needed to seize and retain the initiative once it rejoined the fight in earnest, Gerhardt's staff required accurate and timely intelligence, and the only reliable means of obtaining it was to relentlessly feel and probe ahead until something of value was learned. In the 29th Division's war room tent, the general's attention to detail when he perused Colonel Witte's master situation map was legendary, and if a 115th Infantry patrol provided intelligence of enemy activities that could be exploited, Smith would surely be receiving a telephone call from his boss soon.

In the meantime, if the 29th Division lacked the artillery shells to shower the enemy with steel, there was another method of inflicting a sharp sting upon the enemy, and starting at 12:30 P.M. on Tuesday, September 5, 1944, the amazed members of the 115th Infantry watched a display of that firepower they had never seen before and in all probability would never see again. That memorable show was carried out by a diverse conglomeration of aircraft belonging to the Eighth and Ninth Air Forces,

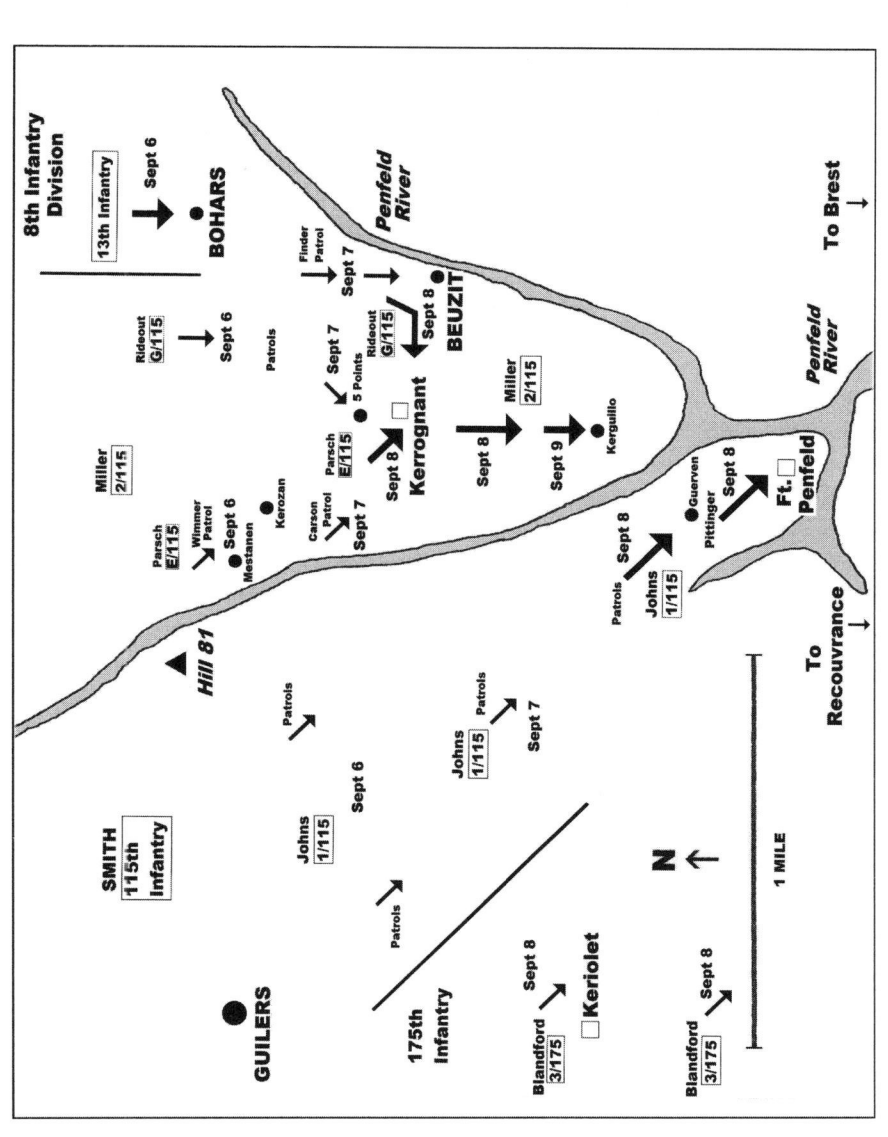

115th Infantry: September 6–9, 1944

as well as RAF's Bomber Command, which pounded the enemy lines at Brest all afternoon and into evening with a deluge of thousands of bombs. The 115th's frontline troops did not have much warning of the impending show, as an 11:52 A.M. entry in Lt. Col. Tony Miller's 2nd Battalion journal revealed: "Battalion notified that air would begin bombardment of targets to our front at Kerrognant and the entire Brest area at 12:30. Companies notified to display [colored] panels prominently." Given past evidence that intense bomb strikes in direct support of the infantry could wreak just as much damage on the Americans as the Germans, that warning was entirely justified—and apparently carefully adhered to, since September 5 records indicate that the air attacks did not inflict a single friendly casualty.

A young and highly perceptive corporal in the 2nd Battalion's Headquarters Company named Art Plaut observed that remarkable event in its entirety from the high ground north of Brest and later noted,

> In groups of four [the P-47s] dove down upon the enemy, their machine guns blazing and spitting a deadly hail of bullets. From the ground we could see the smoke from the tracers long before we heard their sound. . . . Below the level of the trees we lost sight of the planes until they had dropped their demolition and fire bombs and roared skyward. In a constant parade one plane followed another, alternately bombing and stafing. Later in the afternoon the medium and heavy bombers arrived. Now there was none of the fancy acrobatics that had distinguished the fast fighters. The big ships came in high, in perfect formation, aloof and seemingly above the noise and confusion below. . . . The bombers circled the target once and on the second time around they dropped their loads. [Plaut would put his keen powers of observation to good use in the immediate aftermath of V-E Day, when he co-authored the official history of the 115th Infantry in World War II.]

The 2nd Battalion's journal, usually an emotionless daily catalog of unit activities, featured a 5:12 P.M. entry that declared: "B-17s, P-38s, P-51s, P-47s, Lancasters, etc., overhead bombing the hell out of enemy positions to our front." That was a highly evocotive portrayal, for as darkness set in, any 29er who glanced toward the enemy lines and beyond noticed an eerie glow emanating from behind German lines—a product of countless fires in downtown Brest. The sheer power of the aerial display bode well for Smith's 115th Infantry, for it hardly seemed possible that the

Germans could withstand for much longer the type of punishment they had suffered on September 5.

Even the redoubtable Ramcke had to admit that from the German perspective, "The air attacks were appalling. In fact, they were hellish. . . . The bombs rained down from the skies and smashed everything up. The heavy blockbusters knocked everything to blazes, and the whole town immediately became a heap of rubble. There's nothing you can do against that! . . . Our antiaircraft defenses [had] ceased to exist, and they dropped their bombs right in among us."

The bombing of Brest may have been impressive, but when Smith's men finally joined in the 29th Division's offensive again, as sooner or later they must, their mission would be grueling. As usual the crazy pattern of hedgerows and sunken lanes so typical of this area of Brittany entirely favored the German defenders. Furthermore, two of the enemy's toughest strongpoints in the Brest environs were situated squarely in the 115th Infantry's zone of attack: Kerrognant (typically spelled "Kergonant" on U.S. Army maps), a formidable German antiaircraft position constructed for all-around ground defense on high ground about one mile behind the enemy's front line; and Fort Penfeld, a sturdy, nineteenth-century French pentagonal fort located nearly two miles deep in enemy territory.

One geographical reality somewhat troubling to Smith was that his two-mile front was cut right down the middle by a branch of the Penfeld River, flowing through a deep and wide ravine that was a bona fide obstacle to military operations. The 115th Infantry's 1st Battalion, under the command of Maj. Glover Johns, occupied the front line on the ravine's west side; Miller's 2nd Battalion held the line on the east. Consequently, in the event that Johns or Miller ran into trouble, it would be almost impossible for either commander to offer immediate help to his opposite number on the far side. Furthermore, the ravine would have the effect of channeling both battalions' attacks to entirely predictable routes, since clever maneuvers designed to bypass or surround stubborn enemy opposition would be out of the question. As Fort Penfeld lay on the west side of the ravine and Kerrognant on the east, both Johns and Miller would in all probability have to wage stand-alone assaults to penetrate the German lines and push ahead to capture those tough objectives—and even a military mind as brilliant as Caesar's or Napoleon's could not circumvent the obvious detail that those assaults would have to be made frontally. The 29ers had learned from past experience that those kind of attacks could be costly and dispiriting, especially against an enemy that had exhibited not the slightest sign of submission.

But the impressive aerial assault on September 5 did much to encourage the attackers. Even better, a few peeks over the frontline hedgerows on the morning of September 6 hinted to the incredulous members of the 1st and 2nd Battalions that the enemy might have disappeared. A 12:47 P.M. entry in Miller's 2nd Battalion journal noted: "Company E opened fire on enemy positions, but there was no return fire. Patrols being sent forward." One patrol, led by 2nd Lt. William Wimmer and Sgt. Nick Addomio, radioed back thirty minutes later, and the journal indicated their encouraging news: "Patrol reported taking two fields to immediate front of 'horseshoe' [a U-shaped dirt trail on the edge of the ravine, skirting a farm complex known as Mestanen]. Patrol is attempting to take buildings [of the nearby Kerozan farm] to immediate front." (Regrettably, Addomio was killed two days later.)

All across Smith's front on the afternoon of September 6, the 29ers aggressively carried out Gerhardt's requirement for "active patrolling," and the subsequent terrain gains, although defined by Smith as "nothing to get excited about," represented the first forward movement for the 115th Infantry in ten days. Thankfully, casualties were light, but the work was still extraordinarily dangerous because the cunning enemy had left behind booby traps, mines, and even timed demolition charges along trails, as well as in abandoned foxholes and farm buildings.

Miller's left-flank unit, 1st Lt. Robert Rideout's Company G, made a particularly notable advance in early evening when a message from the neighboring 8th Infantry Division signaled that its rightmost regiment, the 13th Infantry, had seized the village of Bohars, the vital crossroads town that the enemy had held resolutely for two weeks. To keep even with the 13th Infantry on their left, Rideout's men pushed ahead more than 600 yards—hardly a blitzkrieg, but by the standards of the past several weeks a meaningful accomplishment that was certain to impress Gerhardt.

The question dominating the thoughts of all 29ers on the 115th Infantry's front was whether the German retreat augured a total collapse, in which case the Americans soon would be herding the enemy into prisoner-of-war camps; or whether that withdrawal was premeditated and orderly. The care with which the Germans had arranged their profuse booby traps hinted at the latter hypothesis. But one prominent warning issued that day to all 29ers—"Treat all civilians with extreme caution for the enemy is reportedly trying to escape in civilian dress"—suggested that the enemy might be disintegrating.

The only way for the 29ers to discover the truth was to go in for the kill and launch a ferocious attack in which every man would be focused on forcing his way into the streets of Brest. Ammunition for that purpose, however, was lacking—so that kind of set-piece offensive must still wait. Therefore, at 6:13 P.M. on September 6, Witte radioed Maj. Harold Perkins, the 115th's executive officer: "Nothing for you to do tomorrow except to keep probing forward with those patrols." According to Gerhardt, that type of activity would conserve ammunition while achieving the dual goals of maintaining pressure on the enemy and enabling the division to discern the enemy's true intent.

On September 7 it did not take the 29ers long to figure out that intent, and their conclusions were not entirely positive. An early morning Company E patrol was decimated by a concealed enemy machine gun near a road junction about 300 yards north of Kerrognant, labeled "Five Points" by the GIs, resulting in the nearly instantaneous death of four men. That kind of evidence revealed that the enemy's withdrawal was hardly panicky, and in fact, as more patrol reports piled up during that morning, Johns and Miller drew the correct conclusion that the Germans were preparing to make a determined stand at Penfeld and Kerrognant. Air photos and interrogations of German prisoners disclosed the obvious detail that if the enemy were given time to thoroughly organize those formidable forts, they would be tough to crack.

The 115th Infantry must concentrate on not giving the enemy that time, and accordingly, in late morning of September 7, both the 1st and 2nd Battalions intensified their patrol efforts to throw the enemy off balance and, assuming Gerhardt decided to resume the offensive the next day, to determine a favorable line of attack against each strongpoint. On both sides of the ravine, Johns's and Miller's battalions managed to accomplish those aims admirably. Johns's 1st Battalion forged slowly but steadily ahead in the wake of its advance guards, which brushed aside scattered enemy outposts. By nightfall, the "Big Red Team," as Johns now and then liked to style his beloved battalion, had Company A scouts in the village of Guerven—just 275 yards north of Fort Penfeld. Johns observed that at sunrise the following morning, "Brest was clearly visible in the middle distance [three miles away]—challenging the men of Company A to take the fort." He later noted with some pride: "This marked the most forward advance of the entire corps as of that date. For that reason I consider it noteworthy."

For Tony Miller's 2nd Battalion, on the opposite side of the ravine, the enemy's Kerrognant strongpoint posed an immediate and vexing challenge on September 7. Kerrognant was close—only a few hundred yards beyond the 115th's front lines—but because of the nature of the terrain, no

29er had yet laid eyes on it save for those who had examined air photos. What those prints revealed were fortifications so daunting that if the enemy could man them adequately it might take weeks to force them out, at a considerable cost in lives. The wise combat veteran from Baltimore therefore aspired to move fast, and on the morning of the seventh, Miller's 29ers faithfully adhered to their commander's wishes.

Shortly before dawn Rideout's Company G sent out a five-man patrol under Sgt. Theodore Finder to investigate the approaches to Kerrognant from the east. Normally, a patrol of such small size was limited to slyly observing the Germans rather than inflicting physical harm. But, in an action defined by the 115th's official history as "one of the outstanding moves of the entire campaign," Finder's little band managed to do both, and as a result the enemy's ability to retain Kerrognant was significantly diminished.

The Germans had constructed an outlying resistance nest about 400 yards east of Kerrognant at the village of Beuzit (spelled "Beuzic" on U.S. Army maps). Both sides comprehended the significance of Beuzit because as long as it remained in German hands, the 29th Division could not possibly flank the Kerrognant position from the east. Amazingly, Finder's patrol managed to approach Beuzit at point-blank range without the enemy's knowledge, and according to the 115th's history, "[The patrol] surprised the German machine-gun crew, who were eating lunch. [More likely it was breakfast, as this affair occurred in early morning.] Before the Germans realized what had happened, Sergeant Finder's men had overcome them and taken over the gun emplacements."

Normally, the patrol would have promptly returned to American lines, but when news of Finder's coup at Beuzit filtered back to Miller's command post, at 10:55 A.M. he boldly declared to Maj. Bill Bruning, the 115th's operations officer: "I'm going to take it." Rideout thereupon dispatched a full rifle platoon to Beuzit, and shortly after noon it reached that village with orders to hold it at all costs. The significance of that achievement was emphasized by the 2nd Battalion journal, whose 1:30 P.M. entry on September 7 was typed by a proud clerk entirely in capital letters: "G COMPANY CAPTURED BEUZIC."

In slightly less dramatic fashion, a patrol sent out on September 7 by the CO of Company E, 2nd Lt. Roderick Parsch, achieved similar results. Moving stealthily around Kerrognant's western side between the strongpoint and the ravine, this seven-man group, led by S/Sgt. Delmar Carson, infiltrated deep behind enemy lines against light resistance for more than 1,000 yards all the way to a German command center in the village of

Kerguillo. Carson reported back to Parsch, and according to a 2nd Battalion report, "[He] did not feel there was any large [enemy] force in the area."

Intelligence of that kind was highly encouraging to Smith and Gerhardt, both of whom grasped that the time to attack Kerrognant was now—ammunition or no ammunition. The job would not be easy: Finder's and Carson's patrols observed plenty of German soldiers "infiltrating back" into Kerrognant, the first sight of which was enough to convert a confident man into a pessimist.

The usual German diligence in defensive works was evident everywhere, including a large concrete pillbox and several dugouts, which according to a report were "cleverly constructed and well concealed . . . manned by members of the 2nd Parachute Regiment, well-known for its clever, dogged, and determined fighting quality." The strongpoint was surrounded by two bands of barbed wire, and according to that report, "For 600–800 yards to the front and flanks of the wire and outlying trenches, the Germans had leveled all hedgerows, trees, and embankments, and there was nothing intervening between the [2nd Battalion's forward] hedgerow and the enemy works except grass and a large turnip patch." Once the Germans opened fire it seemed as if nothing could live in those empty fields. Colonel Smith hinted at the difficulties ahead when at 4:07 P.M. on September 7 he radioed Witte in the war room: "It looks like Kergonant is pretty strongly held."

But Gerhardt realized that VIII Corps was about to open the proverbial floodgates because of a signal from Middleton that an abundant supply of ammunition had finally reached Brittany. Consequently, Gerhardt gave Smith the green light to initiate a major attack by the 115th Infantry's 1st and 2nd Battalions the next day, Friday, September 8, 1944. Ten minutes before that attack was set to commence, the general radioed Smith with some words of encouragement: "Give them the works today. When they drop the artillery on that objective [Kerrognant], holler '29 Let's Go!' and storm that objective!" There was only one response Smith could utter—and that was "Yes, sir!"

Miller's 2nd Battalion would have to deal with the formidable Kerrognant, and orders to seize that place reached his command post at 10 P.M. on September 7: "Jump-off at 10 A.M. on September 8. Main effort to be toward the left [east, where parts of Company G occupied Beuzit], supported by one company [A] of the 709th Tank Battalion."

Although every 29er in the 2nd Battalion would strive to contribute to Kerrognant's downfall, the main burden in the attack fell squarely on the shoulders of 2nd Lt. John Moore, the leader of Company G's 2nd Platoon. Two weeks in the line in Brittany had reduced Moore's outfit from its normal complement of forty-one to less than thirty, and it would soon be the duty of that meager band of 29ers, who lay prone behind a forward hedgerow as the moment of jumpoff neared, to charge across nearly one-quarter of a mile of open ground to take Kerrognant. A post-combat interview of Company G members less than two weeks later revealed: "Beyond the cleared ground the men could see the outcropping of the first line of enemy fire pits, and beyond these a jumbled mass of huts, ramparts, pillboxes, observation posts, and battered works of varying kinds. . . . Rideout walked up and down the [hedgerow] looking at the men: He noted that even the new men were calm, some of them laughing."

When the assault jumped off, ten minutes late, an intense volume of supporting tank, machine-gun, mortar, and rifle fire generated an overwhelming cacophony that seemed like the abrupt arrival of a dozen express trains at once. Even if that fire did not kill many enemy troops, all of whom were under cover, it at least had the effect of keeping their heads down—a meaningful achievement, as the Germans would easily have been capable of mowing Moore's men down with impunity in such wide-open ground had they been able to use their weapons freely. According to witnesses, "Moore yelled 'Let's go!' and [the platoon] went through the hedgerow atop the hill and moved down the slope at a 'dog trot,' firing as they went." It was an unforgettable sight—terrible and magnificent all at once. "We yelled '29 Let's Go!,' Rideout remarked. "Our [German] POWs [later] said it scared the piss out of them."

Normally, a one-quarter mile-sprint while weighed down with standard GI paraphernalia would have been a strain, but the jolts of adrenaline coursing through the veins of those 29ers who partook in this frantic rush more than compensated for their physical burdens. As Moore's men approached Kerrognant, they drifted impulsively to their left to take advantage of a hedgerow close to the German trenches that the enemy had carelessly failed to clear away. According to Sgt. Dudley Floyd, "The [platoon] sergeant told us to build up along the hedgerow . . . but we were winded badly." A few men on the far right of the line ignored the hedgerow and dashed straight toward the enemy position, but they were stopped in their tracks by an unbroken barbed wire fence. For them there was no option except to lay prone and reply to the frequent tosses of potato masher grenades by the nearby enemy with a retaliatory salvo of American grenades.

The 29ers had made it successfully across the lethal open ground, but the much more arduous task of clearing out the enemy from Kerrognant had not even started. With such a small number of GIs at his disposal, Moore surely wondered whether that task could ever be accomplished. For the moment, until someone thought up a sensible course of action, the 29ers would exchange small-arms fire and grenades with the enemy at a range so close that the men could not let down their guard even for an instant. When a fearless German paratrooper tried to set up a machine gun in a nearby trench, Sergeant Floyd noted, "We let him have it. A German medic came along and picked up the machine gun, after pulling in the man's body. We let him get away with it."

A toe-to-toe battle at such a high level of intensity, however, could not last forever, and ultimately, the 29ers must either retreat or advance. That they chose the more hazardous second option was due to the leadership of Moore and Rideout, who sensed victory and did not want to yield their hard-won initiative to the enemy. Moore's prone men crept forward over terrain described as "a sponge of deep bomb craters and covering debris." Yet again, however, the combat evolved into a vicious deadlock that lasted more than an hour, during which the stubborn Germans would not retreat and the equally stubborn Americans could push ahead no farther without risking annihilation. It was the kind of close-in fighting that transpired only rarely, but when it did, it was so intense and horrifying that in truth no one could ever get used to it. As a Company G member, PFC Henry Green, recalled, "I was so scared that I could actually feel the machine-gun bullets cutting me in half."

That the 29ers would eventually emerge victorious from this stalemate could be credited to several factors, one of which was the key contribution by several 709th Tank Battalion Sherman tanks. On that unforgiving ground, it was probably even riskier for a tanker to drive his Sherman forward than it was for a rifleman to attack, for a 33-ton tank had no place to take cover, and the deadly mines, vast bomb craters, and resolute enemy soldiers armed with *Panzerfaust* rocket launchers were perils that could wreck a Sherman in an instant. As the official 709th history observed, "Greater casualties were inflicted by mines and close-in bazooka [*Panzerfaust*] antitank teams than by direct enemy fire weapons."

Nevertheless, when Rideout requested close-in tank support to aid his beleaguered company, one tanker gamely responded in the affirmative. It took some time for engineers to clear a secure path over which the tank could move, but when it finally surged ahead, witnesses reported: "The

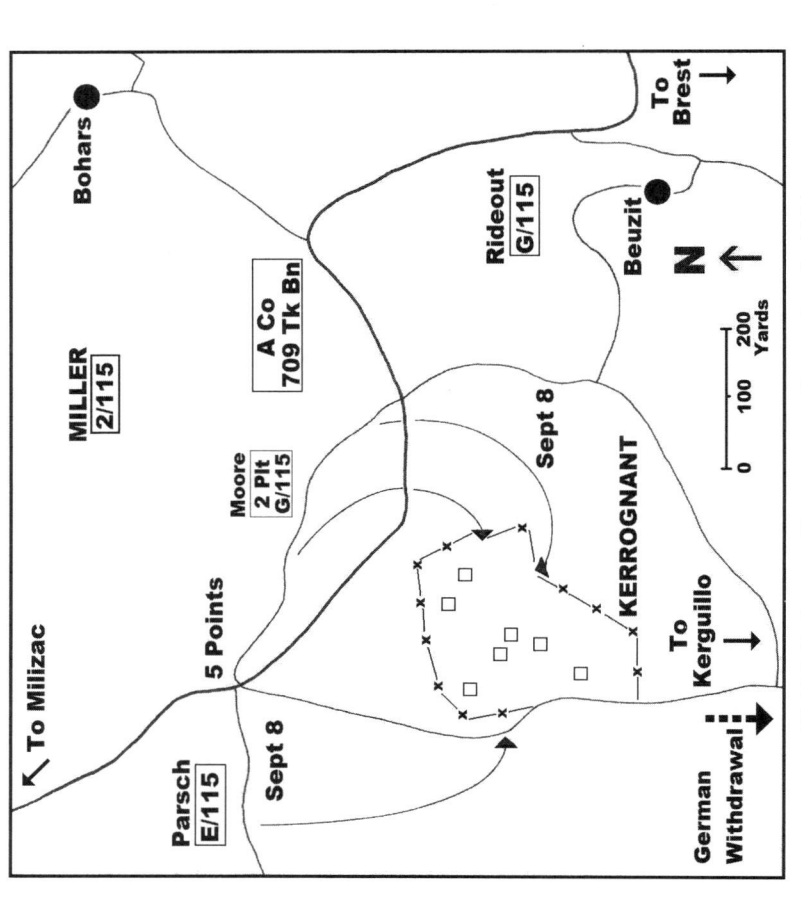

2/115th Infantry: Kerrognant, September 8, 1944

tank put 75mm shell and .50-caliber machine-gun fire into one enemy machine-gun nest on the left flank, then moved over right. In delivering point-blank fire against the enemy on [the right], its blast was so close to [Sgt. Edwin] Sweeney and his men that they had to clear back."

The tank's fire severely punished the Germans, but they soon reciprocated. A well-aimed *Panzerfaust* shot sent a jet of molten metal through the tank's turret, instantly setting its interior on fire. When the five-man crew promptly bailed out, the nearby 29ers noted that they "were stunned and helpless." The U.S. Army historian who interviewed Company G members two weeks later reported, "Sgt. Guy Hazlitt said to Sweeney and Pvt. Morris Low: 'Come on, let's go! Those guys are going to die if we don't.' They crawled out. Those who witnessed it said that bullet fire was whipping the ground. . . . One tanker lay on the ground, blinded. Another had his face burned to a black crisp. They carried both men back to the crater. The second man died while they were bringing him along."

Another factor contributing to the Americans' ultimate victory at Kerrognant was the pressure exerted on the opposite flank of the German defenses by Lieutenant Parsch's Company E. Like Rideout's Company G, Parsch's men learned the grueling lesson that the nearer they approached the heart of the Germans' strongpoint, the more doggedly the enemy resisted. Rideout, however, noted that "I had perfect radio contact with Company E all day, and the two companies always worked together."

The beneficial result of that cooperation was a constantly tightening pincer movement threatening the German defenders of Kerrognant with encirclement. But, as always seemed to be the case when fighting the Germans, that feat was achieved at the cost of many good men. One Company E squad led by Sgt. Carlton Felty was advancing toward Kerrognant from the west with the object of bringing bazooka fire against an enemy emplacement. "The [bazooka] man and his assistant moved to the left along the hedge parallel to the advance," witnesses recalled. "The assistant, Pvt. Walter Thull [a recent replacement from Minnesota], was killed by machine-gun fire when he tried firing his carbine and it jammed. The gunner, Pvt. Gerald Kramer, fell in an exposed position in the field and played dead for several hours, as he was almost in the enemy [lines]. Even his comrades who could see him lying there believed him to be dead." (Kramer is not listed in regimental records as a casualty, so he was probably unwounded.)

By late afternoon, pressure from Rideout's and Parsch's companies was steadily squeezing the enemy out of Kerrognant. The wily Germans, however, had held open a secure escape route until the last moment, so that when the vengeful 29ers finally burst into the enemy's battered dugouts and pillboxes at about 6 P.M., an observer noted with some regret: "Kerrognant was occupied only by the German dead." Despite the lack of enemy prisoners, Miller's terse announcement at 6:05 P.M.—"Have taken Kergonant"—signified a notable victory for Smith's 115th Infantry. The following morning, Gerhardt would acknowledge that fact when he radioed Smith: "You sure did fine. . . . Pat the men on the back."

Furthermore, Miller would see to it that Rideout would receive a Silver Star, the citation for which would note: "On one occasion, when one tank was disabled by enemy fire, Lieutenant Rideout braved the decimating enemy fire while leading another tank into position . . . [and was] a constant inspiration to his men." A North Carolina native, Rideout would gain an Oak Leaf Cluster to that Silver Star on November 19, 1944, during the 29th Division's fall offensive into Germany, but regrettably, that second award would be posthumous.

On September 8, Smith had much more on his mind than just Kerrognant. While his 2nd Battalion was struggling to secure that place, three-quarters of a mile to the west Glover Johns's 1st Battalion was pushing southward to secure the formidable Fort Penfeld. Despite the close proximity of the two battalions, however, the stark ravine dividing them forced Smith to direct each operation independently. During the night of September 7, 1st Battalion scouts had reported to Johns that the enemy was exhibiting no signs of a determined stand at Penfeld. That news was indeed heartening, but also implausible, since under normal conditions the Germans would never give up a position as significant as Penfeld without a fight.

But the tactical situation on the afternoon of September 8 could hardly be categorized as normal. At least on Johns's front, the Germans were apparently on the run, a retreat that was hastened courtesy of the Ninth Air Force's deluge of bombs, including several of the Army Air Force's new jellied gasoline variety, later known as napalm. The encouraging evidence of that destruction in the form of a moonscape of craters was easily visible to members of the 1st Battalion as they approached Fort Penfeld from the north. Even so, many last-ditch German defenders remained, who, according to Johns, "had chosen open ground outside the walls for better fields of fire." Enemy reinforcements were arriving, too—a detail noted by several Company C members who watched in amazement as a German ambulance suddenly pulled into the front lines, only to disgorge eight heavily armed paratroopers, all of whom swiftly disappeared into the hedgerows.

Penfeld was a five-sided fort, surrounded by a moat and constructed with the sturdy earthen walls, wrapped in masonry, so typical of the pre-twentieth-century fortifications near Brest. It was designed to check an enemy attack coming from the north—precisely the direction from which Johns's men must approach—and if the 29ers could not breach the walls or hurriedly obtain scaling ladders, the only way to enter the fort would be to swing around its southern side and break in through the sally port. Late in the afternoon of September 8, a platoon led by T/Sgt. Lennis Pittinger of Company A intended to do exactly that. It stealthily slipped around Penfeld's western side, searching for a seam in the enemy's defenses. By the standards of typical 29th Division riflemen, the twenty-six-year-old Pittinger was an "old" soldier, a veteran of Omaha Beach and almost every brutal battle fought by the 115th's 1st Battalion since. A native of Thurmont, Maryland—just a few miles from President Roosevelt's celebrated Catoctin Mountain retreat known as "Shangri-La"—Pittinger had served with Company A since his enlistment in the Maryland National Guard in July 1939. As of September 1944 that kind of military experience was highly valued by the 115th's riflemen simply because it was so rare.

That Pittinger knew how to lead troops in battle was confirmed at Penfeld when he managed to maneuver his men around the fort and subdue the many enemy machine-gun nests in the adjoining hedgerow-lined fields, after which several members of his redoubtable group penetrated into the fort's interior from the rear. Those 29ers who understood the enemy knew that a counterattack would soon follow, and when it came, according to Johns, it took "two hours of sharp fighting before [the fort] was secured." At one point, Pittinger and his men were cut off from the rest of Johns's 1st Battalion, and as noted by the citation for the Silver Star Pittinger would shortly receive, "When ordered by the enemy to surrender, T/Sgt. Pittinger answered their demands with fire."

By nightfall Penfeld was devoid of German defenders—and another nail had been hammered in the enemy's coffin. The delighted 29ers promptly discovered that the Germans had left behind a bountiful supply of military souvenirs that would make an interesting show-and-tell for the folks back home—assuming those GIs would survive war's dreadful law of averages and get back home in one piece.

On the U.S. Army's 1:25,000-scale maps of Brest, Penfeld was not labeled, leading many of Gerhardt's staff officers to refer to it in war room transcripts simply as "The Unnamed Fort." That was hardly an appropriate name for such an important military bastion, but starting on September 9, it gained the new, if entirely unauthorized, name of "Fort Pittinger" in honor of the Marylander who, according to his Silver Star citation, had "displayed courage and leadership of the highest order."

When there was still some light remaining on September 8, Smith wondered whether or not the 115th should press deeper into enemy lines toward Brest. The successes at Kerrognant and Penfeld were significant, and good commanders had a sense of when to go in for the kill. The Germans in Smith's sector were obviously showing signs of collapse, and penetrating farther ahead toward Brest was tempting, for only 600 yards south of Kerrognant, American air photographs had revealed something unusual. It was a chateau named Kerguillo, set on a hill in a scenic woodland, which the Germans had transformed into some sort of high-level command post. A circular barbed wire perimeter about 200 yards in diameter enclosed the grounds. Local Frenchmen had told the 29ers that the Germans had used Kerguillo as a rest center for submariners upon their return to Brest after their deadly U-boat expeditions in the Atlantic. More recently, however, intelligence information hinted that Ramcke himself had used the Kerguillo chateau as a headquarters.

Such a place was certainly a worthy objective, and at 6:12 P.M. Smith radioed Witte in the war room: "We are pushing down to Objective F [Kerguillo]. . . . If [it] is held, do you want to start a fight there tonight?" Fortunately, Witte's intelligence reports indicated that "there isn't a great deal [of the enemy] in Kerguillo," a detail that emboldened Smith and caused him to issue orders to Miller's 2nd Battalion to resume its southward advance. However, darkness and the severely depleted condition of Miller's outfit after its exhausting fight at Kerrognant forced Smith to call a halt to that advance at about 10 P.M., when Miller's men were just short of the chateau. Smith promptly radioed Witte: "I think we can knock it out in the morning."

They did. At 8:30 A.M. on Saturday, September 9, the cheerful members of Companies E and G jumped off and swiftly discovered that their mission would be infinitely easier than the previous day. Less than thirty minutes later, Company E reported, "No one in the chateau . . . but the area has been strongly fortified with many antiaircraft and '88' emplacements." At 11:20 A.M., a proud Miller radioed Smith: "The battalion mission is complete." Two days later a delighted Gerhardt congratulated Smith: "You've got the best regiment in the division [and] you have the three best battalions."

The 115th Infantry now held the coveted high ground north of Brest, and from that advantageous military perspective, its members could look nearly straight down the ravine of the Penfeld River as it wound its way southward to the sea just three miles away. As the regimental history noted, "The Brest campaign was about to enter its final stage." How easy that stage would be depended on the enemy's vigor. If, as intelligence reports seemed to indicate, the Germans were showing signs of cracking, it was entirely possible that in a matter of days the 29th Division could traverse those three miles and at long last march right into the enemy's nefarious submarine pens on Brest's waterfront—an accomplishment that would shortly trigger such a flood of American troops and supplies into Brest that the Nazis' inevitable downfall would be considerably hastened.

Such a success would delight General Gerhardt, but assuredly, it would delight General Eisenhower even more.

2. KAPUT!

Every 29er realized that the noose around the enemy's Brest enclave was tightening. It would not be long, or so the GIs hoped, before General Middleton ultimately tightened that noose with sufficient force to squeeze the Germans into oblivion. Thus, when one glanced at Middleton's situation map on September 10, 1944, a salient detail emerged: Thanks to the near-continuous pressure exerted by the Americans since the start of the siege, VIII Corps' semicircular front surrounding Brest had decreased appreciably in length as the Germans fell back toward the city. That development was entirely favorable to Middleton, for American combat power was now concentrated on a much more compact front than before. True, Ramcke had less ground to defend, but military logic suggested that an attacker capable of massing supreme effort and firepower on a narrow focal point would hold a significant tactical advantage, and now the Americans needed to prove that point.

Accordingly, soon after the 115th Infantry's successes on September 8 and 9, Middleton consented to a major narrowing of the 29th Division's front lines. His scheme called for Smith to yield the 115th's hard-won gains at Penfeld, Kerrognant, and Kerguillo to the 8th Division's 28th Infantry, which would shift westward to take over Smith's front. Tony Miller's 2nd Battalion pulled out first, on the evening of September 9, followed by Glover Johns's 1st Battalion the next night. Both outfits made a circuitous eight-mile journey by truck behind the front lines all the way to the 29th Division's opposite flank near the village of La Trinité, where the 116th Infantry, and more recently the 175th, had faced a tactical deadlock for more than a week against tough German paratroopers and had made unimpressive terrain gains. At La Trinité, Miller and Johns would join their 115th comrade, Maj. Randy Milholland, whose 3rd Battalion had been attached to the 175th Infantry during the grueling fight for Hill 103 and had helped immeasurably to seize that key objective.

If Gerhardt wished for his division to be concentrated on a narrow front, that wish was now granted. The 29th Division's worn-out infantrymen were now responsible for a sector only three miles in length—shorter by almost a mile than the line held by the 115th Infantry alone during late August. Ordinarily, conditions would have been perfect for a smashing offensive aimed at a critical point in the enemy lines, but September 10, 1944, could by no stretch of one's imagination be categorized as ordinary. When the 115th Infantry shifted to its new sector at La Trinité, six of the 29th Division's nine infantry battalions—including all three battalions comprising the 116th Infantry—were out of the line recuperating from their recent traumatic spells in combat. As a firm believer in the military tenet that time out of the line cured a military unit's ills, Gerhardt still needed a few more days to allow those depleted outfits to recover their physical and spiritual strength. Only when they were revitalized would he deploy them properly for the decisive attack that must soon follow.

The 115th Infantry's appearance in its new sector on September 11 thoroughly raised the spirits of Lt. Col. William Purnell, whose 175th Infantry had shouldered the burden of combat in that deadly locale for longer than any member of the regiment cared to remember. One mile east of Hill 103, in the area known by the locals as Ilioc farm, Purnell's 29ers had been waging a fruitless on-again, off-again struggle since September 5 and had suffered appalling casualties. The 175th's main effort at Ilioc had been on September 8, the same day Tony Miller's 2nd Battalion, 115th Infantry, had waged its monumental battle at Kerrognant. The previous evening at 6 P.M., Purnell had declared somewhat bombastically to Gerhardt, "We are all set for the massacre of the Jerries," to which Uncle Charlie replied: "Give it the works!"

But the hardy Germans had not willingly submitted to any "massacres," and in all likelihood inflicted much more punishment on the Americans than they themselves received. Despite Purnell's statement to Witte at 10:30 P.M. on September 8, "I think in the morning [the Germans] may draw back to their next position," the next day's fighting at Ilioc had been even worse, and when September 9 drew to a close, Purnell had a two-day casualty total of 28 killed and 125 wounded—with no significant terrain gains to offset that severe human cost. Most of the fighting at Ilioc had been carried out by the 2nd Battalion, which had recently been amply infused with replacements. When Gerhardt asked Purnell how it had performed in this kind grueling hedgerow combat, Purnell replied apologetically, "I think if they had been seasoned troops, they would have done a little better."

A member of Company F, Dan Relihan, learned how bizarre warfare could be in the constricted hedgerows around Ilioc. Relihan, a 60mm mortarman, had suffered severe hearing loss on Hill 103 due to the detonation of a shell close by, an ailment that had not gotten any better over the past several days. Soldierly duties in the front lines in Brittany required sharp eyesight and even sharper hearing, and an affliction as bad as Relihan's considerably reduced his ability to survive. He learned that detail one day near Ilioc when he whirled around in his frontline fighting position to discover five Germans, two of whom were medics, staring at him from close range with their hands over their heads. Had the enemy soldiers not been so eager to give up, Relihan's malfunctioning ear drums could have led to his death.

Colonel Purnell's only success during this trying period had come in an unanticipated quarter. On the regiment's left flank, nothing much in the way of significant terrain gains had been expected from the unit covering that sector, Lt. Col. William Blandford's 3rd Battalion, which extended over a front of more than two miles. For a depleted outfit with an acute shortage of experienced riflemen, such a lengthy front had virtually precluded offensive operations. But Blandford's battalion had tied in with the right of Smith's 115th Infantry, and when that regiment had achieved its notable triumphs at Penfeld and Kerrognant on September 8, the Germans on Blandford's front abruptly pulled back to avoid encirclement by the 115th. Thanks to the the Blue and Gray Division's standard practice of "aggressive patrolling," Blandford's battalion had immediately detected the enemy's pullback.

By the evening of September 8, Blandford's men had collectively congratulated themselves on their amazing luck at the enemy strongpoint known as Keriolet. The Germans had successfully countered every 29th Division maneuver to take Keriolet for over two weeks, and the nightmarish memories of the August 27 frontal assault against that strongpoint by the 116th Infantry were still fresh. To the members of the 175th's Company L, no paradox of war could have been more manifest than their cautious entry into that gloomy landscape of bomb craters, corpses, and lifeless trees late on September 8. Not long ago, it seemed as if an entire U.S. Army armored division would be needed to storm that position, but in actuality, it was seized by a handful of Blandford's riflemen, and the enemy did not even make an appearance. One immediate problem, however, had been the crafty enemy's standard tactic of leaving behind hundreds of concealed mines and booby traps. In truth, by this stage of the campaign, the 29ers were used to the German Army's guile, and Blandford immediately called in the experts from Company C, 121st Engineer Battalion, led by 1st Lt. Herbert Williams, to clear and secure those still-hazardous areas.

But the enemy was not so accommodating at Ilioc. In fact, German paratroopers had fortified the sturdy hedgerows and farm buildings there with such fervor that Purnell concluded to Witte, "It's going to require quite a blast to get them out of there." On September 10, Lt. Col. Millard Bowen's 2nd Battalion tried for the third straight day to shove the enemy back toward Brest, but even with all the "blast" the 175th could muster, the Germans hardly budged, and they inflicted about seventy more casualties on Bowen's battalion, a heavy price to pay for its nearly nonexistent gains.

Even worse, by this stage of the campaign the cumulative effect of those steadily mounting casualties—about 700 in the 175th in a little over two weeks—had wholly deadened the spirits of even the most buoyant members of the regiment. The commander of Company F, 1st Lt. Carl Hobbs, observed:

> Seeing comrades fall day after day, moving and fighting with little rest, hopes for eventual survival fading—all these caused values to change. The normal strong will to survive became weak. . . . Often, and possibly for good reason, objectives were given with firm orders from high headquarters—and to us, with not enough support. To the frontline soldiers, it was natural to gripe and wonder what the reason was for that lack of support.

In the immortal words of Bill Mauldin's dogfaces, Willie and Joe, those infantrymen who had survived without a scratch since the 29th Division had arrived in Brittany knew full well that they were "fugitives from the law of averages."

Here was war at its most gruesome. On a daily basis graves registration and medical personnel had the dreadful and highly dangerous duty of combing the hedgerows and pastures for the bodies of dead 29ers. When they found what they were looking for, they initiated a process with which they had become entirely too familiar in recent weeks: secure the dogtags, collect personal effects, note the nature of the wounds, prepare the body for movement back to a temporary cemetery. It was just the start of a long trail of paperwork that would reach its culmination a few weeks later when the dreaded telegram from the Adjutant General of the U.S. Army arrived at an unfortunate family's home: "We regret to inform you . . ."

You could never get used to it. At the height of the Ilioc fighting, a 175th Infantry graves registration officer by the name of 2nd Lt. Fritz

Sandner began the task he had carried out many times before by typing up a list of nineteen 29ers he and his men had gathered over the past two days. He eventually forwarded that list to Sgt. Abe Sherman at regimental headquarters with the somber annotation: "We certify that the above-named officers and enlisted men have been killed in action." Next to one name, Pvt. Louis R. Wiley, Sandner placed an asterisk with an accompanying footnote: "Wiley is to be carried as missing in action until further information can be obtained regarding his death. There was only the right leg of a body found alongside of a bill-fold belonging to Louis Richard Wiley." Not a single trace of Private Louis Richard Wiley, 29th Infantry Division, U.S. Army, was ever found again.

Every 29er comprehended that the fortunes of war were entirely unpredictable. But, much to Purnell's regret, those fortunes had been absolutely pitiless to the 175th Infantry, which in large measure had fought nothing but brutal toe-to-toe slugfests for two weeks against an implacable enemy from Plouzané to Hill 103 to Ilioc. There had been nothing that had even remotely resembled a breakthrough, but that detail had been directly attributable to the fact that Gerhardt had committed the regiment to a locale the enemy was keenly resolved to retain, particularly Hill 103.

By now, every 29er had learned the hard reality that there could be no subtlety in combat operations at Brest. The only option was a relentless and vigorous frontal attack, and even military neophytes knew that the 175th's axis of attack toward its ultimate objective was entirely predictable. The Germans, who certainly were not neophytes, knew exactly where Purnell would attack, and had so far resisted fiercely every step of the way. Something would have to give: At the rate the enemy was falling back and inflicting casualties, the 175th Infantry would cease to exist by the time the 29th Division approached the walls of Brest.

Gerhardt was the type of general who was loath to admit that the despicable enemy possessed a fearsome combat proficiency. He had trained the 29th Division so hard that in a stand-up fight between 29ers and Germans, he was positive the Americans should prevail every time. When they did not, he neither credited the enemy nor blamed the common American fighting man. Instead, from his lofty perspective, the culprit was always poorly trained or irresolute American field grade officers, typically battalion commanders—as he had emphasized time and again during the training days in England.

At the height of the Ilioc battle, Gerhardt was not happy with the 175th Infantry, and he bluntly dwelled on his theory of leadership to its commander. "I think I'll reorganize the division," he remarked whimsically to Purnell. "I thought we'd put [Lt. Col. Anthony] Miller [CO, 2nd

Battalion, 115th], [Maj. William] Puntenney [CO, 3rd Battalion, 116th], and [Lt. Col. Randolph] Millholland [CO, 3rd Battalion, 115th] in charge of your battalions." Somewhat awkwardly, Purnell replied, "If that were possible, we'd take Berlin tomorrow." But the general concluded on a serious note: "I think Blandford and Bowen are too gloomy, and in order for success we must have a spark in the leader. See what you can do about it!"

Things have a way of changing suddenly in combat, and a remarkable series of events was about to occur on the 175th's front at Ilioc that would change Gerhardt's view of the 175th Infantry forever. After the war, the French government would present the exalted Croix de Guerre to Bowen's 2nd Battalion for its laudable behavior in an incredibly complex and volatile military situation, and the U.S. Army would grant an even greater tribute—a Medal of Honor—to a sergeant in Company F, the first time that celebrated decoration would be bestowed upon a 29th Division soldier in World War II.

It all began at 10:30 A.M. on September 11, when Bowen's outfit, for the fourth consecutive day, initiated an attack that was intended to drive the enemy back from the Ilioc sector. This time, to ensure more positive results, Gerhardt launched simultaneous supporting assaults across much of the 29th Division's three-mile front. On the 2nd Battalion's left flank, Lt. Col. Roger Whiteford's 1st Battalion had only hours earlier moved into the line and held orders to advance across a few hundred yards of difficult lowlying ground toward a farm hamlet known as Keriel, about two-thirds of a mile due north of Ilioc. On Bowen's right, Miller's 2nd Battalion, 115th Infantry, fresh from its triumphs at Kerrognant and Kerguillo, had just relocated to La Trinité with orders from Gerhardt to push ahead along the N789 thoroughfare toward the village of Coatuélen. If both Whiteford's and Miller's attacks succeeded, the Germans at Ilioc would be threatened with encirclement, and the 29th Division would be less than three miles from the walls of Brest, poised for a final push straight into the city.

As usual, turmoil and stagnation set in from the start. None of the three attacking battalions made any appreciable progress for several hours. Gerhardt's mood darkened by the minute. At 12:45 P.M. he phoned the 175th's command post to speak to Purnell and lost his temper with a staff officer when he discovered that Purnell was up front with Whiteford. "You tell [Purnell] that I must know where he is at all times!" Gerhardt bellowed. "Get on the telephone and have him call me!"

Gerhardt could hardly be surprised that Whiteford could accomplish little on the morning of September 11, since his 1st Battalion had been thrown haphazardly into an impossible tactical situation. The battalion, which had been severely depleted by the grueling battle for Hill 103, had made three major shifts of position in the last few days. It had thankfully been removed from the line following the Hill 103 fight and placed in regimental reserve, but Gerhardt had then unexpectedly committed it on September 10 in the 116th Infantry's zone at La Trinité with orders to attack eastward along the N789 highway. Just as suddenly, the general had changed his mind on September 11, less than twenty-four hours later, and pulled Whiteford's men out again, shifting them northward to Keriel with orders to conduct an immediate attack in support of Bowen's 2nd Battalion at Ilioc.

It was all incredibly bewildering to Whiteford's 29ers, who by September 11 had been bounced back and forth across the front like a ping-pong ball, and now they had to carry out an attack across deadly ground with which they were totally unfamiliar. Still worse, the terrain over which that attack had to be made was open and flat, and every foot of it was exposed to a devastating crossfire of German machine guns. Understandably, perhaps, the 1st Battalion made no progress whatsoever when it jumped off shortly before noon on September 11 amid a cacophony of enemy machine-gun fire.

Gerhardt, however, would tolerate no excuses, and somewhat heartlessly according to Purnell's staff, the general ordered the assault renewed at midnight. There was no doubt about it now: Gerhardt's hackles were up, and when he was in a mood like this, no one short of Generals Eisenhower or Bradley could restrain him. When Gerhardt later learned that Whiteford's jumpoff was delayed by several hours, he promptly focused his rage on Purnell. "I understand the 1st Battalion did not move until 0630 [on September 12]," Gerhardt declared. "Relieve that battalion commander [Whiteford] if you gave him the order to [attack]. I am very much disgusted with this whole business! Let's get something salvaged from it!"

Purnell endeavored to defend Whiteford, his old friend from the prewar days in the Maryland National Guard, by asserting, "There are some [Germans] between two of Whiteford's companies;" but Uncle Charlie roared back: "To hell with them! . . . The indications are that there was no [enemy] there."

It was not easy to stand up to Gerhardt, but Purnell rejoined: "The CO of Company A [1st Lt. John C. Jones] and also one of my best sergeants [S/Sgt. John Hoopes from Baltimore, who had joined the Maryland National Guard in 1939] were killed down there yesterday." Jones was the second commander of Company A to die in the past two weeks.

Whiteford's men finally took Keriel on the morning of September 12, but Gerhardt's mood did not improve. "I want a full report on this whole thing," he announced. "What I can't understand is why they're not moving

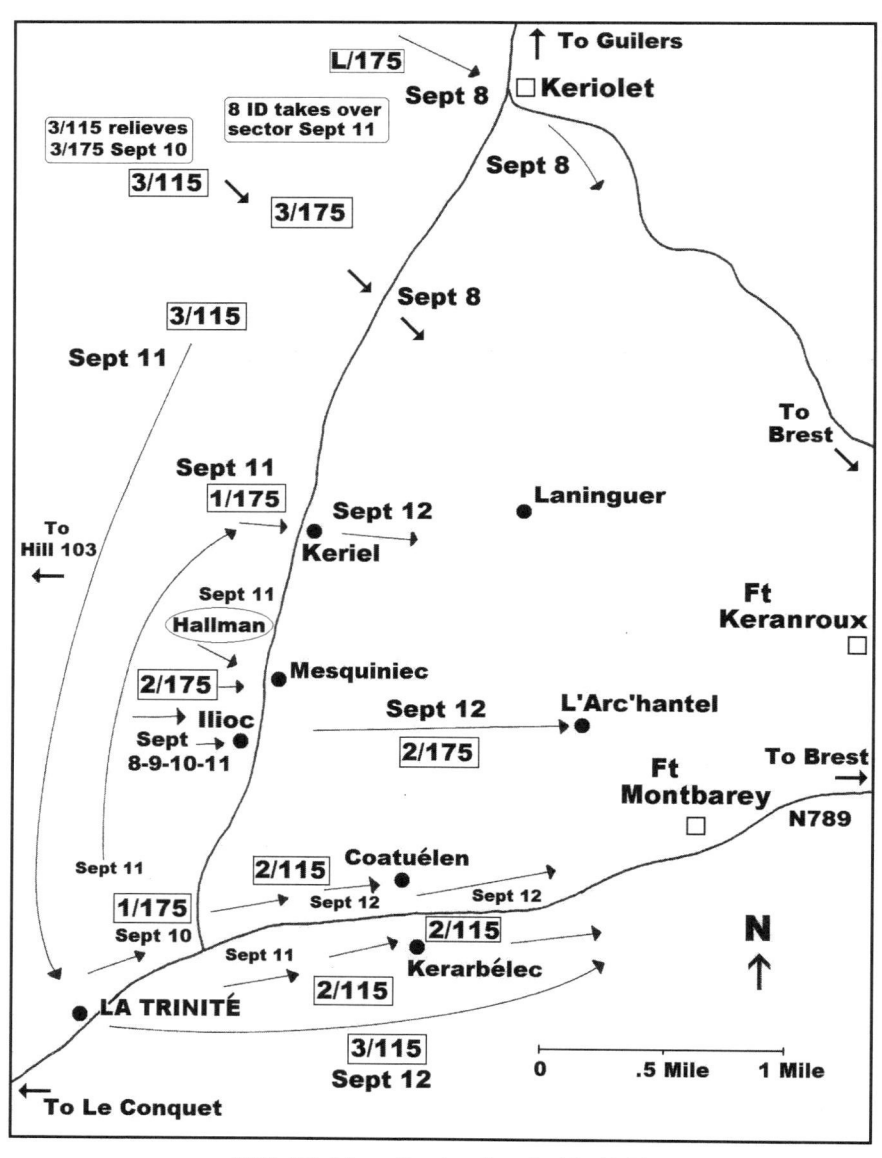

29th Division: September 8–12, 1944

when there is no resistance"—a remarkably uninformed statement given the large number of 175th casualties that were being reported. Later, he remarked to his operations officer, Colonel Witte: "You can see that both of them [Purnell and Whiteford] had no conception of capitalizing on this thing as they should do." Witte, a close friend of Purnell and Whiteford from the old days in the Maryland Guard, said nothing.

The tenacious enemy seemed disinclined to yield to the Americans' intense pressure, a detail that Tony Miller learned on the far right of the 29th Division's line at La Trinité when his 2nd Battalion, 115th Infantry stumbled into a redoubtable enemy strongpoint at Coatuélen. On September 11 his outfit jumped off at 10:30 A.M. with Company G on the right, Company F on the left. The 29ers made it up into a deep ravine about 500 yards west of Coatuélen without any difficulties, but when they pressed on, they ran into deadly mortar and machine-gun fire. A battalion staff officer noted that there were "quite a few casualties from the [enemy] mortars, [and] Company G got up to move and practically had a hand-to-hand battle using grenades."

By late afternoon Miller's men had stalled in the lethal fields west of Coatuélen and a nearby farm complex known as Kerarbélec, but an adamant Gerhardt ordered the attack resumed at midnight. The enemy must have been caught by surprise by the night assault because this time it worked, and both Coatuélen and Kerarbélec were cleared of the enemy by 2:30 A.M. on September 12. With their objectives now secured, the exhausted infantrymen yearned for a rest, but Gerhardt would have none of it. "I understand that there's no resistance on your front and that you propose to stop them on their objective," Gerhardt radioed the 115th's commander, Colonel Smith. "I want them to keep going. . . . Call me back at 0400 as to their progress."

The general's entreaty promptly filtered down the chain of command and triggered an unforeseen interruption in a radio conversation on the front lines between the commanders of Company G, 1st Lt. Robert Rideout, and Company F, 1st Lt. Warren McNulty.

"Hey, 'Ride,'" McNulty asked. "How are you doing? Meeting anything?"

Rideout replied: "Nope, nothing yet. Everything's too quiet. It looks fishy to me. Are you pushing?"

"Yes, but not too fast," replied McNulty. "As soon as I meet something, I'm going to button up."

"OK. Let me know when you stop—and I will too," Rideout declared.

Unfortunately for the two lieutenants, their boss, Lt. Col. Tony Miller, was listening in to the dialogue. "Like hell you will! You'll stop when I tell you to!" Miller roared. "Now you two stop worrying about what might happen and get going!"

When Gerhardt demanded of Smith if he was "prepared to exploit the success with another battalion," Smith responded: "Yes, sir. I have another battalion [Millholland's 3rd] ready." The general concluded, "OK—keep it going and call me at 0500."

Gerhardt had sensed that the Germans were ready to crack, and this time he was right. His relentless pressure on commanders to push their men forward, viewed by many as a callous and heartless posture that did not show an understanding of the realities of frontline combat, would, on September 12, help to produce the most successful day of operations so far in the 29th Division's grueling endeavor to take Brest, a day that even the general would later admit had turned out much better than expected.

Miller's 2nd Battalion hastened forward in the predawn darkness, and suddenly the Germans were gone. By the time the sun rose, the 29ers had pressed ahead on either side of the N789 road for almost a mile, a rate of advance that by the standards of the Brest campaign amounted almost to a blitzkrieg. Miller's men stopped just short of a conspicuous water tower and a deep antitank ditch, beyond which were several fields ominously devoid of their usual hedgerows. The reason for their absence was obvious, for about one-half mile away the leading scouts could perceive the ancient French fort known as Montbarey—a sinister edifice with which the 29ers would soon become entirely familiar. At 11 A.M. Millholland's 3rd Battalion relieved the 2nd and proceeded eastward toward the fort, a place that would later go down in history as one of the 29th Division's toughest objectives in World War II.

No one in the 115th Infantry yet knew that Miller's victory at Coatuélen on the morning of September 12 could be attributed to the stunning success achieved by the neighboring unit on Miller's left, the 175th Infantry's 2nd Battalion under Lt. Col. Millard Bowen. And soon the 29ers would learn that the fate of Bowen's outfit had in large measure been determined by one man, S/Sgt. Sherwood Hallman of Company F.

When Hallman and his comrades opened their 10:30 A.M. attack on September 11, they experienced the same kind of ferocious enemy resistance that had paralyzed the efforts of the 2nd Battalion's neighbors on either flank. By early afternoon, when Bowen's attack dissipated, the battalion had gained only a few insignificant hedgerows and was still not in control of Ilioc and the nearby farm of Mesquiniec. Gerhardt had no intention of stopping, however, and at 3 P.M. he pronounced to Purnell: "I want you to throw the book at them!" The general's plan was to revive the 2nd

Battalion's forward progress from about 4:30 to 7:00, followed by a pause of several hours. Then Bowen's men would resume the attack with an even greater fervor at midnight.

At about 4 P.M. the weary men of Company F were resting behind a forward hedgerow near Mesquiniec awaiting orders. The cynical survivors of two weeks of brutal combat had every expectation that those orders would make little sense and trigger even more casualties. The company commander, 1st Lt. Carl Hobbs, observed: "It was a warm day. We had eaten a noon-day ration while behind the hedgerows. . . . We were at a standstill after having moved forward only 200 or 300 yards that morning. Most of the men were lying around, dozing or asleep. Our guards, of course, were posted."

It was the proverbial quiet before the storm.

Sergeant Hallman was a thirty-year-old native of Spring City, Pennsylvania, just west of Philadelphia, who had been with Company F since its lengthy pre-D-Day training period in Cornwall, England. He had lasted only one day in Normandy before suffering a severe wound due to friendly fire, requiring a two-month convalescence period in England. His D-Day company commander, Capt. Robert Miller, described Hallman as "a determined man—a combat leader and a fighter . . . a good soldier and comrade." When the U.S. Army had inducted Hallman into military service in November 1942—only a month after his first child, Sherwood Jr., had been born—he had been forced to abandon his own business, a highly successful grocery delivery service called "Sherry's Modern Market," featuring a refrigerated food truck painted with the motto "A Store At Your Door." His wife, Virginia, later observed: "I think he would really have been a tycoon."

On September 11, 1944, Sergeant Hallman was about to display initiative at an even higher level than he had exhibited when he generated his own business from scratch. At Gerhardt's order, Company F was about to renew its attack at 4:30 P.M., and to discover a better way to do it than the fruitless and predictable frontal attacks of the past several days, Hallman embarked on a one-man patrol far out in front of his company's left flank, creeping forward along hedgerows and a sunken road until he detected some unwary German paratroopers in an open pasture. "I heard a hand grenade explode, an automatic rifle began firing, and a wild yell," Hobbs remembered. "This was followed by more gunfire, and then suddenly there were yells of 'Kaput! Kaput!' Germans started running toward our right-front, which was bounded by a road. I ordered the platoon leader on that side to get his men to quickly disarm the Germans and herd them together behind a hedgerow." A Company F mortarman, PFC Dan Relihan, had to do just that, as he spotted an enemy soldier coming toward him over a nearby earthen embankment with a terrified look on his face and his hands in the air—followed shortly thereafter by Sergeant Hallman with his BAR. Relihan relieved the German of a pistol and shoved him toward the growing mass of prisoners for which Company F had abruptly become responsible. Hallman had single-handedly energized his outfit, whose members by this time were all shouting elatedly, as if their team was about to win the World Series.

Sgt. Sherwood Hallman had just confirmed Napoleon's maxim: "In war, men are nothing—one man is everything." He had caught the ordinarily ferocious German paratroopers at a highly vulnerable moment, and in an instant expoited that moment to the fullest. According to his Medal of Honor citation,

> Firing his carbine and hurling grenades, Staff Sergeant Hallman, unassisted, killed or wounded four of the enemy, then ordered the remainder to surrender. [Hobbs recalled that Hallman was armed with a Browning Automatic Rifle, not a carbine.] Immediately, twelve of the enemy surrendered and the position was shortly secured by the remainder of his company. Seeing the surrender of this position, about 75 of the enemy in the vicinity surrendered, yielding a defensive [position] which the battalion, with heavy supporting fires, had been unable to take.

Eventually, so many Germans fell into Company F's hands at Ilioc farm that Hallman directed several members of his squad to assist him in moving the prisoners to the rear. When Purnell learned of Hallman's deed, he promptly radioed Witte in the war room: "I think this thing is busted through. We've taken about 30 POWs, and more are coming in. They came out of the hedgerows from every direction."

Purnell was so impressed that, on Hallman's behalf, he would in due course order his staff to prepare and file the complex paperwork the U.S. Army demanded for Medal of Honor consideration. To ensure that a soldier satisfied the Army's strict conditions for "conspicuous gallantry and intrepidity at the risk of life above and beyond the call of duty," that soldier's actions had to be described in a written report, featuring as many tactical details as possible and supported by affidavits by at least two eyewitnesses. That appeal could only be approved by a majority or unanimous vote of a three-member board of senior officers. No matter how scrupulously a unit prepared its report, however, the U.S. Army's well-known stinginess in matters of that kind suggested that the odds of any given appeal yielding a Medal of Honor were extraordinarily low. Even worse, rumors were widespread within the 29th Division that Gerhardt was the type of general who was parsimonious when it came to exalted decorations for valor. One could hardly deny those rumors after examining the division's crop of medals in the aftermath of the historic Omaha Beach invasion. Compared to the 1st Infantry Division's three Medals of Honor and fifty-three Distinguished Service Crosses on D-Day, the 29th Division's twenty-seven DSCs—and no Medals of Honor at all—seemed paltry in comparison, despite the undeniable detail that both divisions' D-Day combat experiences were virtually identical, and both suffered a nearly equivalent number of casualties.

The real heroes of the 29th Division may have gotten a raw deal in the past—but not this time. Sergeant Hallman had personally shattered an enemy defensive line at Ilioc farm that had successfully resisted all American attempts to break it in four solid days of brutal fighting. Purnell and Gerhardt were about to reap huge benefits from that accomplishment, and both resolved to honor Hallman for it. That effort would take months, and unfortunately, by the time the U.S. Army, by General Order 31 on April 17, 1945, granted S/Sgt. Sherwood H. Hallman of Company F, 175th Infantry, the 29th Division's first World War II Medal of Honor, Hallman was dead. In fact, he never even knew of the paperwork submitted on his behalf because he was killed on September 14—three days after his exploit at Ilioc. (A second 29er, T/Sgt. Frank Peregory of the 116th Infantry, would posthumously receive a Medal of Honor as a consequence of his valor in Normandy on June 8, 1944, but the U.S. Army did not grant that decoration until May 30, 1945.)

It would be up to historians to analyze Hallman's actions in detail and place them within the larger context of the 29th Division's effort to take Brest, but because of the proverbial fog of war, that effort would take years. In the meantime Hallman's Medal of Honor citation would summarize the significance of his deed. When that citation was written in 1945, however, the fog had not yet dissipated, which explains why the citation erroneously specifies September 13, 1944, as the date of Hallman's gallant act rather than the actual day of September 11.

From Omaha Beach to Brest, the U.S. Army had recognized hundreds of 29ers—both living and dead—as heroes. Sergeant Hallman, of course, was special, but in a sense he embodied the spirit of all those men— professional soldiers, part-time guardsmen, volunteers, and draftees—who had come together in that unique outfit known as the 29th Infantry Division to establish the truth to a cynical enemy that Americans were not the pushovers Hitler had suggested.

If Hitler and his Nazis still believed that American society could not produce adept warriors, all they had to do to realize their misjudgment was to reflect upon Sherwood Hallman's journey from peace to war, from "Sherry's Modern Market" in Spring City, Pennsylvania, to Ilioc farm in Brittany, France.

3. FROM SUGARLOAF TO MONTBAREY

By early evening of September 11, it seemed as if Sergeant Hallman had either killed or captured every German defender on Company F's front. If any enemy soldier had survived, he had taken off for the rear hours ago. Colonel Purnell's boast to Witte had been valid: The 175th Infantry had indeed "busted through." According to Gerhardt, now was the moment to exploit that dramatic success, and presently, Purnell—urged on by an agitated division commander—roused his men and, in the early hours of September 12, ordered them to move ahead with the exhausted but spiritually uplifted 2nd Battalion in the lead. The 29ers were always wary of intricate maneuvers at night, but this time they had little reason to fret. Facing almost no opposition they pushed forward directly eastward for more than a mile, and shortly after dawn reached a point a few hundred yards past the tiny farm hamlet of l'Arc'hantel.

The leading GI scouts peered ahead directly into the hazy light of the low morning sun, which brightened by the minute as it ascended from the horizon in the east. They looked across green pastures, filled with their elongated, early-morning shadows, and noticed at once that something was different. For soldiers whose experience of war had been limited to the claustrophobic Norman and Breton hedgerow country, the terrain ahead was enough to take their breath away. Directly to their front, a half mile distant, stood a small, old-fashioned earthen fort known as Keranroux, but it was not the fort itself that was troubling. According to a 175th action report,

> Between the 2nd Battalion's position and the fort lay a stretch of terrain approximately 800 yards in width, completely clear of trees and brush, and open to enemy observation from northeast and south. Halfway to the fort an antitank ditch, ten feet wide at the top, ten feet in depth, narrowing to four feet in width at the bottom, completely surrounded the fort. East of the tank ditch

were several concrete pillboxes surrounded by defensive wire. Mines which could be electrically detonated by remote control [and] remote-controlled miniature "pig tanks" dominated every approach to the fort. Dug-in positions beyond the tank ditch were connected by trenches five- to six-feet deep, partially covered and well-camouflaged.

Normally, attacking such a position would have been suicidal. But the top brass had hinted that the Germans were beaten, and it was better for the 29ers to move ahead now rather then giving the enemy a chance to reorganize its defenses. If the Germans offered resistance at Keranroux, Gerhardt growled that the men must "wade right through it," and at about noon he angrily radioed Purnell: "You are going to stay in there until you get down in!" But figuring out how to do it would be tough, for as Company F's Lieutenant Hobbs recalled, "There was no knowledge of the strength of the defense."

At 3:30 P.M., Company F dispatched a twelve-man patrol, which managed to temporarily seize a German pillbox near the fort and take twelve Germans captive. Armed with evidence that a passage across the open ground in daylight was feasible, the 2nd Battalion dashed forward into the open fields in front of Keranroux around 5:30 P.M., and Hobbs's Company F made it into the antitank ditch with no trouble. But there was plenty of trouble after that: The ditch seemed like a perfect place to take cover, but unfortunately every inch of it had been registered by German mortarmen, who promptly demonstrated how proficiently they could use their lethal high-angle weapons against American troops who had made the mistake of bunching up. Purnell understated the case when at 7:32 P.M. he radioed Gerhardt: "White [the 2nd Battalion's codename] is stuck for the moment." Under such an intense barrage it seemed impossible to go forward—or backward—but at nightfall the company managed to return to its starting point, minus about a dozen men. Purnell would have to wait until morning to have another crack at Keranroux.

Late that night Hobbs returned to the antitank ditch when he ascertained that one of his men, whose name he could not recall, was missing. "I went with three of his buddies to search the area where they knew he had been," he remembered. "We could not use a light and went through a barbed-wire entanglement, crawling in the mud, until our low shouts reached him. With our raincoats and rifles a litter was made, and we got him back to company headquarters. It was a blow to learn the next morning that he had died."

About one-half mile northeast of Fort Keranroux stood a great green-grass mound of earth, so prominent that no 29er on the 175th Infantry's front could fail to notice it. The closer the GIs approached, the more disquieting it became, for the mound dwarfed everything in the vicinity—a detail the shrewd enemy would surely exploit to the fullest. It rose so abruptly from the surrounding countryside that the 29ers nicknamed it "Sugarloaf Hill" after the old-fashioned cones of concentrated sugar that used to grace American dinner tables. That the mound was man-made was obvious, and that impression was corroborated when the 29ers learned that prior to the war the French Navy had piled that immense mass of earth at the far end of a 1,000-yard firing range as a backstop, or "butts," for target practice. Indeed, some 29ers would always remember that oppressive mound as "The Naval Butts."

The Germans, of course, had no desire to use the Butts for target practice. Rather, it made a perfect position for observers to adjust deadly artillery and mortar fire on American positions, although by this point in the campaign Ramcke had to admit that his indirect fire ammunition had dwindled almost to nothing. Much more alarming to the 29ers was the evident detail that the Germans had tunneled into the hill like moles to create a sheltered military facility that would in all likelihood be impervious to American fire. High on the mound's western slope—the side facing the 175th Infantry—the enemy had excavated individual firing positions, emplacements for 40mm antiaircraft guns, and concrete observation posts and shelters. An alarmed Purnell remarked that "the mound is a veritable fortress—on the northeast corner is a concrete and steel observation post with a wonderful view. In back of that is a radio room and an arsenal." The mound complex was surrounded by barbed wire, which enclosed communications trenches, pillboxes, and even an underground hospital. To members of the 175th Infantry who had already been drained by the nearly constant fighting at Hill 103 and Ilioc, Sugarloaf Hill seemed an objective that would make the others appear puny in comparison.

A glance at the map yielded a clear appreciation of the hill's significance. A 175th action report defined it as "one of the key points of the defenses," indicating that if Brest was to be liberated, the mound's German garrison would have to be neutralized in the next few days, either by direct frontal attack or by an encirclement that would force the enemy's surrender. That difficult task fell to the 175th's 1st Battalion under Roger Whiteford, a man whose supposed tardiness on the morning of September 12 had provoked Gerhardt's ire.

What Whiteford's men were able to accomplish by nightfall that day, however, would improve the general's mood considerably. Starting at about 11 A.M., the 1st Battalion jumped off and achieved remarkable momentum, progressing eastward more than two miles from Keriel farm all the way to Sugarloaf's outer defenses—one of the most lengthy and rapid advances made by a 29th Division unit during the entire Brest campaign. Whiteford was no longer in the doghouse, a point Gerhardt made clear when he announced early on September 13, "We had a very fine day yesterday—although it didn't look so good in the morning."

What the general failed to note was that it hadn't looked so good yesterday evening either. Late on September 12, on Whiteford's right flank, Bowen's 2nd Battalion had run into the proverbial wall in the open fields and antitank ditch in front of Fort Keranroux and was lucky to extricate itself from a predicament that could have degenerated into disaster. Similarly, Whiteford's men, energized by their unanticipated two-mile advance that afternoon, came to an abrupt halt in front of Sugarloaf Hill that night when the Germans disclosed that they were not yet beaten—a detail that became clear to Gerhardt when someone from Purnell's command post radioed him to report, "Our Red [1st] Battalion has received a hell of a plastering and seems to be in a pretty hot spot unless the fort to our front [Sugarloaf Hill] is knocked out."

To the 29ers it seemed as if some anonymous German commander, probably Ramcke himself, had drawn an imaginary line from Sugarloaf down to Keranroux and on to Montbarey, and pronounced to his men a Germanic variant of Marshal Pétain's famous motto at Verdun: "They shall not pass." From the German perspective there was no alternative: if the 29th Division did indeed pass that line, as it seemed ready to do late on September 12, the Americans could be marching into the streets of Brest in a matter of hours. The 29th Division had smashed into the enemy's last-ditch line of defense, and Gerhardt knew it. That night he radioed Purnell to "fold up at your discretion.... We'll prepare to go at 1000 in the morning [September 13]."

Keranroux and Sugarloaf would surely be tough to capture, but Fort Montbarey would be the toughest of all. That eighteenth-century French fort lay just north of the main east-west road leading into Brest, the N789, and was situated just two miles west of the city walls. Montbarey featured a sturdy masonry wall backed up by a massive earthen embankment forty feet thick, which even the most powerful American weapons could not penetrate. Surrounded by a moat fifteen feet deep and forty feet wide, entrance into the fort was limited to the main gate and a few nearly inaccessible tunnels.

To the 29ers, however, far more unsettling than the fort itself were the defenses encircling it. In truth, the GIs would get nowhere near Montbarey unless they could figure out a way to penetrate an antitank ditch, ten feet deep and thirteen feet wide, lined by a continuous band of barbed wire and fronted by a particularly deadly minefield, 200 yards in width, including buried naval shells so large they could blow a man to smithereens and obliterate a tank all at once. The typical assortment of enemy pillboxes and secreted machine-gun positions, all of which were connected by deep communications trenches, lay scattered throughout the fort's environs. As usual, the U.S. Army Air Force's concentrated efforts to blast the enemy out of Montbarey by means of bombing alone had been impressive—but had not worked. Even so, the bombing had stupefied those Germans defenders who still managed to man the defenses and reduced the area surrounding the fort into a moonscape.

Montbarey fell within the zone of Smith's 115th Infantry, and for a few hours late on September 12, it seemed to Smith and Gerhardt as if the regiment had seized it in one determined lightning stroke. Millholland's 3rd Battalion had traversed the antitank ditch at 11:30 A.M. with little difficulty and promptly pressed on toward the fort. Now the 29ers had to traverse the lethal minefield, but thanks to one courageous 29er, that dilemma was solved in a hurry. According to *Baltimore News-Post* reporter Lou Azrael, Pvt. Herman Kahn, a native of Germany whose family had emigrated to New York before the war, "captured thirty German prisoners [who] showed him the location of the mines. Tape was stretched intricately across the field, showing the safe path."

By 12:15 German resistance had increased appreciably, and across the lurid landscape the battle swayed back and forth, marked by dozens of disconnected combats at deadly point-blank range, each of which involved just a few men on each side. Eruptions of German machine-gun fire, characterized by its distinctive ripping-bedsheet sound, were answered by the clatter of the 29ers' M-1s and BARs. An astute listener could always tell when the antagonists had come to close range because the shooting would be abruptly replaced by the concussive reverberation of grenades.

For a time it was hard to tell which side was winning, but if victory would be determined by who held Fort Montbarey at nightfall, apparently it was the Americans. Somehow or other, Capt. Earl Tweed's Company L had men within rifle-shot range of Montbarey by mid-afternoon, an event that induced Smith to reinforce that unexpected success by committing Glover Johns's 1st Battalion to the fight. Soon men of the 115th Infantry were swarming around the fort—Millholland's 3rd Battalion on the south, Johns's 1st to the north. At 7:41 P.M., Maj. William Bruning, the 115th's operations officer, reported to the 29th Division's war room the astonishing news: "Company L is in the fort."

If true, Bruning's report would mean that the road to Brest was wide open. Many 29ers, however, later came to believe that his report was untrue. Major Tom Dallas, the 116th Infantry commander whose 1st Battalion would soon take over the effort to seize Montbarey, observed: "When we finally blew the side of the fort open [on September 16], we were completely convinced that no other Americans had been in there except two wounded 115th men who had been shot in the outer defense positions and carried in there by the Germans. The fort itself had been occupied by the Germans all the time."

The mystery intensified when in 1945 the 115th Infantry's official history noted that Company L "pushed on into the fort, where well over one hundred prisoners were taken." One member of a Company M machine-gun team attached to Company L, S/Sgt. Angus Morrison, recalled: "Everything went smoothly until we reached and secured the fort. Then all hell seemed to break loose. . . . The Jerries tried to sneak up and occupy our positions. . . . A volunteer patrol made up of men from Company M went into the fort to try to clear it out. The patrol consisted of Lt. Austin Harris, T/Sgt. Ambers Glidewell, Cpl. John Mair, PFC Robert Cox, and myself. All of the men lost their lives except Cox and myself."

Despite Dallas's assertion, in all probability Millholland's battalion did indeed penetrate into Montbarey, but definitive historical evidence proves that it did not have the muscle to secure it and was ultimately driven out, since passages in the regimental journal on the night of September 12 repeatedly refer to "Jerries" inside the fort. One notation observed, "Neither [the 115th nor the Germans] can get enough troops into the fort to control the situation." In fact it would be four more days before those stubborn "Jerries" were kicked out for good.

Even if the 115th Infantry did not control Montbarey, however, the onslaught by Johns's and Millholland's men had placed the Germans in a predicament from which it would be difficult to recover. The 29ers had penetrated the enemy's mine, wire, and antitank barriers with comparative ease, and with that accomplishment the German defenses were swiftly thrown into disarray. On September 12 clear proof of that fact arrived at Smith's command post in the form of hordes of German prisoners.

One machine gunner from Company H, S/Sgt. Donald Van Roosen, was responsible for one of the largest hauls of Germans that day, an exploit that came about almost by accident. When the 3rd Battalion passed through Company H's lines that morning, Van Roosen met two of his friends, T/Sgt. Ambers Glidewell and Cpl. John Mair of Company M. He accompanied the two men forward, taking advantage of a rare period of frontline tranquility to chat. After an enjoyable respite that lasted only a few minutes, Van Roosen wished them luck and turned back toward his company's bivouac area. He had no idea that in an hour or so both Glidewell and Mair would die at Montbarey.

Van Roosen and another 29er, armed with a Browning Automatic Rifle, decided to explore their surroundings, a judgment that promptly led to some amazing adventures. "We went around the end of a [hedgerow] and came upon a German soldier who was shaving on the top step of a stairway leading down to a bunker," Van Roosen recalled.

> Leaving the BAR man to guard the entrance [and the German soldier], I went below into a room filled with armed men. Nothing works like a good bluff, so I pretended I was backed up by a large force . . . and demanded [in German] that everyone get their belongings, leave their weapons, and go outside. There was no hesitation, and some 60 or 70 men filed out. We pointed them to where our battalion was halted, and they marched away into captivity. Encouraged by our success, the two of us continued to look for other bunkers and found three more—where the results were the same.

Van Roosen, who in the next month would be granted a battlefield commission as a second lieutenant, had demonstrated to Gerhardt and Smith that the Germans' fierce resolution to hold Brest was clearly sagging. (At Brest, however, the fortunes of war could turn in a hurry, and Van Roosen himself would become a prisoner two days later.)

While attached to the 115th's 3rd Battalion in the front lines, *Baltimore Sun* reporter Holbrook Bradley noticed more signs of German spiritual collapse: "There was a continuous rustle overhead of our artillery shells as we followed a trail along a telephone line," Bradley wrote.

> There was also a continuous thudding as these shells landed up ahead and filled the air with dirt and flying debris. . . . Then two GIs appeared herding ten dirty, grimy and apparently dazed

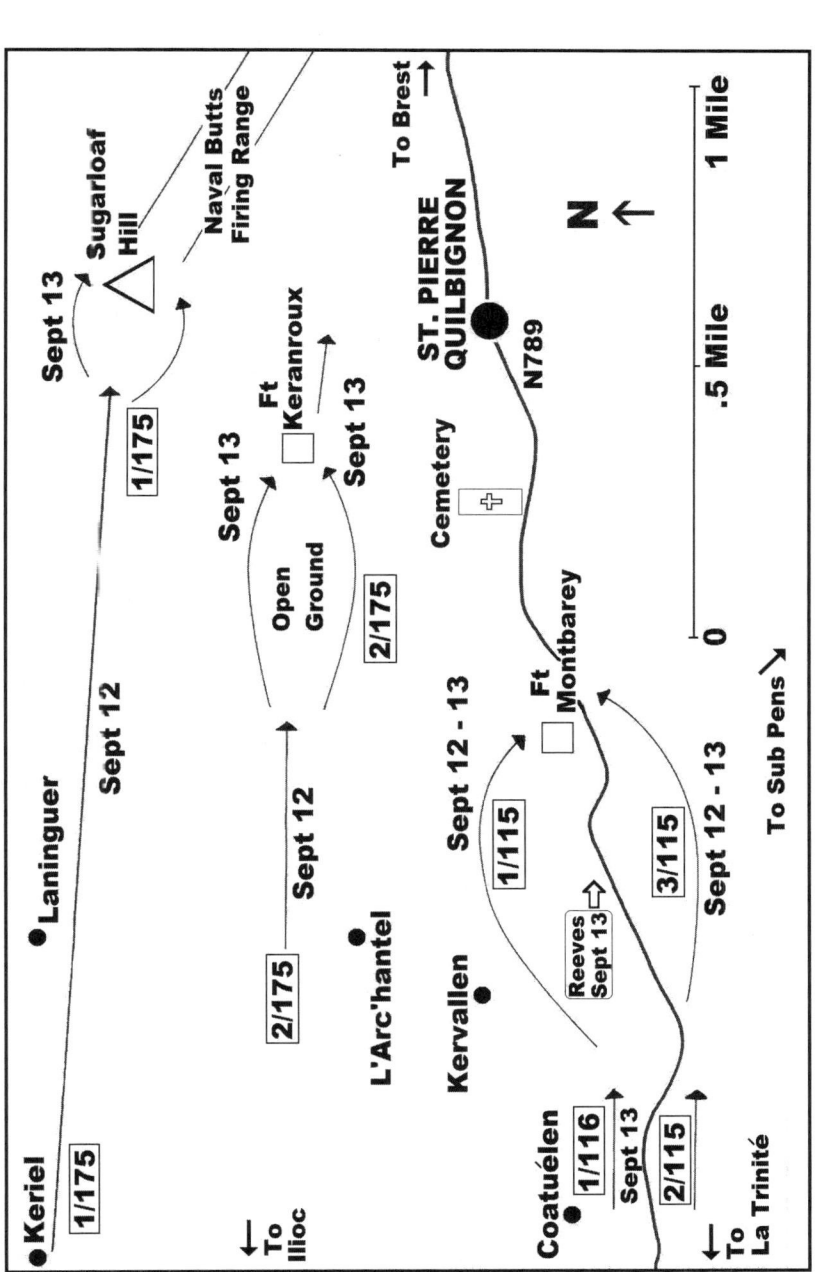

115th and 175th Infantry: September 12–13, 1944

Heinies up the path. They had taken them as they stepped out of a hedge, and none of them seemed sad about being captured. [Later] the leader of our party spotted a German lying in a hole in front of us. He had just finished saying the Heinie was dead when he raised up, and another German appeared from somewhere behind him. We backed off, expecting a hand grenade at least, but none followed, and [David] Scherman [a *Life* magazine photographer] yelled in German for the Germans to come out with their hands up. Just to back him up, our guides fired a couple shots up the trail, and more Germans came running down the path waving a white flag and clasping their hands over their heads.

September 13, 1944, promised to be a historic day in divisional history because that morning the 29th Division would, as Gerhardt used to say, "throw the book at them." The attack was supposed to begin at 10 A.M., but a highly unusual event on the 115th Infantry's front at Fort Montbarey postponed the jumpoff by thirty minutes to 10:30. Apparently, Middleton had been thoroughly impressed by the astonishing number of enemy troops who had recently fallen into American hands, and he proposed to send a delegation into Brest to meet with Ramcke and appeal for his surrender. Those soldiers at VIII Corps headquarters responsible for practicing psychological warfare upon the enemy had recently been bombarding Brest with leaflets urging the Germans to give up, and Middleton surmised that those leaflets were finally beginning to work. One of the most persuasive read, in German: "Your loved ones can receive either of two messages concerning you: Message 1 is a death notice. You know best how this will affect your family. . . . Message 2, delivered through the Red Cross, would tell your family that you are a prisoner of war, but are safe. You know that this is the only way you can get out of the fortress alive and go back to your family."

On September 12, Middleton had composed a blunt letter to his opposite number in Brest and entrusted his chief intelligence officer, Col. Andrew Reeves, with the duty of delivering it the next morning into Ramcke's hands. Middleton and Ramcke were only nine months apart in age, and both had commenced their long careers as professional military men before World War I, when they were both teens. Accordingly, Middleton phrased his letter in the type of language that he sensed a fellow soldier would appreciate. "There comes a time in war when the situation reaches a point where a commander is no longer justified in expending the lives and destroying the health of the men who have bravely carried out his orders in combat," Middleton wrote. "Your men have fought well. Approximately 16,000 of them from this area are now prisoners of war.... I am calling upon you, as one professional soldier to another, to cease the struggle now in progress.... I trust, as a professional soldier who has served well and has already fulfilled his obligation, you will give this request your favorable consideration."

At 8:15 A.M. on September 13 the embattled 29ers on the Montbarey front, who according to the war room journal had "been fighting all night down there," were greeted by the extraordinary sight of a U.S. Army sedan hoisting a large white flag driving eastward down the N789 road straight toward Brest. The vehicle's occupants included the conveyor of Middleton's solemn dispatch to Ramcke, Colonel Reeves, as well as several aides, including an interpreter. Passing through the 29th Division's many frontline checkpoints was slow, and the journey became even more protracted when Reeves had to wait for a U.S. Army sound truck to pave the way, blaring out appeals in German for the enemy to hold its fire as his automobile passed into and beyond no-man's-land.

Reeves and his comrades surely hoped the enemy would practice strict fire discipline, for when their vehicle arrived at the front, wary 29th Division riflemen warned them that even the slightest hint of American movement on or near the N789 could trigger a ferocious German fusillade. The brutal effect of that kind of concentrated firepower on an unarmored staff car filled with several helpless passengers was easy to envisage. Moreover, regardless of Ramcke's response, Reeves's later return to American lines, where any trigger-happy 29er could mistakenly perceive his mission as an insidious Nazi trick, could be equally perilous.

As a consequence of the apparently indiscriminate violence of the front lines, it was hard to believe that Middleton's message would ever reach Ramcke, but somehow or other it did. In fact, a relieved Reeves later reported that throughout his mission he "was only fired on once"—although he did not specify by whom. When he passed beyond the German front lines, some skeptical enemy paratroopers, just as tired and grimy as their 29th Division counterparts, provided a frosty but correct reception and forwarded him to a rear-area command post. There, he would have to wait while a German courier conveyed Middleton's letter to Ramcke's headquarters.

Reeves lingered for several hours for Ramcke's reply, and during that interval, according to Reeves, the Americans enjoyed "a very fine reception and had a dinner at a battalion command post about 500 yards in rear of the lines. The dinner also included drinks." That happy interlude, however, came to an abrupt end at 3:30 P.M., when a German courier arrived, saluted Reeves, and handed him Ramcke's blunt reply. Its simple words surprised neither Reeves nor any other American soldier at Brest—from Middleton down to the youngest private. If Middleton's appeal for Ramcke's surrender was based on the shared credo of military men, in turn Middleton must surely understand Ramcke's response.

It declared: "General: I must decline your proposal."

4. TEAR THEM APART

Ramcke had done his duty, and now it was Middleton's turn to do his. Middleton had offered his opponent what he perceived as an honorable end, but now could extend to him only fury, an attitude he made clear in a circular issued to all American units participating in the Brest effort. "General Ramcke has been given an opportunity to surrender," he pronounced. "Since he has declined what is believed to be a humane and reasonable request, it now remains for VIII Corps to make him sorry for his refusal. Therefore, I ask the combat soldiers of this command to enter the fray with renewed vigor. Let's take them apart and get the job finished."

Now that Gerhardt's boss had clarified that the siege of Brest would end not with the stroke of a pen, but by the mighty force of American arms—just as Gerhardt had always suspected—his 29ers must now execute Middleton's directive. "They declined the offer—so tear them apart!" Middleton radioed to Gerhardt at 5:45 P.M. on September 13. "Ramcke said he was going to fight until the last paratrooper was killed, in honor of the German government. So go in there and give them the works!"

Gerhardt replied, "Yes, sir," but that job would not be easy. Furthermore, by this stage of the Brittany campaign, Gerhardt had become highly disillusioned with his boss, Middleton, an attitude that arose as the result of intemperate words, both written and verbal, the VIII Corps commander had used to describe to his superiors the fighting qualities of his infantrymen. It was bad enough that a September 1 letter from Middleton to Omar Bradley had complained that one of the reasons Brest was not yet in American hands was because the troops Bradley had assigned to VIII Corps were "none too good." But most offensive of all to Gerhardt had been an unannounced visit Middleton had paid to the 115th Infantry's command post on September 11, when Colonel Smith was in the middle of managing a complex and deadly fight at Coatuélen. Middleton's trip had not been cleared through Gerhardt's headquarters, and when Gerhardt found out about it, he was livid.

Nevertheless, the U.S. Army's code of behavior meant that Gerhardt had to swallow his pride. At 7 P.M. on September 11, Middleton telephoned the 29th Division's war room about his visit to the 115th, and an irritated Gerhardt had to listen respectfully to his boss's observations: "I told Smith if he would get on that 90 grid line [a longitudinal line on a U.S. Army map, just short of Fort Montbarey], I would give him six good cigars. Looks like I might have to smoke them myself! . . . I told the boys if they put that artillery on them and then went in, they could take them. Looks like some of the boys are hiding behind the hedgerows. I was down there, and I could see it."

From Gerhardt's perspective those caustic remarks represented a blatant example of VIII Corps interference in tactical matters, which according to standard U.S. Army practices, should not have been the focus of Middleton's attention, or at the very least should have been discussed with Gerhardt rather than directly with Smith. Later that evening Gerhardt complained to Smith, "I understand the corps commander was down there this afternoon. Why didn't you call me?" Smith's reply only elevated Gerhardt's anger: "I thought you gave him our location and he came from [29th Division headquarters]."

"His conversation left me with the impression that he didn't think much of us," Gerhardt responded. "He said he could see our boys behind the hedgerows," but Smith contradicted that assertion: "He couldn't see them from here, for they were moving."

Middleton's meddling in internal 29th Division affairs extended to one of Gerhardt's pet projects, a scheme that Uncle Charlie had only recently implemented to the great benefit of the division's combat efficiency. In Normandy, Gerhardt had seen firsthand how wasteful and heartless the U.S. Army's replacement policy could be, and therefore, at the start of the Brest campaign, he had instituted a division-wide policy that green infantry replacements must not be thrown into the front lines arbitrarily. Rather, they must be assigned to an infantry battalion currently out of the front lines for a rest period of at least three days. The replacements would then have a chance to familiarize themselves with their new unit, get to know their leaders, and, most important, practice with their weapons.

Gerhardt's idea made perfect sense and helped to rectify a problem that had threatened to erode the 29th Division's renowned combat skills. One day, however, Middleton heard the incessant *pop-pop-pop* of M-1 Garands on a rear-area rifle range, and he inquired about it. When he learned that it was one of Gerhardt's reserve battalions practicing its marksmanship, Middleton bluntly expressed his disapproval. According to his biographer, "[Middleton] told Gerhardt to have his men get back into the siege line and do the remainder of their practice shooting on the Germans." An appalled Gerhardt, however, somehow managed to ignore that directive for the rest of the Brest campaign.

On September 13, 1944, the 175th Infantry proceeded to "tear the enemy apart," just as Middleton's orders prescribed. That remarkable accomplishment would soon earn the 2nd Battalion the celebrated French Croix de Guerre with Silver-Gilt Star, and ever since, the 175th's regimental colors have been adorned by a red-and-green battle streamer embroidered with the name that had already become a part of 29th Division history: "Brest." But that morning the men of the 2nd Battalion were so weary that it was hard to believe they could accomplish anything at all. Rifle companies were at about one-third authorized strength, and given Company F's fresh memory of being caught by German mortars in Fort Keranroux's antitank ditch the previous day, one sensed that those companies would soon be reduced to close to zero if the tempo of operations did not slow down.

At dawn on September 13, company commanders were called to the 2nd Battalion's command post to discuss their upcoming attack on Keranroux with Maj. Claude Melancon, the battalion's executive officer. Lieutenant Hobbs of Company F recalled,

> With the foolish attempt to take the fort the previous afternoon, I asked Melancon what kind of artillery preparation and support we would have. He said he had been told that it would be up to the battalion to prepare for the attack with its own smoke and mortar fire. Both Captain Stevens and I were bitterly critical. [Hobbs apparently was referring to Capt. Joseph Stewart, Company E's CO.] [Stewart] said it was stupid and would be a crime to have men killed without better support. . . . Melancon picked up the telephone and asked to speak directly with the regimental commander, Colonel Purnell. He told Purnell he would refuse an order of attack without artillery preparation. He said, "Have me court-martialed if you will—but you know that I'm right."

Purnell did not need any prodding. He requested and promptly received from Gerhardt fire support at a far greater level than the 29th Division had been able to achieve so far in the Brest campaign. So much for the ammunition shortage: Starting at about noon and lasting for about two hours, dozens of American howitzers and mortars bombarded Keranroux non-stop, yielding shell craters that reporter Holbrook Bradley observed "were deep enough to hide a one-room house." For the 2nd Battalion infantrymen in the front lines, it was invigorating to feel the deep percussive thud of their own howitzers firing behind their lines with an intensity they had not experienced since Normandy. Even better was the whistle of friendly shells overhead and, soon thereafter, more thuds as those shells impacted on the enemy lines.

At about 1:45 P.M., the heavy 4.2-inch mortars of Company A, 86th Chemical Mortar Battalion, laid down an intense barrage of smoke shells only seventy-five yards in front of the 2nd Battalion's forward positions. The mortarmen fired nearly continuously for an hour to create a smoke screen sufficiently thick to obscure the enemy's vision and conceal the impending attack, and thanks to a favorable wind, that effort paid off handsomely. Once the mortar fire lifted, the battle's outcome was decided remarkably quickly. As they moved their men across the open ground surrounding the fort, Hobbs and Stewart observed that they "received only a light flurry of small-arms fire, and in about fifteen minutes [just before 3 P.M.] were inside the fort." Company G, led by 1st Lt. Lawrence Maddox, swiftly moved up to and past Keranroux to exploit that amazing success. One notable feature of the 2nd Battalion's attack was the 29ers' use of bayonets, which most of the men had never before affixed to their rifles in battle. Thanks to the persistent clouds of smoke, the riflemen speedily learned that Germans could suddenly appear at alarmingly close ranges, and the men thought it would be best to have their bayonets ready—just in case.

Any 29er who survived the September 13 attack on Keranroux would never forget its surreal and hellish setting: the vaporous clouds of smoke that could suddenly envelop a comrade ten feet away, the shell-torn ground reminiscent of World War I, the grotesque corpses of friend and foe alike. According to a 2nd Battalion after-action report,

> The enemy, pinned down in their positions by the barrage and confused by the smoke, was completely surprised by the assault waves and surrendered in the face of grenades and the bayonet. Approximately 150 prisoners were taken initially. The battalion quickly overran the fort itself. Mop-up squads continued to take prisoners throughout the day, the advance elements continuing to a position 200 yards beyond the fort, where they reorganized and dug in to defend against a possible counterattack.

News-Post reporter Azrael witnessed that amazing assault and observed: "Through [the smoke] the American soldiers, with bayonets poised, went charging. They leaped into a six-foot ditch and scrambled up its slopes, shouting. The Germans, surprised by the direction of the attack, and unable to see any enemy, fired only a few scattered rifle shots before scurrying out. . . . Hundreds of bewildered Germans came rushing out to surrender."

The reassuring smoke may have shielded the 29ers from enemy fire, but it had done nothing to protect them from German mines, which the enemy had buried all over the approaches to Keranroux. To provide its infantrymen with the confidence they would need to traverse those deadly pastures, the 2nd Battalion requested support from the division's 121st Engineers, many of whose members had bravely gone forward before dawn into the fields with detectors and knives to sweep and probe for enemy mines. When their work was finished, they marked the safe paths prominently with white engineer tape. Reporter Bradley later moved through one of those lanes behind the attacking infantry, and he observed:

> The battlefield ahead of us seemed more like one of Cecil B. DeMille's movie sets than anything we've seen so far in France. . . . Fire from both sides cracked overhead. Through the smoke of artillery we could see a few barbed-wire entanglements, a couple of broken and battered trees. In an antitank ditch almost at the base of the fort was the crumpled body of a dead GI machine gunner, his face contorted and twisted. Across in a narrow ravine were four or five Heinies who had been killed. . . . So heavy was the destruction about the fort that it was impossible to trace its outlines until we had climbed on top of piles of dirt that once had been its ramparts.

Just a few days later, Purnell observed: "Fort Keranroux is nothing but a mass of rubble, destroyed buildings, equipment, and motor vehicles strewn over the entire area. Along one side of the fort is a large concrete pillbox and gun position, intact." An interrogated prisoner made a statement that when the fort was bombed, approximately thirty men ran to the lower floor of the fort and were buried when the bombs struck.

From a forward 175th Infantry command post, Gerhardt himself witnessed the 2nd Battalion's assault, and when it was over, the general's customary disparagement of his subordinates' abilities would abruptly evaporate, to be replaced by gushing words of praise and respect. At 5:12 P.M. he telephoned Purnell, "I've asked G-1 [Lt. Col. Cooper Rhodes] to give that battalion a unit citation. Very good. It looked fine—many congratulations!" Later, the general remarked: "It looked just like a movie!"

Even better from Gerhardt's perspective was the fact that he had personally escorted the U.S. Ninth Army's commander, Lt. Gen. William Simpson, to the forward command post to observe the 175th in action. A proud Gerhardt would recall that occasion in a 1964 letter to Simpson: "I met you first at Brest. You came to an observation post to watch the 175th Infantry attack and capture a field position. This they did, and I can see them now rounding up the prisoners in the smoke screen." Gerhardt's enduring displeasure with Middleton also emerged in this letter when he added somewhat caustically, "As I remember, General Middleton was there too, but he took little interest." Evidence from the 29th Division's war room transcripts, however, indicates that Middleton did not personally witness the 175th's exploit, as at 4:10 P.M. that day Gerhardt telephoned him at VIII Corps headquarters to declare: "We got the fort. It was really something watching them take it."

The 175th Infantry had captured Fort Keranroux and now stood only a mile and a half from the ancient city walls of Brest. Hobbs remembered the powerful satisfaction of the moment: "We spent the night in real comfort in the luxurious bunks in the fort—in greater security and comfort than we had enjoyed at any time since the beginning of the Brest campaign. I recall writing a letter home that evening." Hobbs did not realize that this was the last night he would experience as a frontline soldier in the 29th Division because the following day he would be wounded storming an enemy pillbox armed only with a pistol and spend the next fourteen months in the hospital, emerging with permanent disabilities.

The 29th Division, for a change, had carried out warfare according to the methods it had learned in training. Happily, the ammunition shortage was over for good, and the focused and intense firepower that could finally be unleashed upon the enemy had led directly to the highly successful result. Assuming the top brass would keep the 29th Division well supplied in the future, that notable success heralded better times. As a regimental report observed, "The action clearly demonstrated the complete effectiveness of properly coordinated supporting fires with the infantry attack; and the exceptional value of smoke-screening to confuse the enemy."

The Blue and Gray Division fought many actions on September 13, but none of them yielded as much satisfaction to Gerhardt as the success at Keranroux. Roger Whiteford's 1st Battalion, 175th Infantry, began that day just north of the fort, only 350 yards from the looming mass of Sugarloaf Hill, a place the enemy displayed every intention of holding to the last man. In fact, starting at about 7:30 that morning, the Germans sallied forth from the hill's many tunnels and dugouts and displayed some of their renowned "enthusiasm" against Whiteford's exhausted troops. The 29ers doggedly fought back against that counterattack for two hours, and when it was over a liaison officer with Whiteford nonchalantly reported to the war room: "The [1st Battalion] had a little activity this morning between 0730 and 0930, and they lost a little ground. But they picked it right up again." To the men who had to fight off that enemy assault, however, the battle was by no means that easy. Almost all available American artillery and air support had been directed against Keranroux rather than Sugarloaf Hill, and consequently, Whiteford's depleted battalion had to fight minus its normal sources of outside aid. Whiteford would have to wait until the next day to take on the hill, but with Fort Keranroux in American hands, that task would become appreciably easier.

About 1,200 yards southwest of Keranroux lay the even more formidable enemy bastion of Fort Montbarey, which Lou Smith's 115th Infantry had come tantalizingly close to capturing on the evening of September 12. But at dawn the next day the positions occupied by Smith's 1st and 3rd Battalions around the fort were so haphazard that perplexed 115th Infantry staff officers could hardly indicate with certainty on their situation maps where they were located. A hasty reorganization was obviously in order, but as the regimental history noted, "Effective regrouping proved impossible."

The 29ers were so close to Montbarey that Gerhardt momentarily expected to receive a report from Smith that the fort was in American hands. Even if he lacked the cohesive infantry strength to tip the balance, Smith hoped that sheer firepower in the form of air support would do the trick. At 1:45 P.M. on September 13, Maj. Harold Perkins, who had joined the Maryland National Guard's 1st Infantry as a private in 1925 and by September 1944 had climbed to the regiment's executive officer slot, radioed the war room and declared,

> "We would like to get a lot of air instead of the usual four planes. . . . [Maj. Glover] Johns [CO, 1st Battalion] called in and asked for some air, and he says that a massed concentration in front of them would be just the thing." Perkins' request, however, was turned down because, as an observer reported, "We have troops all around the fort, so we can't put anything heavy in there. It's really tough—and it's going to be rough to get out of it."

Just as Smith was pondering whether to press his attack on the fort with his meager force or to "get out of it" and let the fighter-bombers do their deadly work, the Germans intervened. For a few hours, determined enemy paratroopers swarmed around Montbarey, striving to shove Smith's

29ers back and buy time for the fort's garrison to prepare its defenses. The ensuing melee was particularly brutal, a consequence of the jumbled front lines and constrictive terrain, which triggered dozens of small clashes at ranges close enough to use hand grenades—and even bayonets. One such clash cost the life of Company A's commander, 1st Lt. William Todd, a native of Texas.

When darkness thankfully brought the bedlam to an end, Maj. Tom Dallas of the 116th Infantry, whose outfit would shortly relieve Johns's 1st Battalion in the Montbarey sector, observed that the 115th's forward positions "did not compose a line, but a pretzel—with organizations so badly twisted that a clean relief could not be accomplished." As the sun set on September 13, the only thing that mattered to Gerhardt was whether or not the Americans held Fort Montbarey. When he found out they did not, his only course of action was to order Smith to "button up" for the night and shove fresh units, including the 116th Infantry, into the breach the following morning.

For the 29th Division, September 13, 1944, had been a grueling day, one in which both the 115th and 175th Infantry Regiments suffered a casualty count exceeding any of their one-day totals since late August. The 115th lost seventy-one men; the 175th, ninety. In what was supposed to have been a comparatively easy campaign, the two outfits had already expended a combined total of 1,600 men, a strain they could not stand for much longer. The only way to end that suffering was to capture Brest posthaste.

According to Gerhardt, that grand finale was imminent—and it was long overdue.

SIX

They Also Served

1. LE CONQUET INTERLUDE
No American soldier could hope to rise to the exalted rank of general officer without mastering the many dense field manuals and challenging war college courses the U.S. Army offered to its future combat leaders. However, one element of the siege of Brest that General Gerhardt could never have learned to deal with by reading the impenetrable Field Manual 100-5 (Operations) or sitting in a classroom at Leavenworth was the curious military situation he faced in late August 1944 in the Le Conquet peninsula, about a dozen miles west of Brest at the far western tip of Brittany. Much to Gerhardt's surprise, the VIII Corps' swift maneuver to encircle the enemy's Brest garrison had cut off close to 2,000 enemy troops in and near Le Conquet under the command of Lt. Col. Martin Fürst. Since all evidence the U.S. Army had gained so far in World War II about German soldiers indicated that they would not yield unless the Americans pummeled them into oblivion, Gerhardt quickly grasped that the 29th Division would have to fight two entirely different wars at Brest. First, as per Middleton's orders, the 29ers would have to attack Brest proper; second, somehow or other they would have to deal with a substantial body of enemy troops behind their lines.

No war college curriculum could have prepared a future U.S. Army division commander how to wage two separate wars simultaneously, with two distinct lines of American troops fighting back-to-back—one facing east, the other west. That was precisely the situation portrayed by Gerhardt's war room map on August 29, as the 29th Division attempted to attack eastward to seize Brest, while the improvised outfit known as "Task Force Sugar," under the command of Lt. Col. Arthur Sheppe, endeavored to deal with Fürst's Germans in Le Conquet. The solution to that predicament was apparently straightforward: As Brest was by far the more important objective, all Sheppe had to do was contain the enemy's Le Conquet garrison, and eventually, it would wither and die like a plant deprived of water.

But Gerhardt discovered that this scheme could not work. The Germans were present in Le Conquet in much higher numbers than he originally thought; even worse, their formidable Graf Spee Battery just outside the village of Lochrist, consisting of four 11-inch naval guns fixed in massive concrete casemates, was regularly firing with deadly effect into the rear of the 29th Division's main battle line. The Americans' attempt to neutralize that battery by air bombardment and the salvos of a Royal Navy battleship had so far failed, and as the 29ers had learned time and again in Normandy, infantrymen must therefore undertake a job the navy and air force could not fulfill.

It took Colonel Sheppe only a day or two to learn that his Task Force Sugar, as Gerhardt had originally envisioned it, was not nearly strong enough to do the job. By August 29, parts of Lt. Col. James Rudder's 2nd Ranger Battalion had reached the Atlantic coast on the far western tip of Brittany and, on that and the following day, proceeded to capture or neutralize a few scattered German forts on the coastline, but the main enemy enclave in the Le Conquet peninsula, which included the fearsome Graf Spee Battery, remained intact. Obviously, Fürst was resolved to fight. Sheppe managed to seal off the roads leading to Le Conquet, but he was uncertain about what to do next.

The Graf Spee Battery's gigantic shells greatly annoyed Gerhardt, and that annoyance grew appreciably when some of those shells landed with terrifying effect near the 29th Division's war room. Gerhardt determined to solve the Le Conquet problem with all possible speed, and therefore, at 10:30 A.M. on August 28, he appointed an officer more senior to Sheppe, Col. Edward McDaniel, as commander of Task Force Sugar, although Sheppe stayed on as McDaniel's executive officer. McDaniel currently held the lofty post of 29th Division chief of staff, and many staff officers whispered that without him, Gerhardt's sometimes unrealistic schemes could not be carried out with the energy and success for which the 29th Division was renowned. McDaniel's job, however, entailed supervision of rear-area staff officers rather than frontline combat soldiers, and accordingly, his job change promised to be abrupt.

The forty-year-old Alabamian was the perfect man for the job. A member of the Class of 1926 at the U.S. Military Academy, McDaniel was highly respected within the division for his intellect, reliability, and unflappable demeanor. Prior to his overseas deployment, he had served at Washington's new Pentagon building on the War Department staff and had played a cursory role in the design of a new top-secret plan known as "Overlord" in the summer of 1943. Gen. George C. Marshall, the U.S. Army Chief of Staff, thought highly enough of McDaniel to grant him the new and highly valued decoration known as the Legion of Merit. McDaniel, however, yearned for an active command role in an overseas theater, and soon, with Marshall's blessing, he found himself a key member of the 29th Division, with which he would eventually gain a second Legion of Merit—and, later, two Silver Stars.

In the last days of August 1944, McDaniel's highest priority was to figure out where the Germans holding out in Le Conquet were situated and to determine if Task Force Sugar had sufficient manpower to overcome them by direct attack. Gerhardt, however, desired immediate results, and he goaded McDaniel repeatedly to attack the enemy promptly, wherever resistance was encountered, no matter what the odds. On August 28, the general even hatched a scheme in which some of Rudder's rangers would be loaded into boats manned by 29th Division engineers for an amphibious end run around the enemy's Le Conquet strongpoints. As a highly qualified divisional chief of staff, however, McDaniel was a methodical planner who vigilantly weighed risks against potential gains, and he resisted his boss's plan because, as he bluntly stated to Gerhardt, it posed "unreasonable dangers." Lesser men trembled at the prospect of contradicting the boss, but when McDaniel pointed out that "the entire coast is mined," Gerhardt had to admit that he had a point. Even so, Gerhardt wanted the Le Conquet quandary solved in a hurry, and on the morning of August 29, he growled to McDaniel: "Stop fooling around down there and do some fighting and get going!"

The U.S. Army was renowned for its flexibility, and its readiness to create ad hoc task forces as a military situation demanded demonstrated that point. A vexed McDaniel, however, would soon learn that his Task Force Sugar had been an entirely irrational creation. Above all, it was obviously too small for the job at hand. With no more than 1,300 GIs on its rolls—only a small minority of whom were 29th Division personnel—it was little larger than an infantry battalion. Furthermore, the task force was extraordinarily diverse: Most of its non–29th Division units, such as Rudder's 2nd Ranger Battalion, were used to operating independently, outside the normal chain of command of an infantry division, and McDaniel soon discovered the unfortunate truth that under such a hazy command arrangement, his ability to fulfill Gerhardt's directives was problematic. In late August, for example, the general wanted McDaniel to work closely with 800 enthusiastic French partisans under "Commandant Louis," the leader of the local Resistance group, but in reality McDaniel had no command authority over those nonconformist fighters, who tended to adhere wholly to their own agenda. One 29th Division major assigned to Task Force Sugar recalled irritably that the French "caused us more trouble than they were worth."

McDaniel soon realized that if he were to accomplish his goals at Le Conquet, unfortunately he would have to fight outnumbered. With troops as proficient as the rangers and 29ers, that disadvantage could be overcome; even so, a desperate McDaniel obviously needed more men. On August 30, in a Task Force Sugar assembly area, he discovered Battery C, 480th Anti-Aircraft Artillery Battalion, commanded by a Captain Wickland. Although that outfit answered directly to the U.S. First Army and was not officially attached to McDaniel's command, he pressed Wickland's men into service and promptly deployed them in a blocking position astride a key road near the village of Tréméal. With his many rapid-fire 40mm guns and .50-caliber machine guns, Wickland had impressive firepower at his disposal, and since there was virtually no chance that German airplanes would show up in Brittany, McDaniel—with Gerhardt's approval—reasoned that those heavy weapons would significantly enhance the task force's ability to fulfill its mission.

For two days Battery C members fired their formidable weapons against enemy ground targets and conducted patrols. But on September 1 Wickland complained to General Middleton that McDaniel was employing his highly trained antiaircraft soldiers as ordinary infantry, a role for which they were not suited and, more important, that only the commanding general of First Army could approve. Wickland was entirely within his rights, but Gerhardt phoned Middleton in a huff and growled, "You better attach them [to me] or take them away." Middleton replied meekly: "I just found out they are not even attached to me." At 6:30 P.M. on September 1, Wickland's outfit was relieved by Middleton's order, although the battery was directed to "leave its forwardmost guns and personnel in position until they could be relieved by a platoon of rangers from Company A, which would reach the position prior to dark." At sunset, McDaniel visited

Wickland's position and, much to his disgust, "found that the forward guns had already been pulled out of position, leaving no one to hold the ground . . . as the rangers had not yet arrived at this location." The rangers pulled in by truck at 9 P.M., so the Germans' window of opportunity to exploit that slip-up was short, and fortunately, they never even noticed it. Still, Task Force Sugar's journal probably understated the case when it noted that "Colonel McDaniel was very much displeased by this action."

If Task Force Sugar had to carry out a vigorous offensive, Rudder's 2nd Ranger Battalion must bear the primary burden simply because it represented McDaniel's entire complement of experienced infantry as of August 29. On that date two ad hoc ranger groups, consisting of four companies from the 2nd Ranger Battalion under the command of Captains Otto Masny and Harold Slater—both veterans of the D-Day assault on Pointe du Hoc—moved westward out of the village of Locmaria-Plouzané. The two groups consisted of only about 250 men total, so Masny and Slater advanced cautiously, a prudent course of action given that they had not the slightest idea how many men the enemy had and where they would stand and fight. At about noon on the following day, August 30, Slater's group seized an important piece of terrain known as Hill 63, defined by an action report as "a very desirable position, as it was the highest ground overlooking the Le Conquet peninsula and served the main blacktop road [N789] leading from Le Conquet to Brest." From its summit the main object of Task Force Sugar, the enemy's Graf Spee Battery, was easily visible only three miles to the west.

The German response to the rangers' seizure of Hill 63, an intense and enduring artillery barrage, was entirely expected, and consequently, as McDaniel's report later noted somewhat sardonically, "The large amount of [German] artillery in the Le Conquet peninsula had definitely been established." Private Al Baer of Company D, 2nd Ranger Battalion, corroborated that point when he observed: "Hill 63 was a bitch. We didn't do much there—just sat on top of the hill and took some pretty rough shelling."

On the night of September 1, Gerhardt himself was the target of "some pretty rough shelling" when a few of the Graf Spee Battery's enormous shells landed in the immediate vicinity of the 29th Division command post with a gigantic blast effect triggering ground tremors equal to an earthquake. According to Capt. Robert Minor of the 29th Division's G-2 (intelligence) shop, the enemy knew the precise location of the headquarters "from information obtained from a captured 29th Division field order," a security lapse that was certain to cause the general to burst into one of his notorious temper tantrums. Luckily for the war room staff, one

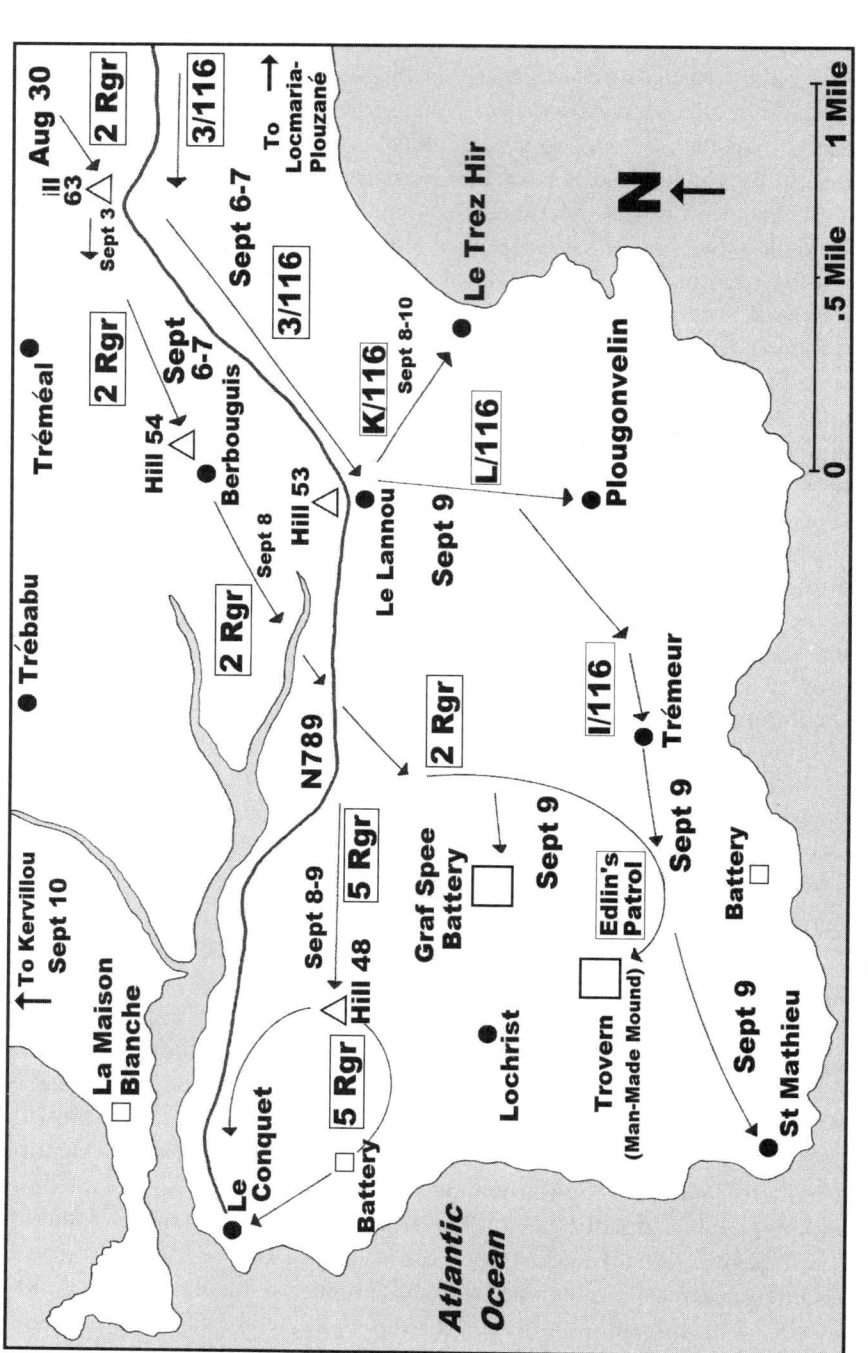

Task Force Sugar: August 30–September 10, 1944

of the 11-inch shells failed to explode. Ultimately, Gerhardt ordered some of his ordnance personnel to remove its ballistic cap, paint its nose with the division's blue-and-gray symbol, and mount it on a wooden pedestal as a war trophy. It can be viewed today in the 29th Division Museum in Baltimore's Fifth Regiment Armory.

Gerhardt responded to the enemy's firepower by allocating McDaniel and Rudder some heavy firepower of their own in the form of four 155mm howitzers of Battery C, 227th Field Artillery Battalion, commanded by Capt. Charles Ward. Those howitzers and the Graf Spee Battery's much heavier guns exchanged fire for several days, but it hardly seemed like a fair fight. The Americans, however, had a much more plentiful supply of ammunition than the enemy. Even better, Battery C had a superb view of the German position, courtesy of an observation post set up on a commanding height by the 227th's S-2, Capt. Cecil Harvey, a veteran of the outfit since 1940, when it was a component of the Pennsylvania National Guard in Pittsburgh.

The opposing batteries endeavored to destroy each other for several days in an exchange that one member of Battery C, Lt. Herman DeMoss, categorized as a "vendetta of nightly shelling." Captain Harvey recalled: "I fired at the German gun for hours. It would elevate; I would see a flash and puff of white smoke; then hear its report, then some seconds later heard the shell going overhead. It sounded like a train passing by. . . . The gun would then depress, load the next shell, then elevate."

Gerhardt would not be satisfied until the Graf Spee Battery was no more, but against such a heavily fortified position, that goal would be difficult to achieve with howitzers alone. Nevertheless, Harvey must try. As for the cannoneers back at Battery C's gun positions, DeMoss recalled: "Although we never received a direct hit, the concussion from the shock waves rolled us out of 10- to 12-inch-deep foxholes, which were impossible to dig deeper because of the rocky content of the hard ground."

Task Force Sugar's after-action report commented that for the next few days the rangers' mission on Hill 63 "was to mop up isolated pockets of resistance to the south, straighten and extend the front lines, and send patrols from their present location [to the west, toward the Graf Spee Battery]." In reality, however, survival in the face of the enemy's terrifying artillery bombardment was the order of each day, as in truth McDaniel and Rudder had nowhere near enough men to press forward in strength past Hill 63.

Rudder learned that hard lesson on September 3, when he attacked at 8 A.M. with Masny's and Slater's rangers. McDaniel offered in support seven M5 light tanks from Troop F, 86th Cavalry Reconnaissance Squadron (an element of the 6th Armored Division), and five Shermans from Company A, 709th Tank Battalion, hoping that this beefed-up force would be sufficient for Rudder to break through.

It was not: Although the rangers gained a few hundred yards of ground, by 3 P.M. Rudder's casualties had reached twenty-seven—a very high loss percentage given that his attacking force consisted of less than 300 men. Even worse, McDaniel's operations officer, Capt. Thomas Neal, reported to Gerhardt, "This Lochrist [Graf Spee] Battery is firing point blank at Colonel Rudder. Air is the only thing that can knock it out." The Army Air Force had tried to knock it out before, and would try yet again—but would fail. That evening, Rudder announced to McDaniel that he was pulling his men back to Hill 63.

When Gerhardt learned of that development, he became livid and spoke of Rudder's setback in particularly harsh terms. The general angrily ordered McDaniel to "button [Rudder's] ears down. I would just as soon can him as not. . . . Get after those rangers and get somewhere!" But "canning" Rudder would of course be an entirely irrational act, as he was one of the most intrepid battalion commanders in the U.S. Army. Furthermore, Gerhardt's boss, General Middleton, admired Rudder greatly, a sentiment Middleton later articulated when he defined Rudder as "one of the finest combat soldiers I ever saw." Clearly, it would be self-defeating for Gerhardt to remove Rudder from command, as such an act would in all probability get Gerhardt himself in deep trouble.

McDaniel defended Rudder by announcing to Gerhardt, "He did good work today," adding that he would direct Rudder "to give you something in writing on this pullback." As for Task Force Sugar's failure to push west from Hill 63 and eliminate the infuriating Graf Spee Battery once and for all, McDaniel correctly pointed out to his boss: "We are spread mighty thin." In truth they were spread so thin that even Gerhardt had to admit that considerable infantry reinforcements would be required if the Germans in Le Conquet were to be overcome. In the meantime, as one of McDaniel's action reports later observed, "The [Task Force Sugar] troops were tired, and September 4 and 5 were spent in rest and rehabilitation while reinforcements were received in preparation for a final assault."

When those reinforcements arrived over the next few days, they nearly tripled the task force's manpower, and still better, they were comprised almost entirely of the one article McDaniel needed most: experienced infantrymen. At 10 P.M. on September 5, the 116th Infantry's 3rd Battalion, under the command of a former cavalryman from Arizona, Maj.

William Puntenney, moved into the lines at Hill 63, allowing Rudder to concentrate his rangers north of that hill on a much more narrow front. At 8:30 the next morning, September 6, Puntenney and Rudder attacked westward on either side of the N789 road, supported by heavier fire from tanks, heavy mortars, and artillery than McDaniel had received since he had taken over from Sheppe on August 28. Their objectives were Hills 53 and 54, two prominent elevations less than two miles east of the Graf Spee Battery.

Urged on by Gerhardt's demand to "do it quick," the 29ers and rangers at first made good progress against only scattered opposition. As they neared the two vital hills, however, the Germans' resistance stiffened considerably. Puntenney's official report later observed,

> Well dug-in positions and defenses were encountered. Types included concrete pillboxes cleverly camouflaged with paint and material, circular one-man dugouts with entrances, dugouts reinforced with heavy logs, machine-gun emplacements dug into hedgerows. . . . Practically all passable roads were mined, and several elaborate antitank ditches and roadblocks were seen. These antitank obstacles were covered by 47mm antitank guns and small-arms fire.

According to Puntenney, "The enemy resisted strongly, but under persistent attack he broke and surrendered." That happy result, however, was not achieved until late afternoon of the next day, Thursday, September 7, when the rangers finally overcame the German strongpoint in the hamlet of Berbouguis on Hill 54. Puntenney's Company L, under the command of Capt. Maurice McGrath, moved onto Hill 53 at the Le Lannou farm, situated directly on the N789 highway. (McGrath, a native of Philadelphia, would gain a Silver Star for heroism in Brittany, but would be killed in action little more than one month later in Germany.) Rudder's and McGrath's accomplishments, however, were not decisive enough for Gerhardt, who phoned Task Force Sugar's command post during the action and barked into the mouthpiece: "Tell McDaniel that he's going too slow! We've got to get results!"

The general would not have to wait long to obtain his "results." But still, his impatience showed on the afternoon of September 7 when he unexpectedly ordered McDaniel to return to the war room to resume his normal duties as the 29th Division's chief of staff, replacing him as leader of Task Force Sugar with Col. Leroy Watson, the 29th's assistant division commander. "We are sending another backfield and change of command at 1300: Colonel Watson," Gerhardt told McDaniel. "I want you back here on the staff—no reflections [on you] or anything." As Watson was older than Gerhardt by two years, and only a few weeks in the past had commanded the 3rd Armored Division at the rank of major general before his abrupt relief and demotion in Normandy, his leadership of Task Force Sugar could have yielded some awkward moments considering Gerhardt's habitually brusque demeanor. Over the next few days, however, both men comported themselves entirely professionally, much to the task force's benefit. "Leroy Watson was a fine gentleman and an able officer," Puntenney remembered. "I liked him and always referred to him as 'general,' even though he wasn't one now. Later on, after we got into Germany, he was promoted to brigadier general."

At 7 A.M. on September 8, Puntenney caught the Germans by surprise by swinging 1st Lt. Elmer Reagor's Company K to the south, around their main defenses astride the N789 road. The fact that the 29ers did not pound the enemy with their standard artillery barrage immediately prior to the assault greatly accentuated the surprise effect of that flank attack, and accordingly, as an action report observed, "The movement brought dividends, as the enemy had concentrated its forces on the high ground overlooking the ridge [on the N789] and had altogether disregarded the woods on its right." Reagor's immediate objectives were the coastal villages of Le Trez Hir and Plougonvelin, formerly seaside resorts featuring quaint summer homes and a stunning crescent-shaped beach, swarming with bathers during the tourist season. Now, however, they were about to become deadly battlefields.

Reagor had no idea how many Germans defended those villages, but he was about to find out. One platoon, led by 2nd Lt. Benjamin Snipas, had orders to clear Le Trez Hir of the enemy. Snipas directed his group, which included some French Resistance fighters, down to the beach crescent, noting that "a careful search was made to determine if we could spot any enemy weapons that might be covering the beach road. Our search paid off, as a large gun—possibly an 88—was spotted on high ground less than 1,000 yards to our front. This cancelled out any attack on the beach side of town."

The platoon tried to resume its advance a little farther inland, but that design too failed to work when a hidden German machine gun opened up and killed one of Snipas's men. It was, as Snipas remarked, "a lousy attack situation," and it took two more days of maneuver and hard fighting for his men, with the assistance of some Shermans from the 709th Tank Battalion, to finally secure Le Trez Hir.

Meanwhile, Company L pushed into nearby Plougonvelin on September 9, although Captain McGrath reported that "the town itself had been mined and booby-trapped." Nevertheless, the 29ers swiftly secured it, an accomplishment that Puntenney's report noted was "the key capture of the [3rd Battalion's] operation." The German defenses of Le Conquet were obviously crumbling, and on the afternoon of September 9, advance elements of Puntenney's battalion dashed westward toward the old lighthouse at Pointe de St. Mathieu, the westernmost point on the French mainland. For Fürst's Germans, it was only a matter of time now.

First Lt. James Myers's Company I bumped into a German antiaircraft strongpoint just outside the village of Trémeur, only a mile and a half east of the St. Mathieu lighthouse. After a short aerial and artillery bombardment, the German defenders demonstrated no inclination to fight, and soon Myers was responsible for a large batch of prisoners. That success would bring the 3rd Battalion's short spell with Task Force Sugar almost to an end. Puntenney's men were needed back on the 29th Division's main front with the rest of the 116th Infantry for the upcoming—and final—assault on Brest. They would depart the Le Conquet peninsula for good on September 10, and whatever laurels remained for American soldiers in that sector would be gained by Rudder and his rangers.

There was, however, one more important issue for Puntenney to deal with. Some German diehards behind his front lines, amounting to fifty-seven troops, had holed up in a beach-front building in Le Trez Hir known as L'Hotel des Bains, but on September 10, a 75mm high velocity round from one of the American tanks accompanying Snipas's platoon rapidly convinced them that if they did not want to die, their only option was to surrender. They did so, and little more than one week later, the 29th Division's 110th Field Artillery Battalion would use that same hotel for a spirited party to celebrate the liberation of Brest.

The hotel's former occupants were not invited.

2. RANGERS LED THE WAY

General Gerhardt was the kind of man who had little inclination to modify a poor first impression of a subordinate. The general revealed that unfortunate trait time and again during the Le Conquet fighting in his highly strained relationship with the commander of the 2nd Ranger Battalion, Lt. Col. James Rudder. From Task Force Sugar's creation on August 25 until September 8, Gerhardt viewed Rudder's performance as plodding and rebellious. According to Gerhardt, Rudder had committed a cardinal sin by his obvious unwillingness to submit his high-spirited battalion to the

29th Division's combat methods. When Colonel Watson took over Task Force Sugar, Gerhardt demanded of him, "How's Rudder?" "He's all right," Watson replied. "We've had a couple of heart-to-heart talks."

On September 9, however, Rudder and his rangers gained a laudable success that abruptly brought the Le Conquet fighting to an end in favor of American arms, an achievement that Gerhardt could not fail to appreciate. No one would ever know whether that feat would alter the general's poor impression of Rudder, as Task Force Sugar would shut down on September 11, and the two adversaries did not cross paths again for the rest of World War II.

Gerhardt's foremost objective within the Le Conquet peninsula was the enemy's Graf Spee Battery, and by the evening of September 8, Rudder's 2nd Ranger Battalion had advanced a mile beyond Hill 54 to bring that vital target finally within reach. Pilots' post-mission reports and air reconnaissance photos indicated that American air power had turned the enemy position into a moonscape, and apparently, aerial bombs and artillery shells had at last managed to neutralize some, if not all, of the German heavy guns—a detail Rudder readily discerned because the frequency of the battery's salvos had diminished considerably. The battery had let loose with a few shots on the morning of September 8, but for the rest of the day remained silent. In fact, that salvo was the last one it would ever shoot.

Evidence that at least one of the guns had been put out of action by 29th Division artillery was later discovered by Capt. Cecil Harvey of the 227th Field Artillery Battalion. "When Task Force Sugar advanced beyond the Lochrist site [on September 10], I was able to go to the emplacement and examine the gun," Harvey wrote. "A direct hit of a shell had struck a trunnion, about which the gun elevates and depresses, and so it became inoperative."

The enemy's guns would menace the 29th Division no longer; but still, more than 1,000 German defenders reportedly occupied Le Conquet even now; and like any good American combat leader who wanted to get this brutal war over with rather than sitting back and watching the enemy starve, Rudder yearned to exterminate them. On the morning of September 9, his rangers set out to accomplish that task. Rudder had learned that Fürst's Germans no longer defended the peninsula in a conventional front line. Instead, they had withdrawn into various self-contained strongpoints, all constructed with the enemy's customary thoroughness for all-around defense.

As far as Rudder could tell the Germans held out in at least six scattered resistance nests, all of which would be extraordinarily difficult to overcome by direct assault. To save time and blood, the Americans' obvious solution would be to convince Fürst that further resistance was useless. To do that, Rudder would have to find the German commander and make that appeal to him directly. But where could he be found?

One of Rudder's ranger lieutenants was about to find out. It all started with a four-man patrol led by 1st Lt. Robert Edlin, a member of Company A, 2nd Ranger Battalion. Edlin's band moved out at sunrise on September 9 with orders to probe one of the enemy's toughest strongpoints, located at an assortment of old farm buildings collectively known as Trovern, just a few hundred yards from the Graf Spee Battery. Rudder did not realize that the distinctive Trovern strongpoint, visible by the Americans from a considerable distance away and known to them simply as the "Man-Made Mound," was the control center for all of the enemy's Le Conquet defenses.

Built as an observation post with highly sophisticated equipment to control the fire of the enemy's heavy naval guns, the structure was so massive that the Germans could make no attempt to camouflage it. An American report described the mound as "an elaborate heavy concrete structure on a man-made hill, fifty feet above the surrounding terrain [with] a commanding view of the entrance to Brest harbor." The edifice was big enough to enclose several levels—some above ground, others below. Reporter Holbrook Bradley entered the mound on the day following Fürst's surrender through a tunnel featuring an electric door, which he observed "was heavily constructed of steel and concrete." He added,

> The rooms below seemed much like those aboard ship. The bunks were in tiers, and there were ship-type washrooms. . . . On the deck above, we found the quarters of the commander [Fürst] and much of his personal equipment. In the officers' wardroom outside there was an American-manufactured refrigerator, still running. . . . The room on top of this structure commanded a wide view of the area all around, and contained some of the most intricate range-finding devices we have yet come across.

What Bradley did not realize was that his leisurely examination of the mound on September 10 was made possible only through the exertions of Lieutenant Edlin and his patrol, which, much to the amazement of Rudder, had induced Fürst to surrender by mere bluster at noon the previous day. That accomplishment was made without the loss of a man—American or German.

Shortly after they moved out at dawn on September 9, Edlin's patrol cautiously traversed a German wire barrier and minefield only to come up against a large pillbox the enemy had sited to guard the approaches to the mound. That the pillbox was occupied by enemy troops was obvious because Edlin and his men could hear them talking inside. As Edlin recalled, it was also evident that the Germans "were ready to quit. The pillbox door was open, and nobody was guarding it." Edlin, accompanied by Sgt. William Courtney and PFC William Dreher—both of whom had been awarded the Distinguished Service Cross for valor on D-Day—burst into the pillbox with guns drawn, a highly perilous action, since it turned out the rangers were outnumbered by about twenty to three. Fortunately, the Germans were entirely docile, and Edlin remembered, "All their hands went up. Nobody reached for their guns. They just stood there."

Edlin demanded to see the enemy commander, and a compliant German officer who spoke English volunteered to present him to Fürst. Normally, American fighting men professed a near-total lack of trust in their cunning opponents, and if this was a trick, Edlin and his three comrades would soon be dead or prisoners of war—so be it. But the submissiveness of this downhearted group of Germans was like nothing the 2nd Ranger Battalion had seen since its landing at Pointe du Hoc and Omaha Beach on D-Day, so perhaps the enemy was indeed ready to give up.

It certainly was worth a try. The German officer led Edlin and Courtney along a safe route through a minefield and into the menacing mound by way of a massive steel door opening up into a dark tunnel. To the two rangers, the interior of the mound was a baffling maze of corridors and rooms, one of which, as Edlin remembered, was a hospital "big enough to hold three or four hundred patients." Within a few minutes, Edlin and Courtney were in a small office, face-to-face with Fürst. The ensuing encounter between the twenty-two-year-old American lieutenant and the German lieutenant colonel nineteen years his senior was a microcosm of their respective nations' fortunes in the current war.

Fürst, who spoke flawless English, was later described by Bradley as "a thin-faced, bespectacled Nazi—the typical German Army officer." Edlin added that Fürst "was very hard-nosed and arrogant," an observation that in truth reflected all American fighting men's analysis of German military officers. The German commander of Fortress Brest, General Ramcke, provided a less caustic portrayal of Fürst when he described him simply as "an old regular soldier from the '100,000-man army'" [the Weimar Republic's all-volunteer force in the early 1920s, limited to that size by the Treaty of Versailles].

Edlin looked Fürst directly in the eyes and quickly came to the point: Fürst must surrender immediately, along with all his men. Fürst promptly refused and, in fact, tried to turn the tables on Edlin by claiming, "You're my prisoners now."

If words could not accomplish Edlin's purpose, actions would. He coolly demanded a grenade from Sergeant Courtney and promptly shoved it against Fürst's abdomen, snarling, "You're either going to surrender, or you're going to die right now!" According to Edlin, Fürst replied: "Well, so are you."

Fürst's retort was persuasive, but it failed to work. There was something about the intensity of Edlin's manner that convinced the German officer that the young American was actually capable of carrying out his deadly threat. Under those entirely implausible circumstances, Fürst gave in—much to Edlin's relief. Only formalities remained, but they would take time. In the meantime, Fürst announced by loudspeaker to the German occupants of the "Man-Made Mound" that resistance was at an end.

The honor of the German Army demanded that an officer who had to undergo such humiliation must do so formally to an officer of equal or higher rank. Colonel Rudder honored that request, and at about noon on September 9, he showed up at the mound with Baptise Faucher of the French Resistance. Fürst recalled that in this, "the most difficult moment of my military life," Rudder's behavior was "chivalrous." In the American camp, however, confusion immediately arose over the extent of Fürst's capitulation: Did it include just the German strongpoints in the immediate vicinity of the mound? Or did it include all German troops in the Le Conquet peninsula?

At VIII Corps headquarters Middleton insisted that the surrender must encompass all troops under Fürst's command. Middleton's operations officer, Col. John Evans, telephoned Witte in the 29th Division war room and demanded, "Put that colonel [Fürst] in a car with a white flag, and get him to go around and force the others to surrender. Be sure you get prompt action. . . . [This will] prevent unnecessary bloodshed." However, at 5 P.M. on September 9, Watson radioed Gerhardt and reported, "Fürst said 'nothing doing' on that deal . . . so I am going to continue the fight." Fürst apparently gave his captors the somewhat halfhearted excuse that since he "was already a prisoner of war," he had no authority to order other German outposts to surrender, and that as German soldiers it was their duty to fight on.

Fürst's contrary attitude made little difference, as all German soldiers in Le Conquet now fully understood that further resistance could not accomplish anything more than killing a few additional Americans—an act that in all probability would lead to the deaths of many more of their own. Duty did not go that far; but even so sporadic fighting continued for one more day after Fürst's surrender.

Two days earlier, on September 7, Gerhardt had dispatched two-thirds of the 5th Ranger Battalion by truck to help Watson and Rudder. That outfit was commanded by Richard Sullivan, who in the first week of September had established his value so convincingly to Gerhardt that the general was about to promote him from major to lieutenant colonel. Upon the rangers' arrival with Task Force Sugar, Watson had assigned Sullivan the mission of cleaning out the northern part of the Le Conquet peninsula, including a radar station on a prominent elevation known as Hill 48 and a four-gun naval battery sited in the peninsula's northwestern corner just south of the picturesque fishing village of Le Conquet.

Sullivan's rangers had already participated in several bitter combats in the Brest campaign, but fortunately for them by the time they shifted to Le Conquet the enemy garrison's will to resist had been almost entirely eradicated. The 5th Rangers had joined the attack in Le Conquet on the afternoon of September 8, and their toughest problem at first was an estuary almost 100 yards wide that would have to be crossed under artillery fire if they were to reach their objectives. That difficulty was solved on the morning of September 9, and soon 1st Lt. John Gawler was leading his Company E forward to the German radar station atop Hill 48. According to a 5th Ranger Battalion action report, "The enemy surrendered without a fight, and about 120 POWs were taken."

Later that day the 5th Rangers, assisted by some of Rudder's men, captured the naval battery adjacent to Le Conquet and pushed ahead into that village against virtually no opposition. The 5th Rangers' report observed somewhat caustically: "The grimness of war seems to be spotted by comedy, and in this case it was the FFI [French Resistance] who furnished the amusement. They had waited outside the town until it was taken, and as soon as the town surrendered, they went marching in, tipping their caps, bowing, and 'bonjouring,' while French civilians cheered them for performing the liberation."

Fürst's surrender did not make much of an impression on several isolated German strongpoints on the Brittany coast north of Le Conquet, but in truth that could have been because those garrisons never learned of it. Accordingly, on the afternoon of September 10—the day after Fürst's capitulation—Sullivan's and Rudder's rangers prepared for the attacks that would finish Task Force Sugar's mission for good. One formidable German fort known as La Maison Blanche was sited on the Pointe de Kermorvan headland jutting out into the Atlantic just north of the Le Conquet estuary. It was connected with the mainland only by a narrow causeway, and therefore attacking it would be little different than attacking an island. At 4 P.M. Sullivan planned to move two 5th Ranger companies over the estuary by raft to attack La Maison Blanche directly, a job that appeared suicidal if the German defenders demonstrated any inclination to fight. Ten minutes before Sullivan's attack was set to jump off, Army Air Force P-47s worked over La Maison Blanche with machine guns and bombs, a traumatic experience for the occupants that finally caused them to crack. At 5:57 P.M., just three minutes before the rangers would swarm into the rafts to begin their assault, the Germans surrendered, yielding 120 more prisoners. This success, however, cost Sullivan seven rangers, who suffered wounds from the enemy's sporadic artillery fire.

One of the last German strongpoints in western Brittany to hold out had been one of the first that Task Force Sugar had encountered nearly two weeks in the past. On August 30, parts of Rudder's 2nd Ranger Battalion had run into a tough enemy position on a rocky cape just west of the village of Kervillou, labeled simply the "Old Fort" on U.S. Army maps. Rudder had reflected that it would cost too many GIs to storm frontally; and since the Old Fort was separated from the main German defenses in the Le Conquet peninsula by more than two miles, it posed not the slightest threat to Task Force Sugar or the rest of the 29th Division. Rudder had therefore decided to contain it with just a handful of rangers and about seventy Russians, all ex-prisoners of war from the Eastern Front who passionately despised their former German captors and, under the leadership of their mysterious commander, "Joseph 351," enthusiastically looked forward to killing some of them in close combat at Kervillou.

They never got that chance. On the afternoon of September 10, when the fifty German occupants of the Old Fort observed that the rangers and Russians were about to launch an assault, they realized that if they wished to live to see another sunrise, they must raise the white flag posthaste. When they did so, all German resistance west of Brest had finally been eradicated.

After Fürst handed over his pistol to Rudder in a formal surrender ceremony at St. Mathieu, Gerhardt ordered Watson to send the German officer up to the 29th Division's War Room so they could chat. Like any typical GI, the general was always on the lookout for souvenirs, and he observed to Watson: "I want a couple of those paratrooper knives."

On the afternoon of September 10, a forlorn Fürst, dressed in a long gray military greatcoat with two bags of his personal belongings slung somewhat awkwardly over his shoulders, was brought before Gerhardt.

This was no ordinary meeting, as Fürst was the highest ranking German officer captured so far in the war by the 29th Division. Gerhardt prepared for the occasion by bringing in a photographer and a correspondent from the division newsletter, *29 Let's Go*. He then dressed in his sharpest field uniform, and as always he fastened his helmet chin strap underneath his lower lip, according to official regulations—just as he expected every member of the 29th Division to do.

The meeting, which took place in front of the war room tent, was described by the correspondent as "formal and brief." He added: "Our general said he was pleased to meet the German commander. He said he was sorry that circumstances were such as they were, but so go the fortunes of war. General Gerhardt told the German that he had put up a stiff fight, and that he was a good soldier. The Jerry colonel expressed his high regard for the ability of American fighting men. That was about all there was to it, except that General Gerhardt had the German sign his guest book before he sent him away."

Gerhardt had maintained that guest book since November 1943 and took great pride in it. The book had been signed by the likes of Dwight Eisenhower, Nancy Astor, Bernard Montgomery, Omar Bradley, B. H. Liddell Hart, and Edward G. Robinson. (Ike had signed in the wrong place, but no one had had the heart to correct him.) The gloomy officer grabbed a pen, and he scrawled, nearly illegibly, "Fürst." Then, in the "Remarks" column, he added: "Not too happy—Heil Hitler!"

It definitely was the only time in World War II anyone would write "Heil Hitler" in the guest book of the 29th Infantry Division.

3. ROMMEL, COUNT YOUR MEN

The demise of the enemy's Brest garrison was imminent; and when that city finally fell, the Germans would surely excuse their defeat, as they always did, by asserting that they had not been overcome on the battlefield in a fair fight by American infantry, which they regarded as poorly trained and timid, but instead had been overwhelmed almost entirely by American firepower. After the fall of Brest, Gen. Hans von der Mosel, Ramcke's chief of staff, somewhat caustically summed up the sentiments of most enemy soldiers when he blurted to a fellow German general in captivity: "The Americans put up a barrage, and when they had done that for a time, they groped their way forward and encountered our fire. . . . Then they went back and put up another barrage."

What the enemy failed to realize, however, was that their American opponents had been hampered by a severe ammunition shortage for the first sixteen days of the Brest campaign, and during that period—when artillery shells were in especially short supply—the American infantry repeatedly had to carry out frontal assaults against prepared enemy positions with much less direct artillery support than the GIs had gotten used to in Normandy.

Generals Bradley and Middleton struggled to make up for this deficit with alternative sources of firepower, such as Ninth Air Force fighter-bombers and corps-level mortar, tank, and tank destroyer units, but within the 29th Division's three infantry regiments, nothing could fully make up for the dedicated 105mm and 155mm howitzer battalions that had served them so well in the past. Indeed, by late summer 1944, U.S. Army artillerymen had become expert at providing much-needed fire support to their beleaguered infantry brethren; and under normal conditions the artillery's forward observers and liaison teams at the front could employ their first-class radios and telephones to request and receive that support faster and more accurately than any other army in the world. However, the logistical circumstances at Brest were anything but normal, and during the siege of that city, the 29th Division's gunners would have to do the best they could during an ammunition deficiency that at times became critical.

From its very first contacts with the U.S. Army in World War II, the Germans had gathered that American cannoneers had expertly learned the complex science of gunnery, a conclusion drawn with some authority since the Germans themselves had revolutionized artillery tactics in the last year of World War I and at the start of the present war. When the Americans combined that new-found skill with their exceptional mobility, near-total command of the air, and seemingly limitless quantities of ammunition, the Germans grasped that their opponents were capable of bringing down a deadly torrent of shells in an instant, with uncanny precision, almost anywhere they wanted within range of their guns. Furthermore, the U.S. Army possessed an impressive array of artillery weaponry, from air-transportable 75mm pack howitzers to immense 240mm cannon. That the Americans had managed to ship all of those thousands of pieces of ordnance and their associated ammunition stocks across the Atlantic to the European theater with almost no loss from enemy U-boats was even more impressive, an accomplishment that guaranteed that the U.S. Army would be able to practice warfare in Europe according to the cutting-edge methods it had learned from field manuals and practiced in stateside training.

When the Germans had been on the receiving end of those methods in Normandy, they glumly acknowledged their effectiveness, but grumbled somewhat unreasonably that the American infantry was over-reliant on supporting artillery. The enemy failed to comprehend, however, that the U.S. Army's highly flexible infantry-artillery techniques essentially amounted to a new approach to tactical warfare, one that was distinctively American and took advantage of the United States's awesome capability to produce artillery hardware at prodigious rates, ship that materiel to the front, and then use it with unprecedented skill.

Brest was the perfect place for the Americans to demonstrate that artillery prowess, even with the severe ammunition deficiency. Middleton had assembled nearly 400 guns of 105mm caliber or greater, and the Germans were trapped in a pocket in which every square foot of ground was within easy range of those guns. Even better, most of that ground was under direct observation by American troops because their lines surrounding the enemy enclave were typically on higher ground than the German defenses. True, the German troops had entrenched and fortified their lines with their usual thoroughness, so that artillery fire would in part be negated; but still, in theory, any time the Americans felt like it, most German strongpoints at Brest could be targeted by an intense and decidedly accurate crossfire of U.S. Army guns.

The man who managed the 29th Division's artillery at Brest was Brig. Gen. William Sands, a crusty fifty-two-year-old Virginia native who had served overseas during World War I with the 80th Division. After that war Sands maintained a law practice in Richmond and Norfolk while simultaneously pursuing a dynamic career in the Virginia National Guard. By 1944 he was the 29th Division's most experienced artilleryman and its senior National Guard officer. Gerhardt, a West Pointer, subjected all his officers with National Guard origins to exceptionally close scrutiny, but Sands's military skills were so impressive that Gerhardt's periodic assessments invariably rated him highly. Sands, however, was fully aware that a single mistake on his part could cause Gerhardt to bust him, and he therefore ruled over 29th Division artillerymen strictly by the book and developed a nasty reputation as a martinet. One of the four 29th Division artillery battalion commanders who worked directly under Sands, Lt. Col. John Cooper of the 110th Field Artillery, recalled, "Sands was afraid of being busted and wanted absolute perfection from his troops."

Cooper himself was a veteran gunner who had joined the Maryland National Guard unit he now commanded as a private in 1929. "For the first time in France, during the siege of Brest the 110th was able to obtain good, long-distance ground observation into enemy territory," Cooper observed. "On the high terrain which circled Brest the cannoneers maintained several observation posts in house attics, frequently using the same buildings in which the infantry maintained battalion command posts. From such points . . . observers could view much of the 8,000 yards, about four and a half miles, of terrain between the 110th and Brest itself. During clear daylight hours, the observers frequently spotted numerous enemy artillery positions, fortifications, troop movements, and supply points. On such targets the battalion observers—sometimes as many as nine—fired all available ammunition." Cooper's second-in-command, Maj. Donovan Yeuell, added: "Every place was an observation post: churches, farmhouses, treetops, crossroads. Practically no mission was unobserved."

Although at Brest the 29th Division's available artillery ammunition rarely amounted to very much, the 29ers' ability to observe a great deal of the enemy's rear-area activities provided them with an ideal opportunity to prove that the highly complex science of modern gunnery they had learned on the firing ranges at Camp A. P. Hill and on Bodmin Moor had been absorbed well. "Brest was a place where the 'book solution' would apply," Yeuell noted. He continued:

> Most of our procedures had been developed to a degree of facile utility. Communications invariably worked; there were few mistakes by the gun crews; the fire direction procedure was smooth, and even the telephone operators could fire a mission. Forward observers and liaison parties were old-timers by now: They knew how to gain maximum effect with minimum effort. . . . On the whole, the battle for Brest was about the most reasonable fight an artilleryman could ask for.

Blue and Gray gunners quickly established that kind of deadly proficiency to the unfortunate German garrison at Brest by means of a variety of methods Cooper summarized as "sniping with artillery." According to one technique the 29ers favored, a keen-eyed American artillery observer would scrutinize the area behind the enemy's front line with a powerful binocular telescope, searching for a key road junction through which German vehicles regularly passed. A gun crew would be assigned to register its 105mm howitzer on that intersection by firing a few trial rounds, and in a matter of minutes meticulous adjustments would yield definitive range and bearing data, enabling the gunners to drop their next 33-pound shell onto that crossroads with deadly accuracy. The crew members would load a shell into the barrel, finalize the appropriate settings on their field piece—and then wait to hear from the observer by telephone. When the observer spotted an oncoming enemy vehicle, he would judge its arrival time at the junction and order the howitzer to fire so that the shell would impact just as the vehicle reached that point. That procedure required split-second timing since the flight time of a 105mm howitzer shell was typically about twenty seconds. Much to the consternation of the enemy, it frequently worked.

Early in the Brest campaign, the 110th Field Artillery had an ideal observation post in the attic of a house in the village of Kervalguen, about four and a half miles due north of Brest. Virtually no blocking terrain between that attic and the city existed, and with their telescopes—which magnified discernible objects by a factor of ten—Cooper's observers could spy on the German garrison all the way down to the city center. Here was a textbook observation post, from which the 110th's gunners could direct pinpoint counterbattery fire against the enemy. Consequently, their German counterparts would soon learn the hard lesson that if they wished to survive, they would be wise to shift their guns swiftly to a new position after firing even a single-volley mission against the Americans.

"I took my battalion operations sergeant, T/Sgt. Paul Bradford [later commissioned as a lieutenant], up to the front lines for a change of scenery and to see some shells land among the enemy," Cooper noted. "We spotted the flash of a German gun southeast of Fort Keranroux, and I took that on. When this enemy gun was silenced, Bradford said: 'Colonel, I've spotted another one.' I told him to conduct fire on it, using my last rounds as a reference. We watched for his first adjusting round and saw a wisp of smoke, which suddenly blossomed into a tremendous column of smoke, pyrotechnics, and debris that must have risen 300 feet in the air. I told him he sure was lucky to hit the jackpot with the first nickel, and he agreed. We knew we had hit something big, as little side explosions were still popping." Such a catastrophic explosion was in all likelihood generated by a direct hit on an enemy ammunition dump, an event that would obliterate that site's entire contents and anyone standing nearby, yielding nothing but a crater of monumental proportions.

The American gunners managed to achieve exploits of this kind with such regularity that Middleton's VIII Corps staff eventually came to the understandable conclusion that German artillery at Brest was taking such a severe beating that it would soon be totally neutralized. Three weeks into the Brest assault, the word filtered down from the top brass that this result had supposedly been achieved. To the GIs at the front, that news, if true, was undeniably encouraging. But wary 29th Division veterans were ready for anything—and given their redoubtable enemy, that precaution turned out to be wise.

Sometime shortly before the fall of Brest, the executive officer of the 175th Infantry's 2nd Battalion, Maj. Claude Melancon, observed two of his radio operators digging a foxhole at the base of a hedgerow. He reminded them that a declaration had been passed down from division that frontline troops would no longer have to worry about the supposedly defunct German artillery. The skeptical GIs continued to dig—an act that may have saved their own and Melancon's lives because only moments after finishing their hole, the enemy demonstrated that the division's pronouncement was premature. According to one of the radio operators, T/4 Jack Montrose,

> Suddenly the entire hillside erupted from a concentrated salvo of large-caliber German artillery. One round landed particularly close, and a large piece of shrapnel zipped a few inches over my head. It sliced off the radio antenna, at a height even with and some twenty inches from Melancon's belt buckle. I will never forget that sight . . . Melancon standing next to the radio, his handset still at his ear, an amazed look on his face. In the foxhole, I braced for the impact of Melancon's weight. But—would you believe—he took time to ask permission: "You guys got room in there for me?" Hartman and I, in unison, shouted, "Get the hell in here!" [Later], Melancon, rather apologetically, commented: "If I ever again tell you guys you don't need a foxhole, don't pay a damned bit of attention!"

But the 29ers could take solace from the evident reality that the perils they faced from enemy artillery were nothing compared to what German soldiers were enduring under the deadly U.S. Army barrage, an onslaught that intensified markedly when the Americans' ammunition shortage vanished in the last few days of the siege. Whenever they fired a 155mm shell into the enemy lines, the American gunners in one corps-level artillery outfit attached to the 29th Division, the 333rd Field Artillery Battalion, bellowed a war cry that fittingly summed up the Germans' plight: "Rommel—count your men!" Admittedly, Field Marshal Rommel was actually nowhere near Brittany at the time; but even that slip-up managed to convey with a fair measure of truth the idea that if Ramcke did not surrender before long, sooner or later he would run out of men.

Commanded by Lt. Col. Hubert Barnes, the 333rd Field Artillery, which had the fitting radio call-signal of "Monster," was attached to the 115th Infantry for much of the Brest campaign, and its twelve 155mm howitzers added a great deal to that regiment's firepower. The U.S. Army in World War II was racially segregated, a policy that produced dozens of units like the 333rd—led mostly by white officers but populated entirely by African-American enlisted personnel. According to Cooper, the black gunners "performed extremely well on all missions." One effective ploy devised by the 333rd at Brest entailed a highly unusual observation technique: Furnished with powerful radios and binocular telescopes, a small team of artillerymen journeyed more than twenty miles by jeep to set up an observation post on the Daoulas Peninsula, a strip of land jutting into Brest harbor south of the city well beyond the 29th Division's zone of operations. The enemy's Brest garrison lay squarely between that observation post and the 333rd's howitzers, so when the observation team spotted a target and radioed for a fire mission, the howitzers' shells actually traveled directly toward those observers' position. According to Cooper that innovative practice "could bring observed fire on many areas otherwise hidden."

After the fall of Brest, the 29th Division and the 333rd Field Artillery Battalion parted ways, but the African-American gunners retained their affiliation with VIII Corps and accompanied Middleton with his command to Belgium in October 1944. Middleton set up his headquarters in a humble Belgian town named Bastogne; and in December would assign the 333rd to support the 106th Infantry Division, freshly inserted into the thin American line in the Ardennes forest. The Germans launched a surprise offensive on December 16, and in the furious fighting that would later be known as the Battle of the Bulge, the 333rd suffered more than 200 casualties and lost most of its howitzers. The remnants of the battalion retreated into Bastogne and fought alongside the 101st Airborne Division in the epic siege of that town.

Another VIII Corps outfit that supported the 29th Division at Brest, the 539-man 771st Field Artillery Battalion, specialized in long-range artillery fire, particularly pinpoint counter-battery work against German heavy gun positions. The 771st was equipped with twelve 4.5-inch guns, an uncommon U.S. Army weapon that had nearly twice the range of the 29th Division's 105mm howitzers and could even hit targets deeper inside enemy territory than pieces of much larger calibers, such as 155mm or 8-inch howitzers. One of the 771st's senior officers was Maj. Joseph Sewell, an old-timer who had enlisted in the Maryland National Guard in 1931 and had risen by 1940 to the exalted position as "Top" (first sergeant) of the 110th Field Artillery's Headquarters Battery—an outfit then commanded by John Cooper. Immediately prior to the 29th Division's February 1941 mobilization, Sewell made an unusual career move when he accepted a commission in the 110th, a step that converted him into a twenty-nine-year-old second lieutenant. Sewell later transferred to the 771st, and at the height of the Brest campaign, he surprised Cooper by paying a visit to his former comrades in the 110th, who welcomed him heartily. The 771st remained with Middleton's VIII Corps after the fall of Brest and, like the 333rd, suffered heavily from the full impact of the enemy's Ardennes offensive in December 1944. After the war, Sewell returned to the Maryland National Guard.

4. BLUE AND GRAY SAPPERS

Almost everything the 29th Division had set out to accomplish in Normandy and Brittany depended heavily on support by U.S. Army engineers. And yet, the division's organic sapper unit, the 121st Engineer Combat Battalion, had gained almost no headlines for the pivotal role it repeatedly played in divisional operations. Hundreds of 29th Division engineers from that outfit had landed in the first hours of the Omaha Beach invasion on D-Day, and their exceptional value to the 29th Division, and indeed to the U.S. Army as a whole, was confirmed when First Army awarded the 121st Engineers the highly prestigious Distinguished Unit Citation. That award noted: "The outstanding performance of duty by this battalion was a substantial contribution to the success of the assault operation." Anyone who had harbored hopes that engineer work would be safer than that of the infantry, however, saw those hopes dashed when, in the first hours of the invasion, the 121st Engineers suffered eighty casualties. Indeed, on D-Day and afterward, the somewhat shocked sappers learned the reason why the Army had inserted the word "combat" in the middle of the battalion's official designation.

The 121st's commander both on D-Day and at Brest was twenty-eight-year-old Lt. Col. Robert Ploger, an Idaho native who had graduated 23rd out of 456 cadets in the class of 1939 at the U.S. Military Academy. Ploger had first reported to Gerhardt in the fall of 1943, when the 29th Division was in England preparing for the upcoming invasion of Normandy. Gerhardt, who had only recently assumed command of the division, had become alarmed by the exceptionally high number of 121st Engineer officers who had requested transfers—a sure indicator that the unit had morale problems. The 121st would need a new commander, and despite Ploger's youth, Gerhardt considered him a prime candidate for the job. In their first meeting the general demanded direct answers to only three simple questions: "Have you attended the U.S. Army Engineer School [at Ft. Belvoir, Virginia]?" "Have you ever commanded an engineer company?" "Have you ever served in a division before?" Ploger replied in the affirmative to all three questions, prompting Gerhardt to assert, "If it's OK with you, I'll put in a request for your reassignment [to command of the 121st]."

The command of a 649-man engineer battalion was a breathtaking job offer for such a young officer, but when Ploger arrived at the 121st Engineers' headquarters in Cornwall to take over in December 1943, he rapidly determined that his new post would be a challenge. Much to his astonishment, many 121st officers, including the outgoing commander, repeatedly and openly spoke callously of General Gerhardt, a practice that Ploger immediately banned. Ploger attempted to tighten up discipline while simultaneously enhancing the enlisted men's morale, a tricky command procedure that in a lesser man's hands would not have worked. Within a few weeks, however, Ploger's natural skill at that sort of leadership emerged, and the 121st Engineers developed not only into a first-class military unit, but also into one that was highly motivated to carry out its exceptionally difficult D-Day mission. If that leadership was hindered in any way by Ploger's youth in comparison to some of the hardened NCOs and officers in the battalion, no one admitted it, but just in case, Ploger grew a mustache, yielding what he hoped would be a more mature appearance. That he was indeed youthful, however, no one could deny; and that trait emerged in the exuberant entry he penned in Gerhardt's guest book on December 3, 1943: "Joining the best d—— Division in the whole Army!"

Like every other outfit in the 29th Division, the 121st Engineer Combat Battalion had National Guard origins. Unlike those other units, however, the 121st did not derive from a Maryland or Virginia National Guard organization. Rather, it had been a key component of the District of Columbia militia since its establishment in 1802 as the "Columbian Brigade," during Thomas Jefferson's presidency. For 120 years the unit had served as infantry, but in 1922 it was converted to an engineer regiment and assigned to the 29th Division. It was called into federal service on February 3, 1941, with the rest of the 29th Division and promptly underwent profound organizational changes. In 1942, its entire 2nd Battalion was transferred out of the division and ultimately shipped to the Caribbean island of Trinidad, a place it had the good fortune to garrison for more than a year. What was left of the 121st Engineers, now much reduced in size, converted to a battalion in March 1942, and transferred to England with the rest of the 29th Division that fall. Like so many other Anglo-American military units, it would have its rendezvous with destiny in Normandy on June 6, 1944.

By the time the 121st Engineers had reached Brest eighty days later, it was a highly seasoned outfit, whose casualty count of 300—nearly half the battalion's authorized strength—confirmed that it had been in the thick of every 29th Division effort since D-Day. In the meantime Ploger had earned Gerhardt's perpetual respect; and indeed the young lieutenant colonel's innovative ideas on helping the infantry bust through Normandy's infamous hedgerows by using prongs welded to the front of tanks had generated deep interest in American military circles as high as First Army.

Since Brittany's terrain was not much different than Normandy's, that knowledge would again prove useful during the siege of Brest; and the 121st's after-action report for September 1944 noted: "One important operation that was decided to become SOP [standard operating procedure] within the battalion was the placing of hedgerow-busters on all tanks attached to the division. The battalion had the mission of equipping nine medium tanks in a limited length of time, which required six welding sets. The tanks were completely equipped for their scheduled attack." A British Army tanker attached to the 29th Division noted with amazement that the engineers jumped into that work with "drive [and] enthusiasm, [with] not one welder, but two whole teams working 24-hours long by shifts."

To read the 121st's action report is to grasp how thoroughly Ploger and his sappers devoted themselves to the enemy's overthrow at Brest. From the moment of the battalion's arrival in Brittany, every engineer, both in and behind the front lines, focused on a seemingly inexhaustible series of tasks that would not end until Ramcke raised the white flag over Brest. Some of the most notable of those tasks were described in the battalion's action report: "All companies were required to prepare pack and pole charges and scaling ladders for the various infantry combat teams. The companies held training [for the infantry] in the passage of enemy obstacles and started repairing and clearance of roads in their assigned sectors. . . . Engineers also assisted in giving instruction in the use of the flamethrower."

One marvelous new piece of military equipment with which the 121st Engineers became entirely proficient in Brittany was the Bailey bridge, the celebrated 1943 invention by a British civilian of that name, which had revolutionized Anglo-American military operations. Water barriers that formerly would have impeded the movement of mechanized forces could now be spanned in a matter of hours by engineers who had been trained to piece together the prefabricated and ingenious Bailey components. Bridge equipment adding up to one 150-foot span could be transported by only twenty-one of the U.S. Army's ubiquitous two-and-a-half ton trucks, and accordingly it was easy for the engineers to dispatch that equipment remarkably quickly to the point where it was needed most. If the western Allies expected to win the war in Europe principally with mobility, they could not hope to achieve that goal by superior motorization alone. It was also imperative that they had the equipment and skills to traverse difficult pieces of terrain, namely rivers, and by so doing swiftly seize the key terrain objectives that would place the enemy in a position from which it could not recover.

In truth, all military engineering tasks in an active war theater—even the straightforward assembly of a Bailey bridge miles behind the front line—entailed risk. Some tasks, however, unquestionably posed much more risk than others. Those members of divisional engineer battalions regularly assumed the worst of those risks simply because their primary mission was to support their infantry brethren in the deadly struggle in the front lines; and when that struggle took on the form of a direct American assault on a fortified enemy position, such as the 29th Division's effort to take Brest, the hazards of engineer work became pronounced. On a daily basis the 121st Engineers fulfilled all those tasks sappers dreaded, such as clearing minefields, using demolition charges to assist infantrymen in their assaults on German pillboxes, and cutting gaps through barbed wire under direct enemy observation.

Of all those activities, mine clearance was probably the most disquieting. The Germans at Brest employed prolific numbers of antipersonnel mines, simple but thoroughly lethal devices planted cunningly throughout the most likely approach routes to every enemy strongpoint guarding the city. Many, including the notorious Schu mine, were almost impossible to locate with mine detectors because they were made predominantly out of wood. Another type, the infamous "Bouncing Betty," featured a highly sensitive trigger mechanism that would propel a mine canister almost three feet in the air, where it would abruptly explode and fling deadly metal balls in all directions over a distance of more than ten feet.

Predictably, locating and neutralizing thousands of insidious weapons of that kind was a chore that appealed to no one. Someone had to do it, however, and within the 29th Division's sector at Brest that job fell squarely on the shoulders of the 121st Engineer Battalion's sappers. It took a great deal of practice to do that sort of work, but as a September 1944 121st Engineer action report noted, practice was hardly any safer than the real thing: "A minefield consisting of Schu mines was located around an [abandoned] enemy strongpoint, and Company C [normally attached to the 175th Infantry] alternated platoons in removing the mines for training purposes. Several hundred mines were removed. During our operations, several different types and arrangements of mines were found, all of which were reported in detail to higher headquarters."

In actual combat the tricky mine clearance procedure often had to be performed at night—sometimes within easy range of the enemy's machine guns. But when that work was done, sets of parallel lines of white engineer tape clearly defined for the attacking infantrymen safe paths through countless German minefields.

To the doughboys that white tape was a wholly reassuring sign that the 121st's engineers had been on the scene, and yet again they had done all they could humanly do to make the infantrymen's lives just a little bit safer.

SEVEN

Brestgrad

1. CROCODILES
Even General Ramcke had to admit that the end was near. Although only recently he had brusquely rejected the Americans' demand for the unconditional surrender of his Brest garrison—for such an ignominious capitulation would clearly violate Hitler's dictum to fight to the last bullet—the Germans were now feeling the wrath of their vengeful opponents. As difficult as it was to admit, the Americans' current line of reasoning, articulated by means of tens of thousands of air-dropped leaflets fluttering down into Brest daily, was beginning to make sense to the weary German fighting men holding out in their last-ditch defensive line just outside the walls of Brest. Those leaflets proclaimed: "Difficult though the postwar period may seem, you cannot choose a cowardly escape into death and leave Germany's reconstruction to your women and children." A sketch of a German soldier's grave, illuminated by a full moon, heightened the significance of the life-and-death decisions those fighters would have to make in the days ahead. Given the experience of the past year, several cynical German fighters became fatalistic, and some even dared to scribble the word "Brestgrad" onto the walls of their pillboxes—an allusion to the catastrophe suffered by the German Army at Stalingrad in 1943.

Ramcke had issued strict orders to his troops that those leaflets must be ignored, but such an order was of course impossible to enforce; and to many apathetic members of his garrison, particularly non-Germans, the Americans' points were truly compelling. Ramcke's chief of staff, Gen. Hans von der Mosel, once had to severely reprimand a German colonel, whom he discovered reading a leaflet. Later, in captivity, von der Mosel insisted that he himself had never read one because "some of its message was bound to stick."

On September 14, 1944, Ramcke prepared for the inevitable by printing thousands of leaflets of his own, labeled with the heading *Soldaten der Festung Brest!* ("Soldiers of Fortress Brest!"). If, "after heroic resistance we have to surrender to the numerical superiority of the enemy, it must be done in an honorable way," the leaflets declared. First, however, Ramcke had to describe to his men the nature of their American enemy.

> In reality, the American today, like once before, is the fighting tool in the hands of the international Jew, who is residing in Wall Street and who from there, assisted by Russian Bolshevism, wants to conquer the world. The inhabitants of the U.S.A. do not belong to one single race. All the races of the globe are represented, good ones and inferior ones. Among the latter are especially the colored and the great number of half-castes. . . . It must be expected that these inferior elements in the American Army will disobey [the Geneva Convention] and, obeying their base instincts, will mistreat defenseless POWs, just as much as the colored vassals of England have done in innumerable cases. [You will oppose] such treatment, in contradiction with existing laws, with your pride as a member of a nation of ancient culture and of the glorious German race.

Ramcke's diatribe said much more about why Nazi Germany had cast the world into a cataclysmic global war than it did about America's incentive to become a participant in it. By this stage of World War II, 29th Division veterans had seen enough of the enemy to understand with perfect clarity the reasons why they had been deployed by the millions across the ocean to fight. However, just in case there were any newcomers to the division who did not entirely grasp those reasons, Ramcke's leaflet would provide a quick refresher course. When hundreds of German leaflets fell into 29th Division hands in mid-September, Gerhardt promptly had one of them translated into English for insertion into the division's monthly

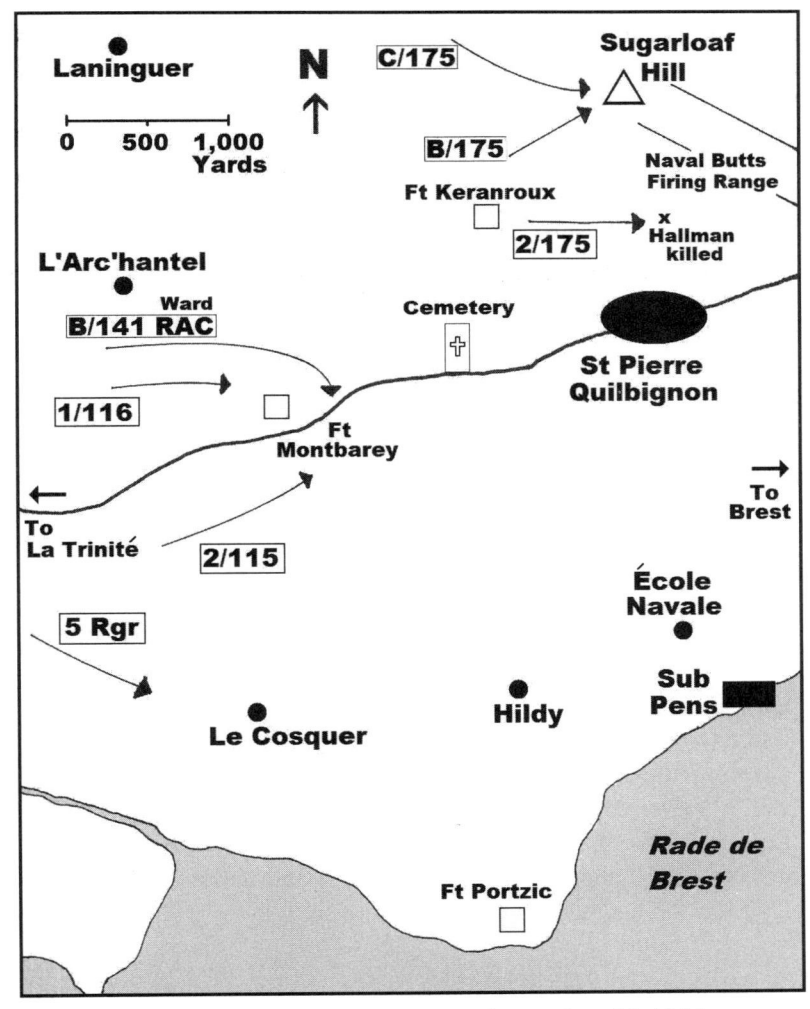

29th Division and 5th Rangers: September 14, 1944

action report. If Ramcke's arrogance and lies could not illuminate to 29ers the issues at stake in the current struggle, nothing would.

Evidence that Ramcke had much more on his mind than just the welfare of his soldiers and the fulfillment of his duty emerged in the last days of the Brest siege. Ramcke was well-known in German military circles as an egomaniac, a man who ardently prized the status that came with military decorations, particularly the legendary Iron Cross that originated in the Prussian Army in 1813. By 1944, Ramcke was already a highly decorated soldier, having received the coveted Knight's Cross of the Iron Cross for his daring leadership during the invasion of Crete; and the Knight's Cross with Oak Leaves for his heroics in North Africa.

Those were honors any German soldier would treasure, but Ramcke craved more. Later, during captivity in England, he revealed to a British Army officer his blunt scheme to get it. "If [I] was ever to get the 'Swords' and 'Diamonds' [two higher grades of the Knight's Cross], it was a case of now or never," he declared.

That statement was followed by an explanation so astonishing that his interrogator shortly put it down on paper:

> [Ramcke] couldn't very well ask for those awards outright, but as he knew he was in favor with the [Nazi] Party—and he had taken great care to see that he was—he decided that if he asked for decorations for some of his subordinates, these would not be refused. He therefore sent a telegram to the Führer recommending that the Oak Leaves should be awarded to Adm. [Otto] Kähler and Gen. [Hans] von der Mosel. These two did not really deserve this decoration [Ramcke commonly referred to them as "nitwits"]. Ramcke, however, knew perfectly well that if they were given the Oak Leaves, he would have to get something higher. Sure enough he got both the Knight's Cross with Swords and Knight's Cross with Diamonds.

Ramcke was one of only about thirty men to receive such lofty honors in World War II.

By September 14, 1944, the Germans at Brest may have known the end was near, but still the Americans faced the predicament of how exactly they would bring about the enemy's downfall. One detail was certain: the final assault would be no pushover. Although the enemy's Brest enclave was small, Ramcke still had plenty of fighters left, and even if only a small portion of them fought to the bitter end, American casualties could be huge. To prevent that, Middleton resolved to strike hard and fast, with no let-up until the Germans at last raised the white flag.

Although the 2nd Infantry Division was already battling block-by-block in the streets of eastern Brest, the neighboring 29th Division had not even reached the ancient and formidable walls on the city's western periphery, encasing a working-class part of town on the Penfeld River's west bank known as Recouvrance. Before the 29ers reached their ultimate objective, however, they would have to conquer three remarkably tough enemy strongpoints standing squarely between them and Recouvrance. The northernmost, only a mile west of the city walls, was "Sugarloaf Hill," that massive earthen mound also known to some 29ers as "The Naval Butts," which had acted as a backstop for the French Navy's gunnery practice in prewar days. That the Germans were not yet beaten was obvious to Lt. Col. Roger Whiteford, whose 1st Battalion, 175th Infantry, had on September 13 seen dozens of enemy troops suddenly emerge from the mound and launch a determined counterattack, which the 29ers had only barely contained. The next morning, September 14, it would be the Americans' turn to attack.

Two miles south of Sugarloaf lay a striking rocky headland known as Pointe du Portzic, featuring an 1848 octagonal lighthouse that in more peaceful times had employed its brilliant light to guide ships up to twenty-two miles out to sea into Brest harbor. In September 1944, however, the lighthouse was dark and abandoned; and the Germans had occupied the entire headland in force, taking advantage of an old French coastal strongpoint known as Fort du Portzic. Gerhardt would assign the job of taking that fort to one of his favorites, Maj. Richard Sullivan, commander of the 5th Ranger Battalion. Little more than 1,000 yards due east of Fort du Portzic lay the German Navy's infamous submarine pens, that massive structure of solid concrete that was a masterpiece of military engineering. If anything symbolized the German hold on Brest, it was those sub pens, and if the 29th Division could capture them, the battle would be as good as over.

But by far the toughest German strongpoint standing between the 29th Division and Recouvrance was Fort Montbarey, the aged French citadel that Ramcke had apparently classified as a position from which his troops must not retreat under any circumstances. They had so far carried out that order faithfully, although on September 12 and 13 the Americans had come very close to smashing their way into the fort. Located about halfway between Sugarloaf Hill and Fort du Portzic, Montbarey sat just north of the main N789 east-west highway leading into Brest, and it blocked access to the city exactly as its designers had intended hundreds of years in the past.

If ever there was a case of an irresistible force striking an immovable object, it was at Montbarey on September 14, 1944. The outcome of that paradoxical physical relationship would determine how soon—and at what cost in lives—the 29th Division would take Recouvrance. To generate an attacking force that was irresistible, Gerhardt pumped two fresh infantry battalions into the line on the night of September 13. On Montbarey's northwest side, the 116th Infantry's 1st Battalion, which had been out of the front lines for six glorious days, relieved the 1st Battalion, 115th Infantry. Meanwhile, south of the N789 road, the 115th Infantry replaced its 3rd Battalion with the somewhat rested 2nd Battalion, led by one of Gerhardt's favorites, Lt. Col. Tony Miller. It would be Miller's job to clean out the profusion of enemy pillboxes and resistance nests south of the N789, while the mission of taking Montbarey itself fell to the redoubtable new commander of the 1st Battalion, 116th Infantry, Maj. Tom Dallas.

The thirty-year-old Dallas was the perfect choice to fulfill that challenging task. Commissioned as a lieutenant in the Virginia National Guard after spending seven years as an enlisted man, Dallas had been one of the most notable characters in the 116th Infantry since its mobilization in 1941 and had indisputably proved himself as a solid combat leader since coming ashore with the first wave on Omaha Beach. He was large and somewhat portly, with a cherubic face that belied a ferocious temperament—a trait he had repeatedly revealed to alarmed victims and onlookers alike since training days at Fort Meade. Fortunately for the 29ers, by September 1944 most of that anger was focused on the enemy, a group for which he expressed a fanatical hatred. The Germans had inflicted terrible carnage upon Dallas's men on D-Day, and now he felt not the slightest pang of regret when verbalizing his revulsion for them. His fellow Stonewall Brigade battalion commander, Maj. Charles Cawthon, observed that "Tom was never one to make a muted effort; his demands for artillery and self-propelled gunfire to keep the Germans' heads down [at Fort Montbarey] while the engineers worked could probably be heard at the regimental command post without benefit of telephone."

What Dallas and his men were about to accomplish at Montbarey could not have been done without the active participation of a group of British Army soldiers with whom the 116th had been training behind the lines over the past several days. Those men were members of B Squadron, 141st Regiment, Royal Armoured Corps, also known as "The Buffs," who had brought fifteen flame-throwing Crocodile tanks to Brittany on U.S.

Army tank transporters to help the Yanks storm Brest's many concrete strongpoints filled with obstinate German defenders. The prospect of that support uplifted Dallas, and he promptly established a close working relationship with Maj. Nigel Ryle, B Squadron's highly competent and courageous commander.

Dallas's skills as a soldier were obvious to the British, one of whom noted in the squadron's history that he was "one of the few, so very few, absolutely fearless men who can stand unperturbed in a hail of bullets and mortar fire and bear a life that is doubly charmed." That observer added: "Dallas never gave out the location of his command post. It was invariably with the leading platoon—himself, a runner, and a guy with a telephone. 'I guess then, if folks really want to see me, well, they'll come and see me,' [said Dallas]. We hand it to Major Dallas in a big way." Dallas returned that compliment in full when he later described Major Ryle to a U.S. Army historian as "the best soldier I have ever known." Those who knew Dallas intimately grasped that he was not a man who routinely offered praise of that kind, and thus his admiration for his British Army counterpart was entirely genuine.

That the British did things a little differently than their American allies immediately became evident to the 29ers in the bivouac areas behind the front. The 116th Infantry's intelligence officer, Capt. Robert Walker, observed, "On a visit to the British one afternoon, at their command post, I noted that they had changed from battle dress, had tea in the late afternoon, and a late dinner in a tent on a table covered with a clean white tablecloth. They were cheerful and charming. They had earned a reputation as fearless fighters."

Dallas would gladly take all the help he could get, and since his was a mission of vital importance, Gerhardt offered him much more than just B Squadron in support of the Fort Montbarey effort. In a February 1947 letter to Joseph Ewing, the author of the classic divisional history *29 Let's Go!*, Dallas remarked,

> Supporting my battalion were, in addition to normal artillery [of the 111th Field Artillery Battalion], a platoon of the 644th Tank Destroyer Battalion [with four self-propelled M-10 tank destroyers], part of Company B, 121st Engineer Combat Battalion, Company B, 86th Chemical Mortar Battalion [with twelve 4.2-inch mortars], and some 105mm cannon from the 116th Infantry's Cannon Company. . . . We worked together as a closely integrated unit—otherwise we would never have been able to rip the fort open in three days.

Dallas had to figure out a way to get his infantry and Ryle's flame-throwing Crocodile tanks safely over the wide German antitank ditch guarding Montbarey's western approaches. An even more perilous threat, however, was the deadly enemy minefield encasing the fort, which according to an American intelligence report consisted of "buried 300-pound naval shells equipped with pressure ignitors" that could wipe out an unlucky Crocodile and all its occupants in an instant.

If ever there was a job for combat engineers, this was it. Late on September 13, therefore, Dallas directed the 121st Engineers' Company B, under the command of Capt. Sidney Smith, to carry out that taxing task in preparation for a combined infantry-tank attack the following day. Smith's mission would have been suicidal in daylight, for every German weapon within range would have opened up on the defenseless sappers, who by necessity had to work in the open. The engineers therefore would begin their work at 11 P.M. under the cover of a night sky that an account later described as "quite dark." An action report defined the engineers' two-fold mission as "clearing two 8-yard-wide paths, 50 yards apart, through the width of the minefield [approximately 200 yards] so that tanks could proceed safely; and putting a road across the 13-feet-wide and 10-feet-deep antitank ditch." (Another engineer report specified that the ditch was actually 20 feet across.)

To lead the way, Smith selected a thirty-man platoon under the command of 1st Lt. Shelton Clemmer, who in 1943 had learned the value of initiative in battle as a member of the short-lived 29th Ranger Battalion. The job ahead could only be executed with proper equipment, and platoon members burdened themselves with mine detectors, white engineer tape, picks, shovels, batches of C-2 plastic explosives, and many miscellaneous tools. Among those diverse utensils were bayonets, which the engineers noted with some trepidation would have to be used to probe for mines that were immune to detectors.

At the stroke of H-Hour, 11 P.M., the sappers slipped into no-man's-land and hurriedly began their work under eerie and gloomy conditions more evocative of World War I than the present war. Probing with metal detectors and bayonets for 300-pound mines, fused with hair-trigger pressure igniters and concealed in severely cratered ground, was an adventure that sappers could later relate to their grandchildren if they survived. Years after the event, the intense strain of such work would be almost beyond words, and certainly no embellishment would be necessary to convey the nature of that strain to an awestruck listener.

The official report of the operation by the 121st Engineer Battalion observed:

The detecting was done by three-man teams. The first man operated the detector. The second man marked the extent of his sweep with white tape. The third man did the probing, using a bayonet for this work and thrusting in, always easily and at an angle. The men all worked in a crouching position, and the detector was used with the handle removed. All work proceeded in silence, and to further lessen the possibility of detection, the resonator [the device that beeped when metal was detected] was removed from the detector and reliance was put exclusively on the luminous needle. The ground was so littered with metal from shells, bombs, and enemy material that a suspicious object was encountered in practically every yard of each lane.

Sometimes the sappers would work for a quarter of an hour on a supposed mine only to discover that it in truth was just a large shell fragment—or in one case a discarded German bayonet, buried in the soft earth. But when a 29er definitively located an enemy mine, his work immediately became infinitely more dangerous, for now he had to discern the best means of neutralizing it. The 116th Infantry's commander, Col. Philip Dwyer, reported to division headquarters that such a task would be tricky: "The engineers can't lift [the shells] out because the men have to stay too close to the ground—and if they blow them up, they leave craters for the tanks." Despite Dwyer's report, the engineers had perceived that it would be much too dangerous to defuse the mines where they found them; and they therefore determined that their only feasible option would be to blow them up from a safe distance. Afterward, they would speedily have to fill in the resulting craters with earth.

The 121st's report specified,

> The aerial bombardment had put so many craters over the field that no mine pattern could be described. Some of the mines were buried too deeply to register on the detectors; one was so shallow that Pvt. Charles R. Lake stumbled over it before it had registered on the detector. . . . Four mines were discovered, three in one lane and one in the other. . . . A one-pound charge of plastic explosive was placed on each shell and tied into the primacord main.

At 8:30 A.M., Clemmer shoved the handle down on his igniter, an act that instantaneously detonated all of the carefully placed charges, including those designed to blow in the walls of the antitank ditch so that a road could swiftly be bulldozed across it. If the Germans had not yet figured out their opponents were up to something, the staggering series of explosions that resulted would certainly provide a hint that they must instantly prepare for an American assault.

The massive explosion triggered by Clemmer neutralized several German mines, but regrettably also revealed at least one German naval shell buried so deep that neither detectors nor bayonets had pinpointed it. Pvt. John Nelson, a Kentuckian, spotted the shell in one of the two paths to be used by the British Crocodiles and charged forward, aiming to place a charge on the shell and detonate it before the tanks pushed ahead. He drew the attention of the Germans, who felled him with a burst from a machine gun. Nevertheless, he pressed on, placed a charge on the shell, and withdrew to detonate it. Nelson survived; and for this act of "outstanding courage and devotion to duty, which materially contributed to the success of the assault," the 29th Division granted him the Silver Star.

The entire mine-clearing operation had been fulfilled with a loss of one engineer, a private by the name of William Berkowitz. (A second, Pvt. John Fogelsanger, later died of wounds received that night). The 121st was populated heavily by New Englanders, one of whom was Private Berkowitz, a native of Massachusetts. Late on the night of September 13, Berkowitz volunteered to shoulder a rifle and provide forward security for his fellow sappers who had to focus their full attention on locating and neutralizing enemy mines. In the eerie gloom he crept ahead of his comrades, down and up the innumerable craters splattered across no-man's-land, to a site very close to German lines. He must have let down his guard for an instant, for an enemy sniper soon shot him dead. His buddies later saw to it that Berkowitz would receive a posthumous Silver Star, the citation for which noted that he displayed "unflinching courage and unselfish devotion to duty."

Had the Germans been more alert on the night of September 13–14, the human cost to the 121st Engineers would certainly have been much worse than just Berkowitz and Fogelsanger. An engineer account noted, "The enemy put up a few flares during the approach—but these ceased after the engineers got up to the ditch." Even if they failed to directly observe the Americans, however, the devious Germans had done everything in their power to kill or maim any GI who dared to enter no-man's-land. One 29er reported, "In going through the craters, the engineers discovered that the Germans had emplaced four-pronged impaling devices at the bottom, each spike being about eight to ten inches long. One infantryman had become impaled and badly hurt when he flopped on one of these spikes during the afternoon."

Ultimately the engineers would be judged on the quality of their work; and according to an American statement, "Lieutenant Clemmer was so certain that he had done a perfect job on the minefield that he offered to have his enlisted men ride on the outside of the Crocodiles when they went through. The [engineers] didn't think this was quite the sporting touch—and the ride wasn't made."

The British were exceptionally proud of their unique flame-spewing "Crocs," all of which were painted with names beginning with the letter "S" ("Sudan," "Scimitar," "Squirt," and "Sheridan," for example); and now was the time to show the Yanks how they could materially contribute to final victory at Brest. As a British observer correctly noted, however, "The Americans had little experience of close cooperation with tanks, and none with flamethrowers—in particular how to apply them over this extraordinary ground. Nigel [Ryle] and the American staff hammered away and produced the drill, then down to training in real earnest."

To ensure their tanks would be properly employed for the September 14 attack, the British tankers had performed several hazardous "recces" (patrols) on foot of the German defenses. One memorable patrol led by Capt. Harry Cobden, the tank squadron's second-in-command, had included seven American sappers from the 121st Engineers, and the conduct of one of those 29ers, Sgt. Edward Humphrey, particularly impressed the British. Humphrey was already a legend within the 121st as a result of his July 1944 heroics at St. Lô, where he had been awarded the Silver Star. At Montbarey, he was about to gain an Oak Leaf Cluster to that impressive decoration. The British squadron's postwar history noted that Humphrey did several "hair-raising recces, clearing paths through the minefields in broad daylight the whole way along for the Crocs, and escaping in some miraculous way with his own life though his men were falling right, left, and center all around." Unhappily, that British writer did not realize that less than three weeks later, Humphrey's luck would run out on a mine-clearing operation on the Dutch-German frontier, where he was captured by the enemy; his comrades never again saw him alive.

It was never easy for the leader of a combined tank-infantry force to decide who should lead an assault: the tankers or the riflemen. For the attack on Montbarey on the morning of September 14, Dallas settled on the latter because innumerable German defenders still occupied concealed positions outside the fort's walls, and if those enemy troops were not wiped out they could easily pick off the British tanks with their lethal *Panzerfaust* antitank rockets at pointblank range. Consequently, as Dallas noted in his 1947 letter to Ewing, "For the opening of the attack I committed Company C only, with a mission of attacking due east and cleaning out all open emplacements on the west side of the fort up to the moat." When Dallas's men jumped off at 8 A.M., they harbored hopes that the Germans had withdrawn from Montbarey, since the enemy's customary heavy mortar fire was almost completely lacking. One 29er at the front reported to Gerhardt at 5:47 A.M.: "Everything's quiet . . . too quiet, they say."

But the enemy was there—and, as usual, ready. When the attack opened the 29ers successfully made it through the minefield and across the antitank ditch, but all hell broke loose when they got into some enemy communications trenches connecting several pillboxes immediately west of the fort. "Company C was engaged all day in hand-to-hand, bayonet, and grenade fighting, but in spite of heavy casualties, they had completed their mission by about 4 P.M.," Dallas recalled. "They occupied all outer defenses on the west side of the moat when they completed their attack."

Company C's notable success was due in part to the outstanding leadership of its commander, 1st Lt. Joseph Adams, a native of Georgia. According to the citation for the Silver Star Adams would earn for gallantry, "From the time of the initial assault at 0800 hours until the late afternoon, the company was engaged in a fierce, moving, close-combat engagement. . . . [Adams] traveled from one platoon to another under grazing enemy machine gun fire, directing each phase of the attack. . . . His courageous leadership and his audacious determination inspired all his officers and men to a successful accomplishment of their mission."

But from the very start of Company C's assault, Dallas was not moving nearly fast enough for Gerhardt, who at 9:26 A.M. loudly complained to Dallas's boss, Colonel Dwyer: "I'm getting sick of this slow stuff!" The variance between the reality of front-line combat and Gerhardt's perception of it had always been a sore point among his subordinates; but on this occasion, at least, Gerhardt's annoyance was apparently entirely inappropriate, for his assistant division commander, Col. Leroy Watson, had been at Dallas's side all morning and reported back to the War Room at 1:40 P.M. that the 116th was "moving very well."

The infantrymen's progress could, in part, be attributed to the vast amount of suppressive fire the Americans were placing on Montbarey, including an effective barrage of white phosphorous smoke laid down by the 86th Chemical Mortar Battalion. According to Dallas, "The smokescreen was started about 1 P.M. and was kept up for about four and one-half hours. We really gave the mortar crews a workout that day. The screen was effective and aided considerably in that it blinded distant observation, resulting in our not receiving any artillery fire from the Germans."

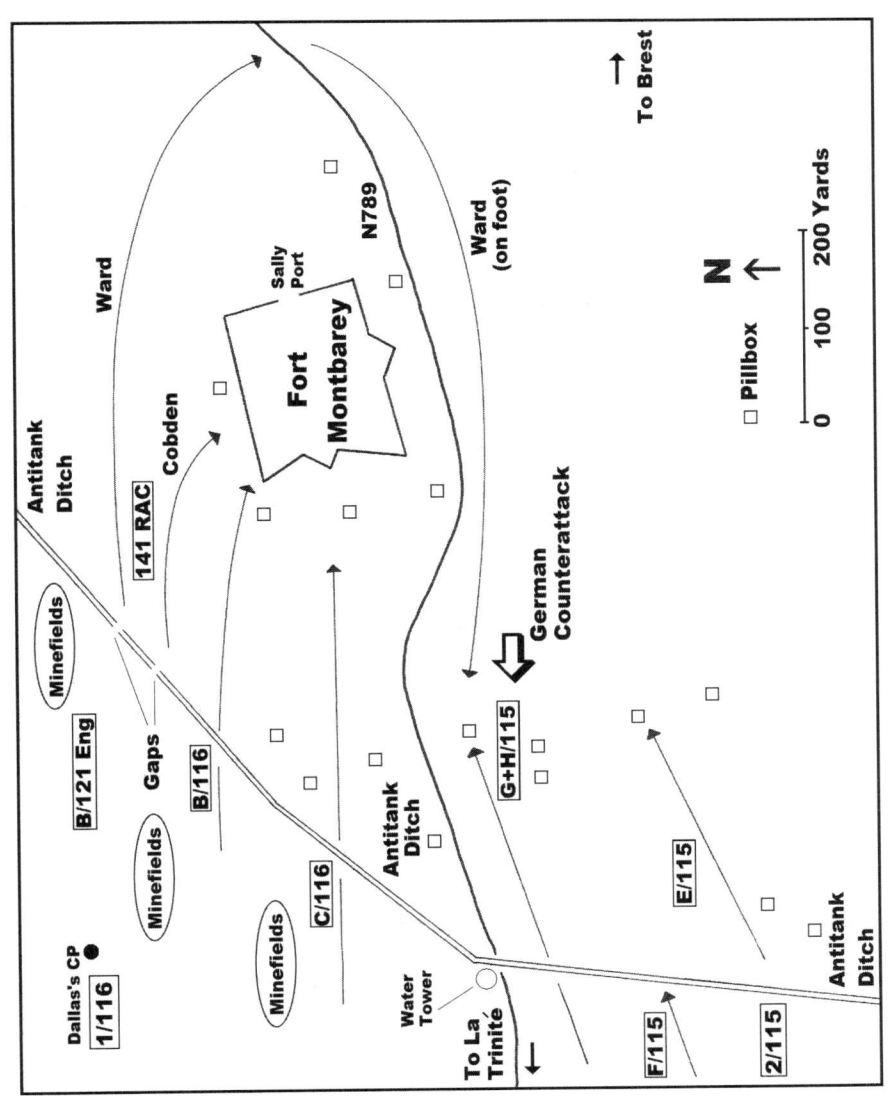

The assault on Ft. Montbarey: September 14, 1944

At about 2 P.M. there was a short lull in the fighting, during which the 29ers were astonished to observe a German medic emerge from Montbarey carrying a white flag. Some GIs escorted him to Dwyer's command post, and there he handed a crumpled note from the German commander of the Montbarey garrison to Captain Walker. A hasty perusal of the message indicated to a disappointed Walker that its purpose was not to initiate surrender proceedings. Rather, it was a straightforward appeal to Dwyer to demonstrate compassion for both sides' wounded. "I have with me an American soldier who is severely wounded and needs medical aid," the note began. "I beg you to give me an opportunity to transport to you this man as well as a few of my own wounded. I appeal to you to send back to me my medics. Yesterday my medic was shot as he was rendering aid to a wounded American soldier."

Walker reported this development back to the 29th Division's senior intelligence officer, Lt. Col. Paul Krznarich, who made the kind of pitiless reply that unfortunately had become the norm in a war of such unceasing brutality: "We had trouble with this before—keep him [the wounded American soldier] as a prisoner."

Now it was the British tanks' turn; and when they jumped off, Dallas and his men eagerly looked forward to discerning how effective their remarkably impressive petroleum flame-jets would be when they splattered up against Montbarey's walls and poured through the enemy's firing embrasures. That would be a sight to behold, and the impact upon the enemy should be terrific, but first the tanks had to negotiate the ditch and the minefield safely to get within flame-throwing range.

At 4:45 P.M. three Crocodiles, under the command of Lt. Hubert Anthony Ward, lined up one behind the other at the forward edge of the minefield. Behind them were four conventional tanks, armed with either 75mm or 95mm cannons, which would provide Ward's group with covering fire. Upon a hand-signal from Ward, the drivers revved up their engines and cautiously started forward through one of the paths marked by the 121st with white engineer tape. As indicated by technical information provided by the British to the 29th Division, "Each Crocodile tank tows an armored trailer containing 400 gallons of petroleum fuel and five nitrogen tanks under 2,500 pounds per square inch pressure to force fuel through the tube to the tank and project it about 80 yards in front of the tank. The ignition [of the fuel] is by electric spark. The gunner, seated to the left of the driver, may fire 120 to 160 one-second bursts, aiming with a telescopic sight." Each tank had also been provided with a frontal hedge-cutter courtesy of the 121st Engineer Battalion.

The Crocodile was slow and extraordinarily heavy, but one of its strongest traits was that it could traverse broken ground more adroitly than lighter tanks. That characteristic would come in handy at Montbarey since the terrain surrounding the fort had been mangled into a moonscape by aerial bombs and artillery; and no matter how intensely the 29th Division's engineers worked to smooth it out, the ground would have been treacherous for tanks even had no enemy been present. Lieutenant Ward, known to his brother officers simply as "Tony," led the way with his Croc, and although the ground was as rough as expected, for a minute or two it seemed as if the plan would work with no hitches. But then disaster struck when the tank behind Ward's, commanded by Sgt. Leslie Morley, ran over one of the enemy's buried naval shells. According to the tank squadron's history,

> There was a colossal explosion, and the whole track wrapped itself over the turret. The driver, L/C [Lance Corporal] D. Moore, was killed outright. Sergeant Jake [Leslie] Morley, Trooper [Guy] Thorne, Trooper [Harry] Adams, and Trooper [Leslie] Worthy were hellishly battered and spent many months in hospital—Thorne and Worthy having both legs broken amongst other things. This completely blocked the whole column behind . . . [and] the engineers began desperately clearing a further passage around the dead Croc.

Captain Cobden, who occupied a command tank behind Ward's column, observed that "Sergeant Morley's tank blew up on a buried naval shell in the center of the marked gap in the minefield, just a few yards in front of me." That misfortune was certainly a profound shock to the 29th Division engineers, who had professed confidence that their mine-clearing work had been thorough. But the British tankers were experienced combat veterans, well aware of the chaos and uncertainty of modern warfare; in their postwar accounts of the Montbarey battle, they expressed not the slightest lack of confidence in their American comrades-in-arms. On the contrary, they had seen firsthand the perils of the engineers' task, and one British tanker declared they had carried it out with "superb courage." Still, how did it happen? The most likely explanation is that the American mine detectors failed to locate several buried shells, a detail corroborated by the 121st's official report, which stated: "Some of the mines were buried too deeply to register on the detector. . . . Those too deeply buried were discovered only when exploded by sympathetic detonation." Unluckily for the Americans and their allies, one of those shells was located squarely in the middle of the path used by Ward's Crocodiles, buried deeply enough so that it was neither picked up by the detector nor revealed by a nearby explosion—but shallow enough so that its exceptionally sensitive fuse would be ignited by the overhead pressure exerted by a passing forty-ton Crocodile. Another less likely possibility is that the Americans had indeed detected the buried shell, but the primacord and plastic explosives fastened to it somehow had failed to detonate it.

Historians could explain it all later. The only detail that mattered at 5 P.M. on September 14, 1944, was that Tony Ward's Crocodile was now all alone. Still, Ward directed his driver, Trooper George Clare, to keep going straight for Montbarey in a latter-day version of the Charge of the Light Brigade. Unlike that renowned 1854 debacle, however, Ward's dash was anything but futile, and much to the satisfaction of Major Dallas, who observed the action firsthand, it soon would accomplish significant military benefits.

In the Crocodile's wake Dallas sent his Company B forward, which promptly started collecting frightened German soldiers as prisoners as they emerged with their hands held high from the various pillboxes beyond Montbarey's walls. The 29ers could plainly see that just a few jets of flame from Ward's tank had been all the inducement the enemy needed, and ultimately nearly eighty of them surrendered to Company B—all of whom, as a 116th Infantry narrative maintained, "were completely terrified and incapable of action." According to the British squadron's postwar history, Ward went

> through the minefield and on to the tricky antitank ditch, over it by the skin of his tracks, then a very pretty game of in and out of the craters, scything his burning track of death through the rich harvest of machine guns and light antiaircraft and antitank guns. Driving and commanding were and had to be superb. . . . Right up to the sunken road on the north side [of the fort], from where he flamed and shot the infantry in the German positions along the whole length of the wood surrounding the fort. Then over to the left and around the corner, flaming and blasting until the doughboys were in possession of the eastern wooded fringe as well—drill working famously, infantry right up behind and cashing in one hundred percent.

Ward and his intrepid crew had not only reached Fort Montbarey, but gone beyond it—more than half a mile beyond it, in fact, until it seemed for a few glorious moments that they would charge into Recouvrance by themselves, spewing deadly flame at any enemy redoubt daring to offer resistance. But soon Ward's Crocodile used up its trailer's entire load of petroleum fuel, so it was no longer possible to flame the Germans; and even worse, Ward had been using his main 6-pounder gun and single turret-mounted Besa machine gun so aggressively that he had finally run out of bullets—and shells, too. At that point Ward's tank was a declawed and defanged lion that could no longer inflict hurt upon its quarry. Besides, Ward had gotten well ahead of his supporting infantry, and logically there was nothing to do now except to return to the 116th's lines. He started to do that by coming around the fort's southern side rather than returning on the north side from whence he had come.

However, his astonishing journey came to an abrupt end when his Crocodile tumbled sideways into a large depression, at the bottom of which was a large enemy bunker filled with thirty-nine petrified Germans apparently eager to surrender. But when they gradually grasped that Ward's tank was practically impotent, some of them changed their minds. In the words of B Squadron's history, "The tilt of the tank was forcing the petrol out, and fumes were filling the tank. Worse still, the fall had released a methyl-bromide extinguisher inside the tank, and this was now discharging at full speed. One by one the crew were starting to pass out, and Tony felt more than ever that without a breath of fresh air, life just wasn't on. So what does the brave little lad do but pop his revolver out of the hatch . . . and in his best Yorkshire German yells 'Hände hoch!' [Hands up!]."

The odds against the beleaguered British tank crew were great, but Ward's audacious action worked. It didn't hurt that one of Ward's tankers produced a 20-pound Bren light machine gun from the tank's interior, fully armed with a thirty-round magazine, which according to a witness Ward test-fired with "fearsome abandon." Meanwhile, Majors Ryle and Dallas had become concerned by Ward's apparent disappearance, and they resolved to find and rescue him posthaste. In truth, however, Ward found his rescuers before they found him: He abandoned his tank and moved on foot with his crew across that deadly ground back into American lines— minus his beloved Crocodile, but with an impressive haul of prisoners.

In the meantime three more British tanks roaming no-man's-land and flaming the walls of Montbarey became immobilized: two by tumbling down into unseen craters; and another by throwing one of its tracks. Captain Cobden occupied one of those tanks, and he recalled: "I found it necessary to get out of my tank in order to extricate it, and two others. . . . A 40mm gun spent its time sniping in my direction, and I leaped into a convenient crater, there to meet an American. I had a few words with him, only to find he would not again be conversing on this earth."

By herculean effort, Cobden and others managed to free all three tanks and head back to American lines—somewhat hindered by the large batches of German prisoners wishing to follow them. What was about to happen, however, revealed that the British tankers had much more to fear from inanimate German objects than they did from live ones. According to Cobden, "Things became confused. . . . Halfway through the minefield the tank behind mine [commanded by Lt. Neal Hare], following in my tracks, blew up on yet another undiscovered naval shell. This so upset our American passenger [guarding the German prisoners] that he accidentally shot himself through the thigh with his own pistol."

The mine's explosion was an appalling spectacle that immediately drew the attention of everyone in sight, for the massive force of the blast actually separated the Crocodile's turret from the hull and blew it and its three occupants into the air. It hardly seemed possible, but all three—Hare, Lance Sgt. Albert Cowe, and Lance Cpl. Jack Rayman—survived. All were seriously injured, although according to a British observer, "Lance Cpl. Rayman, with a broken thigh, was as cool as a cucumber as they picked him up." Unfortunately, the two drivers positioned in the hull, Troopers E. Guy and A. Frudd, were much more severely hurt since they were closer to the source of the explosion. Guy died immediately, and Frudd expired the following day.

By the time the surviving Crocodiles made it back to American lines, the sun had almost descended to the western horizon. That night, when the tankers gathered in their bivouac area and calculated the cost of the battle, they were disheartened by the realization that two of their comrades were dead and eight gravely wounded, one of whom would die the next day. Two of the seven tanks committed to the action had blown up on German mines, and a third had been smashed up in a huge crater. It was a high price to pay, and when Captain Walker of the 116th Infantry wandered into B Squadron's camp that night, he sensed that some of the tankers were distraught over the loss of their friends.

But on September 14 the squadron had materially contributed to a vital tactical success at Fort Montbarey, a detail Major Dallas substantiated a few days later when, in a conversation with a U.S. Army historian, he said of Ward's intrepid dash around Montbarey: "It was as bold an act as I have ever seen." If Gerhardt would judge the combat by the damage inflicted upon the enemy, the British had done remarkably well. In the words of B Squadron's history: "Six officers and 116 ORs [other ranks] taken prisoner, several guns knocked out, a hell of a lot [of Germans] killed, a hell of a lot put to flight, and a daring penetration to Recouvrance.

[Ward had not in fact made it all the way to Recouvrance.] Not bad for a lone Croc—in fact probably a record."

Gerhardt agreed, and he promptly penned a letter to Ryle commending the members of his tank squadron for their "superior service" at Montbarey. He concluded his letter by affirming, "The troops of this division were always most enthusiastic as to your combat efficiency"—words of praise the general had only rarely employed when alluding to his own 29ers since D-Day.

Gerhardt ordered an aide to initiate the required paperwork for the award of a U.S. Army Silver Star to Ward—an exceptional recognition for a member of a foreign army. The commander of the Ninth U.S. Army, Lt. Gen. William Simpson, approved the award in November; and on January 2, 1945, in the Dutch village of Bergeyk, Simpson himself would pin the Silver Star on Ward while Simpson's aide, reading from the citation, recounted Ward's "intrepidity, aggressiveness, and devotion to duty." Thirteen other members of B Squadron, 141st Regiment, Royal Armoured Corps (The Buffs)—including Major Ryle—were awarded the Bronze Star.

2. A DANGEROUS PLACE TO BE CAUGHT

While Dallas's infantrymen and Ryle's tankers were waging their fierce battle for Fort Montbarey on September 14, only one-third of a mile away Lt. Col. Lou Smith's 115th Infantry was fighting an entirely different kind of war south of the N789 road. Dallas's struggle at Montbarey may have been tough, but for the next few days the 115th's fight was even tougher. Smith's men would have to overcome enemy fortifications just as formidable as those Dallas had to deal with—minus Ryle's flamethrowing tanks. As the members of the 115th were about to learn, German soldiers would apparently rather face the hazards of American bullets and artillery shells than deal with the prospect of immolation in a confined pillbox from a Crocodile's flamethrower. In fact, for a short time on September 14, the 115th completely lost the initiative due to the enemy's unforeseen "enthusiasm," a detail that caused Gerhardt to yet again push back the date when he expected the 29th Division to enter Brest.

At an assembly of his senior commanders, Gerhardt had once declared: "The rifle battalions carry the division the whole way. A properly trained combat battalion can do any damn thing in the world. Their leader has got to have some imagination, some skill, some knowledge. With those things, there are no limits to his success." On September 14 the 115th's 2nd Battalion, led by Lt. Col. Tony Miller, would determine if that statement was valid. On a broad front of over 800 yards, Miller's men jumped off at 8 A.M. with orders to penetrate the belt of German fortifications south of Montbarey, but they ran into immediate trouble. At 9:30 A.M. the regimental journal noted, "Jerry very well entrenched and has some 20mm and 40mm antiaircraft guns—and is using them. Have used WP [white phosphorus] on us. [Some 29ers later claimed that the WP came from the 2nd Battalion's own mortars.] Jerry has many machine guns firing crossfire from the flanks."

Miller tried to overcome the enemy resistance nests with a 1:45 P.M. air strike by four P-47 Thunderbolts, and for awhile that support helped. An intense barrage by 110th Field Artillery Battalion howitzers, expertly prearranged by liaison officer Capt. Frank Steele from Miller's forward command post, also provided vital assistance to the haggard infantrymen. At 2 P.M. the attack resumed with Company G on the left and Company E on the right. The commanders of those same two companies, Lieutenants Robert Rideout and Roderick Parsch, had successfully guided the 115th's laudable September 8 attack on the German strongpoint at Kerrognant; but only six days later, both outfits were worn out and severely understrength. One 29er described the terrain over which Company G had to attack as "open [and] flat as a billiard table, with no cover at all except for the tank trap [ditch]—which was a dangerous place to be caught in."

Thanks to the air and artillery support, Miller's men managed to push ahead a few hundred yards beyond the antitank ditch. On the left, parts of Rideout's Company G stumbled into an enemy pillbox-bunker complex only 300 yards southwest of Fort Montbarey. The Germans should have been able to hold on to it for a considerable period, but the 29ers seized it at 3:15 P.M. along with more than a dozen prisoners. Among those tough enemy paratroopers held in reserve in the Montbarey sector, however, that success triggered a reaction that the Americans had experienced many times before and should have expected this time as well. It was the standard German counterattack, or "enthusiasm," as Gerhardt referred to it, which hit Company G hard just before sunset. The Germans continued to press their attack after dark, and the 2nd Battalion's journal ominously noted at 11:15 P.M.: "Company G is in a bad spot."

One depleted rifle platoon and a pair of machine-gun teams from Company H were in such a particularly bad spot, in fact, that the Germans were demanding their surrender. That beleaguered group of 29ers had found itself besieged in one of the captured enemy pillboxes when friendly units on both flanks had been driven back by the paratroopers' assault. Intense close-range fighting persisted in the area around the pillbox all night long. The leader of the Company H machine-gun teams—

and de facto leader of the entire group—S/Sgt. Donald Van Roosen, recalled: "Around the pillbox we were sheltered by deep trenches and the underground bunker we had captured earlier in the morning, [but] the paratroopers had infiltrated troops all around us."

Miller needed to mount a rescue attempt in a hurry; and at 2:30 A.M. on September 15, the 2nd Battalion journal noted, "Company F attempting to advance to retake pillbox, but fear enemy is holding it strongly." That was an accurate assessment of the situation, for Company F stalled at the antitank ditch and could not get restarted. As Van Roosen later lamented, "It was only 200 yards from where we were," but by then it was too late. Van Roosen and twelve other 29ers fought on for a time, but finally, sometime near sunrise, they yielded to unrelenting German pressure and surrendered. Their captors marched them down to the Brest waterfront, little more than a mile away, and placed them in the submarine pens under guard along with dozens of other American captives.

One of the prisoners, PFC Joe Rockman, was apprehensive about his treatment because he was Jewish, but in the sub pens Rockman experienced an amazing coincidence. A German doctor who had once lived in Brooklyn, New York, and known Rockman spotted him and greeted him warmly; and from that moment until the Americans captured the sub pens three days later, the German behavior toward Rockman was entirely correct. The thirteen 29ers would thankfully experience only a short period of captivity, but still it was spent in much hunger and discomfort. The sub pens' solid concrete ceilings and walls, however, at least provided safety from the unceasing deluge of American bombs and shells.

What one battalion could not accomplish, maybe two could. At about 11 A.M. on September 15, Colonel Smith committed Maj. Glover Johns's 1st Battalion to the fight with the mission, as Johns recalled, "To dig the Germans out [of the pillbox complex] again and rescue the captured men of the 2nd Battalion, if possible." For Johns, a more challenging mission could hardly be imagined: His depleted outfit had only recently been pulled out of the line for a rest, but that recuperative period had lasted only a single day. In the bitter September 13 fight on Montbarey's northern side, one of his company commanders, 1st Lt. William Todd of Company A, had been killed; another, 1st Lt. Arthur Chadwick of Company B, had been seriously wounded.

Johns moved the 1st Battalion into position, examined the ground, sent out scouts—and promptly concluded that the only way he would have any chance of success was to attack after nightfall. That attack jumped off at 10 P.M., with Company B in the lead. "It went in fast, under artillery, and for several hours the situation was very vague," Johns observed. "But at 11 P.M., 1st Lt. Luke Padian, in command [of Company B] for the first time, announced that the pillbox was secure . . . over two hundred prisoners were taken." It did not take a military genius to determine why the enemy had been able to frustrate the advance of the 29th Division for so many days in that sector: At least six concrete pillboxes and underground bunkers were scattered among the fields, and much to the astonishment of the 29ers, the electric lights within still glowed. In one of the bunkers was a large subterranean hospital, but, as Johns remarked, "The only remaining patient was very dead."

The 1st Battalion captured a proud German major, who promptly insisted that he be brought before Johns. "It seemed he was very perturbed over the fact that his personal luggage and his striker [orderly] had not been brought out with him, in accordance with promises made by a party that had been attempting to negotiate the surrender of the entire Fortress Brest," Johns recalled. "He was informed that such promises did not cover small units that were routed out at bayonet point after a fanatical counterattack that had inflicted some loss on our troops."

A frustrated Gerhardt by now sensed that his men would have to kill or capture virtually every German soldier in the Montbarey area before the 29th Division could march into Brest and declare the city secure. He longed to do that soon—but would the Germans hang on for much longer? Any American soldier with a decent grasp of military operations suspected that they could not. The enemy, however, had defied American expectations countless times in the past, and would continue to do so this time.

On September 14, while Dallas and Ryle were smashing up against the walls of Montbarey, only a mile to the northeast Col. William Purnell's 175th Infantry was punching through the enemy's last-ditch defensive line west of Brest. The most prominent component of that line was the man-made Sugarloaf Hill, on and around which German paratroopers had been holding out against a forceful attack by the 175th's 1st Battalion's for several days. The enemy's hold on the hill, however, was shattered when the 1st Battalion's commander, Lt. Col. Roger Whiteford, directed two of his rifle companies to move in for the kill at 10:30 A.M. on September 14: Company C would assault the hill itself; Company B would deal with the numerous pillboxes that lay scattered in the fields to the south.

By this stage of the Brest campaign, the 29ers had learned that if a direct infantry attack against a prepared enemy position were to succeed, the assaulting infantrymen had to move up against the enemy as quickly and closely as possible following a friendly artillery and smoke barrage.

At times that tactic appeared nearly suicidal, but it was far better than being caught in the open by enemy machine guns. Now that the American artillery ammunition shortage was nothing but a memory, the 29ers had a chance to prove just how effective such a tactic was, and on September 14, a platoon in the 175th's Company B, led by T/Sgt. Bruce Barnum, did exactly that.

South of Sugarloaf the German occupants of three pillboxes demonstrated a clear intent to hold fast against the 175th's assault, but in the immediate aftermath of intense shelling courtesy of the 224th Field Artillery Battalion, Barnum's platoon was upon them before they realized what was happening. Only one week later Barnum observed, "We were right with them, mixing it up close." So close, in fact, that grenades were the weapons of choice. As Barnum related the action in the division newspaper, *29 Let's Go*, "The platoon ran out of grenades and began pitching Jerry's. In their hurry to take cover underground, the Germans had left stacks of ammunition in the communication trenches between the pillboxes. The Americans heaved enough of Jerry's own ammunition at him to make him cry for mercy." According to the *29 Let's Go* account, Barnum's platoon captured forty-three enemy prisoners, plus a vast assortment of weapons, ammunition—and whiskey. It was, as the soldier-reporter noted, "The stuff the Krauts thrive on."

Those "Krauts" still occupying the many tunnels and bunkers within Sugarloaf's massive earthen mound may have had many of those items available in profusion, but by noon on September 14 they were almost surrounded and could not hold out much longer. A determined advance by the 175th Infantry's Company C, led by 1st Lt. Grant Darby, worked around the hill's southern side in the early afternoon and finally forced its way inside some of those seemingly impenetrable defensive structures. According to the citation for the Silver Star Darby would gain for his exploits, he displayed "expert leadership and unflinching courage, [and] was constantly at the head of his troops, encouraging and inspiring them to maximum effort." (Remarkably, this was Darby's second Silver Star in less than two weeks, as he had also earned one at Hill 103.) Thanks to Darby and his intrepid 29ers, the German defenders finally gave up at 2:15 P.M.; and with that success the 175th now possessed a dominant observation post only one mile distant from Brest's western walls.

September 14, 1944, may have been a remarkably successful day in the annals of the 175th Infantry, but it was also one in which the names of two key soldiers were removed from the regiment's rolls. In the midst of the Sugarloaf battle, Roger Whiteford—a fixture in the 175th Infantry (formerly Baltimore's "Dandy 5th" of Maryland) for more than twenty years—had to yield command of the 1st Battalion when he suffered his second serious wound since D-Day. At first Purnell underestimated the severity of that injury when he reported to Gerhardt that Whiteford would be out "only for a few days." In truth Whiteford's wound was much worse than that, and he would not return to the regiment until Christmas, when the 29th Division was fighting in western Germany.

Whiteford's replacement would be Lt. Col. Lawrence Meeks, a native of Roanoke, Virginia, and a longtime member of the Virginia National Guard. Meeks had landed on Omaha Beach on D-Day as commander of the 116th Infantry's 3rd Battalion, and like so many other survivors of that cataclysm, had been shaken by the experience. Immediately before the liberation of St. Lô, Gerhardt had replaced him as CO of the battalion with the legendary Tom Howie, but he had remained with the 29th Division as a supernumerary officer and for two months had performed highly useful service as a stand-in commander, including executive officer for Task Force Sugar. Gerhardt, however, wished to find a permanent replacement for Meeks as soon as possible. Blunt as always, the general complained to Purnell: "You can't count on Meeks—he's no good when it comes to getting something done. . . . Shop around and let me know."

The loss of the second soldier was much more devastating to Purnell because it was permanent. Staff Sgt. Sherwood Hallman of Pennsylvania was only one of twenty-five men in the 175th killed in action on September 14, but his death in combat amid the hedgerows east of Fort Keranroux, just short of the 175th's final objective of Recouvrance, was especially heartrending to his Company F comrades because he had expertly guided bewildered riflemen through the terrors of combat innumerable times in the recent past. Hallman was irreplaceable—one of those rare men who could be snatched out of the civilian world by the draft and emerge from the mind-numbing experience of U.S. Army basic training with a proclivity for decisive and courageous leadership on the battlefield. He had proven that fact conclusively on the morning of September 11, 1944, when he single-handedly shattered the enemy's defensive lines at Ilioc, an event that led directly to the fall of Fort Keranroux two days later. After three consecutive weeks of brutal combat at Brest, the battered 175th was on the verge of final victory, but sadly Sergeant Hallman would not live to see that gratifying moment. No one in the 29th Division yet realized it, but the U.S. Army would shortly agree with Company F's assessment of Hallman's superb leadership qualities by granting him a posthumous Medal of Honor.

Maj. Gen. Charles H. Gerhardt Jr. and Baptise Faucher, FFI commander at Brest. Gerhardt was about to pin a U.S. Army Bronze Star on Faucher when this photo was taken.

General Gerhardt salutes Gen. Dwight D. Eisenhower at an inspection of the 29th Division shortly after the siege of Brest.

The 29th Division band performs in the Le Conquet area. The tune: Cole Porter's "What Is This Thing Called Love?"

Lt. Col. William Purnell (*at left*), CO 175th Infantry, sits atop the old walls of Brest next to Maj. Sherwood Collins, XO 224th Field Artillery Battalion, Sept. 16, 1944. Hundreds of enemy POWs are seated in the moat at the base of the wall.

General Gerhardt and Maj. William Bratton, outside the 29th Division "war room" tent.

Part of Brest's wrecked harborside after the German surrender.

General Gerhardt presents an award to Col. Charles Canham, CO 116th Infantry, in England prior to D-Day. At Brest, Canham was a brigadier general, the 8th Division's assistant commander, and accepted Ramcke's surrender on September 19, 1944.

Maj. Gen. Charles Hunter Gerhardt Jr., commanding general of the 29th Infantry Division, July 1943–January 1946.

In England in late 1943, General Gerhardt (*at left*) speaks with an unidentified Medical Corps officer (*center*) and Maj. Randolph Millholland (*right*), then CO of the 29th Ranger Battalion.

Maj. Tom Dallas, CO 1st Battalion, 116th Infantry, at Fort Montbarey.

A street in Recouvrance, looking toward the harbor, after the German surrender.

Lt. Col. Louis Smith (*at right*), CO 115th Infantry, dictates surrender terms to German emissaries in St. Pierre Quilbignon, Sept. 18, 1944.

The landward side of the German submarine pens at Brest, viewed from the top of the bluff where the École Navale (Naval Academy) was situated.

The École Navale on top of the bluff just north of the submarine pens, the site of the enemy's last-ditch defenses at Recouvrance.

British Army crews of two Crocodile flamethrowing tanks from B Squadron, 141st Regiment, Royal Armoured Corps ("The Buffs"). This unit played a pivotal role in the capture of Fort Montbarey.

The house in St. Pierre Quilbignon where Lt. Col. Lou Smith of the 115th Infantry dictated surrender terms to the enemy on Sept. 18, 1944.

An aerial view of the German submarine pens at Brest. The École Navale is visible on the bluff behind the sub pens.

An aerial view of Brest's submarine pens and harbor breakwater.

An aerial view of Fort du Portzic, just west of Brest. The sub pens and breakwater are visible in the background.

Four artillery officers examine a map in a 29th Division fire direction center. The three soldiers wearing helmets have their chin straps buckled on the point of their chins, as per the orders of General Gerhardt.

Brig. Gen. William Sands, 29th Division artillery chief, who took over command of the division during Gerhardt's absence after the fall of Brest. Sands, a former member of the Virginia National Guard, was the division's senior National Guard officer.

A sketch by Pvt. Charles Murphy, 121st Engineer Battalion, of the Chateau de Kervataux, occupied by the rear echelon of 29th Division headquarters during part of the siege of Brest.

Gen. Hermann-Bernhard Ramcke, the German commander of Festung Brest, captured by troops of the 8th Infantry Division on Sept. 19, 1944.

A British soldier reads a copy of the 29th Division newsletter, *29 Let's Go*.

"Herman the German," the POW used as a courier by Maj. Tom Dallas of the 116th Infantry to carry messages into Fort Montbarey.

Lt. Col. Martin Fürst, commander of German forces in the Le Conquet peninsula, departs Gerhardt's tent after signing the 29th Division's guest book, Sept. 10, 1944.

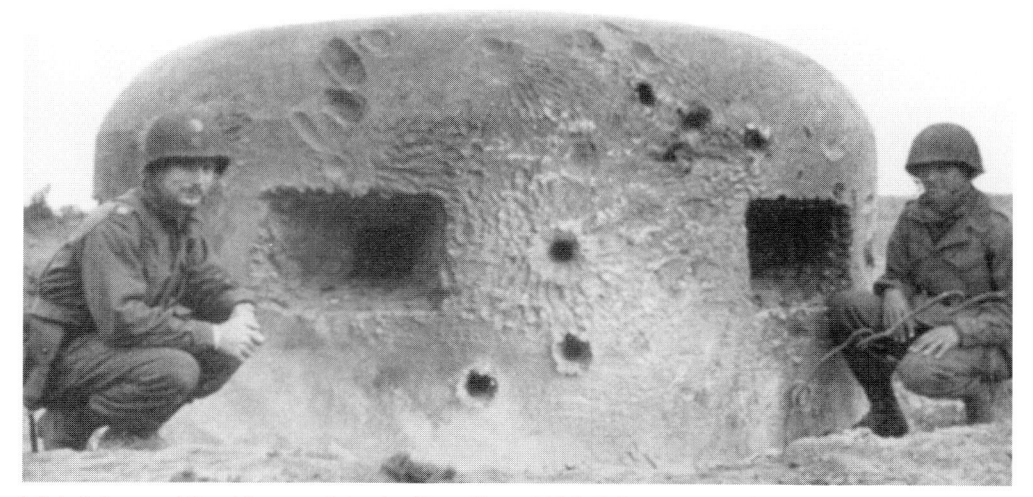

Maj. Johns and Lt. Ahrens of the 1st Battalion, 115th Infantry, examine one of the enemy's formidable steel turret pillboxes near the village of Hildy, a part of the enemy's last-ditch defense north of the submarine pens.

The leaders of the 115th Regimental Combat Team. *Front row, from left:* Lt. Col. John Cooper (CO 110th FA); Maj. William Bruning (S-3 115th); Lt. Col. Louis Smith (CO 115th); Maj. Glover Johns (CO 1/115); Lt. Col. Anthony Miller (CO 2/115). *Back row, from left:* Maj. Harold Perkins (XO 115th); Maj. Randolph Millholland (CO 3/115); Maj. William Bratton (S-2 115th).

An aerial view of Fort Montbarey after its capture by the 116th Infantry. The breach blown in the north wall by Company B, 121st Engineer Combat Battalion, on September 16, 1944, is visible. The N789 road to Brest can be seen in the background.

An air photo of the subterranean oil storage tanks near the village of Hildy. The École Navale buildings are visible on the left, and just above them the submarine pens and breakwater can be seen.

U.S. Army rangers, members of the 29th Division's Task Force Sugar, confer with members of the FFI in the Le Conquet area.

Troops from the 29th Division take cover amid the wreckage of a bombed-out street. A Thompson submachine gun lies next to the soldier in the foreground.

Troops of the 175th Infantry move toward the walls of Brest after the capture of Fort Keranroux on Sept. 13, 1944.

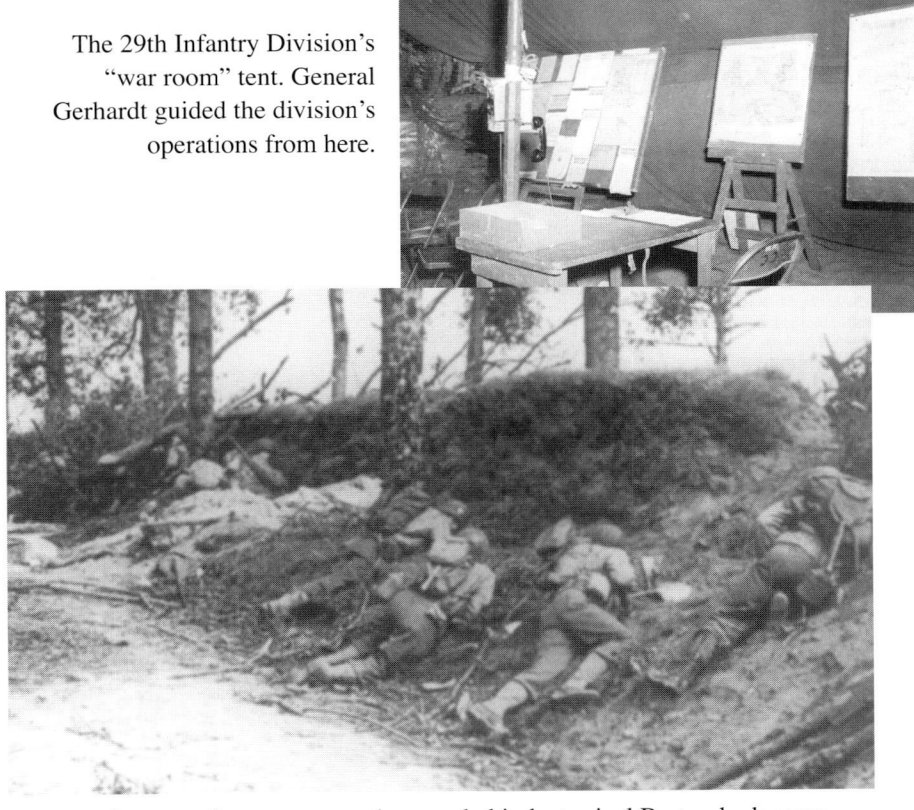

The 29th Infantry Division's "war room" tent. General Gerhardt guided the division's operations from here.

Troops take cover from an enemy barrage behind a typical Breton hedgerow during the siege of Brest.

General Ramcke (*second from left*) enters captivity, holding his Irish setter, on September 19, 1944. Brig. Gen. Charles Canham (*center*) is facing the camera. The commanding general of the 8th Division, Maj. Gen. Donald Stroh, is on the right, facing Ramcke.

A sketch by Pvt. Charles Murphy, 121st Engineer Battalion, of the panorama west of Brest visible from the summit of Hill 103. Sugarloaf Hill is in the upper left; the large water tower near Fort Montbarey can be seen in the upper right, and next to it the rooftops of St. Pierre Quilbignon.

3. I'LL BLOW YOU TO HELL

For three days the frazzled German garrison of Fort Montbarey had withstood a deluge of aerial bombs, a cascade of howitzer and mortar shells, an immeasurable number of bullets, and streams of liquid fire. On the morning of September 15, 1944, General Gerhardt could scarcely believe that the enemy could still hang on to that battered fortress, but evidently the occupants, led by an Oberleutnant (first lieutenant) by the name of Flöter, a member of the 6th Company, 2nd Parachute Regiment, still had plenty of fight left.

One detail that cheered up Gerhardt, however, was that Flöter's catalog of woes could be amplified by the undeniable fact that Montbarey was now completely surrounded. That accomplishment had been achieved by Maj. Tom Dallas of the 116th Infantry's 1st Battalion, when on the afternoon of September 14 he had swung his Company A in a wide flanking maneuver around Montbarey's north side to a point about a half mile east of the fort. Even better, Maj. William Puntenney's 3rd Battalion had paralleled Company A's movement in an even wider arc, eventually reaching an ancient cemetery in the village of St. Pierre-Quilbignon just a mile from the walls of Brest. That cemetery was situated just off the N789 road, which was Flöter's lifeline to Brest. Montbarey was now thoroughly cut off, and neither a rescue nor breakout attempt stood the slightest chance of success. Dallas and his British comrade, Major Ryle, were now free to blast Flöter's garrison into oblivion if it was foolish enough to continue the fight.

Had the Americans been practicing war by the book, however, there would have been no need for Dallas and Ryle to attack Montbarey at all. The 175th Infantry was already well beyond that citadel, ready to plunge into Recouvrance and bring the deadly Brest campaign to an end in a matter of days. Montbarey's dazed German defenders apparently were few in number and would have been promptly gunned down by the surrounding 29ers had they attempted a sortie. Dallas and Ryle could therefore have waited patiently for Ramcke to surrender Fortress Brest, but the western Allies had learned long ago that war by the book varied drastically from reality. There was something symbolic to all 29ers about Montbarey; and as they knew full well, Gerhardt was mesmerized by military symbolism. A lot of good 29ers and British tankers had given their lives to expel the Germans from the fort, and there could be no doubt that Charles Hunter Gerhardt Jr. was resolved to raise the Stars and Stripes above Montbarey's ramparts before the Brest campaign reached its grand finale.

Still, it hardly made sense to waste American and British lives in a direct assault. The ultimate object could be achieved with much more subtlety, and accordingly Dallas and Ryle spent most of Friday, September 15 figuring out how to do it. Such methodical planning time promised to yield considerable benefits, for the two men reckoned that if they could maneuver the Crocodile flame-throwing tanks freely around the fort at close range, the enemy might yield to an accurate and nearly incessant barrage of flame-jets through Montbarey's firing ports. The immediate problem, as Dallas noted, was that "quite a bit of engineer work was necessary in order to get the tanks in position all around the fort so that we could flame it from all sides. All day long [on September 15] the engineers worked hard improving the gaps in the minefield and grading approaches to the moat for the tanks."

That daunting work again fell to the sappers of Capt. Sidney Smith's Company B, 121st Engineer Battalion, who promptly jumped behind the controls of massive bulldozers, grabbed picks, shovels, and mine detectors, and carried forward boxes of explosives to fulfill the tasks Dallas and Ryle had insisted upon. That the work had to be carried out in the open within pistol-shot range of the fort's walls indicated that the human cost could be high, but the covering fire provided by Dallas's nearby riflemen was so intense that only one of Smith's men, T/5 Mack Gosiewski, was wounded. Smith would soon receive the Silver Star for his bold management of this hazardous operation. The Silver Star recommendation written by the 121st's commander, Lt. Col. Robert Ploger, noted: "Captain Smith directed Cpl. [Shirley] Williams to move his bulldozer to the moat of Fort Montbarey and lent moral support to the operator by personally being at the site during the entire time he was working. Captain Smith was lying on the ground near the bulldozer under enemy small-arms and sniper fire." Williams, along with fourteen other members of the company, would be granted Bronze Stars for their gallantry in action on September 15.

Thanks to the engineers, the assault Dallas hoped would bring this exasperating battle to an end jumped off early on the morning of September 16. A troop of three British Crocodiles under the command of Capt. Roy Moss plunged forward over the churned-up ground within point-blank range of the fort, and according to the squadron history, "They fanned out on the northern side at the edge of the moat . . . [and] the troop emptied its trailers [of petroleum fuel] in the moat and across the other side in one glorious conflagration of flame and smoke."

Still no reaction from the enemy. As the 29th Division's historian, Joe Ewing, observed: "It was actually the moat and walls rather than enemy action that was keeping the infantry out of the fort." A frustrated Dallas would therefore try to blast the walls down, particularly the main gate

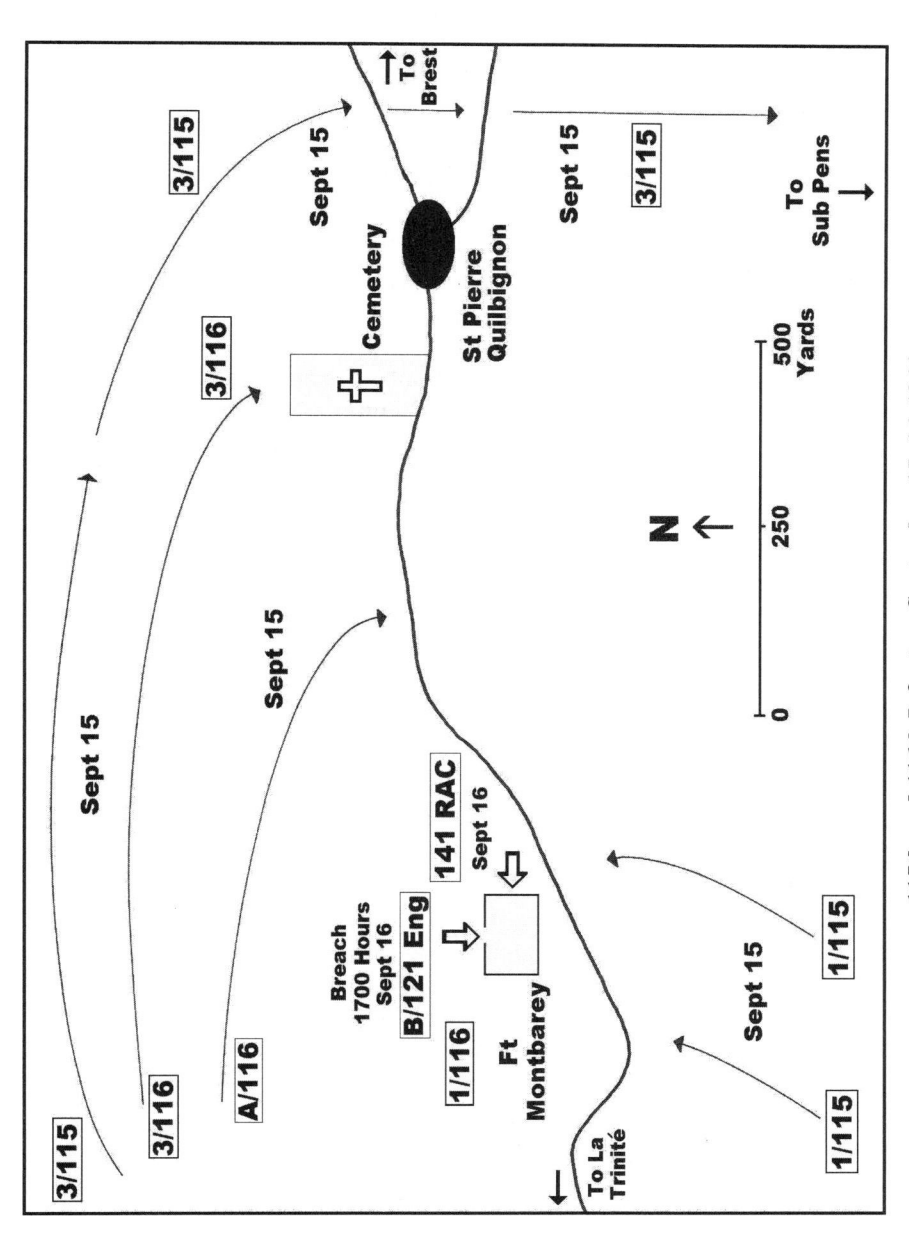

115th and 116th Infantry: September 15–16, 1944

located on the fort's eastern side. "All the walls were so thick that nothing could shoot through them, so it was apparent that if I placed any fire inside the courtyard of the fort, it would have to be through the main gate," Dallas recalled. "The entrance was heavily barricaded by scrap metal, rock, and other debris. . . . I placed a tank destroyer there, and it fired about fifty rounds of ammunition into the barricade."

Still nothing. Another three Crocodiles came up and, according to the squadron history, "used up the whole of their high explosive and flame in one mad outburst"—followed immediately by yet another three "who piled in just as heavy." Afterward, Major Ryle remarked that "the entire moat and walls on the north and east sides were set on fire." That apparently was not enough, so the 116th Infantry's commander, Col. Philip Dwyer, went further by ordering up a 105mm cannon from the 116th's Cannon Company. Under the direction of the company CO, Capt. Robert Ziegler, the cannon's crew manhandled their piece forward until it was positioned at the astonishing range of twenty yards from the gate. "This gun fired over 150 white phosphorous rounds pointblank through the gate and made the inside of the fort a shambles," Dwyer recalled.

By noon, back in the 29th Division's war room, Gerhardt's legendary temper was close to snapping. He radioed Dwyer and snarled, "Why not get a lot of explosives up there and blow the thing in?" Fortunately at that moment Dallas had discerned a perfect opportunity to do exactly that. Smith's engineers had noticed that an enclosed, stone-arched passageway traversed the moat on the fort's north side, connecting an interior and an exterior tunnel. If his riflemen could not penetrate Montbarey's main gate, Dallas reasoned that the passageway might be used instead to infiltrate men into the courtyard.

An M-10 from the 644th Tank Destroyer Battalion fired point blank at the passageway and achieved a penetration through its masonry walls that Dallas observed was "large enough for a man to enter." The hole was of course also large enough for a man to exit, a detail that was established a few moments later when Dallas noticed a white flag projecting from it. "We held fire on that spot, and twelve Germans came out," Dallas wrote. (The renowned U.S. Army historian S. L. A. Marshall later noted that the number was actually three, not twelve—all of whom were wounded.) "The lieutenant in charge of this group [it was in fact a senior non-commissioned officer] said that the cannon fire and flame were driving them all crazy," Dallas continued. "He stated that the CO of the fort, an SS officer [it was Oberleutnant Flöter of the paratroopers, who was not an SS member], would not give up—but that he and his group could stand it no longer."

S. L. A. Marshall provided a more illuminating version of that incident. According to Marshall, "One of [the captives] said to Dallas's interpreter: 'If you don't stop that cannon fire, the inside walls of the fort will collapse.' Dallas replied: 'What more can I ask?'" Armed at last with solid evidence that the Anglo-American effort to subdue Montbarey was close to fulfillment, Dallas would make one more effort to talk the enemy into surrender. If that did not work, he resolved to close out the siege in the cataclysmic way Gerhardt had suggested; and if any Germans would be lucky enough to survive it, they would never forget the experience.

On the previous day Dallas had stopped a passing 115th Infantry jeep that had been transporting an enemy paratrooper to a rear-area prisoner-of-war enclosure. The German spoke a little English, and Dallas therefore snatched him as a go-between at Fort Montbarey. According to Dallas, "Herman the German"—as the 29ers promptly christened him—"at first refused to take my messages into Fort Montbarey, but a little persuasion with my .45 between his eyes convinced him that he should do as I said."

Around noon on September 16, the guns and flamethrowers around Montbarey fell silent, and Herman cautiously marched into no-man's-land waving a white handkerchief. Escorted by two 29ers and carrying a message in his pocket from Dallas to Flöter, he approached the hole in the passageway on the fort's north side. The Anglo-American firepower display directed at Montbarey that morning had been intense, and Dallas's message declared: "That was only a sample of what you're going to get." Unfortunately, when Herman emerged a few minutes later, the enemy's reply was equally blunt: "If that's all you've got, we'll hold out a while."

Only one more message was necessary, and that was from Dallas to Flöter: "I intend to blow you to hell!"

As for "Herman the German," Dallas recalled: "He seemed to be thoroughly enjoying the show."

That "show" was about to reach a denouement because Dallas, who muttered to his staff, "We've tried everything else," now fully intended to fulfill his pledge to blow up the fort. The 29th Division's assistant commander, Col. Leroy Watson, was present at Dallas's command post during the preparation, and at 2:52 P.M. he phoned the war room:

> We have 2,000 pounds of dynamite. [Dallas had somewhat unrealistically requested 10,000 pounds.] We have located a tunnel under the wall of the fort. We have three more flamethrowers coming up.... We have seven forty-foot ladders. Here's the plan: When the dynamite gets [delivered] up, the engineers are going to

go down into the moat and place it in the tunnel. They will be covered by the flamethrowers and also by our fire from the edge of the moat. We expect the dynamite to blow a breach in the wall, and if it does we'll rush right into the fort. If not, we'll use ladders to go over the wall.

Hauling a ton of dynamite in sixty-pound crates across battle-scarred no-man's-land and into the moat would not be easy. An even greater challenge would be squeezing more than thirty of those crates and several sappers through the minuscule hole in the stone passageway so that the explosives could be properly positioned at the pivotal point underneath Montbarey's massive north wall. Even if Ryle's Crocodiles and Dallas's riflemen could keep up a steady stream of covering fire, the Germans would probably manage at least some return fire when they discerned their opponents' intentions. Furthermore, the engineers had not the slightest idea what reception the enemy would offer when the GIs tried to sneak their TNT boxes into the covered passageway leading into the fort. Past experience promised that that reception would be extraordinarily violent.

The old adage that effective military command depends on not taking counsel of one's fears was adhered to by Captain Smith, the engineer officer who took charge of that grueling mission. In the recommendation for Smith's Silver Star, Ploger noted: "He personally directed the operation and was the first officer in the moat of the fort before the demolition was placed.... Captain Smith [was] an inspiration to his men. He has always led his men and has shown the true and primary quality of leadership: 'Follow me!'"

A 121st Engineer Battalion deuce-and-a-half truck loaded with the requisite crates of dynamite managed to approach within 150 yards of the north passageway; and as soon as Smith gave the signal and rushed forward toward the moat, his men did indeed follow him. According to an interview conducted by S. L. A. Marshall with the engineers a few days later,

[a] tech sergeant, who had worked his way up to the front of the carrying party, accompanied Sgt. Edward Humphrey and Pvt. Frank Geiger, and the three men dropped down through the hole in the passageway. [Marshall's unnamed tech sergeant was probably John Lacosky, who was actually a staff sergeant at the time.] Geiger was armed with a tommy gun, and he sprayed fire forward as he proceeded [down the passageway], and then fired in both

directions down the connecting passageways [underneath Montbarey's north wall]. Humphrey threw several grenades into the courtyard. Behind these three came [1st Lt. Shelton] Clemmer with the detonating equipment and [PFC Melvin] Borenstein with the first load of explosives. The space below was cramped, and the hole in the top restricted easy passage. So Pvt. Mike Galecio (the company barber), Borenstein, and one other man worked in the hole setting the charge. The others brought up the TNT and passed it through the hole. In about twenty minutes the charge was complete. Borenstein was the last man out. Captain Smith then sent him back into the hole again to make a reconnaissance and make sure that all had left the passageway.

The massive pile of dynamite, apparently amounting to somewhat less than the 2,000 pounds ordered up by Watson, was ready for detonation. However, two unforeseen factors conspired to momentarily postpone the explosion. The first was the possibility of further negotiations with the fort's garrison, a point evidently brought to Dallas's attention by a German prisoner. Dallas brushed this aside with his habitual bluntness: "Fuck 'em! Blow them all up!"

The second factor, however, genuinely troubled Dallas. Somewhere close to the spot where Smith's engineers had penetrated into the passageway, the body of 2nd Lt. Durwood Settles of Company B, 116th Infantry, lay crumpled in the moat. Settles had been killed two days previously, on September 14, when Dallas's battalion had opened its attack on Montbarey. Those who knew Tom Dallas well understood his intense sense of loyalty to all members of the 116th Infantry. Furthermore, they knew that his devotion extended particularly to Settles, a prewar Virginia National Guard comrade from Company H, whose armory was located just north of the North Carolina border in the town of Martinsville. Consequently, Dallas would not allow the engineers to set off the charge until Settles's body was recovered. A graves registration lieutenant from division headquarters by the name of Kelton volunteered to recover Settles's corpse; and in Marshall's words, "Kelton personally climbed down into the moat and came up carrying Settles' body in his arms."

At about 5 P.M. on September 16, 1944, the tenacious Dallas issued the order he had promised the despised enemy he would soon carry out: "Blow them to hell!" One of Smith's engineers set off the charge, and the deafening blast and blossoming cloud of debris and smoke drew the prompt attention of every American and British soldier within earshot, most of whom in all likelihood noted with approval that the Germans in Montbarey were finally getting what they so richly deserved. When the cloud dissipated, the 29ers could see that the blast had had its desired effect: the entire central part of the fort's north wall had collapsed so completely that ladders were not needed to enter the courtyard through the breach.

If the Americans moved fast, the enemy could not recover. Captain Smith was one of the first 29ers to enter the fort, and as Marshall noted, "The Germans still remaining alive were so stunned that not one shot was fired by the defenders [and] the assault force did not lose one man." Several Germans started to emerge from their hideouts just off the courtyard, waving white flags, but the covering fire from American tank destroyers and British Crocodiles was so intense that the act of surrender was more lethal than staying put. A British observer noted that as Smith's engineers dashed into the breach, there was "an absolute crescendo of flame, 75s, Besa [machine-gun fire], and smoke." Eventually, the 29ers had to pound on the Crocodiles' hulls to warn the tankers that the Germans were finally ready to lay down their arms.

It would not be easy for the Americans to navigate through the labyrinth of tunnels underneath Montbarey, but presumably several obstinate Germans were still slinking about somewhere down there, and sooner or later the 29ers would have to root them out. Smith and a few engineers pressed warily ahead down one dark and narrow passageway and realized they were close to their prey when they heard two men conversing in German at the far end. As Smith noted in a letter to his father a few weeks later, "[I fired] a few bursts from my Tommy gun, which they didn't like, and they came out pronto." Smith had made a valuable catch, for the German duo consisted of an officer—in all probability Oberleutnant Flöter, the garrison commander—and an enlisted aide. Smith promptly dispatched the pair under guard to Dallas's command post.

According to a witness, when an engineer sergeant brought the bedraggled German officer before an equally unkempt Dallas, the enemy soldier blurted: "I'm a German officer and expect to be treated as such." Dallas roared back, "You're a prisoner of war! Get your hands above your head!" A 116th Infantry action report noted that "Dallas made him go back into the fort and in person remove all of the mines that had been set by his men."

Meanwhile Dallas's men initiated the lengthy but undeniably intriguing process of stripping the enemy captives of all items of military significance. The 29ers had always prized German war souvenirs, of course, but this opportunity was something special. The capture of Fort Montbarey had been a brutal and costly struggle, and the Americans, all of whom were understandably in a foul mood, took grim satisfaction in the discomfort of their hated enemies. Accordingly, the 29ers did not perform this task gracefully, and the obvious fact that the haul of items taken off the German paratroopers went far beyond the limitations specified by the July 1929 *Geneva Convention Relative to the Treatment of Prisoners of War* surprised neither friend nor foe. Article 6 of that Convention stipulated: "All effects and objects of personal use except arms, horses, military equipment, and military papers shall remain in the possession of prisoners of war, as well as metal helmets and gas masks." The objects snatched by the 29ers, however, included watches, wallets, money, photos, Iron Cross decorations, paratrooper insignia—even shaving kits and soap. The surly and resentful German reaction was entirely ignored by the fuming 29ers, who acted as if their opponents should consider themselves fortunate to still be alive. Even more to the point, in a prisoner-of-war camp back in the States, the Germans would learn to live without the items the 29ers had just lifted off them.

While being frisked, supposedly by Dallas himself, one senior enemy non-commissioned officer blurted out the word that German soldiers commonly employed to categorize their American opponents: "gangsters." For this transgression, a nearby 29er used his fist to strike the paratrooper hard in the face, after which the German repeated his insult and was struck again. The Germans did not think highly of the U.S. Army's legendary melting pot, and that same enemy NCO recalled that one of Dallas's 116th Infantry interpreters was "one of those neo-Americans, a real Jew from Vienna . . . with a Vienna accent."

That the 29th Infantry Division's incentive to fight was only fueled by comments of that sort did not seem to occur to the German NCO. In any case, he would soon be out of the Blue and Gray Division's hands and on his way to the United States for a comparatively comfortable life in a stateside prisoner-of-war camp. There, he would witness a way of life that would be utterly alien to Germans who lived under the Nazi regime, and that experience would in all probability make him a better man.

In the meantime, the 29th Division was on its way to Brest.

EIGHT

Giving Them the Works

1. FRONT AND HOMELAND

By mid-September 1944, in the brutal battle for Brest, the ordinary pleasures of life had all but vanished for 29ers. Within the minds of the weary combat soldiers, a mere hot cup of coffee, a few meager shavings of chocolate from a D-ration bar, or a letter from home stood out as glorious highlights in the repetitive and miserable cycle of brutality that had defined the Brittany campaign for three terrible weeks. When the evidence of battle so clearly pointed to the deduction that a man might not live to see the next sunrise, it was amazing how meaningful such simple joys could be.

One item every 29er in the front lines always eagerly looked forward to was his copy of *29 Let's Go*, the daily division newsletter churned out at the "Special Services" section of division headquarters by a witty and artistic corporal by the name of Jean Lowenthal. Printed by a mimeograph machine on both sides of a single, flimsy sheet of legal-size paper, *29 Let's Go* was the antithesis of a typical U.S. Army publication. Its writing was humorous and chatty, and the front page was habitually livened up by a cartoon that regularly featured what 29ers missed most—attractive American women on the home front.

General Gerhardt did not make a habit of staying in touch with many corporals, but he made a point of maintaining a special relationship with

Corporal Lowenthal. The general realized *29 Let's Go* spoke the language of the ordinary fighting man, and as long as Lowenthal relentlessly promoted the 29th Division's exploits, Gerhardt did not meddle with his style that had proven so popular among 29ers. Uncle Charlie commonly took a few moments out of his busy schedule to give Lowenthal a call and suggest a suitable topic for a new story, but his involvement did not get much deeper than that. Occasionally, Lowenthal would even phone the general and ask: "Got anything for us today, sir?" Gerhardt was so impressed by Lowenthal's work that he awarded him a Bronze Star "for meritorious achievement" during the Brest campaign. The general directed Lowenthal to mention that honor in *29 Let's Go*, but the modest young corporal declined to do so.

One of Lowenthal's typical *29 Let's Go* tidbits at Brest that so amused the 29ers noted: "'D-Day' [General Gerhardt's dog] has finally become a full-fledged soldier. He took his first flight in an L-4 artillery observation plane today [September 11, 1944]. The trip was made over Le Conquet peninsula, and D-Day made this remark: 'What took you so long?' After returning to the airfield, in appreciation for his splendid trip, D-Day lifted his leg and left his initials on the Air OP's command post tent."

Most 29ers grasped the well-known truth of military life that events beyond the confines of their small platoon- and company-size units were of little interest. Why pay much attention to what you could not possibly understand? In the recent past the 29th Division's ordinary fighting men had fought hard to secure places such as St. Lô, Vire, and Hill 103 because their leaders had ordered them to do so; but in truth most of the troops did not grasp the military significance of those exploits. Apparently, only generals could understand that. Even 29th Division officers as lofty as battalion commanders complained that they knew less of the "big picture" than rear-echelon troops—and much less than civilians back on the homefront. If the GIs could not even discern what was going on in their little corner of the world, how could they hope to stay informed about events in the rest of the European theater of operations—not to mention Russia and the Pacific?

Lowenthal's *29 Let's Go* tried to rectify that lamentable situation in a style that was unique to the 29th Division. Gerhardt had always asserted that the Blue and Gray Division was special, and *29 Let's Go* did its best to establish the uncontestable truth of that assertion. Amid all the carnage of the battlefield, the newsletter was persistently upbeat, but by no means annoyingly so. In fact, Lowenthal's sporadic bouts of bluntness only served to endear him to the fighting men. One such frank report on September 12 noted: "We're having a hell of a time of it. Regardless of air support, artillery, or anything else, in the end it will take the second squad of the third platoon to get in there and take [Brest]. And the boys all know it." As events developed, Lowenthal's prediction was highly accurate. Two days later in *29 Let's Go*, he candidly described the 175th Infantry's capture of Fort Keranroux: "It was a bitch!"

Almost every issue of *29 Let's Go* featured a light and informal article about a notable 29er, ranging from a private recently decorated for heroism to the commanding general himself. Occasionally, Lowenthal would highlight the work of individual 29th Division units, as varied and obscure as the division headquarters' Finance Section, led by Lt. Col. Louis Lucas; or the 729th Ordnance Company, commanded by Capt. Harold Price. It was Lowenthal's combat stories, however, that made the most riveting reading, and they remain absorbing more than sixty years afterward. Writing for an audience of hardened soldiers was not easy, but Lowenthal had a flair for it because he concentrated on people rather than on military strategy or tactics; and simultaneously he conveyed a genuine sympathy for the plight of the front-line combat soldier.

29 Let's Go, along with the omnipresent *Stars and Stripes*, also provided an enlightening if somewhat pithy account of events beyond the realm of the 29th Division. That service was invaluable to the 29ers because it helped to instill in them the confidence that all U.S. Army generals required of their troops if they were to fulfill their arduous objectives. With death and destruction enveloping them daily, the 29ers did not find it easy to maintain that confidence; but somehow or other when one perused the stories in *29 Let's Go* about the highly encouraging developments all across the globe in the war against the Axis, assurance in ultimate victory suddenly became much more pronounced. As one of the 29th Division's most renowned characters, the 175th Infantry's forty-six-year-old Sgt. Abe Sherman, once remarked to Lowenthal shortly before the fall of Brest: "We're coasting now—the war's in the bag, and we're coasting. This f—— war is not gonna last long."

If the war news as reported in *29 Let's Go* were accurate, Sherman's prediction would soon come true. On September 14, 1944, as the 29th Division closed in on Brest, Lowenthal reported the astonishing news, "The American First Army has captured Rötgen, the first German town to fall into Allied hands, and is driving into the Siegfried Line defenses." That delightful intelligence was accompanied by a report that "RAF Mosquitos last night attacked Berlin, the fourth night running." Both of Lowenthal's notable stories were positioned adjacent to a cartoon of two American beauties conversing on a beach, each in a skimpy bathing suit.

One woman says to the other: "You and your sunrise swimming! There's not a man in sight. . . . We might as well swim now!" The 29ers loved it.

The 116th Infantry became somewhat miffed with Lowenthal when, on September 15, the regiment closed in on Fort Montbarey and captured several Germans in an outlying pillbox. One 29er who frisked a German prisoner was amazed to discover that September 14 edition of *29 Let's Go* inside the enemy soldier's uniform. As Lowenthal recounted the story in the next day's edition, "On the day the prisoner was taken, the 116th had not yet received its distribution of the September 14 issue. Col. [Philip] Dwyer, commander of the 116th, says that General Ramcke, commander of the German Citadel Brest, must be on the priority list to get *29 Let's Go* ahead of his outfit."

The informality and frankness of *29 Let's Go* surely astonished those Germans who could read a little English. Their army did not do things that way. In contrast, those of Gerhardt's 29ers with a smattering of German who had the opportunity to examine the German Army's version of *29 Let's Go*, a pamphlet called *Front und Heimat* ("The Front and the Homeland"), were not in the least impressed. As Lowenthal remarked at the close of the Brest campaign,

> Our American paper is written to satisfy 10,000 individual preferences; that of the Hun is directed at satisfying one. We of the American Army look forward to a variety of opinions and reading matter in our paper. We are interested in news headlines from the four corners of the world; in news of politics and sports; of entertainment and finance; of military events and radio programs; even the funny papers—take your pick. The Boche *Front und Heimat* features none of these things. It is out to sell one commodity—mass thinking. . . . It's the old Kraut song. He's been singing it down through the centuries. Five years ago, he *sieg heiled* it in the great halls of Berlin as his destructive hordes swept across the face of Europe. This is what he loves. . . . The whole rotten business is a vicious circle.

2. IT SEEMS TO BE A HABIT

The September 16 edition of *29 Let's Go* reported, "Yesterday was the 115th's day." There was a great deal of truth in that statement: Maj. Glover Johns's 1st Battalion had made a dynamic nighttime attack on September 15 that had cleared the enemy from the fortified zone surrounding Fort

Montbarey, a success that helped immeasurably in the fort's downfall the next day. The 3rd Battalion, under the command of the highly respected Maj. Randy Millholland, also joined the fray in the afternoon of September 15 with orders from Colonel Smith to advance eastward from its reserve position at Coatuélen and swing in a wide arc around Fort Montbarey on its northern side. After successfully bypassing Montbarey, Millholland's men entered the village of St. Pierre–Quilbignon against only light resistance, and there they turned sharply 90 degrees to the south, heading straight for an array of about two dozen massive subterranean oil storage tanks, about a half mile distant, which the French Navy had constructed long before the war on a narrow ridge overlooking Brest's inner harbor. If they could capture that ridge, they would be just a long rifle shot away from the infamous submarine pens, which intelligence had reported was the nerve center of the enemy's Brest defenses.

Darkness slowed the 3rd Battalion's progress, but escalating enemy resistance slowed it even more. At about 9 P.M., Millholland reported to Smith that he was "stopped by heavy fire from the right and front." Smith replied: "You will resume attack at 1000 hours, 16 September 1944, to the south to capture Objective 'E' [the oil tanks and the adjacent village of Hildy]. Active patrolling to the front during the night." Although the 3rd Battalion had executed a complex maneuver of nearly two miles in length in a highly perplexing tactical situation, Gerhardt was still not satisfied. On the morning of September 16, he complained to Smith, "I understand Millholland didn't take advantage of his time yesterday." In the threatening tone that all 29ers feared, the general growled: "Tell him about that!"

September 15 may have been the "115th's day," as Lowenthal wrote, but on that date the 5th Ranger Battalion made an equal contribution to the 29th Division's success. Over the past few weeks, the top brass had shuttled that elite ranger outfit all over western Brittany like a billiard ball caroming off a pool table's cushions, but by now the 5th Rangers, under the command of the redoubtable Lt. Col. Richard Sullivan, had settled down and held the right of the 29th Division's battle line, where the land dropped down to the sea in an alternating series of spectacular ravines and promontories. For Sullivan, however, such scenic beauty was unhappily also a tactical nightmare, since the Germans had thoroughly fortified that area and had fully taken advantage of the abnormal terrain.

Gerhardt assigned Sullivan the mission of seizing Fort du Portzic, the formidable coastal fortification that sat on the southern tip of a headland jutting out into the entrance of Brest harbor. Not many places in the Brest environs were more vital than Portzic, and accordingly the Germans prepared some surprises there should their opponents dare to attack it frontally. By this point in the campaign the Americans were thoroughly used to the hazards of attacking the enemy's fixed fortifications, but the new style of defenses Sullivan's rangers first encountered at Portzic elevated those hazards to an entirely more difficult level.

On the sharp ridges between the submarine pens and Portzic, the Germans had constructed dozens of circular steel pillboxes resembling turrets housing heavy guns on a warship. A 121st Engineer Battalion report noted:

> Each turret was made of cast steel, twenty inches thick, with an outside diameter of twelve feet. They were set in concrete foundations with reinforced concrete aprons projecting about eighteen feet on all sides. Turret tops projected about five and a half feet above the surface of the ground, and no attempt had been made to camouflage them. Six firing ports permitted all-around fire. These could be closed by port covers, six inches thick. Turrets were armed with two LMG [light machine guns] on track mounts so that they could be readily moved from port to port. [Those machine guns could be fired remotely by means of a periscope.] Steel ladders connected the turret with underground quarters for the troops and with an extensive tunnel system, which connected all permanent defensive positions in the locality, as well as giving passage to the underground hospital at the subpens.

Sullivan's 5th Ranger Battalion, however, could not even approach Fort du Portzic without overcoming an enemy strongpoint in the village of Le Cosquer, situated at a key road junction a little less than a mile north of the ancient Portzic lighthouse. At about 2 P.M. on September 15, the arrival of the 115th Infantry's Company L in the rangers' zone allowed Sullivan to concentrate his men against Le Cosquer. At 7:11 P.M., supported by the high-velocity three-inch guns of the 644th Tank Destroyer Battalion and a battery of self-propelled 155mm guns from the 557th Field Artillery Battalion, the rangers launched their attack. According to the battalion's monthly after-action report,

> Company D advanced rapidly across open ground and entered the town at 7:30 P.M. During the attack this company was subjected to intense machine gun and mortar fire from the pillbox south of Le Cosquer, but only suffered four casualties. . . . The enemy was

definitely surprised by the rapidity of the assault, for many were killed in their foxholes by the assault men of Company D. Sixty-nine prisoners were immediately taken. This total was increased to 215 after the companies mopped up the town.

That night and the following morning, Sullivan's rangers pressed on—and got their first taste of the Germans' fearsome steel pillboxes. The results were not encouraging. The commander of the 5th Rangers' Headquarters Company, Capt. John Raaen, observed to Colonel Witte in the 29th Division's War Room: "Those pillboxes are strong as hell. The 155s [from the 557th Artillery] bounce right off them." Witte replied, "The general doesn't want you to get all shot up assaulting [them], so you had better have Sullivan call us up and give us his survey of the situation."

The 5th Rangers were what GIs used to refer to as a "bastard" outfit, only temporarily attached to the 29th Division. Those kinds of units never felt entirely comfortable taking orders from strangers, and for Sullivan's battalion that problem became acute when a series of unfortunate events developed on September 15. Those events caused an irritated Sullivan to take the unusual and risky step of complaining openly to his current boss, Gerhardt. On the night before the Le Cosquer assault, he had protested loudly to the war room that a company from the 115th Infantry had withdrawn from the front without informing him, thereby leaving one of his ranger outfits dangerously in the lurch. On September 15, Gerhardt learned of that row and initially described Sullivan's behavior as "snooty" and "like a spoiled boy." A few hours later, however, the general learned the true facts and bawled out Colonel Smith for the snafu—although Smith stood up for his men and denied any wrongdoing on the 115th Infantry's part.

That the rangers wanted simply to be left alone to perform the task they did best—killing Germans—was obvious. But unhappily, in the aftermath of the seizure of Le Cosquer, Sullivan's men suffered a much more serious intrusion into their affairs that made them suspect that no one in the 29th Division was watching out for their welfare. At about 9 P.M., as related by the 5th Rangers' action report, "A heavy concentration of friendly artillery fell on the troops in Le Cosquer, creating a very demoralizing effect on the men." Sullivan phoned Witte and asked wearily: "Is there a possibility of keeping people from calling for fires in our area? It seems to be a habit."

Witte traced the source of the fire to a nearby chemical mortar outfit, but that discovery failed to solve the problem as quickly as the rangers would have liked. An exasperated Sullivan phoned Witte back and demanded: "Can I be assured I'll not be fired on again? We were getting 4.2-inch mortar fire, white phosphorus, and also some high explosive was going over my head, landing around the town. . . . We are not tied in with anybody, out here by ourselves. I came back through that [115th Infantry company] that relieved us and came under fire. . . . It sounded like American M-1s."

For the rangers an assault against the enemy's formidable pillboxes was difficult enough without the added quandary of friendly fire. But an even more challenging problem was Sullivan's shrinking manpower. The 5th Rangers' normal complement of about 500 men had been considerably diminished by more than two weeks of nearly continuous combat; and even worse, Gerhardt had snatched two of Sullivan's companies—about 30 percent of his strength—to operate with the 29th Reconnaissance Troop to help secure the division's left flank as the 29ers pushed ahead into Brest. Gerhardt returned one of those companies to Sullivan on the evening of September 16, but still an assault against Fort du Portzic with so few men hardly seemed feasible. For most of September 16, Sullivan and his staff pondered the seemingly impossible mission Gerhardt had demanded of them, and they decided to initiate their assault during the afternoon of the following day.

Meanwhile, just a glance at Lou Smith's situation map revealed that the 115th Infantry's war had changed profoundly. Instead of slamming ahead field by field, hedgerow by hedgerow, into the western walls of Brest, the regiment's battle line had swung 90 degrees and faced south rather than east. Now the sea, rather than the city, was Smith's real objective; and on the morning of September 16 his 1st and 3rd Battalions were positioned less than a mile from that goal. However, a quick glance at the enemy's steel pillboxes, situated squarely between the 115th Infantry and its objective, convinced Smith's men that advancing across that interval would not be easy. But on the bright side, the Germans were backed up against Brest harbor and therefore had no place to retreat, a reality that cheered the 29ers immensely because whatever happened next must finally bring their involvement in the Brest campaign to an end.

The enemy's massive submarine pens on Brest's harborside were close—so close that on the evening of September 15, Middleton phoned Gerhardt and declared, "You might finish it up tomorrow." However, even such a dedicated optimist as Gerhardt had learned not to make firm promises to his boss in matters upon which the Germans could exert their considerable influence. As a reply, all Gerhardt could come up with was "Could be."

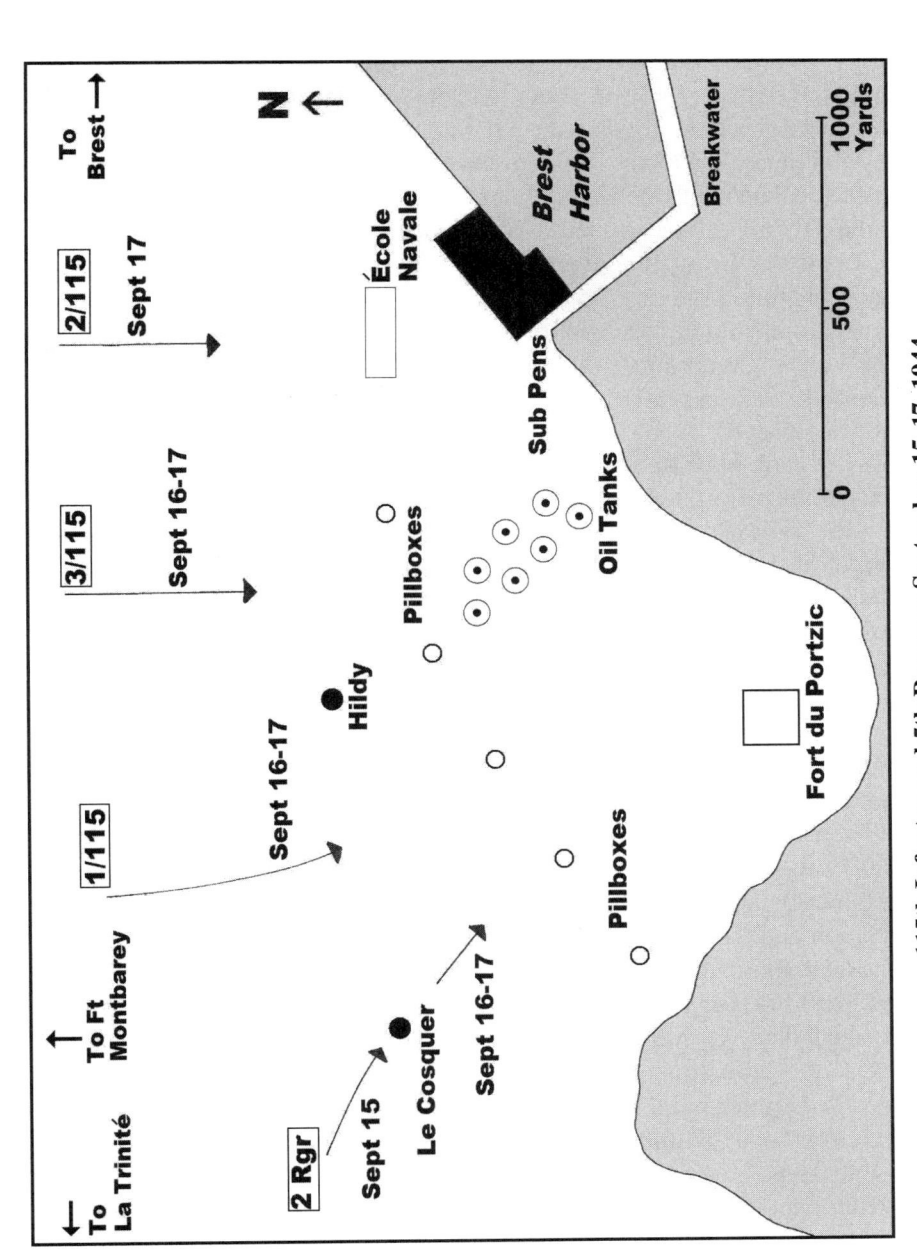

115th Infantry and 5th Rangers: September 15–17, 1944

At 10 A.M. on September 16, the 115th Infantry launched an attack, with Glover Johns's 1st Battalion on the right, tied into Sullivan's 5th Ranger Battalion at Le Cosquer. Meanwhile, Randy Millholland's 3rd Battalion joined the fray on the 1st Battalion's left. There was only one way Smith could signal success to his boss Gerhardt, and that was for his men to push through the enemy lines speedily and reach the shoreline, just as the general had demanded. Unfortunately for Smith, this last stage of the battle for Brest, like every other stage coming before it, did not go according to plan.

As Johns noted, "In front of us, the entire battlefield lay like a set in Hollywood." According to the 29th Division's daily G-3 summary, "This attack was met with very heavy small-arms fire, emanating from pillboxes, and was stopped." The 29ers tried again at noon, this time with the support of a five-tank platoon of Shermans from Company A, 709th Tank Battalion, but that effort, too, made no appreciable progress.

The following day, September 17, Smith took the unusual step of committing all three of his infantry battalions to the battle simultaneously when he ordered Tony Miller's 2nd Battalion to join the attack on the 115th's left, less than one mile due north of the submarine pens. In the words of the 115th's official history, "The regimental front was extremely narrow, and all three battalions were crammed into so small a space [approximately one mile] that flanking and similar maneuvers were almost impossible. The main line of the attackers was not more than 1,000 or so yards from the water, and yet that distance was studded with German pillboxes, mines, wire entanglements, and antitank ditches and obstacles."

For the men of the 115th Infantry, the sight of those enemy defenses, particularly the distinctive steel-turret pillboxes standing between the 29th Division and the sea, yielded the distressing thought that the last stage of the Brest campaign was apparently going to be the toughest. The 115th had lost fifty-four men on September 16, and would lose sixty-five more the next day. At that rate the regiment—already severely depleted by weeks of near-continuous fighting—would not have many men left to witness the Germans' final collapse. Even the regiment's wisest old veterans had never seen anything like those pillboxes before and did not have the slightest idea how they could be overcome. The regimental adjutant, Capt. Lucien Laborde, managed to get hold of a French civilian who had helped construct them, but the intelligence he provided only served to indicate the severity of the challenge ahead.

Laborde, however, was an experienced interpreter of air reconnaissance photographs, and when he examined images of those pillboxes, he reckoned that since none of them had a discernible means of entry at ground level, they must be connected by a maze of underground passageways. To neutralize the pillboxes, Laborde reasoned, the 115th would have to locate one or more entrances into that tunnel system, which in all likelihood would be found somewhere near the base of the cliffs and bluffs lining the shoreline near the sub pens. When those openings were discovered, Laborde recommended that his boss, Colonel Smith, call upon the British flame-throwing Crocodile tanks that had worked so well for the 116th Infantry at Fort Montbarey. If the tanks could shoot their flame-jets into the tunnels, the effect on the defenders would be overwhelming, and might even result in the asphyxiation of dozens of Germans occupying the pillboxes. Smith and his perplexed battalion commanders were willing to try anything, and Laborde's idea was as good as any other. Gerhardt agreed and ordered the British tanks to shift to the 115th's front, but they would not be ready to attack until the next day, September 18.

There must be no break in the 115th's assault, Crocodiles or no Crocodiles, so for the September 17 attack, Smith's battalion commanders would have to try different means of cracking the pillboxes' solid steel. The high-velocity three-inch guns of supporting M-10 tank destroyers tried first, but according to Glover Johns of the 1st Battalion, who watched the show from about 800 yards distance, "They did not hurt them at all." The 29th Division's chief artilleryman, the cantankerous Brig. Gen. William Sands, tried to help out by bringing up a self-propelled 155mm "Long Tom" gun, a weapon renowned for its accuracy and power. A disappointed Johns observed this fire and noted, "The 155 put eight direct hits on a box, which I think accounted for some ripples on the surface [of the steel]."

From the second-story window of a house near the Long Tom, Lt. Col. John Cooper of the 110th Field Artillery, along with Maj. Al Warfield, executive of the 115th Infantry's 2nd Battalion, peered toward the target with binoculars to help adjust its fire if necessary. According to Cooper, "When the first round of the big, self-propelled 155mm gun went off only twenty feet from the building, most of the wall on the enemy side of the house fell out, leaving the two observers 'naked,' much to the amusement of those nearby. Needless to say, the officers left the house rapidly!"

Johns eventually moved up three high-velocity 57mm guns from his antitank platoon, under the command of 1st Lt. Sorrel Abramson, and ordered their crews to open fire with armor-piercing ammunition on one of the pillboxes at nearly point-blank range. Johns recalled that the 57s did some "pretty good shooting," and managed to put a few shells directly into one of the pillbox's deep apertures. The only appreciable result of those bull's-eyes, however, was to render the sliding steel door cover of the firing-port inoperable. For all the 115th Infantry's efforts, that was not much of an accomplishment. A few days later, after the enemy's surrender at Brest, Johns learned that several German occupants of the pillboxes had been killed by the concussion produced by direct shell hits, but that result had not been sufficient to trigger a collapse in the enemy's last-ditch defensive line.

On the 2nd Battalion's front, on the far left of the 115th Infantry's line, those 29ers who peered out of their frontline foxholes could perceive the massive buildings of the École Navale (Naval Academy), which sat on a lofty cliff looming over the submarine pens. Those buildings had once been the pride of the French Navy, but now, according to Cpl. Art Plaut of the 2nd Battalion, "[They] had been blasted by shells and bombs and their interiors gutted by fire so that only the walls remained." Plaut also observed that the surrounding area was "the preconceived idea that most soldiers had of what war's no-man's-land resembled . . . bomb-pitted, torn-up fields, wrecked tanks and vehicles of both armies, smashed pillboxes and gun embrasures, taped paths through mine-strewn rubble, antitank ditches and barricades, and all types of equipment scattered everywhere."

That locale may have seemed like a vision of hell, but on the evening of September 17 it was obviously about to become appreciably worse. The frustrated members of the 115th had made virtually no progress that day, and their only solution to the tactical impasse was to apply more and more firepower, concentrated on the tiny area into which the enemy had been cornered. At 7 P.M. the 2nd Battalion journal noted, "Planes over again—bombing and strafing installations in Naval Academy and sub pens. All kinds of armored stuff, guns, etc., moving into position to fire on enemy positions in Naval Academy."

It was such an obvious target that the 29ers could not miss, but for a time they hesitated. The 29th's assistant division commander, Col. Leroy Watson, had reported to the war room, "I have an airplane photo that shows two Red Cross buildings among a group of buildings I would like to use artillery on. . . . It will just be unfortunate if the Red Cross buildings get hit. Right now they're just holding us up." Witte replied: "I think [the artillery] should fire on the academy if we are getting fire from there. . . . Tell them to go ahead, and I'll handle it from this end."

He did, and soon there was nothing more for the front-line infantrymen to do except sit back, enjoy the firepower display, and wait for the next morning to resume the attack. By that time, the British Crocodiles' flame-jets just might convince the German defenders that further resistance was useless.

Just beyond the 115th Infantry's right flank, the men of the 5th Ranger Battalion had worried more on September 16 about the impact of friendly fire than they did about shells emanating from the German lines. Happily that problem had been solved by nightfall, but on the morning of the 17th Sullivan's rangers held direct orders from Gerhardt to press on to Fort du Portzic by tackling the same dominating lines of enemy pillboxes that were giving the men of the 115th Infantry fits. The rangers were celebrated for their unusual solutions to tactical dilemmas, and they established that the 115th Infantry's method of blasting the pillboxes with point-blank cannon fire was not for them. Rather, their more daring and enterprising approach was based on the assumption that the only way to deal with those ingenious enemy fortifications was by direct human contact.

Sullivan had his choice of explosives from the abundant inventory of Lt. Col. Robert Ploger's 121st Engineer Battalion, and at 3 P.M., he sent forward a Company E platoon under the command of 1st Lt. Richard Aust to determine what a 40-pound pack charge of C-2 plastic explosive could accomplish when applied directly into one of the firing ports of a pillbox. According to the 5th Rangers' action report, "At 1506 hours the charge was blown, and the platoon withdrew under withering fire into the town [Le Cosquer]. The pillbox suffered no visible damage, but two Germans outside the box were killed. The platoon lost three men—two killed and one seriously wounded."

Seven hours later, when complete darkness had set in, Sullivan tried again. This time an eleven-man patrol from Company E, led by 1st Lt. James Greene, intended to place three C-2 pack charges on the pillbox rather than just one; and for good measure the rangers planned to douse it with twenty gallons of an oil-gas mix. It was not easy to do that hazardous work in the dark, but the gloom helped to shield Greene and his men, who managed to get in quickly, place the charges, and return to Le Cosquer with no casualties. Apparently it worked, for a witness observed, "The explosion came at 2210 hours, and the burning pillbox lit the sky for forty minutes." Shortly after midnight a Company A patrol attempted to repeat that performance, but could not get close to its target because of heavy German fire. As the 5th Rangers' action report noted, "The Jerries were evidently quite nervous, for they fired mortars and machine guns into the area surrounding the pillboxes during the entire night."

It had taken a lot of work to destroy just one German pillbox, but one wrecked turret was better than none. Between the rangers and Fort du

Portzic, however, many more of those evil turrets still survived, and their occupants demonstrated not the slightest sign that they were ready to quit.

3. GOOD GOING

Uncle Charlie was not the type of general who would allow many words of praise to pass his lips, but as the Brest campaign neared its inevitable conclusion, the astonished staff officers of Bill Purnell's 175th Infantry could not help but wonder if their regiment had suddenly become the division commander's favorite. Gerhardt had personally witnessed the assault by the 175th's 2nd Battalion on Fort Keranroux on September 13, a stunning success the general would insist was worthy of some sort of special unit award. The 2nd Battalion had to wait six years for that recognition, and when it finally came, in 1950, it was granted not by the United States government, but by the French, in the form of the exalted *Croix de Guerre avec Étoile d'Argent*. The red and green Croix de Guerre streamer, embroidered "Brest," is still carried on company guidons of those units of today's 175th Infantry directly descending from the 2nd Battalion in World War II.

Further evidence of Gerhardt's favoritism soon emerged when the general forwarded an impressive recommendation to the U.S. Ninth Army that a 2nd Battalion soldier, S/Sgt. Sherwood Hallman, be awarded a posthumous Medal of Honor. So far in the war no 29er, living or dead, had gained that prestigious decoration, and the 29ers were beginning to wonder whether or not anyone ever would. Ultimately, the Army would bestow only two Medals of Honor to World War II 29ers, and the first of these would go to Hallman of the 175th for his extraordinary display of gallantry in the last week of the Brest campaign.

The super-critical Gerhardt had even begun to display grudging respect for the leadership abilities of Purnell, the Harvard-educated lawyer whose military upbringing in the Maryland National Guard over seventeen years had at first triggered nothing but cynicism in the commanding general's mind. Over the course of his combat career within the 29th Division, however, Purnell would earn the remarkable total of two Silver Stars and six Bronze Stars for valor. Gerhardt granted one of those awards to Purnell in the last week of the Brest campaign, when Colonel Watson observed Purnell's conduct in the regiment's approach to Keranroux and reported to the war room: "Just south of Laninguer, when his regiment was engaged in action, one company of the 2nd Battalion was held up, and the enemy was jumping plenty of artillery on them, Colonel Purnell personally went up under fire and got two companies started around the flanks." Gerhardt admired that kind of leadership—and ultimately would reward those who carried it out successfully.

Gerhardt's new-found respect for Purnell was particularly notable because in the closing stages of the Brest campaign the 175th Infantry faced a series of daunting combat missions that would have severely challenged the abilities of even a highly experienced regimental commander. After shattering the German defenses at Ilioc on September 11, Purnell had pushed the 175th forward to the daunting enemy strongpoints at Keranroux and Sugarloaf Hill. Much to Gerhardt's delight, both of those vital positions were in American hands by September 14—one of the rare cases in 29th Division history in which a mission was accomplished as quickly as Uncle Charlie had demanded. Only a mile beyond those objectives, however, lay the even more challenging obstacle of Brest's ancient city wall, an impressive military edifice that to the 29ers appeared somewhat dated, but which was still a formidable barrier the wily Germans would surely exploit to the fullest. Beyond the wall lay Purnell's ultimate objective, that portion of Brest west of the Penfeld River known as Recouvrance. For Purnell's men, a new combat experience lay ahead: in July, at St. Lô, the 115th Infantry had experienced true city fighting, and a few weeks later the 116th had faced the same test at Vire; but for Purnell's 175th Infantry the tightly packed row houses and narrow streets of Recouvrance would be the regiment's first encounter with the enemy in an urban environment.

The 175th could not enter Recouvrance unless Purnell could first figure out a way for his men to traverse the wall, but at noon on September 15, as the regiment pressed steadily forward, Purnell confessed to Gerhardt that he had "no dope on the wall," and could not even see it from his command post because the terrain ahead dropped down precipitously into the Penfeld River valley. Those 29ers with a sense of history could not fail to note the irony that throughout French history Brest's walls had never been tested by an invader but were now being defended by the Nazis, the despised occupiers of Brittany who were striving to keep out the city's would-be liberators. By nightfall Lt. Col. William Blandford's 3rd Battalion was out in front and had cleared the enemy from the old French naval firing range, a mile-long finger of wide-open ground originating at Sugarloaf Hill pointing straight as an arrow at the 175th's final objective of Recouvrance. At 8:20 P.M., Purnell reported the promising news to the war room, "We've taken quite a few prisoners;" but added: "That's as far as [the 3rd Battalion] ought to go. . . . Maybe if everything goes well, we'll wind things up tomorrow."

The 175th got its first look at the walls of Brest early in the morning of September 16, when a patrol from Company B probed beyond a large cemetery only a half mile west of the Penfeld River. The patrol eventually had to turn back after running into enemy opposition, but its members described what they saw to the regimental operations officer, Capt. Henry Reed. In turn, Reed reported to Witte at the war room: "They could see the wall, and it varied from fifteen to thirty feet high. They could see an opening [probably a gateway], but couldn't see the thickness."

That kind of information was not sufficient for Gerhardt, who phoned Purnell at 8:31 A.M. and declared, "I want to get down there and find out about this wall. We'll pick our own spots to go through." Determining exactly where "to go through" was Purnell's problem, but it did not help matters when the general added the caustic and immaterial comment: "I saw a truckload of your soldiers without chin straps yesterday. Don't you go set a bad example!" Purnell needed no reminder that his boss was hard to please; and the only sure way to force him to think about matters more urgent than chin straps was to break through the city walls with all possible speed.

On the 175th's front, the wall zigzagged on a north-south axis for more than a mile, but it would take only one narrow breach to allow the entire regiment to pour into Recouvrance like water through a broken dike. *Baltimore News-Post* reporter Lou Azrael followed the regimental commander in the closing stages of the Brest siege, and he observed, "Purnell seemed to know by instinct where and when and how to attack. He picked a spot on the wall and ordered artillery to pound it." The point chosen by Purnell to make that breach was in the wall's northernmost sector, simply because, as he later related, "I had a feeling the Krauts would be weak in that section."

He was right. About midday on September 16, Purnell ordered the 2nd Battalion forward on the regiment's left, or northern flank. Company G, commanded by Capt. Lawrence Maddox, and Company E, led by 1st Lt. Louis Hecht, paved the way in an assault many hoped would bring the Brest campaign to an end at long last. There were only three possible ways for the 29ers to traverse the wall: by going over it; by blasting their way through it; or by going under it. The last method appeared the most unlikely, but it turned out to be the technique used by the 2nd Battalion to enter Recouvrance. At about 6 P.M., when Company E reached the deep moat at the foot of the wall's western side, Hecht could see a large arched doorway opening into a tunnel leading under the wall. He hastily consulted with one of his experienced NCOs, Sgt. William Lee, and they decided that the tunnel just might present an easy opportunity to get into Recouvrance. As the *Baltimore Sun*'s Holbrook Bradley reported, "With a rifle in one hand, a grenade in the other, Lee clambered down the sides of the moat, across a short open space on the bottom and then to the door of the tunnel. . . . Lee poked his head into the door and yelled for the Huns to surrender. Twenty-seven filed out, hands high above their heads. That was only the start, for Lee [later] returned with his squad, and in the space of an hour had accounted for more than 250 prisoners."

That evening Hecht and Maddox pushed their companies through the tunnel, and the 29ers emerged into the hellish pile of ruins into which Recouvrance had been transformed by American and British bombs and shells over the past month. The following morning Bradley passed into Recouvrance through the tunnel, and he marveled at "how [Sergeant Lee] and the few men with him had been able to make it with as little trouble as they had. Heavily fortified passageways within the inner quadrangle seemed a good place to hold out indefinitely."

The riflemen promptly fanned out into the maze of rubble-strewn streets and headed for the harborside. At first American artillery shells, which were still landing in the city with regularity, posed more danger to the GIs than the Germans; but a sharp word from Gerhardt to General Sands to "call off the artillery" swiftly put a stop to the fire. At sunset Purnell made it down to the wall and later reported to Witte:

> It's just one of those old medieval walls with a moat around it. It's about twenty feet high. You can see the docks and cranes over to the right. We have the thing secured. . . . I didn't hear any German fire while I was down there, but Ivanhoe [the call name for the nearby 2nd Infantry Division] was still getting some machine-gun fire. We must have at least a couple of hundred prisoners. They are all over the place. I have given K Company orders to move against the wall too.

When Gerhardt heard that happy news, he relayed a simple message to Purnell: "Hang on! Good going!" Later, when the general learned more details of the 175th's impressive accomplishment, he added, "That's damn good! Gee, that's swell!" Gerhardt was apparently willing to forgive the 175th's many chin-strap transgressions—this time.

As for the mounting number of enemy prisoners, Bradley observed, "Far from the tough, sometimes arrogant, fighters they have been on occasion, this group of Nazis seemed subdued, ready to give up and get out of the fight. There was little noise; only a few talked among themselves as GI guards paced up and down before the group." As all 29ers grasped, if the enemy defenders of Brest had descended to that level, the end was imminent.

While Purnell focused on the problem of shoving his regiment across the walls of Brest on September 16, only two miles to the west Col. Philip Dwyer of the 116th Infantry was concentrating on the equally difficult predicament of Fort Montbarey. The 116th's 1st Battalion, under the redoubtable leadership of Maj. Tom Dallas, had struggled for three days to overcome that strongpoint's stubborn German defenders, who finally yielded on the evening of the sixteenth, just as the first members of Purnell's 175th Infantry were advancing into Recouvrance underneath the city walls.

Meanwhile, as Dallas's outfit labored to secure Montbarey, Dwyer had swung Maj. William Puntenney's 3rd Battalion around that fort, soon to be followed by the 2nd Battalion under the command of Maj. Charles Cawthon, and by the morning of September 16, Gerhardt had deployed those two battalions in the gap between Purnell's 175th Infantry in the north and Smith's 115th Infantry to the south. When that movement was accomplished, anyone who glanced at the war room map could not fail to draw the conclusion that the end was indeed near. The entire 29th Division was concentrated into a front less than three miles in length, curved like a crescent moon, with all three regiments in line, each holding direct orders from Gerhardt to attack until the job was finished.

Those orders brought the 116th Infantry's 2nd and 3rd Battalions directly into the sprawling Brest suburb of St. Pierre Quilbignon—and their first experience of city fighting since Vire. As the division's action report for the month of September 1944 noted, "Progress was necessarily slow, as house-to-house fighting was the type [of combat] engaged in; but resistance was generally light." That adjective, however, would certainly not have been one that would have been used to describe the Germans' will to resist by the 29ers who probed cautiously into the rubble of St. Pierre on September 16. Pvt. James Trethewey, a fresh replacement in Company F who experienced his first taste of combat in St. Pierre, recalled:

> We started forward to attack, but were soon pinned down by heavy machine gun fire and sniper bullets that cost us a few casualties. I spent a very uncomfortable night [September 16–17] in a shallow foxhole behind an orchard wall. Sleep was almost impossible—in addition to standing guard for two hours, rain fell almost continuously. German automatic weapons kept up constant firing, and the steady stream of bullets over the orchard wall sometimes lit up the place as bright as daylight for minutes at a time. The

gray, dismal light of dawn revealed the only casualty in our orchard—an old cow that had spent the night there was badly wounded in the lower jaw and leg. She stood perfectly still, apparently shocked from the wounds and gunfire.

Dawn on September 17 in St. Pierre revealed a devastated town, enveloped by an odor that Cawthon remembered as a combination of "cordite, dust, and charred wood." The devastation, however, did not seem to impact Gerhardt, who telephoned Dwyer at 8 A.M. and cheerily announced, "It's a nice day. We're going to roll them up today!" The enemy had abandoned vehicles and piles of equipment everywhere, and an observer with the 3rd Battalion reported, "There are few buildings not completely gutted. . . . Here and there are houses which still have some semblance of their former shape, but even they have great holes in their walls, glass all smashed."

During the night enemy aircraft had attempted to drop supplies by parachute to the beleaguered German garrison, but the Americans had squeezed the defenders into such a small area that many of those supplies fell into the 29ers' hands. "I saw a soldier coming down the road with a box under his arm," Puntenney recalled. "He was passing out something to anyone he came into contact with. He had gotten the box from one of the [enemy's] supply drops that fell in our lines. It was a box of Iron Cross medals intended for the Germans."

Unfortunately for Gerhardt, German artillerymen were much more proficient at their jobs than their Luftwaffe brethren. At about 5 A.M. on September 17, the 29th Division's nerve center, the renowned "war room," was the target of a furious and uncannily accurate half-hour barrage, consisting of 192 howitzer shells of 105mm caliber fired by a German battery situated on the Crozon peninsula, across Brest's massive harbor. Much to the amazement of Gerhardt and the division headquarters personnel, the enemy was not quite dead, but luckily, the barrage inflicted no casualties. As always, the general would later insist that every hole made in the war room tent by a German shell fragment must be patched and then painted over with a miniature Nazi swastika.

One tricky problem Gerhardt had to keep in mind on September 17 was that at 3 A.M. all Allied clocks and watches throughout the European Theater of Operations must be set back by one hour, thereby repeating the sixty-minute interval from 2 to 3 A.M. Under ordinary conditions such a time change would have triggered no special concerns, but since all three 29th Division regiments were set to attack at 10 A.M., the general's staff had to ensure that all units did indeed adhere to the prescribed change. Late on September 16, Witte asked Gerhardt if "we should change the time [of attack] for tomorrow, since we have to move the clock back one hour." Gerhardt replied: "No—it's all right the way it is."

Purnell's success at Recouvrance provided Gerhardt with the ammunition he needed to goad his other two regimental commanders to shove their commands forward relentlessly and at long last bring the siege of Brest to the roaring finale the general craved, one which he hoped would mark the 29th Division's greatest accomplishment so far in World War II. In his regular morning telephone conversation with Dwyer, Gerhardt declared: "You know Purnell got over the wall? . . . Give them the works!"

The 116th began its September 17 attack at 10 A.M. with the 3rd Battalion on the right, 2nd on the left, both pushing southward straight for the dry docks and jumbled port facilities on Recouvrance's harborside. Those objectives were close—so close that Puntenney and his Company L commander, Capt. Maurice McGrath, could clearly see them from atop the 3rd Battalion's command post in one of the rare buildings in St. Pierre remaining intact. The officers used their binoculars to peer toward the harbor area, but the vista seemingly consisted of nothing but huge piles of debris. It hardly seemed possible that an essential military objective existed somewhere in that massive pile of wreckage, but orders were orders.

The 3rd Battalion fought through St. Pierre at a pace described by the regimental journal as "heartbreakingly slow." When the outfit emerged into open terrain, Puntenney recalled, "All that confronted the infantrymen now was a lifeless stretch of level ground." On the far side of that open space lay a belt of the enemy's dreaded steel-turret pillboxes, the same kind of defenses that had thwarted the 115th Infantry and the 5th Ranger Battalion over the past two days. The men of the 3rd Battalion did no better against those German fortifications than their neighbors, but at 8:30 P.M. on September 17, Puntenney came up with the brilliant idea that if bullets and explosives could not overwhelm the enemy, maybe words could. He suggested to Dwyer that loudspeakers mounted on trucks should be brought up to the front, manned by GIs fluent in German who would reveal to the last-ditch enemy defenders the stark choice they now faced: surrender or die. Gerhardt liked the idea and promised the trucks would be ready on Puntenney's front the next morning.

The other half of the 116th Infantry's relentless attack on September 17 was carried out on Puntenney's left flank by Cawthon's 2nd Battalion, using Company G on the left, Company F on the right. As Cawthon

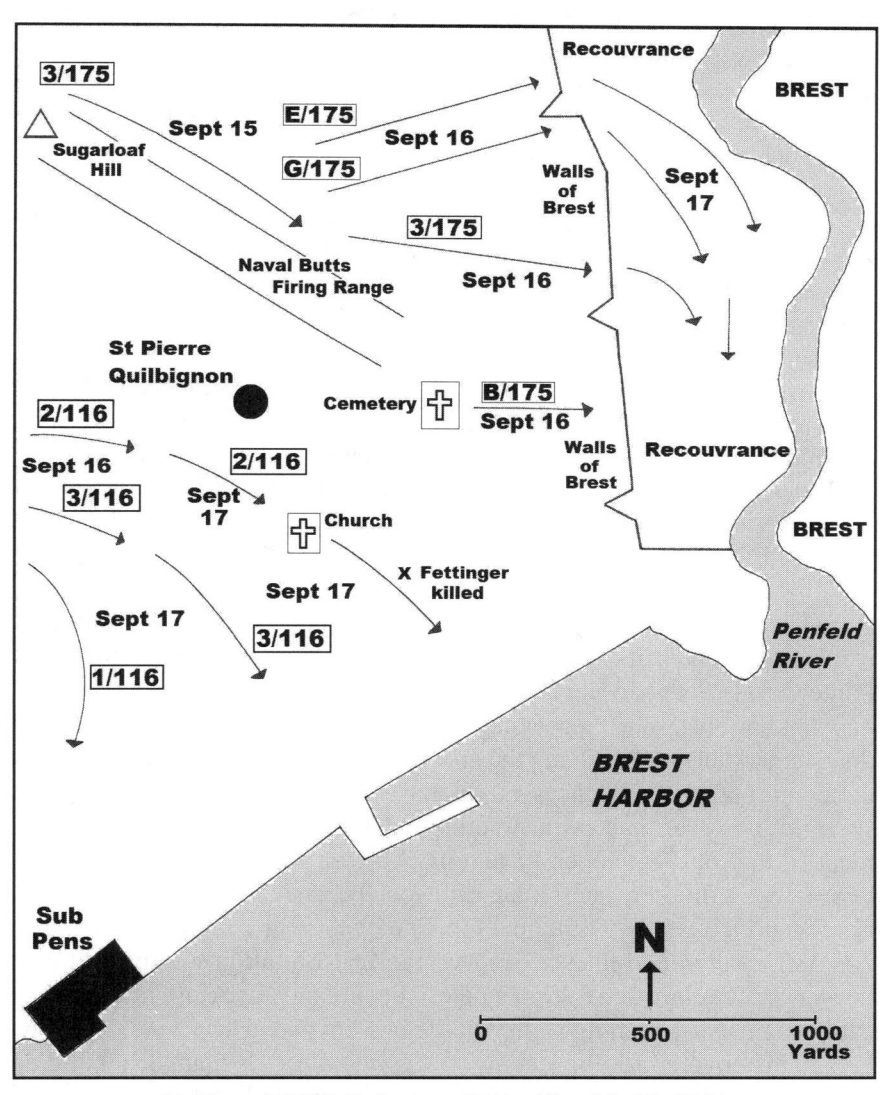

116th and 175th Infantry: September 15–17, 1944

remembered, "Not all opposition had faded, but it dwindled by the hour." Company F, under the command of Capt. Edward Mahaney—a new replacement officer from Rochester, New York—plunged into a built-up area of Recouvrance and ran into vigorous German resistance on a block dominated by a battered old church and an equally smashed theater next door. The antagonists exchanged heavy fire for a time at incredibly close range, but according to Pvt. James Trethewey,

> [a] German soldier appeared in the doorway of the theater waving a large white flag. He came over to us and said that some of the Germans wanted to surrender. We told him "OK," and he went back. The Germans then started walking out of the theater and nearby woods in groups of twos, threes, fours, and fives. They were hesitant about giving up and probably feared they would be fired upon. Another member of my squad, PFC Louis Whittall, and myself stood in the road waving them on. A total of fifty-six gave up in the space of about fifteen minutes, some of them gibbering excitedly that "Today it is finis!" All of them were damn glad it was over.

Mahaney shoved Company F beyond the church, and by dusk it reached the same belt of open ground on the southern outskirts of town that Puntenney's 29ers had run into a few hundred yards to the west. Mahaney may not have had much leadership experience in combat, but his outfit had done remarkably well, driving the enemy out of several tough positions that under normal circumstances might have taken days to overcome. The struggle, however, had been grueling, as Trethewey confirmed when he recalled that on September 17 his platoon lost half its men. Regrettably, less than one month later Mahaney, too, became a casualty—killed in action on October 13 while leading Company F in combat in Germany.

As Cawthon and his staff moved the 2nd Battalion's command post deeper into Recouvrance, sticking close behind the attacking infantry, they came upon an astonishing sight. On the block where Mahaney's Company F had just overcome the enemy strongpoint, more than one hundred French civilians were filing warily out of the church to take a first look at their liberators. The astonished 29ers learned that the civilians had lived for six weeks in the church basement while Allied bombs and shells rained down on their homes, an effort that had altered the once-quiet neighborhood into a clutter of rubble the shocked locals no longer recognized. Such violent acts on the Americans' part would change the lives of those unfortunate people forever, but if that was the price that had to be paid to eliminate the hated Nazi occupiers, then somehow the locals would accept that cruel fate.

Some young Frenchmen rummaged through their secret hiding places and managed to produce American and French flags, which they hung near the church door. Then, as Trethewey remembered, "Someone inside the church played the French and American national anthems on the organ." It was a poignant moment, one that symbolized in just a few minutes why the 29th Division had come to France in the first place. "There was in these people, who had endured four years of occupation, climaxed by the destruction of their city, an impressive dignity and quiet," Cawthon observed. "In their presence, I felt in no way a liberator; it seemed more fitting to express regret than to accept appreciation."

If the war news as reported by *29 Let's Go*, was to be believed, World War II could be over by the time Brest fell and the U.S. Army managed to organize sufficient transportation assets to move the division from Brittany to the main battle front, nearly 500 miles distant on the German frontier. Indeed, even as the 116th Infantry was pushing toward the Recouvrance waterfront on September 17, a giant Allied airborne force and a veteran corps from the British Second Army were initiating Operation Market-Garden, Field Marshal Montgomery's daring scheme to cross the Allied armies over the Rhine and end the war in one dazzling masterstroke. If that plan worked, and the Soviets could repeat the spectacular success of their offensive in the summer of 1944, the 29th Division could be going home before any of its members set foot in Germany.

Still Brest had not yet fallen, and although the enemy garrison was obviously about to give up, a 29er would have to survive the next few days if he wished to see home again. The odds were good, but all infantrymen recognized the brutal truth that survival at the front was purely a matter of luck; and in the last twenty-four hours of the Brest campaign, lamentably, many 29ers' luck finally ran out. One of those was T/Sgt. Ted Fettinger, the twenty-one-year-old platoon sergeant from Company G, 116th Infantry, who only five days in the past, in a bivouac behind the front, had eloquently related his D-Day experience on Omaha Beach to the renowned U.S. Army historian, S. L. A. Marshall. There were hardly any D-Day veterans left in Company G, or in Cawthon's entire 2nd Battalion for that matter; and accordingly, Fettinger's savvy in combat was highly valued by his Company G comrades, especially by its many members who were fresh replacements. That expertise, however, was put to the test on September 17 as Company G, under the command of Capt. Daniel Keyes, assumed the left flank position in Cawthon's battalion and moved into the dense urban setting of Recouvrance—an experience that almost no members of the outfit had faced before.

A Company G rifleman, PFC John Pelchuck, remembered that "Fettinger always looked after his men and taught them everything he could about how to take care of themselves in a combat situation." In Recouvrance, Fettinger practiced that trait with particular care because of the unusual nature of the battlefield. "As we went from house to house, he cautioned us to keep our heads down, for there were snipers all around," Pelchuck recalled. "As we were clearing one house, he neglected to follow his own advice, and he was shot through the head by a sniper."

A few weeks later, Keyes penned a V-Mail letter to one of Fettinger's old friends currently serving in the U.S. Army Air Force.

> My tour of duty with the company has not been long, but I was lucky enough to have Ted with me during some of that time.... His men adored him and insisted on carrying his body back themselves. That is the only time I have known that to happen. It was not until they had personally contacted the chaplain and assured themselves that Ted would have the best care taken of him that they returned to their duties. His loss was a great blow to the company, not only because he was a superior leader, but because on top of that he was a swell fellow—solid gold.

At 1 P.M. on September 17, Gerhardt telephoned Dwyer and declared, "Commit your whole regiment. Let's get going! I want to finish this thing off today!" Thirteen minutes later Dwyer's staff received a much more formal directive from the war room's G-3 shop, which was about as straightforward as a military order could be: "Your mission is to continue the advance to destroy all enemy within your sector by killing or capturing them and advancing to the beach. All the resources of the division will be available to you. Make request for what you want."

Dwyer thereupon committed to the fight Maj. Tom Dallas's 1st Battalion, fresh from its terrible ordeal at Fort Montbarey; and with that commitment every infantry unit in the 29th Division was in the front lines, either attacking or preparing to attack. That kind of all-out effort was almost unprecedented in the annals of the 29th Division, but by this point Gerhardt no longer had to wage war by the book and maintain a reserve because the enemy was powerless to counterattack. The general therefore resolved to end the campaign not with a whimper, but with a resounding demonstration of the 29th Division's combat power. Every available infantryman must be in for the final kill.

By nightfall the regiment had accomplished all that Gerhardt had demanded of it. All three of Dwyer's battalions had made it to the edge of the lofty bluffs lining the shoreline west of Brest, and from there the 29ers had a spectacular view in the gloaming of Brest's immense harbor. The Germans no longer had anywhere to hide, but as any GI could plainly see from his commanding position atop the bluffs, the enemy, at least for the moment, still had a place of refuge. On the far side of the harbor, little more than a mile distant, the 29ers could make out the Crozon peninsula, specifically the rocky promontory known as the Pointe des Espagnols, projecting like an extended finger straight at Brest. That the Germans still controlled that promontory was evident due to the steady stream of small boats making their way across the harbor from Brest to Crozon. In fact, American intelligence had reported that Ramcke himself had recently transferred his command post from Brest to Crozon.

The 8th Infantry Division was in the process of clearing Crozon, and much to Gerhardt's disappointment it would be that outfit rather than the 29th Division that would gain the honor of capturing the notorious Ramcke two days later. During the night of September 17–18, Gerhardt ordered the 116th to help halt the flow of enemy boats between Brest and Crozon by firing illuminating flares at thirty-minute intervals directly over the inner breakwater of Brest harbor. The artificial light provided by those flares enabled 29th Division artillery observers to direct the fire of every American howitzer within range against any German vessel in sight, a massive firepower display that surely convinced those waiting to escape that it was safer to wait for the inevitable end in Brest than to shift to Crozon.

The freshly drawn regimental boundary lines on Gerhardt's war room map showed that section of Recouvrance enclosed by the old city walls as the responsibility of Purnell's 175th Infantry. Company E had slipped under those walls on the evening of September 16, and as company after company followed that night and the next morning into the narrow, battered streets of Recouvrance, the riflemen fully anticipated a tough day of house-to-house fighting throughout Sunday, September 17, against resolute enemy paratroopers who had over the past three weeks proved that they would rather die than surrender.

As Purnell's men quickly learned, however, Brest would be no Stalingrad. Small patrols of 175th men fanned out across Recouvrance throughout the 17th and now and then ran into moderate resistance centered in the many sturdy factories and warehouses lining the Penfeld River's west bank. Steadfast enemy defenders could have held out for a considerable time in the warren of cellars and tunnels comprising that industrial area, but the Germans' behavior clearly indicated they had lost the will to resist. Most of those paratroopers who had resolved to fight to the death were by now indeed dead or in prisoner of war camps; and virtually all of the Germans remaining alive in Brest no longer had any motivation to die in a hopeless cause. The 29th Division had experienced just such a spiritual collapse on the enemy's part twice before—first at St. Lô, later at Vire—when the prospect of brutal house-to-house combat swiftly evaporated as the Americans cautiously entered those cities, only to discover that their only chore was a simple mop-up operation. Happily that defeatist attitude on the enemy's part was exposed yet again at Recouvrance; and a day that some worried could have been among the toughest faced by the 175th Infantry during the Brest campaign turned out to be one of the easiest.

The experience of a three-man patrol led by S/Sgt. Pete Jimenez of Company E epitomized that amazing day in regimental history. Jimenez, a twenty-seven-year-old native of Colorado, was described by a Company E comrade as "a Mexican-American, with a short, squat build, who was always smiling and seemed like an individual in whom you could place enormous trust." Jimenez led his men warily forward to explore what he remembered as a "cave," but which was in all probability a tunnel entrance or opening to a large storage cellar. Suddenly, the fire of a nearby German 20mm antiaircraft gun pinned them down. Jimenez tried and failed to take out the gun with a bazooka, but some well-aimed shots from his M1 killed two members of the crew and silenced the gun. Small groups of German soldiers then tried to dash out of the tunnel, but the fusillade of rifle fire from Jimenez and his men put a stop to that. Shortly thereafter, an astounded Jimenez watched the Germans come out of the tunnel by the hundreds with their hands in the air. As he recalled, "The Germans formed a column approximately five or six abreast and one and a half city blocks long. . . . As we brought the prisoners in, a lieutenant approached me and congratulated me for a job well done. He then said, 'Here, Sarge, have a drink from the old man's private [cognac] stock.'" The provisional government of the French Republic recognized Jimenez's exploit by awarding him the prestigious Croix de Guerre with Etoile de Bronze (Bronze Star) on January 25, 1945.

By the afternoon of September 17, Purnell was worried less about enemy resistance than he was about his ability to handle the thousands of German captives who had fallen into his regiment's hands. "We're raking in prisoners right and left," he exclaimed to Gerhardt. "We've got the whole thing mopped up except for a few snipers here or there—but the city is under our control. You had better get some MPs down here. . . . As far as we're concerned the thing is about over." Later, the 175th's intelligence officer reported, "The [German] administrative troops in the tunnels surrendered upon contact and had been instructed to do so. Much food and other supplies were taken."

Proof of that fact was provided by reporter Lou Azrael, who followed the 175th into Recouvrance to cover what he hoped would be the final combat action at Brest. Azrael wandered into a dark tunnel he assumed had been cleared, and he was about to be surprised. In a flippant September 17 "letter to the editor," later published in the *Baltimore News-Post*, Azrael wrote:

> This is to report that your war reporter today was forced to capture two German soldiers who interrupted him while he was looting liquor. . . . I was making my way through [the tunnel] when by the light of a candle I saw some empty bottles and some straw, which often protects liquor bottles. It seemed to me this situation required reportorial inspection. I was right, too. I found an unopened bottle of cognac and several bottles of wine and benedictine. . . . I saw two German soldiers, and one had a pistol on his belt. In an emergency, man uses any weapon he has at hand. And in my hands were two bottles of liquor. So I vaguely pointed one bottle at the Nazis and shouted in German, 'Hands up!' . . . I shall have wine with tonight's supper. Wish you were here.

The march of the German troops into captivity was described by Holbrook Bradley as "one of the shabbiest processions we've seen . . . more like a refugee army than part of the Wehrmacht." For the moment the 175th crammed the German prisoners into the moat just beyond the city wall, and from a temporary regimental CP atop that wall, a proud Purnell and his staff watched that swarming mass of downhearted men grow by the minute. Here, at last, was tangible evidence of the 175th's battle prowess.

Purnell fervently wished Gerhardt could see it firsthand. If so, the general wouldn't be giving him hell about chin straps anymore.

NINE

The Tragedy Is Complete

1. HEINIES TO THE END

The general knew the end was in sight, and at daybreak on September 18, 1944, his staff noticed with a combination of trepidation and excitement that he had apparently awoken in a state of agitation that made his customary behavior seem serene in comparison. As soon as the general strode into the war room and completed his morning routine, he grabbed the phone to specify to his chief subordinates exactly how the Germans should meet their end: "There will be no terms or anything," Gerhardt barked. "Just keep on firing until you see the white flag!" Like a modern-day version of Ulysses S. Grant, Uncle Charlie fairly hollered his surrender terms into the mouthpiece: "Unconditional! . . . If they want to surrender, they put up a white flag and come marching out! You just let them know that if they want to surrender, [they must] get in groups of 500 and come out with their hands up! There is no talking any peace terms!"

No 29er who witnessed the events of September 18 at Brest could ever forget them. The setting was surreal: The Germans were out there somewhere, hidden for the moment behind the typical early morning haze. The tranquility of this eerie dawn was in sharp contrast to the crashing sounds of a battle that had endured with deadening regularity for so long now that no one could remember any longer when it had started. As the haze steadily dissipated, the 29ers could only hope that the calm signaled the enemy's willingness to give up, but for the moment, the only discernible certainty among frontline riflemen was that they were situated in the middle of a gloomy landscape dominated by the grotesque debris of war.

That nightmarish setting was abruptly accentuated by the arrival at the front of several U.S. Army trucks armed with bulky loudspeakers, which began to blare deafening messages in German to the invisible foe. Those messages were blunt: If the Germans wished to live to see another sunrise, they must come out immediately with their hands in the air. More to the point, if American loudspeakers could not draw the enemy out of its hiding places, American bullets would.

So the rumors filtering down from the 29th Division war room through battalion command posts all the way to the 29ers in the front lines were apparently true: the enemy must be near the breaking point. Could today be the day? The latest solid evidence of the enemy's imminent collapse came from a 29th Division medical officer who had entered a German hospital in Recouvrance the previous night. There he observed, "The Germans had broken into their liquor supplies for a final fling," and added, "They were all drunk—patients and everybody else, and they were wandering up and down the halls singing and having a swell time. It looked like a fraternity house party after a football game."

Almost all 29ers held to the logical line of reasoning that there could not possibly be many Germans left unscathed in Brest as a consequence of the deluge of bombs, bullets, and shells poured into enemy lines by the Americans over the past three weeks. As reality set in on this amazing day of days, however, the fighting men coolly watched thousands upon thousands of bedraggled and compliant enemy soldiers, sailors, and airmen materialize magically from their hiding places with their hands up—just as Gerhardt had demanded. In truth, so many captives marched into 29th Division lines that the division's seventy-one-man military police platoon assigned to guard them could not possibly fulfill its job.

No 29er would fail to take pride in the spectacle. If three tired and depleted U.S. Army divisions had overcome that horde, maybe this costly siege had been worth it. Only time would tell; but in the meantime, all 29ers agreed that if the countless columns of scruffy enemy soldiers typified the current state of the German Army, the war couldn't last much longer.

If the beginning of the end at Brest could be defined by a single moment, that moment came at 7:45 A.M. on Monday, September 18, 1944. At sunrise the alert 29ers of the 115th Infantry's Company E, under the command of 2nd Lt. Roderick Parsch, had peered through the ground fog toward the massive, fortresslike buildings of the French Naval Academy, the focal point of the enemy's last-ditch defensive line in front of Brest's inner harbor. The GIs were on edge, for they held orders to execute a frontal attack against those buildings at 10 A.M., and they knew the assault, which would have to be carried out across 600 yards of wide-open no-man's-land, would be grueling and costly in lives. But as sunlight gradually dissolved the mist, Parsch's men observed an astonishing sight. Someone was waving a large white flag back and forth from a window of the academy. It was an electrifying moment, and the 29ers willingly held their fire as four Germans emerged from the academy and steadily tramped toward the American lines. As they came closer the riflemen could see that all four were officers, probably high-ranking ones, representing all branches of the enemy's armed services: army, air force, navy. Only one of the four spoke English, and according to Cpl. Art Plaut of the 115th Infantry: "When the German emissaries came into the lines, they demanded to see the general in charge of the troops to their front. They were informed that the attacking troops were commanded by Maj. [actually Lt. Col.] Anthony Miller, the 2nd Battalion CO, and the Germans agreed to meet with him although they expressed disappointment."

Parsch passed the news on to Miller, who promptly ordered the enemy emissaries to be escorted back to his battalion command post. Not surprisingly, Miller and his staff were in an angry mood when the Germans arrived, and neither side expressed the slightest hint of cordiality when salutes were exchanged. The helmets worn by the four Germans for the dangerous journey across no-man's-land appeared incongruous with their full-dress uniforms, some of which featured spotless shirts and ties. One officer even sported old-fashioned baggy riding breeches with a leather seat. Corporal Plaut also noted with amazement: "The Germans smelled of expensive perfume." If so, the enemy must have been revolted by the odor emitted by the Americans, all of whom had spent nearly one month in the front lines with no substantive break and currently appeared utterly disheveled.

Presently, Capt. Frank Steele, a liaison officer from the 110th Field Artillery attached to Miller's staff, blindfolded the four Germans and steered them by the arm into waiting jeeps, which would take them behind American lines to meet Lt. Col. Lou Smith, the 115th Infantry's commander. (Later, a photo of Steele blindfolding the German officers appeared in the October 16, 1944, issue of *Life* magazine, featuring the sultry actress Lauren Bacall on the cover.) Gerhardt had dictated to Smith that there must be no negotiations with the reviled Germans; but still, if the enemy wished to surrender, the details of that capitulation had to be worked out. Smith would meet the Germans in St. Pierre, in a three-story stone house that had only recently been transformed from a grand edifice into a battered wreck, featuring a massive hole in its side from a heavy artillery shell, bullet pockmarks by the hundreds, and a dozen or so shutters hanging crazily from window frames.

There was a grim determination to the 29ers that must have disheartened the enemy. Stern-faced 29th Division MPs guarded the house; and the portly Smith, dressed in full battle gear—helmet chin-strap hooked underneath his lower lip, just as Uncle Charlie demanded—established without delay that the 29th Division would only accept an unconditional surrender. Smith insisted that this blunt message be passed back immediately to whoever was currently in charge of the Germans' defenses. Other than that simple detail there was not much to talk about. Plaut observed, "[The Germans] made it clear that they wanted an honorable, orderly surrender, and to save face they wanted us to send a token force into the grounds of their headquarters at the Naval Academy to bring them out. They wanted time to assemble their forces, and they wanted assurances that their wounded would be properly cared for."

While not strictly "unconditional," that arrangement suited Smith, and in less than fifteen minutes the meeting was terminated. Blindfolds were reapplied, jeep engines revved up, and by 8:45 A.M. the Germans had been deposited back in no-man's-land, where they forlornly trudged back toward the Naval Academy. The guns were strangely silent now; and for the return trip, all four no longer felt the need to wear their helmets. Just in case a vengeful 29er felt the temptation to open fire, however, the German naval officer continued to carry the large white surrender flag, raised high so that everyone in the vicinity could see it. Sometime that morning, seven staff officers of the 115th Infantry's 2nd Battalion, led by Miller and his executive, Maj. Al Warfield, tore a piece of cloth from that flag as a souvenir, and ultimately all seven signed it. Nowadays that simple piece of cloth is a treasured 29th Division memento at Maryland National Guard headquarters in the Fifth Regiment Armory in Baltimore, Maryland.

On Miller's right flank, Glover Johns's 1st Battalion held orders to seize the French Navy's old subterranean oil storage tanks on the bluff overlooking Brest's harbor. The attack was preparing to jump off when Johns received a phone call from the front: Company C was reporting a white flag within the enemy's lines. "I reported this fact to regiment and took off for the [oil] tanks," Johns related. "I found a German captain and lieutenant, who explained that they had been under no-fire orders since 8

A.M. I asked why a sniper had shot at me on the way down. They didn't have a good answer to that."

It was just a matter of time now, but if the 29ers had to wait long for the Germans to come out with their hands up, the 115th Infantry was prepared to resume the offensive—and this time it would be merciless and final. For ninety minutes Miller and his staff gazed across the desolate waste toward the Naval Academy, while Johns and his cohorts did the same at the nearby oil storage tanks. According to reporter Lou Azrael, "We saw German soldiers come out and hurl things into the water. We saw them break their rifles and scatter the pieces around. We saw them stack documents and small pieces of equipment on the ground and burn them. Dozens of fires, hundreds of small explosions, were all around." Those actions by the enemy incensed many 29ers, who believed they violated the agreement just struck by Colonel Smith with the German delegation. "Maybe the right thing for our troops to have done, under the circumstances, was to obey their impulse and turn machine-gun fire on the place," Azrael observed. "But there were no orders to that effect."

At 10:26 A.M., the 2nd Battalion journal noted: "Companies E and G reported a white flag flying from the École Navale, and that the enemy were breaking up their weapons and assembling on the academy grounds." For the next hour that assemblage of humanity swelled so rapidly that the single rifle company Miller had alerted to guard the prisoners appeared wholly inadequate. As Plaut observed, "Instead of the 200 or 300 prisoners that we had supposed we would have to handle, we saw men from every branch of the German armed forces, running into the thousands." The 29th Division's provost marshal, Maj. Vern Johnson, also commanded the division's military police platoon, and it was imperative that he get a sense of the enormity of his upcoming mission. He gamely plunged straight into German lines with an escort of only four men, three of whom were unarmed journalists, including a photographer from *Life* magazine. One of those journalists, Holbrook Bradley, remembered that moment as "one of the tenser moments in our lives. . . . From where we stood it looked as if German soldiers, sailors, and marines were everywhere."

Major Johnson, a native of Grand Forks, South Dakota, had learned the value of boldness in his younger years as a highly accomplished collegiate boxer. Somewhere near the cliffside behind the Naval Academy buildings, he and his four accomplices fearlessly plunged into what Bradley remembered as a "mineshaft" and eventually emerged into a veritable subterranean military city. Countless passageways branching off from primary tunnels led to a series of cavernous barracks, officers' quarters, offices, kitchens, and dozens of supply rooms of various kinds. A vast hospital situated in the lower reaches of this amazing complex contained over 600 wounded, cared for by a staff of overworked female nurses with wholly inadequate medical equipment.

The astonished Americans quickly grasped that the enemy's mastery of military architecture had allowed Ramcke and his subordinates to function throughout most of the siege with little interference from the Allies' cascade of bombs and shells. As difficult as it was for Johnson to admit, the 29th Division's immense effort to render the lives of Brest's defenders as uncomfortable as possible had apparently impacted the enemy in this locale hardly at all. As Johnson wandered through the vast warren of tunnels, the glaring evidence of that detail was provided by the humming cacophony of underground generators, still functioning normally and still providing sufficient electricity to illuminate and ventilate each room. Meanwhile, as Bradley remembered, German troops "seemed to stare a moment, then go on with their talking.... We got very much the feeling of being on board ship, for the rooms on either side looked like staterooms aboard a vessel."

Johnson needed to find any German officer familiar with the surrender terms, and that search brought him before a major of paratroopers acting as adjutant for Generalmajor (Brigadier General) Hans von der Mosel, the one-time commander of Fortress Brest who had been relegated to chief of staff upon the arrival of Ramcke in August 1944. The German major extended his arm to shake Johnson's hand, but Johnson abruptly rejected the offer, declaring that he had come to accept a surrender, not to attend a social gathering. Johnson and a few enemy officers thereupon took their seats at a table to commence negotiations, but according to Bradley, "The Germans hardly looked at us." They promptly demanded that talks be postponed for at least thirty minutes so that German troops could finish lunch. Further demands of that kind triggered the Americans' wrath, and Bradley finally blurted out, in German, "Who's surrendering here: us or you?"

Ultimately, the German major declined to escort Johnson to his boss, von der Mosel, since, as Lou Azrael noted, "Johnson was not a direct representative of the commanding general of the conquering force." Johnson could not argue with that line of reasoning, as up until that time von der Mosel's emissaries to the 29th Division had dealt only with Smith and Miller of the 115th Infantry. That potentially explosive situation, however, vanished with Miller's arrival at about 11:30 A.M. Accompanied only by his operations officer, Capt. Robert Boyd, and a single radio operator, Miller came straight to the point and demanded to see the man in charge.

1/116

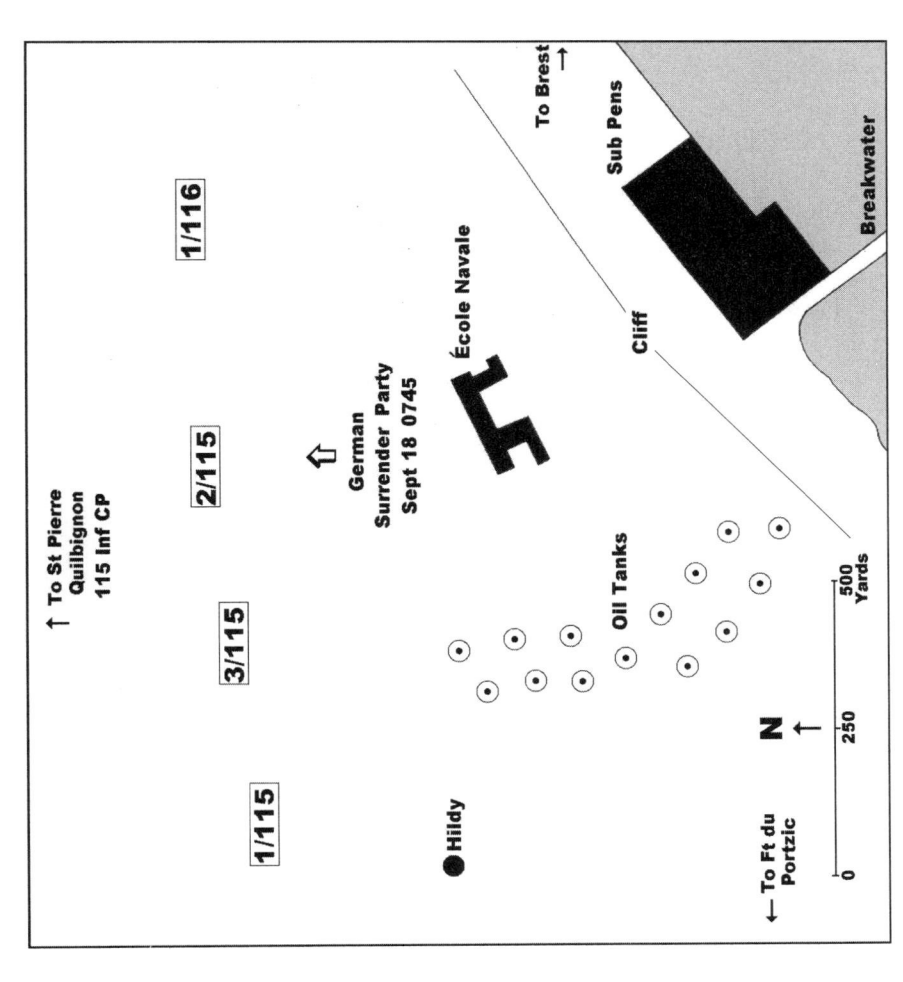

2/115

German
Surrender Party
Sept 18 0745

École Navale

↑ To St Pierre
Quilbignon
115 Inf CP

3/115

Oil Tanks

Sub Pens

To Brest →

Cliff

Breakwater

1/115

● Hildy

N ↑

0 — 250 — 500 Yards

←— To Ft du
Portzic

The Surrender: September 18, 1944

This time, von der Mosel's adjutant complied, and he led Miller's party down through the underground complex, out into the open air through a large opening at the cliff base, across a concrete esplanade, and into a side entrance of the enemy's infamous submarine pens.

A dejected von der Mosel, who had only recently been promoted from colonel to general officer rank, was waiting somewhere inside; but as Azrael wrote, "The Nazi general's adjutant expressed anxiety that not many persons should enter the room where the general sat, so men who had accompanied Miller remained in an adjoining room, and only Miller, an interpreter, a magazine photographer, and I entered." It was one of the great moments in the history of the 29th Infantry Division. The thirty-one-year-old former private in the 5th Maryland Infantry, a resident of 30 North Bernice Avenue in a modest west Baltimore neighborhood, was now face-to-face with a career German Army soldier fifteen years his senior. As Azrael recalled, "The general was the type a movie director would pick for a Nazi officer. He was about fifty [actually forty-six] years old, tall, lean, with a hawklike nose, thin lips, sharp chin."

Ramcke would certainly not have agreed with Azrael's assessment. According to Ramcke, von der Mosel was

> a poor, deaf, dull-witted soul, who had been made commandant of Brest [well before Ramcke's arrival on August 9, 1944] to get rid of him. . . . I reported to the Reichsmarschall [Hermann Göring] that after a careful and accurate consideration of all the circumstances, I could state with full justification that if my 2nd Parachute Division hadn't taken over full control on August 11 of the defense of Brest, then on August 15 the fortress would have fallen to the enemy.

The apprehensive von der Mosel, who according to Azrael participated in the surrender proceedings with "eyes half closed," wished to carry out his distasteful duties as quickly as possible. In truth, von der Mosel and Miller had little to discuss, and the proceedings mercifully endured for only about twenty minutes. The general yearned to evade the humiliation of surrendering his sidearms, but a resolute Miller insisted upon that symbolic gesture, and von der Mosel promptly handed over two pistols. Next, von der Mosel requested an assurance from Miller that his men would be treated humanely in captivity. Miller growled a simple and direct reply: "We know the rules of the Geneva Convention and abide by them."

It was all over by noon. Miller granted von der Mosel ninety minutes to evacuate his non-wounded men from the submarine pens and all adjacent underground facilities. As Miller's battalion journal noted at 1:30 P.M., the Germans met that deadline: "Prisoners in groups of hundreds, under the command of their own officers and escorted by Company F guards and division MPs, marching to POW points." Even when reinforced by Company F's riflemen, the 29th Division's MP platoon would obviously be vastly outnumbered by its prisoners. In fact, when Major Johnson prepared his monthly action report several days later, he noted that the total number of captives his men had herded into prisoner of war enclosures on September 18 alone came to 5,477. "Prisoners were generally of a higher type, both in appearance and discipline, than those taken previously by the division," Johnson reported.

That detail was later corroborated by Azrael, who watched in amazement from the esplanade outside the submarine pens as hundreds of Germans formed up to march into captivity, all of whom were enthusiastically belting out the patriotic anthem "Die Wacht am Rhein" ("The Watch on the Rhine"), with its stirring chorus: "Dear Fatherland! Put your mind at rest! Solid stands the watch on the Rhine!" Azrael observed: "There was no note of regret at surrender in their faces." Any 29er who had seen the 1943 film *Casablanca*, starring Humphrey Bogart, could not fail to be rankled by that offensive German hymn, for in one of the film's classic scenes a group of arrogant Nazi officers dining in Rick's Café Americain had burst into "Die Wacht am Rhein," only to be drowned out by French patriots in a spontaneous and rousing rendition of the French national anthem "La Marseillaise." Regrettably, outside the submarine pens at Brest, no patriotic Frenchmen showed up to overpower this insufferable German display of fidelity to the fatherland.

The commander of the 116th Infantry's 2nd Battalion, Maj. Charles Cawthon, observed: "No Stalingrad or Bataan, this; no starving, disease-ravaged skeletons doomed to a fate as terrible as the one from which they had just escaped. Instead, the men Hitler had ordered to defend Brest to the death were well-fed, cleanshaven, and well-turned-out."

One could hardly imagine a crueler blow to a German general's pride than handing over two pistols in surrender to a scruffy American lieutenant colonel. That mortifying act was a disgrace that could only be marginally alleviated by a formal capitulation to an opponent of general officer rank, an event that would at least allow the adversaries to exchange salutes as equals, and share, if only for a moment, the burdens of high command in war lesser men could not possibly grasp. With luck the German commander might even gain some sympathy from an opponent who would commiserate with him over the fortunes of war and how, on occasion, even the best commanders could fall victim to cruel fate. With those thoughts in mind, Generalmajor Hans von der Mosel, accompanied by the commander of the 2nd *Fallschirmjäger* Division, Generalmajor Hans Kroh, and the German naval commander at Brest, Konteradmiral [Rear Admiral] Otto Kähler, were ushered at 3 P.M. into the command post of the U.S. Army's 29th Infantry Division, commanded by Maj. Gen. Charles Hunter Gerhardt, Jr.

One of Ramcke's most trusted colleagues, the thirty-seven-year-old Kroh was a highly experienced paratrooper who had assumed command of the division when Hitler had promoted Ramcke as commandant of Fortress Brest little more than one month in the past. Kroh's companion, Kähler, was a fifty-year old seaman with a lofty reputation within the German Navy due to his exploits in the armed merchant cruiser *Thor* (known to the Royal Navy simply as "Raider E"), which Kähler commanded on a 1940–41 cruise that endured for nearly a year and resulted in the destruction of a dozen Allied merchant vessels. Ramcke, however, did not think much of Kähler, who he noted "just sat in a shelter" throughout the siege of Brest.

Gerhardt was the kind of man who was indeed capable of offering some solace to subjugated enemy commanders, for he had been a soldier for more than thirty years and respected others—even Germans—who had devoted their lives to military service. He never got that chance, however, because within their first few moments in the war room, the Germans violated one of Uncle Charlie's most prized rituals: They stubbornly refused to sign the 29th Division's guest book when prompted to do so by Gerhardt's interpreter, 1st Lt. Hans Kohler. Gerhardt cherished the guest book because it contained the signatures of many distinguished visitors to the war room: Eisenhower, Montgomery, Bradley, and dozens of others, including Lt. Col. Martin Fürst, who only one week in the past had surrendered the Le Conquet peninsula to the 29th Division. Perhaps an even more galling gesture was made by von der Mosel, who clicked his heels and gave a Nazi salute when he was brought before Gerhardt's appalled 29th Division staff.

Gerhardt occupied an adjacent tent and was waiting for a theatrical moment to emerge, but when he learned of the Germans' behavior from his aide-de-camp, Lt. Bob Wallis, he became enraged and refused to see them. According to the eminent 29th Division historian Joseph Ewing, "It was a rebuff by a defeated enemy who was not sufficiently supine. 'What? They won't sign?' [Gerhardt] barked. 'Well, then! Take 'em away! If they don't want to be sociable, send 'em up to corps. Get them out of here!'" Later that day, Gerhardt muttered to the editor of *29 Let's Go*, Cpl. Jean Lowenthal, "We asked those fellas to sign the guest book, and all they said was, 'Thank you very much.' They were Heinies to the end."

Several days later, by means of a well-placed eavesdropper in a prisoner-of-war camp in England, the Allied high command learned that von der Mosel and Kähler held some dark secrets they had held back from their interrogators. According to the transcript of a conversation in a holding pen, Kähler whispered to von der Mosel: "Just wait and see! I can tell you there will be a terrific row if they find the fifty-five corpses in Brest harbor. You can say what you like—it won't be believed."

General von der Mosel replied, "That's quite possible. . . . Or if they find the corpses that haven't been cleared out of the galleries [in the submarine pens and underground hospitals]."

It certainly sounded like a war crime, but unfortunately, General Gerhardt never found out what they were talking about.

2. THE FRUITS OF VICTORY

On the afternoon of September 18, throngs of 29ers made their way down to Brest's harborside to witness history. By far the most memorable detail of that journey was that even greater throngs of Germans were marching precisely in the opposite direction. The war was over for those enemy soldiers, and weighed down by duffel bags and suitcases stuffed with personal possessions, thousands of them trudged inland up the steep hills of Brest toward the prison camps that would soon become their temporary homes. The wreckage of a defeated army was everywhere; and according to Corporal Plaut of the 115th Infantry, that detritus multiplied significantly as "many [Germans] discarded everything after they realized that they would have to walk several miles to the prisoner of war collecting point."

Lacking their helmets and weapons, the disheveled enemy troops hardly carried themselves like the fearsome warriors who had held the 29th Division at bay outside the walls of Brest for more than three weeks. In truth, however, virtually all of the most fearsome of those warriors were by now either dead or too badly wounded to move. Those prisoners now on parade before the victorious 29ers were apparently of a different warrior caste; and such a vast number of them presently fell into the division's grasp in a matter of hours that many Americans wondered aloud why the Germans had not been capable of holding out for several more weeks. One of Miller's staff officers, 1st Lt. Robert Henne, recalled that he was "stunned" by the size of the enemy procession, and that "we didn't know how to handle them. Someone said that if the Krauts had all spit at one time, the 2nd Battalion, 115th Infantry, would have drowned."

The sights and sounds of the brutal combat at Brest over the past three weeks had understandably triggered emotional despair in the minds of many frontline 29ers. On September 18, however, those feelings vanished in a flash, to be replaced by joy and pride at the realization of what the 29th Division had just accomplished, and the much more blissful thought that the division would now surely be out of combat for at least a week—and maybe forever if Nazi Germany was truly in its death throes. Gerhardt regularly urged the 29ers to "flaunt their patches of blue and gray," an entreaty that typically meant little to hardened combat veterans focused only on survival. At Brest, however, the general's appeal for displays of unit pride seemed entirely sensible. On the afternoon of the 18th, a German officer emerged from an underground shelter in Recouvrance and entered the 116th Infantry's lines, offering to surrender his command of 300 troops as long as that act could be accomplished honorably. According to Pvt. James Trethewey of Company F, 116th Infantry, "Looking around for someone of equal rank to whom he could surrender, the German commander pointed to the 29th Division insignia on my shoulder and asked if that meant I was an officer." Trethewey replied: "Hell, no. That's the insignia of the division that walloped hell out of you."

Trethewey's regimental commander, Col. Philip Dwyer, had a wholly different way of expressing unit pride. The 116th's intelligence officer, Capt. Robert Walker, observed the setting when three German officers were brought before Dwyer to surrender their commands on the Recouvrance waterfront:

> Colonel Dwyer, big and portly, unshaven, and wearing a wrinkled field raincoat, the front of which was stained with tobacco juice, sat hunched over a card table. [The three Germans] were all in immaculate dress uniforms, highly polished boots, and gleaming brass and decorations. They snapped to attention, heels clicking. Dwyer didn't look up. Nothing was said until [Maj. Tom] Dallas [CO, 1st Battalion] told Dwyer he had brought the officers so they could surrender to him. Dwyer hardly moved, but spat tobacco juice and uttered, "Ask 'em why the hell they didn't surrender long ago."

Countless images of human suffering had been etched into the 29ers' minds at Brest, but as the fighting men pushed through the city walls and advanced down to the waterside on September 18, the near-total desolation of the city left a lasting impression upon the men that was equally bleak. In the September 21, 1944 edition of *29 Let's Go*, Lowenthal wrote:

There is not a human emotion that is quite equal to the terrible, pitiful scene unfolding before your eyes. . . . A death-like pall hangs over the city proper—the quiet of no-man's land after battle. The thoroughfare is deserted. Plots of every conceivable kind of debris are strewn in the side streets where they fell. Buildings sag. Those which have received direct hits are stripped of their last vestiges. Some, which were constructed of more durable stuff, are just jagged masses of their own blasted composition. The city is a shambles. The tragedy is complete. The Hun is gone. The ravages he brought down are left behind him.

As the 29ers made their way gingerly through the rubble, they were disheartened to discover that one of the Hun's ravages had been applied to the magnificent American monument on the ramparts of Brest, dedicated in the 1920s to U.S. Navy sailors who had served on the transatlantic run in World War I. That granite tower, standing more than 100 feet high, had been one of about a dozen impressive memorials in France established by the American Battle Monuments Commission during the interwar years under the leadership of its first chairman, the legendary AEF commander Gen. John J. Pershing. Sadly, the tower had now been reduced to nothing but a pile of debris.

Pershing still ran the Commission in 1944. The eighty-four-year-old general, although feeble, naturally still upheld an unshakable interest in the welfare of the American World War I memorials built under his guidance. Indeed, from the apartment the Army had specially constructed for him at Walter Reed Hospital in Washington, Pershing had written to his one-time subordinate Eisenhower following the liberation of France to determine whether or not the Germans had damaged or destroyed his beloved memorials during the occupation. On September 11, 1944, Eisenhower had replied: "I am happy to report to you that our first hasty surveys of American battle monuments and cemeteries, constructed under your personal supervision, indicate that they are intact and undamaged."

But Ike's message had been written a week prior to the liberation of Brest, before conclusive evidence pertaining to the fate of the U.S. Navy memorial tower had emerged. That the monument was no more was obvious. Now it was up to the Americans to determine whether the enemy's explanation for its demise was plausible. According to Gerhardt's chief intelligence officer, Lt. Col. Paul Krznarich, it was not. "The Germans reported for propaganda reasons that the monument had been destroyed by an air raid by the RAF," Krznarich observed. "According to a multitude of French civilians, it is credibly and reliably reported and concluded that the monument was prepared for demolition by the Germans and the demolitions were executed during a raid by RAF planes."

If the Germans could sink to such depths, what else could they do? Evidently, quite a bit: A few weeks later, in captivity in Britain, Ramcke described some more of the ravages he himself had ordered his people to perpetrate on Brest. "I had the houses, the railways, and the railway bridges blown up," he declared. "All the locomotives were burned out and smashed up; and the harbor installations, the quays, barracks, and water towers, power stations, gas works, and all the tramways were smashed up—it was nothing but a heap of rubble! . . . We didn't leave a crane or anything standing." It could have been worse, as Ramcke related with a chuckle to a fellow German general: "I told Middleton, 'Unfortunately I was lacking chemicals. If they had been available, I should have made the open roadstead off Brest stink for the next ten years.'"

The enemy had abandoned weapons and equipment in such profusion in Brest that an anonymous writer noted in *29 Let's Go*: "Souvenir hunters had a field day." In fact, according to Plaut, "When word reached the rear that the fortress had fallen and the Germans were surrendering, every road leading into the area became clogged with vehicles and personnel from every outfit within miles around." Curiosity had its risks, however, as the cunning enemy had scattered booby traps everywhere, which killed at least one 29er and injured many more. It was one thing to lose a comrade to a German bullet, but after a man survived countless fusillades of those bullets over the past several weeks, the irony of losing a buddy to a seemingly harmless bicycle parked against a wall, or a discarded Luger on a heap of stones, produced within the 29ers only revulsion for their prostrate opponents.

All 29ers who desired a memento of the Brest campaign realized that the best place to find it was in the submarine pens. Those amazing structures were practically the only intact edifices in Brest, and the odds were good that the Germans had packed into them all the things a GI fresh out of combat longed for: liquor, food, Nazi medals and daggers—and perhaps even women. Lowenthal accompanied Tony Miller's party into the sub pens, and he observed in a September 19, 1944, edition of *29 Let's Go*: "Down deep in their lair the Nazis have been living like kings. They have had every conceivable luxury."

Unhappily, only hours after the Germans had capitulated, those 29ers who eagerly looked forward to a few hours scavenging in the sub pens were stopped dead in their tracks at the entryways by conspicuous U.S. Army signposts featuring the two simple words fighting men had come to detest: "Off Limits." According to Plaut, the humorless MPs who stood guard next to those signs "prevented any but their own from entering the grounds." Those GIs who did not trust the top brass were convinced that Middleton and Gerhardt were apparently resolved to deny the fruits of victory to the men whose actions had secured the triumph.

For some 29th Division combat soldiers, the challenge of getting past those MPs and into the off-limit sub pens was one that could not be passed up. Capt. Frank Steele, the 110th Field Artillery liaison officer attached to the 115th Infantry who on the morning of September 18 had blindfolded the four German emissaries as they passed into American lines to discuss surrender terms, was renowned throughout the 110th for his mischievous exploits during the 29th Division's lengthy training period in England. One of those deeds in spring 1944 was a mock raid on Abbotsfield Hall, the site of Gerhardt's headquarters on a hill in Tavistock, Devon. Steele had conclusively proved that security at 29th Division headquarters was nonexistent, for he managed to make off with a weapons-carrier, a 400-pound safe filled with secret documents, and several trinkets from the general's private desk. Just to make sure Gerhardt would know intruders had been present in his office, Steele had stopped the general's clock at exactly twelve midnight.

For someone as cunning as Steele, entry into the sub pens was easy. One facet of military life Steele had observed over time was the code of behavior practiced by U.S. Army MPs who manned checkpoints. He noted with amazement that officers who approached checkpoints carrying a pen and a clipboard, to which several sheets of inscrutable U.S. Army forms were attached, invariably were waved through that checkpoint by deferential MPs. At the Brest submarine pens, Steele tried that method, and it worked. Sitting in the front passenger seat of a 110th Field Artillery jeep, his driver approached the entranceway and came to a halt as the MP guarding the checkpoint raised his hand. Steele kept his pen and clipboard in plain sight and maintained a confident manner so the MP would be impressed by his supposed authority. He was fully prepared to mutter some double-talk with official overtones, but the MP waved him right on through.

Steele thereupon wandered freely through the sub pens, searching for something that was not supposed to be there. According to a September 17 report by a 29th Division liaison officer at Middleton's VIII Corps, "Two [train] car loads of liquor are stacked in the U-boat pens, and if Brest falls before they are consumed, they are to be shoved into the water." Steele correctly assumed that no American soldier in his right mind would carry out Middleton's order, but still speed was essential since GIs were sure to descend on the forbidden liquor like a pack of wolves on cornered prey. Steele therefore moved quickly and managed to scrounge about forty bottles of first-class alcoholic beverages of all kinds, which would come in handy for the 110th Field Artillery's highly anticipated victory party in the coastal resort village of Le Trez Hir that Colonel Cooper was currently organizing.

For those fortunate few who managed to get past the MPs by fair means or foul and gain access to the sub pens, their first steps through the massive portals yielded an astonishing sight they would remember for the rest of their lives. "The submarine pen is perhaps the strongest thing of its kind that has ever been constructed by men," Lowenthal wrote in *29 Let's Go*. Here was clear evidence of the Nazis' expertise at war. The sheer size of the cavernous interior, seemingly large enough to hold all the personnel, vehicles, equipment, and supplies of several U.S. Army divisions combined, was like nothing the 29ers had ever seen before; and it was difficult to conceive the monumental amount of labor and materials the Nazis must have applied to its construction. The futuristic design, obviously influenced by the Art Deco style that had dominated European and American architecture during the interwar period, was wholly utilitarian in a military sense.

A vast main corridor, hundreds of yards long, was illuminated mutedly by electric lights on a soaring ceiling; and as one might expect in an edifice housing ocean-going vessels, the musty odor of stale sea water saturated the air. So many secondary passageways and staircases branched off from the main corridor that, lacking a guide or building layout, it was easy to get lost. Unfortunately, it was also easy to get killed, as the devious enemy had attached booby traps to several doors, set to explode when innocent GIs opened them. Thankfully, the Germans did not have sufficient time to activate them all, and those few they did manage to arm were neutralized effortlessly by the 29ers, who by this time had grown used to the enemy's deadly tricks.

One thing the 29ers could not fail to notice was the sub pens' thirteen enormous interior docks, each of which was designed to hold two U-boats. Regrettably, none of those notorious vessels epitomizing the Nazi war machine in the war's early years still occupied the pens when the Americans arrived. Later, the 29ers learned that the last one, U-256, had departed Brest only two weeks previously.

The enemy's effort to construct the sub pens had obviously been prodigious, and the fact they had been designed to protect only a tiny fraction of the active U-boat fleet from Allied aerial attack demonstrated how much Hitler cherished his submarines and how urgently he craved victory in the Battle of the Atlantic. By September 1944, however, the Germans' five-year attempt to cut the transoceanic sea lanes had clearly failed, a failure that had contributed markedly to Nazi Germany's imminent demise. Indeed, the very soldiers whose arrival in Europe the U-boats had been designed to prevent were now about to conquer the U-boat haven that a short time ago had symbolized the immense power of the German submarine fleet.

For the 29ers who had struggled since D-Day to hasten the enemy's defeat, it was vastly satisfying to note that although the sub pens' reinforced concrete ceiling, twenty-five feet thick, had withstood virtually everything the U.S. Eighth Air Force and RAF Bomber Command had dropped upon it, that ceiling had proved irrelevant when the 29th Division arrived at the gates of Brest. As usual, the 29ers noted with a touch of disdain, if Ike needed a tough job fulfilled, the doughboys had to do it. And as Germans marched out of the sub pens by the thousands and the Americans marched in, the enemy's generals and admirals could not fail to ponder the futility of Nazi Germany's immense effort to make those structures indestructible. True, the U-boat pens were still intact; but the flag flying over them was no longer the swastika. It was the Stars and Stripes.

If, as Tony Miller had firmly declared to von der Mosel, the Americans fully intended to fulfill their obligations as dictated by the July 1929 *Geneva Convention Relative to the Treatment of Prisoners of War*, the U.S. Army must immediately assume responsibility for care of German wounded. That task would obviously be taxing, as the Americans could only presume the pounding they had inflicted upon the enemy over the past month had caused thousands of casualties. For a day, or at most two, it would be the duty of the 29th Division's 104th Medical Battalion not only to look after German wounded, but to evacuate them as soon as possible from the fetid underground hospitals the enemy had established deep inside the coastal bluffs to more healthful hospitals managed by VIII Corps and Ninth Army.

The 104th had cared for German wounded in the past, but never on a scale close to the numbers the outfit encountered at Brest. Lou Azrael and a surgeon by the name of Capt. William Heffner, a member of the 115th Infantry's medical detachment, were the first Americans to enter one of the underground German hospitals, an experience Azrael later described in a *Baltimore News-Post* article: "Over 600 wounded men were lying there. Girl nurses were there. Heffner and I went about to the wounded. Some did not know the garrison had surrendered. They thought we were prisoners." Heffner and others helped to stabilize those German troops who were critically wounded and, a few hours later, supervised the transfer of the wounded into ambulances provided by the 104th Medical Battalion for movement to a location in the interior.

The 29th Division had experienced plenty of ironies in combat since D-Day, but none was more striking than the situation faced by the division at Brest on September 18. One moment 29th Division infantrymen were striving vigorously to kill as many German soldiers as possible; and the next, 29th Division medical personnel were laboring with equal effort to look after those same Germans' physical well-being. According to a September 1944 report, "The VIII Corps surgeon reported a total of 5,500 prisoner of war casualties in Brest, most of whom were ambulatory." The necessity for providing care to such a large number of enemy wounded could of course be explained by the 1929 Geneva Convention, which specified: "The Power detaining prisoners of war is bound to provide for their maintenance."

The Convention also mandated, "Prisoners who refuse to answer [questions] may not be threatened, insulted, or exposed to unpleasant or disadvantageous treatment of any kind whatever." Any whimsical 29er familiar with those rules must have wondered why, back in the training days at Fort Meade and in England, his company first sergeant had not been so compassionate.

3. LIMESTONE COVE

Soon after the fall of Brest, Maj. Jim Morris, the executive officer of the 116th Infantry's 1st Battalion, dashed off a letter to his family back home describing in a few simple lines what his outfit had recently endured. "[We] just finished a tough job and will be getting another one soon," Morris began. "The sooner the better because we all want to get this thing over with. . . . It is a hell of a strain . . . but we must keep after the 'paper hanger' [Hitler] while he is on the run."

Hitler may have been on the run, but every 29er, including Gerhardt, relished the thought that fresh outfits from the States would assume their fair share of the fighting while the 29th Division finally took a substantive break from combat. On the morning of September 19, the general phoned Corporal Lowenthal of *29 Let's Go* and proudly announced: "This division has been locked up since May 15, 1944, and at the present time it is in better shape than it has ever been. The standards are high, and everyone tries like hell. . . . We took 6,000 POWs yesterday, including a general and an admiral. The division is moving into a rehabilitation area and all towns are on limits."

Before the festivities began, however, Gerhardt had an unpleasant duty to carry out. The general readily absorbed virtually every detail contained in the countless reports his staff forwarded to him daily, and on September 18 one of those details had disturbed him. It was a succinct memo contained in a type of report known to the war room staff by its three-letter abbreviation: "PWI," for "Prisoner of War Interrogation." Regimental intelligence officers regularly forwarded PWI reports to Gerhardt so the general could get a feel for the enemy's morale. At 9:50 A.M. on September 18, Gerhardt telephoned Maj. Harold Perkins, the 115th Infantry's executive officer, and angrily demanded: "Have you read the PWI report—the last one? Did you see that about the forty Americans surrendering? That was G Company of the 115th Infantry. We are just going to raise ——— [word left blank in original] about that, so get ready for the storm."

Apparently one or more German soldiers who had fallen into American hands on September 17 had reported to their U.S. Army interrogator that three days previously they had been involved in the capture of a small group of American infantrymen in and around a pillbox near Fort Montbarey. That interrogator's PWI report has never been located, so no historian can determine with certainty the information it contained; but according to Gerhardt the gist of the report was straightforward: "The reason we were beaten is that in the middle of the fight our men quit firing to hunt for enemy souvenirs." Now that all American prisoners at Brest had been released by the subjugated Germans, the general was determined to locate those 29ers who had committed that cardinal sin "so [as Gerhardt affirmed] that nothing of this kind will ever happen in the 29th Division again."

Regrettably, Gerhardt proceeded to judge that supposed incident with raw emotion rather than logic; and as a consequence triggered an episode that cast negative aspersions on his leadership style, which, as every 29er knew, was characterized by an uncompromising demeanor and a tendency to micromanage affairs that should have been left to subordinates. As difficult as it was for the accused 29ers to believe, the evidence at the general's disposal stipulating that they had let down their guard to hunt for enemy souvenirs had apparently originated solely from the enemy—a source that under normal circumstances Gerhardt would hardly have trusted. When it came to the sensitive subject of 29th Division soldiers falling into the enemy's hands, however, the general's exceptionally critical mind jumped into action; and evidently in this instance he was willing to believe the Germans' account that his men had not acted in a soldierly fashion—even though no solid evidence whatsoever existed to corroborate that unlikely story.

That an unfortunate group of Americans was about to face Gerhardt's wrath became evident at 12:10 P.M. on September 17, when an order came down from division headquarters to the 115th Infantry's command post: "Recaptured Americans are to be held separately back at the kitchen trains until interrogated and released by Latitude [the 29th Division headquarters' codename]." During the afternoon of the following day, only hours after the Germans had freed all 29th Division prisoners held in the submarine pens, the 115th Infantry conveyed a group of thirteen disheveled 29ers, all freshly released prisoners of war, to division headquarters by truck. Despite Gerhardt's assertion to Perkins that the supposed souvenir-hunters from the 115th Infantry had been members of Company G, all thirteen 29ers brought before the irate general were instead members of Company H, a heavy weapons outfit.

According to S/Sgt. Don Van Roosen, the ranking member of that group, "We were deposited at the bottom of a grass-covered, bowl-shaped area and told to wait. [The group] watched as the entire division staff filed out of the chateau and lined up in their pressed uniforms and shined boots. . . . Our curiosity, concern, and wonder grew as the staff stared down at us, and we stared back in our dirty uniforms, unshaved faces, and grubby boots." The thirteen 29ers had no idea why they had been brought before their commanding general under such curious circumstances, but when Gerhardt regally approached his deferential staff, they did not have to wait long to find out. If, as Gerhardt insisted, the 29th Division's reputation within the U.S. Army as a first-class fighting outfit was tarnished by such a frivolous act as souvenir-hunting in the midst of combat, he must make an example of the transgressors—and do it in such a degrading way that it would never happen again. The general thereupon turned to the 29th Division's chief intelligence officer, Lt. Col. Paul "Murphy" Krznarich, and ordered him to conduct a public interrogation of Van Roosen's little group, in full view of the entire 29th Division staff.

Gerhardt did not seem to contemplate the possibility that the thirteen 29ers might be wholly innocent of the allegations he had made against them. According to a witness, as Gerhardt finished speaking, those men were "seething [and] several tried to arise." Van Roosen signaled them to remain silent and spoke for them all, beginning with the humble request: "Do I have the general's permission to speak, sir?" Gerhardt apparently did not expect defiance from those men who were about to become the target of his scorn, and with some surprise he exclaimed, "Why, of course."

Sergeant Van Roosen proceeded to eloquently preserve his men's repute: "I told him how we had maintained our position, that we had many wounded, and had received no support; that I had been captured by having a gun shoved in my back and had not meekly surrendered," he recalled. "Then I stopped talking and glared at the general. . . . He rudely spun on his heel and marched off without a word of apology."

And that was that. Their honor intact, the thirteen 29ers were trucked back to Company H's bivouac, where they were the recipients of countless questions from their curious comrades. Gerhardt was not the kind of man who could readily admit he had made such a gross mistake, a trait he displayed by failing to make a formal apology to the maltreated party. Nevertheless, he did the best he could. The general divulged the story to Lowenthal, and in the September 23 edition of *29 Let's Go*, all thirteen Company H members were the subject of a highly laudatory article clarifying the events of their capture on September 14 and 15. That their reputation was indeed secure was confirmed by the fact that the article made no reference whatsoever to a search for German souvenirs. "Doggedly, with pistols, carbines, and a submachine gun, the Americans held to their positions until darkness came [on September 14]," Lowenthal wrote. "They were pinned down tight, and their casualties were mounting. Grenades were rolling in on them. . . . The alternatives were death or capture. At the last moment two men escaped with one of the machine guns. Those who could not get away surrendered."

Less than one month later, Uncle Charlie's somewhat roundabout mea culpa in this awkward affair was complete. Sergeant Van Roosen, the leader and spokesman for the now celebrated knot of Company H men, found himself on October 13, 1944, at 29th Division headquarters in the Staatsforst woods in western Germany. This time, rather than facing Gerhardt's anger, he was there to accept one of the U.S. Army's most exceptional rewards—a battlefield commission as a second lieutenant.

No one could accuse Gerhardt of being entirely negative with his men in the aftermath of Brest. One division staff officer observed, "General Gerhardt told his headquarters officers a few days after the surrender that he had been well satisfied with the work of the division in the operation. In commenting on his troops' fighting ability, the general said that he believed the training conducted by the division in methods of attack on fortified points had been invaluable, and that if the training had not been held he would have found it hard to steel himself to order his men against the German defenses."

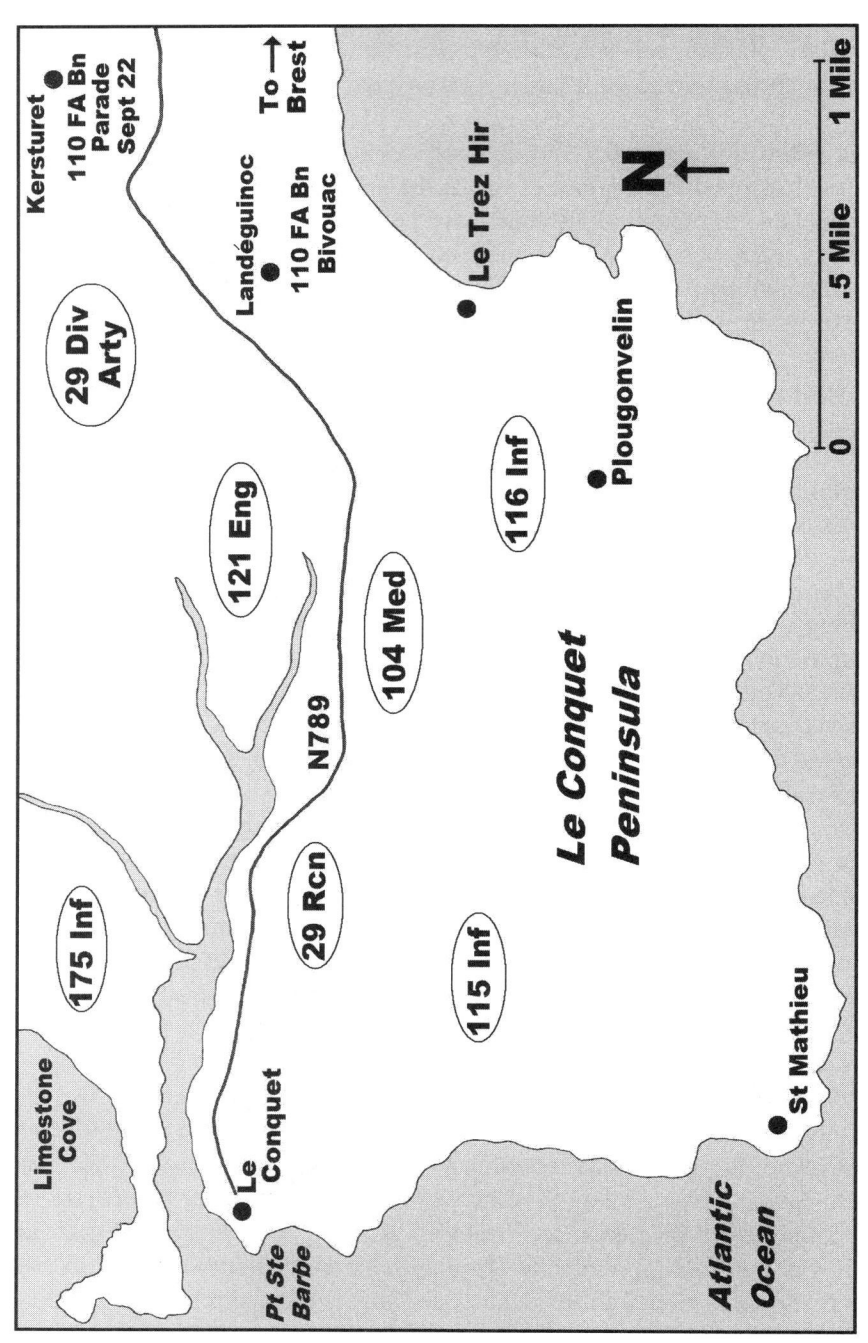

29th Division Rest Areas: September 19–24, 1944

The sight of thousands of German prisoners streaming westward down the N789 thoroughfare from Brest to La Trinité was, not surprisingly, a signal for the 29th Division to start celebrating. As the old World War I veterans used to say, there was nothing quite like the celebration carried out by soldiers fresh out of combat. The incalculable psychological release; the blissful realization that in all likelihood one would live for at least a few more weeks; the pent-up desire to defy unreasonable U.S. Army discipline that had controlled one's life for years: all of these factors were about to come together in a raucous discharge of human emotion. "The night of September 18–19 was a wild one of celebration," Corporal Plaut of the 115th Infantry wrote. "A number of horses made their appearance in St. Pierre, and riders rode them up and down the street all night long. [One memorable, although anonymous 29er did so wearing a fancy derby hat and smoking a cigar.] A few civilian autos and German Army Volkswagens were found in the fort, commandeered, and driven at a reckless pace by happy GIs."

The devastated and depressing city of Brest was not a place in which a worn out infantryman could unwind, so Gerhardt resolved to send the 29th Division in its entirety to a much more tranquil locale as soon as possible. The scenic Le Conquet peninsula, fifteen miles to the west, was the perfect spot. Task Force Sugar had done some hard fighting there in the recent past, but fortunately the many picturesque resort villages on the coast were for the most part undamaged. Even better, Gerhardt insisted that all three of the division's infantry regiments must be bivouacked as close as possible to the coast so that no soldier would have to walk more than a mile to reach one of the many beaches and secluded shoreline coves scattered throughout the westernmost tip of Brittany. True, many of those sites were still littered with hundreds of the enemy's grotesque beach obstacles and lethal mines, but 29th Division engineers would address that problem soon.

How much time would the men have before the whirlpool of war sucked the 29th Division back into combat? On that fundamental question the 29ers were almost unanimously optimistic: "Everyone expected the rest period to last between seven and fifteen days," recalled Lt. Col. John Cooper of the 110th Field Artillery. Just how restful that rest period would be, however, was the subject of some debate; for as a member of the 115th Infantry noted, cynical 29ers had learned that "previous 'rest' periods had found the men training and digging during daylight hours with little time for relaxation." But Gerhardt made it clear from the start that this break was the real thing. True, he insisted each unit must conduct one hour of close-order drill or calisthenics per day, just so that the men did not forget they were still members of the U.S. Army, but aside from that trifling requirement, the general intended that his men's interlude from combat—however long it turned out to be—would rejuvenate them both spiritually and physically.

The 29th Division was used to doing things quickly, and fortunately that policy extended to transferring its members out of Brest and into their Le Conquet rest camps. By the evening of September 19, little more than twenty-fours hours after the German surrender, virtually the entire 29th Division had reached its magnificent new assembly area. Thankfully, most outfits got a lift out of Brest in deuce-and-a-half trucks, but a few unlucky ones, such as the 115th Infantry's 1st Battalion, had to make the journey on foot. Whether one marched or rode, that journey was memorable. When the 110th Field Artillery moved out, Cooper observed: "En route, the cannoneers passed the 29th Division's prisoner of war cage, which was situated south of the town of St. Renan. Here many thousands of Germans had already been collected in open fields surrounded by barbed wire and guarded by military police. Standing as close to the fences as they were allowed, hundreds of French civilians gathered to view with obvious satisfaction the sorry plight of Hitler's 'supermen,' most of whom were a filthy, mole-like color from a continuous existence in holes in the ground."

Only time out of combat would cure the 29ers of the dull spiritual ache permeating their psyches after more than three months of cruel and nearly continuous battle. Happily, that time finally came in that stunning corner of far-western Brittany known as Le Conquet, where a few glorious days of rest, devoid of any military responsibilities and beyond earshot of gunfire, would help to reconstruct their battered souls.

If time could help cure the 29ers' spiritual ills, then so, too, could nature. The 29ers had never seen anything like the sheer physical grandeur of the Le Conquet, from the foamy surf surging incessantly into the rocky headland at Pointe de St. Mathieu, to the serene beach at Le Trez Hir, to the glorious spectacle of multicolored light at sunset overlooking the vast expanse of the Atlantic from Pointe Ste. Barbe. For fighting men who had spent much of the recent past in claustrophobic hedgerow country, stalking the elusive enemy in countless green checkerboard pastures that had a monotonous uniformity, the dazzling vistas of the Le Conquet were rejuvenating. That so many 29ers had not lived to behold those sights was of course tragic, but as the old soldiers used to say, funeral wakes were not part of the U.S. Army's repertoire, and the war had to go on come what may until Hitler was at last dead. When that great day would occur was anybody's guess, but in the meantime, there was no better place to linger than the rest camps at Le Conquet.

Some 29ers may have had doubts about Gerhardt's sympathy for the ordinary fighting man, but when the GIs got their first look at their surroundings on September 19, they agreed that the general knew what he was doing when it came to rest and recreation. Uncle Charlie's promise that all towns in the Le Conquet would be "on limits" was one that all 29ers intended to take advantage of. It had been a long time since the 29ers had been allowed to put aside their helmets and weapons, jump in a hot shower, receive a clean uniform, and strut about freely so that the local populace could see what a real American fighting soldier looked like. The fortunate members of the 175th Infantry woke up on the morning of September 20 after their first sound sleep in weeks to discover that the ancient fishing haven of Le Conquet, the town from which the peninsula derived its name, was only a mile distant from camp. As the men of the regiment promptly ascertained, it was a place of timeless charms: old-fashioned streets, pervasive sounds and smells of the sea, and down-to-earth residents—all of whom seemed genuinely delighted to have the 29ers in their midst.

One place where the GIs hoped they could meet some of those locals of the female persuasion was at a nearby beach the members of the regiment had christened "Limestone Cove," after the 175th's radio call signal. As related by *29 Let's Go*, "Lt. Herbert Steinberg and Lt. Sheldon W. Dennis have developed this spa for the benefit and recreation of their men. They had the engineers check the beach for mines and clear the place of danger. Then they rolled in a snack bar, right down to the beach—everything is on the house. Yesterday they hauled two truckloads of St. Renan lovelies down there to join in the big swim with the boys."

If the 29ers wished to purge their minds of gloomy thoughts of war, the only way to do it was to experience lengthy stretches of unadulterated pleasure. There had of course been virtually no pleasure in the men's lives over the past several months, but a few days in the Le Conquet would abruptly reverse that trend. The cheerful 29ers were presented with so many opportunities for pleasurable diversions that any man who did not thoroughly enjoy himself was either not trying very hard or more interested in dozing than having fun, but for many the opportunity to sleep for extended periods was more enticing than anything Gerhardt could offer.

The men managed to get hold of sports equipment and staged impromptu softball and touch football games; trucks shuttled the men back and forth from the camps to nearby towns, such as St. Renan, Le Conquet, and Plougonvelin; cooks acquired fresh ingredients and concocted hot meals that were an entirely agreeable change from C- and K-rations. Many took the time to fill out the absentee ballots their first sergeants had recently handed out for the upcoming presidential election in November between President Roosevelt and New York governor Thomas E. Dewey. Some 29ers with a sense of history even walked the still-smoldering battlefields outside Brest they had just fought for, and their leisurely inspection of the enemy's formidable pillboxes and heavy coastal guns helped to emphasize the undeniable fact that the 29th Division's latest exploit had been grueling—but amazingly impressive.

And then there were the parties. It seemed that every battalion and regimental staff in the 29th Division managed to commandeer a local resort hotel for a dance, limited to officers—and as many local women as the planners could round up. The 110th Field Artillery's bash at the Hotel des Bains in Le Trez Hir was particularly successful, thanks to Capt. Frank Steele's recent penetration into the sub pens and his abduction of forty bottles of liquor. "The battalion's first social affair on the continent was gay and happy," Cooper wrote. "Present were a few American army nurses, three young French school teachers on vacation, and the hotel proprietor's family, including many of his relatives. Since some officers of the 115th Infantry and the other artillery units in the division also were guests, the gathering consisted of about sixty men and fifteen ladies."

Throwing a dance party in a war zone so soon after active operations had ceased posed some challenging problems, the foremost of which was the essential issue of clothing. Naturally, neither the 29ers nor the locals had access to smart-looking apparel, a detail corroborated by Maj. Charles Cawthon, who attended a 116th Infantry party and later observed: "The French girls undoubtedly did their best, [but] their frocks showed the effects of four years of occupation-enforced austerity. . . . The officers wore unpressed olive drab and combat boots with unshinably rough surfaces and composition soles with no glide qualities whatsoever."

There could of course be no dance without music; but in western Brittany in fall 1944, music-makers, be they mechanical or human, were in remarkably short supply. Very few Le Conquet residents possessed functional phonographs, and even if they did, their collection of Glenn Miller, Tommy Dorsey, Artie Shaw, and Benny Goodman records would surely be minimal. Accordingly, almost overnight, the sixty-man 29th Division Band went from one of the most unnoticed outfits in the division to one of the most popular. When the request for musical support for various 29th Division dances suddenly surged starting on September 19, the musicians formed spur-of-the-moment ensembles and strove to provide each affair with at least a small cadre of experienced dance-band players, many of whom could expertly play more than one instrument, including those not normally featured in a military band, such as the piano, violin, viola, cello, and accordion.

For the 29ers, winning over members of the opposite sex in Brittany was a wholly awkward procedure. The problem was not necessarily the language barrier, which assertive soldiers had long since learned to cope with even though they could neither speak nor understand a word of French. Rather, the real challenge was to dodge the girls' mothers, most of whom had taken the entirely sensible precaution of acting as chaperones for their daughters at all social gatherings involving American troops. Ultimately, the frustrated 29ers learned that the sturdy Breton matrons were almost as tough to overcome as the Germans.

4. BLUE AND GRAY RIDING ACADEMY

The World War II incarnation of the 29th Division dated to February 3, 1941, when President Roosevelt called into federal service all of its diverse components from the Maryland, Virginia, and District of Columbia National Guard. That moment was little more than three years in the past, but to the pitifully small number of 29ers still remaining with the 29th at Brest who had been called up that momentous day, it probably felt more like three decades. The 29th Division in February 1941 had been woefully understrength, populated entirely by guardsmen whose experience of military life consisted of one drill night per week and two weeks of summer camp. The 29th's social fabric had changed dramatically over the years, first as a consequence of the Army's infusion of thousands of draftees to fill the division's ranks to authorized strength; and later, in England, due to the influx of replacements to take over the jobs of those who had transferred to other outfits or had not been able to maintain the 29th Division's notoriously stringent physical standards. But starting on June 6, 1944, combat at a level of intensity the 29ers could not have foreseen had caused that influx to swell to a torrent; and when Brest fell on September 18, more than 12,000 new men had joined the 29th Division as replacements—the vast majority of them infantrymen.

Since at any given time the 29th Division had no more than 14,000 men on its rolls, by the time the 29ers pitched their tents in their new rest areas at Le Conquet on September 19, 1944, all of those men fully understood that the division that had landed on Omaha Beach on D-Day had nearly vanished, to be replaced by an organization with a vastly different makeup. In truth, the current version of the 29th Division was an authentic example of the legendary American melting pot in full boil. No one needed to look beyond a typical rifle company to discover that truth. For example, those devoted company commanders who habitually familiarized themselves with the 200 men under their command often learned with astonishment that their outfit's repertoire included fluency in a dozen or more languages other than English. Such proficiency often came in handy in this bizarre war, in which the 29ers had noticed that masses of the German Army's soldiers did not even speak German.

That there was much to grumble about in matters concerning military life had been demonstrated by American soldiers since the 1775 birth of the U.S. Army. By 1944, however, grumbling by American soldiers had been elevated to an art form for the fundamental reason that the Army had expanded almost fiftyfold over the past four years, and the vast bulk of its recruits, freshly snatched out of the civilian world, had not the slightest zest for the Army's seemingly irrational routines. One of those routines that 29th Division grumblers incessantly griped about was close-order drill. They had a point: What sense did it make to practice the manual of arms or precision marching when the ultimate object was to craft skilled American soldiers who could defeat a formidable enemy on the battlefield? Nevertheless, Gerhardt was a stickler when it came to the old-fashioned military arts and even insisted that his 29ers practice them in their Le Conquet rest camps.

When several 29th Division outfits decided to hold ceremonial parades after the fall of Brest, the 29ers found out why the U.S. Army valued close-order drill. The fighting men had learned that combat was an inherently lonely endeavor: How could one get a sense of belonging to a sizeable, first-class military organization from a frontline foxhole? Under normal combat conditions, almost everyone beyond an infantryman's twelve-man rifle squad was anonymous and nearly impossible to befriend. But when a unit formed up in neat ranks for a review, officers and color- and guidon-bearers out front, one could not fail to be impressed by the outfit's obvious solidity. The faces of the men comprising it were visible to all, and each face was unique and identifiable. Company or battery designations and U.S. Army branch insignia were emblazoned on the treasured fork-tailed guidons: dark blue for infantry; red for artillery and engineers; green for MPs; orange for signal; red-over-white for cavalry. The even more prized battalion and regimental colors featured an impressive representation of the American national emblem, a bald eagle clutching arrows in one talon, an olive branch in the other. Ultimately, the highly meaningful symbolism involved in putting a unit together in one place for a review helped immensely to foster unit loyalty and demonstrate to the fighting men they were not alone.

The 110th Field Artillery Battalion proved that point on September 22, 1944, when it paraded in full battle dress for a ceremony in honor of its men who had been killed in action since D-Day. For many of the 29ers in that outfit, it was one of the war's most memorable moments. Cooper wrote:

> With standards and guidons flying against a beautifully clear sky, the battalion marched to stirring music by the division band to a parade meadow near Kersturet, about a mile up the country road [from Landéguinoc, the 110th's rest camp, one mile north of Plougonvelin]. Each man felt a deep pride in his country, in his division, in his outfit, and in his friends around him. He felt, too, a humble gratitude for his own safety, mixed with a deep sorrow for those who had given their lives or had been wounded in the great cause. . . . On this occasion the 110th presented a splendid appearance, for every man had done himself proud in honor of his fallen comrades and of his unit. As the cannoneers marched back to their bivouac, they felt a surge of unity, solidarity, and strength.

The glorious Le Conquet breather freed the 29ers from their incessant focus on war, with all its violent emotions and implements, and instead allowed the troops to ponder the assorted opportunities available for having fun. As one might expect among such a diverse group of young American males, the 29ers' relentless pursuit of happiness over the next several days varied from soldier to soldier, a process that was exemplified by the members of Company B, 104th Medical Battalion. A former Maryland National Guard outfit from Baltimore, Company B had been caring tenderly for the 116th Infantry's wounded—and dead—since H-Hour on Omaha Beach on June 6, 1944, a herculean effort that had resulted in nearly twenty casualties among the 135 unarmed doctors, litter bearers, and other medical personnel populating the unit. By late September 1944 only a handful of Maryland guardsmen still occupied key positions within the company, such as Sgt. Arnold Levin, the highly resourceful supply sergeant and acting first sergeant; Sgt. William Becker, the senior NCO in the litter platoon; and Sgt. Harry Garner, the mess sergeant.

The 104th occupied a central location in Le Conquet, no more than a mile and a half from that locale's main attractions: the picturesque villages of Le Conquet and Plougonvelin, and the stunning headland at Pointe de St. Mathieu. Sgt. Bobby Johnson, a skilled soldier whose laudable heroism in combat in Normandy had caused a rifle company commander to recommend him for a Silver Star, promptly liberated a functional German motorcycle so he could visit those attractions in style. (A Company B surgeon, Capt. Joseph Shelley, later recalled: "Some jackass reduced [Johnson's] award to a Bronze Star.") Sergeant Johnson quickly became greatly attached to his German motorcycle, but later, when the 29th Division had to pack its belongings and prepare to move back to the front, Johnson was devastated when an order came down from division headquarters that captured German vehicles could not be driven in U.S. Army vehicular convoys. Captain Shelley, however, swiftly solved that problem: "Bobby came to me, almost in tears. I said not to worry. I made room in our kitchen truck for his cycle."

Company B's rest area was in the heart of some of the most beautiful and unspoiled farmland in the Le Conquet, a detail that delighted those members who had rural roots. Pvt. Pete Tarko, an ambulance driver, had been employed by a western Pennsylvania dairy before the war, and Shelley—who remembered Tarko as "a great guy"—noted that he practiced his expert milking skills on the local cows whenever the opportunity arose.

During the Le Conquet rest period, several other members of the Company B melting pot also resumed those practices they had mastered in civilian life. Pvt. Stanley Slowik of Pennsylvania, a litter-bearer, was renowned as the best tailor in the 29th Division, a reputation that drifted as high as division headquarters and caused General Gerhardt himself to send uniforms to him for alterations. Consequently, the locals, as well as jealous 29ers, would note that Company B soldiers were always the smartest dressers in the 29th Division. Shelley, however, observed that one incorrigible Pennsylvania draftee, Pvt. Louis Spizzirri—known to many as "Sad Sack"—"was the worst-looking soldier in the Army. He could bathe, shave, press his uniform, shine his boots; and when he was finished, he looked like he had slept in his uniform for a week." Naturally, every company in the 29th Division had its own version of Spizzirri.

Any soldier who wanted to look well-groomed had to pay sharp attention to his hair. Over the past month, however, Company B members were much too busy to allow time for a haircut at the hands of an experienced barber. That unfortunate state of affairs at last came to an end in the 104th Medical Battalion's rest camps, when T/5 Thomas Sypek, a barber in civilian life back in Pennsylvania, grabbed his tools and skillfully cut and combed his comrades' locks in preparation for the men's upcoming social outings to Le Conquet's coastal villages and beaches. There might be U.S. Army nurses, Red Cross girls, and even some attractive local women who could be courted at those delightful locations, so Sypek's expertise with scissors was a highly valued blessing.

Slowik, the tailor, and Sypek, the barber, were particularly attentive in their work for T/5 Joseph Gondek, yet another Pennsylvanian who everyone agreed was the smartest-looking soldier in the company. As Shelley remembered, "He could look like a general when he got all dressed up." Furthermore, Gondek was blessed with an exceptional voice, and those who heard him use it in song concurred that he seemed like a professional. In fact, in the training days back in England, Gondek had actually performed with a local opera company.

If the 29ers were focused almost entirely on a pursuit of pleasure over the next few days, Gerhardt came up with an extraordinary idea to satisfy that quest. His scheme triggered one of the most memorable tales in the history of the 29th Division, one that virtually all 29ers who survived the Brest campaign would later relate countless times with varying degrees of accuracy to astonished listeners. Ultimately that anecdote would be elevated to the status of a legend, and like all legends, it was a mix both of fiction and fact—much more heavily weighted to the former than the latter.

Only one detail in the story is known beyond doubt, and that was that Gerhardt desired female companionship to be made available to his weary and dispirited men by means of an official establishment he somewhat gingerly described to his staff as a "Riding Academy"—otherwise known more coarsely as a whorehouse. Proof of this fact derives from the 29th Division war room journal at 9:40 A.M. on September 18, 1944—even before the Germans at Brest surrendered—when Gerhardt declared, "We will move east sometime later on. In the meantime we will have a break. [We will] set up all recreational facilities that we can, including the 'Riding Academy.'"

The establishment of official brothels by conquering military forces for the diversion of their soldiers and sailors was a centuries-old practice, one with which the Germans were entirely familiar. As one of the major U-boat bases on the Atlantic coast, Brest had been a temporary home for thousands of German submariners, many of whom had returned to port after grueling Atlantic patrols of several months' duration, looking forward eagerly to one or more visits to the many local brothels that thrived under German military occupation. Senior German commanders, however, had realized that those unsupervised houses of ill repute were both health and security risks, and accordingly they established certified brothels where those risks could be managed directly. It was one of those German brothels Gerhardt had in mind when he brought up the "recreational facilities" he intended to establish after the fall of Brest. When the enemy finally surrendered, the general aimed to reopen the German brothel under new American management. In the end, however, General Bradley unexpectedly called the 29th Division back to the main battle front on September 24, so the 29ers had to depart Brittany for good after only four days rest. That was hardly enough time for the "Blue and Gray Riding Academy"—if such an institution ever actually operated—to draw many patrons.

Was Uncle Charlie's Riding Academy ever really in business? Numerous reliable observers, including 29th Division chaplains and newspaper reporters, insisted that it was. It is noteworthy, however, that none of those observers ever actually laid their eyes on the supposed brothel, nor could they ever identify its precise location. Furthermore, as far as is known, no veteran ever stepped forward in later years to confess that he himself had taken advantage of its services. Nevertheless, at postwar reunions apocryphal stories flourished pertaining to the Riding Academy, the most typical of which claimed that patient 29ers waited in lines longer than those at a Grand Central Station ticket office at rush hour outside an unnamed chateau for their turn at female companionship. That those stories may indeed have been true, if somewhat embellished, was corroborated by Cpl. Conley McMullen, a chaplain's assistant in the 116th Infantry, who observed that "trucks from the divisional engineer battalion were shuttling GIs back and forth from the Riding Academy." Historical evidence is therefore reasonably trustworthy that at least one 29th Division brothel did indeed exist somewhere on the Le Conquet peninsula, and that it stayed open to 29ers for three, or at most four, days.

The management of a brothel, however, was most decidedly not a part of the U.S. Army's repertoire, and there were many people, including 29th Division chaplains, high-ranking generals at U.S. Twelfth Army Group headquarters, and politicians on the home front, who could never accept that an American general could propose such a profane scheme. The 29th Division's senior chaplain, Maj. Harold Donovan, known to all simply as "Father Mike," was well known within the division for enjoying a good party and a stiff drink, but as a Roman Catholic priest of high standing back in Baltimore, it was hardly surprising that from his perspective the Blue and Gray Riding Academy went much too far. According to McMullen and Capt. Manuel Poliakoff, the 29th Division's Jewish chaplain, Donovan met unofficially with other chaplains to discuss Gerhardt's design and concluded that it was thoroughly immoral. He therefore resolved to oppose it, and he carried out that resolve by telephoning chaplains at higher headquarters to inform them of the astonishing development in the 29th Division's rest camps in Brittany. According to some witnesses, Donovan also penned letters to influential Maryland politicians back on the home front. Donovan's response, however, ended up having more symbolic than meaningful impact, for by the time any general or politician learned of the Riding Academy, it had already been closed down as a result of Bradley's order to move the 29th Division posthaste to Holland to join the U.S. Army's fall offensive into western Germany.

Under normal conditions, a general who had just completed a successful battle could expect a career boost and enhanced name recognition. In the immediate aftermath of the Brest campaign, the unfortunate Gerhardt received plenty of the latter, but none of the former, for when the word spread around the U.S. Army of the Riding Academy business, as well as some other improper goings-on at 29th Division headquarters, the general's superior officers could not help but take notice. As a result, to many exceptionally powerful American soldiers, Gerhardt would eventually become a marked man who must not be allowed to ascend any higher in the U.S. Army's hierarchy. As a career soldier Gerhardt fully understood that if he was to achieve coveted promotions, he had to play the game according to the Army's rules, but now that he had broken those rules, and superiors had found out about it, his only option was to wait for judgment.

Meanwhile, the ever-fastidious and detail-oriented Gerhardt continued to watch over his 29ers' welfare in a stern but fatherly way. One day, he phoned Colonel Smith and brusquely announced that the physical appearance of some of the members of the 115th Infantry would not reflect well on the 29th Division's reputation if they were to be seen by the local populace on an outing. "We conducted a physical inspection for bathing," Gerhardt declared. "Sixty of your men were checked and seven needed a bath. That doesn't mean send them to Paris! Have them get a helmet or bucket and take a bath!"

TEN

Here Are Our Credentials

1. YOU'LL END UP IN HOLLYWOOD
Only one act in the drama remained, and that was for the Americans to locate the infamous Ramcke and send him summarily into captivity. As much as Gerhardt fervently yearned to be the instigator of that act, that honor would fall not to the 29th Division, but to Maj. Gen. Donald Stroh's 8th. Ramcke had recently abandoned his troops at Brest to their inevitable fate and fled by boat across Brest harbor to the Crozon peninsula, just two miles southwest of the submarine pens. By the morning of September 19, 1944, he and his last-ditch defenders were cornered deep in an underground bunker in a coastal artillery position on a rocky promontory known as Pointe des Capucins.

By then, Ramcke had acknowledged that only three options remained open to him: death, capture, or escape. He could fight to the death in his bunker, and take a few more American soldiers with him, just as so many members of his garrison had already done at his insistence. Death would also come to him, probably swiftly and brutally, if he were captured and somehow fell into the hands of the French Resistance, whose members were still seething from the alleged atrocities committed by Ramcke's paratroopers in Brittany in the aftermath of D-Day. Otherwise he would end up in an American prisoner-of-war camp in the States. That Ramcke had no desire to share the fate of his garrison, be it by death or capture, was a detail already grasped by many of his fellow German generals, one of who observed cynically that Ramcke was a man who "knows how to look after 'number one.'"

Ramcke resolved to flee Brest and escape from the clutches of the U.S. Army. Later, in a prisoner-of-war camp, he would defend that decision to his fellow high-ranking prisoners by inflating his own importance to the Nazi war machine. "The Führer wanted me to get away," Ramcke insisted. "No E-boats were available at Lorient, so escape by sea was impossible. Then a message came back saying I would be fetched by seaplane and should set up five beacons by the bay south of the cape [Pointe des Capucins]. . . . The enemy broke through and at 6 P.M. [September 19] had surrounded my dugout. If that had happened two to three hours later, in the darkness I should have gotten down the cliffs and taken up my position there and would have gotten away. As it was, there was nothing left for it but to send a message: 'Too late; you can no longer rescue your friend!'" That the Germans were indeed operating lone aircraft off Brest right up until the surrender was corroborated by the 29th Division war room journal, which reported on September 18, "Unidentified seaplane flew low over Brest harbor."

By late afternoon on September 19, American troops from the 8th Division were swarming just outside Ramcke's bunker, and their behavior indicated that a direct assault was imminent. One of Ramcke's staff officers finally waved a white flag and called for a parley with the Americans. Ramcke later claimed, "I had no embrasures in my bunker and no arms." So there could be no escape; it must be surrender.

That surrender was achieved with no direct involvement on the part of the 29th Division. However, the key player in that final act, the 8th Division's assistant division commander, Brig. Gen. Charles Canham, had been a well-known character in the 29th Division for years, having fearlessly led the 116th Infantry ashore on Omaha Beach on D-Day—an act for which the U.S. Army rewarded him with a Distinguished Service Cross. Over two months had passed since Canham had departed the 116th at St. Lô for the 8th Division, but his stern and rigorous leadership style had left an indelible impression on the regiment that no participant in the training period in England or the 116th's pitiless Normandy battles could ever forget.

The words General Canham were about to utter in Ramcke's bunker would leave an even more indelible impression on the U.S. Army as a whole. Canham was an irascible creature who firmly believed in the philosophy that to wage war successfully, American soldiers must learn to loathe the Germans. He had told the members of the 116th Infantry on D-Day "to have no mercy on the enemy," and at Brest he planned to practice what he preached.

According to the German Army's standard practice in the disagreeable matter of capitulation, Ramcke intended to mitigate the humiliation of his surrender by demanding to deal with a senior U.S. Army officer, someone such as General Middleton, who could communicate with proper military protocol only career soldiers could understand. When Canham and his entourage descended seventy-five feet into the dark and dank German command post, Ramcke needed only one glance at the scruffy, pencil-thin American brigadier general to know that this particular opponent was definitely not the kind of man to whom a general of Ramcke's stature could surrender. Only a few days in the past, Ramcke had famously announced to his troops in a leaflet that the U.S. Army contained many "inferior elements," who could be expected to obey their "base instincts" when taking German soldiers captive.

Ramcke took one look at Canham and his scruffy accomplices and growled in English, as arrogantly as he could, that he must see the American's "credentials." Canham did not have to ponder the demand for more than a moment to furnish the perfect riposte, one that Ramcke could not possibly misinterpret. According to the official 8th Infantry Division history, "General Canham pointed to the eager dogfaces crowding the entrance with their M-1s. 'These are my credentials.' This blunt phrase put the Nazi in his place."

The story of Canham's utterance spread like wildfire among American troops and soon became the motto of the 8th Infantry Division and the title of a late 1944 booklet detailing the story of the division so far in World War II. More than a half century later, in a slightly modified form— "Soldiers are our credentials"—Canham's reply became the motto of the U.S. Army from 1995 to 1999 during the tenure of Chief of Staff Gen. Dennis Reimer.

Ramcke almost certainly never found out how Canham's words impacted the 8th Division, but even if he did, he certainly would have poked fun at the Americans' quixotic fantasies. Ramcke later referred to Canham as a "nut," and claimed that in the surrender negotiations he "played a big trick on the enemy." According to Ramcke, Canham arrived in his bunker as German signalmen in an adjacent room were coding and transmitting a seven-page typewritten report prepared by Ramcke for Hitler, Göring, and Goebbels, detailing the vast destruction the Germans had inflicted on Brest's harborside. Ramcke had turned Brest into "nothing but a heap of rubble," and it was vital to him that Hitler appreciated that he had done his duty.

Had Canham realized what was going on in the next room, he could have put a stop to it immediately, but according to Ramcke the Germans diverted his attention with three glasses of Cointreau—an orange liqueur, 40 percent alcohol—and a request that Canham send a few American officers to inspect some nearby German strongpoints. By the time the drinks and inspections and other formalities were complete, a smug Ramcke knew that his report to Hitler had been coded and sent out in its entirety.

Poking fun at the doltish Americans would later entertain his fellow German officers in Allied prison camps, but Canham's celebrated hatred of the enemy leads one to the conclusion that Ramcke was more than willing to exaggerate his craftiness to lessen the sting of defeat. The U.S. Army would discover that aspect of Ramcke's personality presently; and indeed one of the first American officers to interrogate him would bluntly note: "General Ramcke is an egotistical, conceited Nazi."

American military policemen eventually transported Ramcke to VIII Corps headquarters, where he would be introduced to a soldier with far more elevated credentials than Canham: Gen. Troy Middleton. The 29th Division maintained a liaison officer at the VIII Corps' command post, Maj. Charles Custer, who keenly observed the interaction between Ramcke and Middleton and promptly reported his assessment to Gerhardt.

From the details provided by Custer, Ramcke was clearly more comfortable in Middleton's presence than he had been in Canham's. Custer wrote:

> General Ramcke, along with his adjutant, four orderlies, a one-ton trailer full of personal baggage, and leading his dog—a thoroughbred red Irish setter—was brought to corps headquarters last night [September 19]. His uniform was certainly not one becoming to a general, as it was dusty and wrinkled. Instead of leggings or boots, his trousers were tied at his shoe tops. With rosy cheeks and gold teeth shining when he smiled—which he did very frequently—he certainly did not look the part of a hard-shell Nazi. [The following morning, September 20], Ramcke, with his aide and dog, posed for numerous photographs for a total of twenty-one photographers. Numerous remarks were passed back and forth between Middleton and Ramcke while the photographers were taking different poses. Middleton: "No wonder you're smil-

ing: Your work is over, you can take it easy now, and you'll probably end up in Hollywood." Ramcke: "I deserve a rest. I have been at this game for thirty-nine years now." Middleton: "This is my second trip over here. I was here in 1918, and I believe this will be my last trip." Ramcke shrugged his shoulders at this remark and said: "I don't believe it."

Even Ramcke had to admit that by now the downfall of Nazi Germany was inevitable, and he openly professed his opinion to all who cared to listen that "the real war would start after the defeat of Germany when the Anglo-Americans and Russia will clash on the Oder River." But much more fighting in the present war remained, and Ramcke declared to his captors:

> I maintain that it is better to go down with honor, better to fight to the end—then you can wipe us off the face of the earth. In my frank opinion, I should consider it to be a mistake to capitulate without more ado. I did not just capitulate in Brest, but fought to the last round of ammunition, and I hope from the bottom of my heart that my German people at home will maintain sufficient strength to the end to defend every foot of ground, every bridge, every mountain ridge, and every town to the last. Then you can blot us off the map and destroy us; that would not matter, as then at least we should have gone down with honor.

A Ninth Air Force Troop Carrier airplane flew Ramcke and his party to England that afternoon, and ultimately the U.S. Army shipped him to a prisoner-of-war camp in the United States. A disappointed Gerhardt had missed the whole show. The general assuredly would have liked to meet Ramcke, but it was probably for the best that the opportunity never materialized. Gerhardt's beloved spaniel, "D-Day," definitely was more fond of people than he was of his fellow canines, and had he laid eyes on Ramcke's Irish setter he surely would have triggered a fracas that would have been remembered in 29th Division history books forever.

Uncle Charlie would have relished that moment.

2. ENTHUSIASM VERSUS JUDGMENT

The whole sordid Blue and Gray Riding Academy affair had been driven by Gerhardt's well-intentioned desire to get his weary men's minds off the brutal realities of war. True, the creation of a divisional brothel was hardly the way to do it. But still the general understood that those 29ers who had been fortunate enough to survive Normandy, and later Brittany, had undergone physical and mental distress beyond description, for even though the 29th Division had only been actively involved in the war for little more than three months, some of the toughest and most brutal fighting in the annals of the U.S. Army had occurred during that period. The general resolved to do something—anything at all—to alleviate the anguish triggered by that kind of intense combat.

The freedom to wander the Le Conquet peninsula and lounge in rest camps for a few days was certainly agreeable, but far more glorious would be genuine furloughs, officially stamped by 29th Division headquarters, which would allow the bearers to travel beyond the realm of the 29th Division for several days, or with luck even for a week or more. Gerhardt grasped that many 29th Division old-timers, particularly the scant number of D-Day veterans still with the division, had a burning desire to take a substantive break and visit Britain, a place where many had met English women during the preparations for D-Day and formed strong romantic relationships, including some that had resulted in marriage—and even children.

On the morning of September 18, even before the Germans had surrendered at Brest, Gerhardt phoned Corporal Lowenthal, the editor of *29 Let's Go*, and hinted at his plans: "There is a strong likelihood that people will begin to get furloughs." The following morning, the general added the key detail, "Priorities [for furloughs] will be given to men from D-Day and then long-combat men. This may include furloughs to the UK."

No one could ever accuse Gerhardt of making a unilateral decision on the matter of 29th Division furloughs without consulting his immediate superior, Middleton. At 5:30 P.M. on September 19, Gerhardt contacted VIII Corps headquarters by phone about what he defined as "the leave business" and inquired of Middleton if he had any objections to granting a considerable number of furloughs to 29th Division personnel. Middleton declared, "No—no objections at all. How many do you plan to let go?" Gerhardt replied, "About 15 percent, most of the D-Day personnel." Middleton responded, "All right," giving Gerhardt the consent he needed to implement his plan.

Just to make sure, a few minutes later Gerhardt phoned Ninth Army headquarters to speak to its commander, Lt. Gen. William Simpson. "We would like to turn loose up to 15 percent of our people [approximately 2,000 men]," Gerhardt asserted. Simpson responded with a simple "OK."

Armed with the authority he needed to issue furloughs, including many to distant England, Gerhardt directed his staff to inform every battalion-size unit within the 29th Division of the happy news. According to Cooper of the 110th Field Artillery Battalion, "Unit commanders and clerks worked feverishly to select the lucky ones and to prepare the necessary papers." Maj. Charles Cawthon recollected his thought process when considering who among the members of his 2nd Battalion, 116th Infantry, would receive the coveted furloughs: "Knowing how much I depended on the riflemen, I decided they were the most equal among equals. I also went so far as to suggest to Lt. Col. Harold Cassell [the 116th's executive] that I might be available [for a furlough]. He suggested that I forget it."

The very first person to depart the 29th Division on an extended furlough was Gerhardt himself. With the full knowledge and permission of General Simpson, Gerhardt left the war room late on September 19 for a good night's rest and by dawn was settled into the rear seat of his command car, chauffeured by his trusted driver Sgt. Robert Cuff, for the long ride back to Normandy. There he anticipated catching a C-47 back to England to revisit the division's old training areas in Devon and Cornwall. The general fully understood that the 29th Division would ultimately be called back to the main battle front, but he did not know exactly when. As Gerhardt had remarked to Simpson, "General [William] Sands, my artillery commander, is perfectly capable, and I could rejoin the outfit on the way up." Simpson replied: "I think that's all right." Gerhardt added one more sentence, one that would soon come back to haunt him: "I'll go first thing in the morning [of September 20] and keep in touch with the situation."

Unhappily for Gerhardt, General Bradley made some critical decisions at Twelfth Army Group headquarters on the very day of Gerhardt's departure for England that would drastically impact the 29th Division. Bradley's first judgment indicated plainly that he was not happy when Simpson informed him of Gerhardt's plan to issue seven-day furloughs for up to 2,000 29ers. At 10:57 A.M. on September 20, only a few hours after Gerhardt's departure, Col. Edward McDaniel, the 29th Division's chief of staff, telephoned the division's interim commander, General Sands, and declared with alarm:

> [Ninth Army] informed me that the authority granted on leaves to the UK has been revoked. When he gave the authority, General Simpson was unaware of a letter that had arrived from [Twelfth] Army Group giving the following reasons a seven-day leave may be granted to the UK: 1. Death of a family member or close relative, in which a seven-day leave will be granted; 2. Serious illness

of immediate family, in which a seven-day leave will be granted; 3. Marriage, in which five days will be granted. They can only be granted by Army Group. He also directed us to contact General Gerhardt and tell him to return, but if he had already left for the UK, he could continue. We are only authorized to grant 48-hour passes.

The second weighty decision reached by Bradley on September 20 was made at a meeting in Paris at the Georges V Hotel between Bradley, Simpson, and Lt. Gen. John Lee, the commander of the U.S. Army's Communications Zone. The situation on the main battlefront on the German frontier was becoming critical, and according to Simpson's diary, Bradley ordered "that the 29th Division, near Brest, be sent to First U.S. Army." In this and following orders, Bradley made it clear that the exigencies of the moment necessitated that the 29th Division's move to its new sector in southern Holland be made speedily.

Despite his promise to "keep in touch with the situation," Gerhardt did not learn of these startling new developments for four days, a period during which 29th Division staff officers repeatedly attempted to locate him with mounting urgency. Their first effort was made shortly before noon on September 20, when Lt. Col. Cooper Rhodes, the 29th Division's G-1, informed Maj. Murray Little, the divisional signal officer:

The chief of staff [McDaniel] is preparing a message to be sent to General Gerhardt in care of Beachmaster, Omaha Beach. [According to] the best info we have, the general was to go to Omaha Beach by motor and then to the UK by boat. [Gerhardt did indeed proceed to England, but it was by airplane.] The general might have left from Omaha Beach already, and then again he might not have. [McDaniel] wants you to get this message out the fastest way possible, either by wire, telegraph, or telephone, as it is very important.

Despite every possible effort that afternoon and throughout the following day, a frustrated Major Little failed to reach Gerhardt. On September 22, for the third straight day, he was continuing those efforts when Brig. Gen. James Moore, Simpson's chief of staff at Ninth Army, telephoned McDaniel in the 29th Division war room at 11:56 A.M. to ask if Gerhardt had returned. When McDaniel replied in the negative, Moore retorted irritably: "I talked to the big boss [Bradley], and he wants General Gerhardt to come back right away."

Less than one hour later McDaniel sent the following message to the U.S. Army commander of the Normandy Base Section, Col. Benjamin Talley, who was requested to forward it directly to Gerhardt: "The commanding general directs that you return at once to your command per direction of higher authority. I am sending this message also care of Gen. [Charles] Thrasher [the commander of a base section in England] in Salisbury. Request verification." McDaniel also added a postscript to allay any alarm on Gerhardt's part that his beloved division might be in trouble: "Everything OK."

The phrases "right away" and "at once" could not possibly be misinterpreted by an experienced U.S. Army soldier, but Gerhardt could not respond for the simple reason that the critical messages containing those phrases failed to reach him for the next fifty hours. The urgency of the situation was palpable, for by September 22 Gerhardt had already been out of touch with his division for over two days, while two senior U.S. Army officers, one in Normandy and the other in England, held orders to find him immediately and return him to his proper place at the helm of the 29th Infantry Division. Thrasher and Talley energetically but unsuccessfully labored to locate Gerhardt on September 22, throughout September 23, and into early afternoon on September 24. Their failure aroused much displeasure in Bradley, who was left to wonder how it was possible for not a single American soldier in the European theater of operations to have any idea where the commander of one of his most eminent infantry divisions was located for five days running. Even worse from Bradley's perspective was that Gerhardt's disappearance occurred at a critical time when the Anglo-American high command was striving to finish off the Nazis by Christmas.

At 2 P.M. on September 24, General Thrasher contacted McDaniel at 29th Division headquarters with discouraging news: "So far unable to locate Maj. Gen. Gerhardt," Thrasher wrote. "He is supposed to phone this headquarters today. Request immediate reply as to any action you want us to take. Will notify you when message [to Gerhardt] is delivered."

Under normal conditions that news would have caused the 29th Division's chief of staff to intensify his efforts to locate his commanding general, but in truth McDaniel had recently been handed a mission much more vital than hunting for a mere division commander. That mission was the immediate movement of the Blue and Gray Division 650 miles from Brittany to Holland to rejoin the Allies' main military effort on the western front, and McDaniel's ability to carry it out successfully and swiftly would be judged by U.S. Army leaders as lofty as Eisenhower and Bradley. He therefore had no choice but to focus his undivided attention upon it. Fortunately for the 29th Division—and its missing commanding general—the brilliant McDaniel was the perfect man for the job.

McDaniel was the kind of old-school soldier who would never allow himself to express an opinion about orders received from above, but when his incredulous staff learned how the top brass intended to use the 29th Division over the next few days, several could not hide their frustration and anger. Thousands of contented 29ers had only just begun to settle in to their rest camps in the Le Conquet when Colonel Witte, the division's chief operations officer, paid a visit to Ninth Army headquarters near Rennes on September 20. There he had learned the outcome of the meeting between Generals Bradley, Simpson, and Lee at the Georges V Hotel in Paris that morning; and at 4:35 P.M. Witte radioed the lamentable news back to McDaniel at 29th Division headquarters that the division was needed in Holland straight away and must depart Brittany less than two days hence, on the morning of September 22. "It will be a combination rail and motor [move], and we go back to 'Armor' [Maj. Gen. Charles Corlett's XIX Corps codename]," Witte reported. McDaniel replied: "All right. You come on in then."

Planning for such a lengthy movement of more than 14,000 men and all their equipment across the roads and railroads of war-ravaged France was an incredibly complex challenge, but that was the type of work McDaniel thrived on. This time, however, he would be under intense time pressure, for as Lt. Col. Louis Gosorn, the 29th Division's chief logistician, announced the following morning after consulting with senior transportation officers from General Lee's Communications Zone, "The rush seems to be to get us moving." Furthermore, in Gerhardt's mysterious absence, McDaniel would have to fulfill his task with little direction from above.

No 29er, including McDaniel, could possibly view the war from Bradley's lofty perspective, and therefore when the news of the division's impending movement broke, the GIs' ordinary grumbling about the top brass's perpetual insensitivity toward fighting men would be dramatically accentuated. True, there might be an entirely justifiable need to transfer the 29th Division back to the front promptly; but given what the 29th Division had endured since D-Day, a break from combat of just three days hardly seemed fair when so many fresh and unseasoned U.S. Army divisions—nine in August and September alone—had been thrust into the

European theater of operations to join the effort to bring about Hitler's demise. The most strident of the 29th Division's malcontents would assert that Bradley could surely do without the Blue and Gray for a few more days, but as company first sergeants pointed out with regularity: the U.S. Army did not conduct polls among enlisted men on strategy.

What the malcontents could not understand, however, was how profoundly the military situation on the western front had changed in the three and a half weeks since the 29th Division had begun its assault on Brest on August 25. The exhilaration triggered in the Anglo-American camp by the liberation of Paris that same day, the subsequent blitzkrieg across France, and the first penetration into Germany on September 11, had left a lingering impression in most Allied soldiers' minds that the war would not last much longer. The western Allies had crushed the notorious German Army, and according to the prevailing mindset of those heady days, fighting might continue as the enemy retreated into its homeland, but the Allies' ever-increasing confidence and military power would ensure that the Germans could not recover. The 29ers' former commander from the early war days at Fort Meade, Maj. Gen. Leonard Gerow—now elevated to the command of V Corps—expressed the sentiments of all when on September 17 he penned a letter to his troops prior to his departure on special military business to Washington, D.C., for a period he presumed would not last long. "It is probable the war with Germany will be over before I am released to return to the V Corps," Gerow wrote.

But that sort of confidence vanished in a flash in the last two weeks of September as the Allied high command absorbed two hard lessons of military operations. First, boundless optimism and supreme military power could not overcome the irrefutable limits of logistics. Second, the enemy must not be written off, no matter how desperate his condition, until Hitler and all his henchmen were dead and the Allies occupied Berlin. At Brest, the 29th Division was too focused on seizing enemy strongpoints such as Hill 103, La Trinité, and Fort Montbarey to notice that on the main battle front the Allies' pursuit had started to slow down due to lack of gas, just as the frantic Germans were striving with some success to organize a coherent defensive line on the German frontier from the Alps to the North Sea. If the 29ers did not notice those developments, however, almost every other American soldier caught up in the drive toward Germany, from Eisenhower to the youngest GI, did.

That the Allies' successful war of maneuver had suddenly been brought to a standstill was obvious. The chief issue of the moment was whether it would return soon; if it did not, would the stagnant and gruel-

European Theater of Operations Ports

ing positional warfare of Normandy replace it? The one detail evident to all was later articulated by Charles MacDonald, a participant in this campaign and one of the U.S. Army's most eminent postwar historians. "From the British front in the Netherlands all the way down to the Third Army's battleground at Metz, the enemy was rebounding almost miraculously," MacDonald wrote.

By September 21, 1944, the day after Witte had conveyed the news to McDaniel that the 29th Division would be needed back at the front to help reverse the enemy's "miracle," only a select few in the war room were privy to the distressing news that the division's magnificent rest period in the Le Conquet would be cut short. Official orders, which arrived at the war room at 7:45 P.M. on September 22, stated: "Move 29th Division with 29th CIC [Counter Intelligence Corps] and 821st Tank Destroyer Battalion attached from present location by rail and motor to area Valkenburg-Heerlen-Gulpen, all in Holland. Seven thousand troops to go by rail to Liege railhead on September 26, balance by motor in two echelons on September 24 and 25. Division relieved from attachment to VIII Corps upon arrival."

McDaniel promptly disseminated those orders down the 29th Division's chain of command, and they were received, as expected, with varying degrees of disappointment. The division would soon be back in combat—where exactly, no one yet knew. But for those who looked upon the bright side of life, it was good to know that the high-ranking general who had churned out the 29th Division's movement order for Holland had possessed enough empathy to postpone the division's departure from Brittany by two days, from September 22 to September 24. (Those 29ers who were scheduled to move by rail, however, would later have departure date moved up by one day, from the 26th to the 25th.) Accordingly, every 29er would enjoy at least five consecutive days in the Le Conquet rest camps before starting out for Holland. That was not nearly as much time as the rank and file had expected and longed for, but still it was not bad.

Colonel McDaniel and his haggard staff, however, would hardly have a moment to rest, for it was obvious Bradley was impatient to get the 29th Division into the front lines in Holland. On the evening of September 22, Gosorn reported to McDaniel, "The truck movement . . . will be continuous day and night [and] can drive with lights [at night]. Eagle [Bradley's Twelfth Army Group headquarters] sent in an urgent call for that today." Later that night, the Ninth Army chief of staff, General Moore, phoned the harried McDaniel and declared, "[Bradley] wanted recommendations about the possibility of cutting out one of the stops and linking the distance between bivouac areas in order to save a day in the movement to the destination."

In Holland the 29th Division would be returning to XIX Corps, the command to which the division had been attached throughout most of the Normandy campaign. Gerhardt would be delighted by this news—whenever he could be found—for he had always worked well with XIX Corps' commander, Maj. Gen. Charles Corlett, a man who knew and respected the 29th Division's spirit and combat prowess. The XIX Corps had been paralyzed for days in early September because of lack of gas, but it soon recovered and, on September 12, near Maastricht, had managed to achieve the U.S. Army's first penetration into Holland. Corlett's command currently held the U.S. First Army's left flank and was the northernmost American corps on the western front.

McDaniel needed only one glance at a situation map on September 22 to grasp why Bradley needed the 29th Division so urgently. The most obvious detail was that Corlett had only two divisions under his command, whereas every other corps in First Army had three. Corlett's 30th Infantry Division and 2nd Armored Division, both of which had operated side-by-side with the 29th Division in Normandy, had pressed steadily deeper into Holland, but by September 20, when they reached the Dutch-German border, the enemy's resistance suddenly stiffened. Without substantial reinforcements, Corlett's two divisions would never be able to smash through the enemy's formidable West Wall fortifications, which lined the border between Holland and Germany.

The gravest predicament on both Bradley's and Corlett's minds, however, was not the West Wall, but the gaping nine-mile break in the Allied front lines north of XIX Corps. That gap had developed as a direct result of Field Marshal Montgomery's Market-Garden operation, a daring assault deep into Holland by Anglo-American airborne and ground forces that had been launched on September 17. Montgomery had intended to exploit the enemy's supposed disorganization by dropping thousands of parachutists and glider troops behind enemy lines and thrusting a powerful mechanized column through the narrow corridor those airborne soldiers would strive to hold open. The ultimate goal was to gain a bridgehead over the Rhine River at Arnhem, but by September 24, the Allied high command recognized that the plan had failed. As the British and Americans had learned time and again since D-Day, the German Army turned out to be much less demoralized than the top brass had at first thought.

Operation Market-Garden had triggered a paradox in XIX Corps headquarters because Corlett's axis of attack diverged dramatically from Montgomery's. While Monty's troops plunged toward the Rhine in a northerly direction, Corlett's attacked almost due east; and consequently as XIX Corps penetrated into Holland, and eventually Germany, the interval separating the Americans from the British would widen. In short, the greater Corlett's success in pushing into Germany, the more he would have to worry about his unguarded left flank.

By September 24, when the 29th Division began its long journey from Brittany to Holland, the zone between Corlett's left and Montgomery's right was so vulnerable that if the Germans managed to procure fresh troops, they could push several panzer divisions through that gap against no opposition. Corlett yearned to fill the breach promptly with the 29th Division, an outfit that had served him so well in Normandy, and according to Bradley's urgent September 22 directive, the division must proceed to that gap with all possible speed.

The orders had been cut; and on September 24 at 6:30 A.M. Colonel McDaniel would dispatch the first of the 29th Division's truck convoys from Brittany to Holland just as Bradley had directed. But as the truck drivers sped off on their protracted journey to the east, McDaniel still faced one daunting problem: no one had the slightest idea where General Gerhardt was located. Early that afternoon, back in England, General Thrasher had signaled McDaniel that his search for Gerhardt had so far been fruitless. McDaniel must of course go ahead with his plan anyway, whether Thrasher could find the 29th Division's commanding general or not.

Later that afternoon Thrasher sent another message from his Salisbury headquarters, and it was finally one that brought good news. "Major General Gerhardt has received the info," Thrasher declared. "He has already left for the far shore [France]." At 3:30 A.M. on September 26 the general arrived back at 29th Division headquarters at last, and McDaniel promptly brought him up to speed on the division's ongoing truck and rail journey to Holland. McDaniel had planned that exceptionally challenging movement so thoroughly that its execution was remarkably smooth, and Gerhardt could only sit back and watch it unfold. As he did so, the general surely realized that in McDaniel he had the perfect chief of staff, one who had just possibly saved Gerhardt's job.

Had any of Gerhardt's superior officers demanded an explanation for his six-day absence from the 29th Division, Gerhardt would have been entirely correct had he pointed out that Generals Middleton and Simpson were both fully aware of his furlough plans and had indeed approved them. Gerhardt could not have known that only hours after his departure from Brittany, Bradley had vetoed the 29th Division's plan for seven-day furloughs for selected personnel, pointing out that Middleton and Simpson had the authority to grant only forty-eight-hour passes—even to a general of Gerhardt's stature.

The undeniable fact that Gerhardt was unaware of Twelfth Army Group rules was a legitimate line of reasoning that under normal conditions would have yielded leniency on Bradley's part. But one aspect of Gerhardt's behavior in this unfortunate episode Bradley could never forgive, and that was Gerhardt's failure to let anyone in the 29th Division know where he was heading on his furlough and how he could be contacted in an emergency. When Bradley revoked all 29th Division furloughs, and the war room staff frantically endeavored to find their commanding general, McDaniel did not even know whether Gerhardt was currently in England or France, a detail that made the attempt to find him much more difficult.

From Bradley's perspective an even more inexcusable sin was that throughout his furlough, Gerhardt failed to contact 29th Division headquarters. In truth, had it not been for McDaniel's and Thrasher's intervention, Gerhardt's absence from his division during this critical period would have been even more prolonged. Ultimately, Bradley did nothing in the immediate future to discipline Gerhardt for his lapse of judgment, a reflection perhaps of the great esteem the U.S. Army top brass had for the 29th Division's fighting prowess—a trait that in part had been effected by its commanding general's extraordinary vigor. Nevertheless, Bradley's displeasure was obvious; and unhappily for Gerhardt, the man who had been an upper-class teammate on the 1915 West Point baseball team, and who would soon become U.S. Army chief of staff—and still later the first chairman of the Joint Chiefs of Staff—had an exceptional memory.

In the postwar U.S. Army, Bradley's ability to recall his former subordinates' moral and intellectual character would shape the careers of hundreds of career soldiers—some positively, others negatively. Later events would prove that Bradley's view of Gerhardt was apparently in the latter category, a detail that was established a few years after World War II when Bradley made the acerbic remark in his memoirs, *A Soldier's Story*, that "[Gerhardt's] enthusiasm sometimes exceeded his judgment as a soldier." In late 1945 the U.S. Army sent Gerhardt home from Germany at reduced rank, a clear indicator that the peak of his military career had passed. The Army never assigned him to the command of a combat outfit again.

Under normal circumstances, any soldier who had commanded a unit as celebrated as the 29th Division could expect his career to flourish in the form of an important leadership position in the postwar U.S. Army. Gerhardt needed to look no further than his West Point class of 1917 to see clear evidence of that fact. The youngest member of the 1917 class, Joseph Lawton Collins, who had led the 25th Division in combat in the Pacific and later rose to corps command in Europe, was the most obvious example: In 1949, at the age of fifty-three, Collins was named as Bradley's successor in the U.S. Army's preeminent post as chief of staff. Another of Gerhardt's classmates, Matthew Ridgway, raised and led the renowned 82nd Airborne Division throughout much of World War II, but that command was just a precursor to much greater things. In 1951 he took over the reins of Far East Command from Douglas MacArthur at the height of the Korean War, and later succeeded Collins as chief of staff in 1953. Still another 1917 classmate, Frederick Augustus Irving, had commanded the 24th and 38th Divisions during World War II and in 1951 would be appointed to the highly prestigious post as superintendent of the U.S. Military Academy.

A soldier who had held division command for eleven consecutive months of combat, starting out on Omaha Beach on D-Day, should have reaped similar career honors, but unhappily for Gerhardt, those honors never came. After returning home from Germany, the Army dispatched him to Brazil at the rank of brigadier general as part of a short-lived American military mission. In 1947 he joined the Second Army's staff at Fort Meade, Maryland, as G-2 (Intelligence) officer, a post he held for five years before retiring in 1952. In his many encounters with the members of the postwar 29th Division, which often fulfilled its National Guard training requirements at Fort Meade, Gerhardt experienced an awkward role reversal. The 29th Division's new commander was Maj. Gen. William Sands, Gerhardt's former artillery chief during the war years, and the man who had assumed command of the division at the rank of brigadier general when Gerhardt disappeared from Brest on furlough on September 20, 1944. At Fort Meade, however, Sands, now a two-star general, outranked Gerhardt, who served on the Second Army staff as a mere brigadier.

As a rule, as long as a soldier neither violated the U.S. Army's sacrosanct regulations nor ran afoul of civilian authorities, what he did on furlough was his business. The Army apparently held to that policy in Gerhardt's case, for there is no record of any inquiry into the general's activities during his six-day absence from the 29th Division in late September 1944. When the detail emerged that General Thrasher had located Gerhardt in southwestern England, however, many officers in the U.S. Army's high command, including in all probability Bradley, wondered why Gerhardt had traveled so far from Brittany to spend his furlough—and, even more important, why it had been so difficult to find him. The fact that Gerhardt offered no official explanation of his behavior generated malicious rumors within the highest reaches of the U.S. Army; and the fact that many eminent American soldiers came to believe those rumors in all likelihood heavily contributed to the negative impression of Gerhardt that had been building up among the American top brass since Bradley's Twelfth Army Group had abruptly revoked Gerhardt's furlough plans back on September 20.

Only Gerhardt himself, his driver Sgt. Bob Cuff, and whoever hosted his visit in England knew the truth, and presently none of those people had any inclination to speak of it candidly. At least for the moment no one would force them to, for the obvious reason that the momentous military matters on the western front far outweighed the extracurricular affairs of a single U.S. Army major general. The war must go on, regardless of Maj. Gen. Charles Hunter Gerhardt, Jr.'s conduct.

Like every other Allied soldier in the European Theater of Operations, Gerhardt yearned to bring about the end of the war by New Years Day, 1945. For him the battle to accomplish that goal would resume when the 29th Division rejoined the fight in Holland, and when it was over, perhaps Gerhardt would be invited to march in the victory parade in Berlin with all his beloved 29ers—the men who had contributed so much to the Nazis' downfall.

3. WHAT THE FUTURE MAY BRING FORTH

The 29th Infantry Division had done its job, and now it was time for General Eisenhower to do his. Ike was the chief executor of Operation Overlord, and had that monumental design for the liberation of western Europe been carried out strictly according to plan, Eisenhower would now be extolling the 29th Division, and all other VIII Corps outfits, for their triumphal role in the seizure of Brest, an objective Ike had routinely professed was one of Overlord's many essential pillars. In that event, U.S. Army engineers and port construction troops would have poured into Brest by the thousands and promptly embarked on the prodigious task of clearing wreckage, defusing mines, and repairing damaged harbor facilities so that troopships straight from the United States could dock and disgorge the men and materiel Ike would need to overwhelm the German Army and push on to Berlin.

But Operation Overlord had not progressed according to plan. It took the Allies seven weeks longer than expected to capture Brest, and by the time 29th Division troops entered the city on September 18, 1944, the strategic situation on the western front was entirely different than the Allied top brass had foreseen. The Overlord design had assumed that by that date, Allied armies would have progressed only as far as Paris and the Seine River; but in actuality American and British spearheads had pushed more than 200 miles beyond those points and were already moving into Germany. Two crucial ports that had not figured in Overlord plans, Antwerp and Marseille, were now in Allied hands. The German Army in Normandy had been crushed, and Eisenhower and his chief subordinates could not help but seriously contemplate the gratifying possibility that the war would be over by early 1945 if the Allies could maintain their momentum.

How all those remarkably positive developments would impact Eisenhower's perception of Brest was anybody's guess. No soldier familiar with the complex science of military logistics could write off Brest without considerable justification, for it featured one of Europe's most impressive harbors and dockside facilities—attributes that under different circumstances Allied generals would have ardently craved. True, the main battle front on the German frontier was now situated more than 450 miles away, but that essential detail had also been true during World War I when the U.S. Army had used Brest as its main entry point into France.

Eisenhower was the final arbiter of such weighty matters, and ultimately he must make a tough decision. When he did, at the end of September 1944, he chose to send no engineers and port construction personnel to Brest to restore its exceptional harbor facilities and open it up for Allied shipping. What had only recently been one of Ike's highest priorities apparently was now wholly irrelevant, and accordingly, not a single American vessel would dock in Brest for the remainder of World War II. It was a reversal of monumental proportions, one that would trigger a contentious debate that would endure for decades.

By the time Eisenhower made that weighty decision, the 29th Division had journeyed to Holland, deployed across the border into Germany, and was just beginning to reenter combat against a rejuvenated enemy. That the division's prodigious endeavor at Brest, which had resulted in more than 3,000 casualties—including nearly 700 deaths—might now be perceived by some as a complete waste, took some time to sink in. The

29ers had assumed with genuine sincerity that their recent triumph would assist in some significant way to bring about a swift end to the war in the Allies' favor, but evidently that assumption was flawed. The rank and file had to admit that the business of strategy was strictly up to the top brass, and what Ike would do with Brest was his business. Still, Eisenhower's decision to write off Brest seemed curious given the intensity of the 29ers' attack to capture the place, an effort that had only reached its dramatic conclusion little more than a week in the past. Why would the 29th Division have been ordered to do the Brest job in the first place if Eisenhower could not use it?

In his 1946 official report to the Anglo-American Combined Chiefs of Staff, Eisenhower provided a one-sentence answer: "When at last the Allies gained possession [of Brest], they found the port installations so completely wrecked as to be capable of rehabilitation only to a minor degree, and our plans for the introduction of trans-Atlantic troop convoys to the once magnificent harbor had to be abandoned." However, what Ike's report failed to mention was that, given adequate time, the Germans habitually and thoroughly wrecked any port they had been forced to yield to the Allies. The first substantive port to fall into Allied hands after D-Day, Cherbourg, was so devastated that essential repairs took about a month, and a more thorough restoration considerably longer than that.

A September 29, 1944, U.S. Navy survey concluded that the port of Brest could not return to a functional state unless a major reconstruction effort was made over a period of about two and a half months. That endeavor would have been difficult, but by no means impossible; and therefore Eisenhower's implication that the refurbishment of Brest was not a viable strategic option was somewhat misleading. The truth was that had Eisenhower still valued Brest as a major intake port for troops and supplies at the close of September 1944, he could have committed the resources to repair it, and it probably would have been functional by early December.

A more plausible line of reasoning concerning the contentious Brest issue was that the main battle front was now so distant from Brittany that the conveyance of troops and supplies over that considerable distance would have strained to the breaking point both the mangled French railroad network and the Allies' limited truck capacity. By late September 1944 the Allies controlled several French and Belgian ports, most notably Antwerp, Marseille, Le Havre, and Rouen, whose combined capacity could more than make up for Brest, and even better, were much closer to the front. True, the Germans had also smashed up those ports to some degree, and the most important one, Antwerp, could not be used at all until the Allies undertook the challenging task of clearing the German Army from the banks of the Scheldt estuary, which controlled the lengthy approaches to Antwerp's massive harbor.

Furthermore, the Allies' capacity to repair damaged ports was finite. Thus, if Eisenhower had to be selective in his commitment of limited port repair resources, he would have to abandon any hope of rebuilding all available ports and concentrate on the repair of only the most vital few. That Brest fell into the category of those ports that would have to be written off was certainly unfortunate in the World War II chronicle of the 29th Division, but had the 29ers been capable of viewing the war from Ike's lofty perspective, they would have ultimately agreed that his Brest decision was entirely rational. As one of Eisenhower's preeminent biographers, Carlo D'Este, observed: "Ultimately Brittany became a monument to the notion that in war campaigns rarely evolve as planned."

From the 29th Division's standpoint, the only issue of significance was timing. If Ike had written off Brest as a major logistical base before or shortly after the division launched its attack on August 25, 1944, in retrospect it would have been utterly deplorable that so many 29ers lost their lives in a battle that, from the moment of its commencement, the top brass knew would have no impact whatsoever on the outcome of the war. On the other hand, if Eisenhower had decided to dispose of Overlord's grandiose plans for Brest after the enemy's capitulation on September 18, from the 29ers' perspective that decision would have been regrettable but entirely understandable given that the war Eisenhower was managing was almost unthinkably grandiose. No one had foreseen how profoundly the military situation on the western front would change in the aftermath of the Normandy breakout. In the twenty-six-day period Middleton's VIII Corps needed to take Brest by direct assault, that situation transformed so dramatically that it was inevitable that Eisenhower's outlook on Brest would change, just as it had changed on so many other issues of grand strategy due to shifting circumstances.

Historical evidence is irrefutable that Eisenhower did not abandon the idea of using Brest until well after the German garrison there had surrendered. Unfortunately, much of that evidence has been disregarded by postwar historians, who have sought to establish that the American effort to take Brest was grossly irrational from the start; and that Ike should have known before the 29th Division commenced its attack on Brest, or shortly thereafter, that Brest's harbor would be of no value to the Allies. As a basis for their thesis, those revisionists have repeatedly evoked inaccurate and misleading statements by Generals Bradley and Patton that appeared in print in the years following World War II.

For example, in his 1951 memoir, *A Soldier's Story*, Bradley wrote:

> This costly siege of Brest has since been described by some as a wasteful and unnecessary campaign, executed primarily because of blind obedience to an outdated Overlord plan. . . . [With] the capture of Antwerp, one of the largest and best ports in the world . . . we wrote off Brest as surplus. . . . Why then did we spend three divisions on Brest at a cost of almost 10,000 in American dead and wounded? . . . The difference lay in the nature of enemy resistance. For the garrison at Brest was totally unlike those of the other ports. Spiked with troops from the 2nd Parachute Division, the garrison was commanded by Maj. Gen. Hermann Ramcke, too aggressive and fanatical a solider to sit contentedly in that concrete pile. . . . Thus the decision to take Brest was not dictated by any outdated Overlord plan of maneuver. I went ahead with the costly siege of Brest, with Eisenhower's approval, not because we wanted that port, but because Ramcke left us no other solution.

Bradley's recollection is remarkably disingenuous on several counts, the most noteworthy of which is his assertion that the fall of Antwerp directly led to Eisenhower's decision to abandon the Overlord plan for Brest. A careful examination of Ike's correspondence in the aftermath of the British liberation of Antwerp on September 4, however, reveals that that event made no immediate impact on his firm resolve to capture Brest. In a September 9 report to his superiors on the Combined Chiefs of Staff, five days after the fall of Antwerp, he noted that he had assigned his "Central Group of Armies"—namely, the U.S. First, Third, and Ninth Armies—four priorities, and the *first* among them in his list was: "Capture Brest." Later, nine days after Antwerp's liberation, in a September 13 cable to Bradley, Montgomery, and other senior commanders, he reemphasized that resolve: "The Central Group of Armies must quickly reduce Brest so that this place may be available to us for staging troops [directly from the United States]." In fact Ike did not discard the idea of using Brest as a "staging" port until the end of September—twenty-six days after the liberation of Antwerp—and even then that decision was forced on him because he lacked the resources to repair it. Brest may therefore have been "surplus," as Bradley declared; but it did not become so in Eisenhower's mind until well after the Germans had surrendered the city.

Bradley's somewhat more controversial contention that the American effort at Brest was driven not by logistics, but by concern over the large and belligerent German garrison, was articulated by him in a much different way in his 1983 autobiography *A General's Life*.

> We might well have been advised . . . to give up the good fight and let Brest remain in German hands, contained by our newly arriving green infantry divisions or by the French Forces of the Interior. Brest had taken on a symbolic value far exceeding its utilitarian value and, perhaps imprudently, I was stubbornly determined to capture it. . . . Middleton's VIII Corps suffered 9,831 casualties—killed, wounded, missing. That was far too high a price to pay to maintain illusions of invincibility.

In Patton's postwar memoir *War As I Knew It*, published posthumously by his widow in 1947, he noted that on September 9 he and Bradley "had quite a conversation about the Brest operation." According to Patton, "We both felt that the taking of Brest at that time was useless, because it was too far away and the harbor was too badly destroyed. [On that date Brest was still under German occupation, so Patton and Bradley could not have known the condition of the harbor definitively.] On the other hand, we agreed that, when the American Army had once put its hand to the plow, it should not let go. Therefore, it was necessary to take Brest." In the *Patton Papers*, published in 1974, Patton quoted Bradley's somewhat more blunt view of that issue: "We must take Brest in order to maintain the illusion of the fact that the U.S. Army cannot be beaten."

Therefore, if Bradley's and Patton's incredible statements are to be believed, they knew that the monumental struggle for Brest would be a waste of effort and lives nearly from the start. When their analysis, truthful or not, sunk into the 29ers' minds in the years after World War II, it not surprisingly cast unequivocally negative light on Bradley's judgment as a general, for "symbolic" victories do not win wars, and, even worse, they expend lives for little purpose. The 29th Division's loss of more than 3,000 men for symbolic rather than practical reasons could not fail to disgust any 29er who had risked his life on the fighting line and witnessed the death of his cherished brothers-in-arms. That attitude was especially poignant within a division such as the 29th, which even before Brest had suffered an enormous toll of human lives, and whose members desperately yearned for a substantive break from combat.

Could Bradley's recollection of Brest possibly be true? Fortunately for his military reputation, it was not. In terms of Anglo-American strategy in western Europe, Bradley was not the supreme authority—Eisenhower was. A thorough examination of Ike's wartime correspondence and his 1946 official report to the Anglo-American Combined Chiefs of Staff does not contain the slightest hint that from his perspective Brest's strategic value was symbolic rather than real. Indeed, throughout much of September 1944, Eisenhower routinely professed to both superiors and subordinates alike that the requirement for Brest's capture was not only practical, but critical from a logistical standpoint. Therefore, Bradley's statement in his 1951 autobiography that "I went ahead with the costly siege of Brest, with Eisenhower's approval, not because we wanted that port, but because Ramcke left us no other solution," was apparently entirely untrue.

Furthermore, Bradley did not manage U.S. Army logistics in the European theater; Lt. Gen. John C. H. Lee, the head of the Communications Zone, did. It was not until September 14, 1944—only four days before the fall of Brest—that General Lee first recommended to Eisenhower that Brest should be struck off the U.S. Army's list of primary objectives in western Europe. But even then, as noted in the 1958 book *Logistical Support of the Armies* by the official historian of the Communications Zone, Roland Ruppenthal, "[Eisenhower] was not yet ready to abandon Brest in view of the need for reception facilities to handle the accelerated flow of divisions [from the United States]. Furthermore, the condition of the port was unknown even at this time, for it was still in enemy hands. SHAEF for the moment therefore directed that Brest should be developed to the extent needed to receive troops and their organizational equipment."

In fact, Eisenhower did not learn of the conclusions drawn by the U.S. Navy's survey of Brest's damaged harbor until the last day of September, and then, according to Ruppenthal, "Brest was now given the lowest priority [for reconstruction], and was eventually abandoned altogether." In the matter of the Brest operation, therefore, the historical chronology of events clearly reveals that the city was captured not for purely "symbolic" reasons, as Bradley asserted seven years later, but out of genuine military necessity. True, the strategic situation in the late summer and fall of 1944 changed so swiftly and profoundly that that necessity evaporated before any troops set about to repair Brest's harbor facilities; but still, as the members of the 29th Division were laboring mightily to liberate Brest for nearly four weeks that August and September, their great endeavor was obviously not viewed at the time by the highest reaches of the Anglo-American high command as meaningless, despite Bradley's postwar claims.

Nevertheless, if generals are judged by the results generated by their decisions, Eisenhower's recurring directives to his chief subordinates from late August through mid-September 1944, all of which repeatedly emphasized the importance of Brest, bring his generalship into question for the obvious reason that the Brest operation in actuality yielded few, if any, strategic benefits for the Allies. In retrospect, therefore, the paramount historical question relating to Brest is not if VIII Corps' achievement in liberating that city was symbolic rather than real; rather it is whether or not Eisenhower should have foreseen long before he actually did that the monumental effort to seize Brest and restore its harbor were not feasible schemes. Had he concluded in late August 1944 or earlier that those ideas were impractical, for example, the impact of that decision would have been considerable: Only a small fraction of VIII Corps, which would in all likelihood not have included the 29th Division, would have been deployed there; little or no effort would have been made to assault Ramcke's German garrison directly; and American casualties would have been light—or even nonexistent.

The Brest campaign triggered a historical controversy that has raged since the end of World War II; not surprisingly, since then many historians have suggested, with some intensity, that Eisenhower blundered badly by directing Bradley to adhere to original Overlord plans and take Brest as soon as possible following the Normandy breakout. Further, those historians have asserted that the consequences of that misstep were worsened by Ike's unwavering commitment to Brest even as the effort to capture it intensified, VIII Corps casualties mounted, and the strategic situation in western Europe changed dramatically from day to day.

In his classic work *Eisenhower's Lieutenants*, the eminent historian Russell Weigley wrote:

> The excessively cautious concern of the planners for the post-invasion buildup and thus for ports had turned the Third Army into Brittany from Avranches at the beginning of August, when far greater opportunities beckoned to the east. . . . The battle for Brest reflects the excessive caution of the planners, and of a generalship that persisted in relying on the Overlord plans. . . . When the opportunity to leap the Seine proved irresistible even to field commanders otherwise so cautious that they played out the whole Brest drama to its tedious conclusion, the still more cautious logisticians proved never to have considered that flexibility might be a military virtue.

One of Eisenhower's recent biographers, Carlo D'Este, was even more scathing. He categorized the American effort to capture Brest as "a huge military embarrassment to the Allies" and claimed that once the

Allied armies rushed eastward across France following the Normandy breakout, an "outdated" Overlord plan should have been scrapped or significantly modified by eliminating Brest from Eisenhower's list of the Allies' foremost military objectives.

The fact that Ike did not indeed remove Brest from his strategic priority list until the end of September exposes how differently generals and historians ponder military strategy. It is axiomatic that momentous decisions must be made by a general under severe stress, lacking foreknowledge of their results. In contrast, a historian has the much more comfortable task of judging those decisions with full knowledge of their outcome. Not surprisingly, the Brest campaign initiated much second-guessing and criticism of American generalship by postwar historians given that Brest's harbor was ultimately not used by the Allies after Middleton's VIII Corps had expended so much effort, with tragic human cost, to capture it.

However, an entirely dissimilar assessment of Eisenhower's judgment emerges when one carefully scrutinizes Ike's command decisions based strictly on what he knew of the strategic situation—and, more important, when he knew it. Under that form of analysis, one could present an entirely cogent argument that by remaining faithful to Overlord's commitment to capture Brest, Eisenhower did what any prudent commander would have done in the same circumstances. That argument was articulated by Martin Blumenson in his official U.S. Army history, *Breakout and Pursuit*, which in part deals with the Brest campaign.

> The serious problem of port capacity had prompted the Brest operation. The Allied commanders who had initiated the operation had not been able to foretell exactly when and to what extent the Channel ports would alleviate the situation. Thus they looked upon Brest as a port in reserve. The fact that capture of neither the destroyed harbor of Brest nor the Channel ports proved to be an immediate solution did not vitiate their wisdom and vision. . . . If it seemed in retrospect that the commanders erred in starting the siege of Brest, they did so on the side of caution, preferring to be safe rather than sorry.

Logistics was the key. If Eisenhower and his staff did not master that intricate military science, Montgomery could never mount the "one really powerful and full-blooded thrust toward Berlin" that he craved; nor could Patton hurl his Third Army over the Rhine toward that same objective. In short, above and beyond setting straightforward military objectives for his combat formations, Ike had to ponder how many men he had to arm, equip, and feed; the quantity of reinforcements he would receive; how many tons of supplies could flow into France on a daily basis through the ports and artificial harbors currently under Allied control; and, perhaps most important, the means of conveying those supplies to the frontline troops.

Postwar critics of the Brittany campaign leveled the exceptionally harsh charge that Bradley's commitment of the 2nd, 8th, and 29th Infantry Divisions on August 20 and 21, 1944, to capture Brest, as specified in Overlord plans, was a grave error because those three experienced divisions could have been more profitably employed elsewhere. But at that time the only substantive port under Allied control in France was Cherbourg, and its quaysides were bursting under the strain of supplying the ever-increasing number of Allied troops in Normandy. Furthermore, Bradley had needed three U.S. Army infantry divisions to crack the Germans' formidable Cherbourg defenses in June, and as the enemy's resolution to hold Brest would in all likelihood shape up to be equally robust, the employment of three American divisions at Brest at the time appeared entirely reasonable.

Unless the Allies swiftly seized additional ports in the aftermath of the Normandy breakout, their logistical crisis could only get worse as autumn weather set in and their ability to disgorge materiel over the Normandy beaches and artificial harbors inevitably diminished. True, at the time the 29th Division set out for Brittany, the breakout had blossomed into a triumphal Allied victory; but still, Paris had not yet been liberated, and the only port in northern France that had fallen to Allied attack since Cherbourg was St. Malo, which was not nearly of sufficient size to influence the looming logistical predicament.

Brest was certainly one of France's most prominent ports, and as of August 21, 1944, its significance to the Overlord plan still held firm. That Brest even then held such importance in SHAEF's eyes may have been viewed by many as unwise, but judged by the Allies' exceptionally strained logistical situation as of that date, if Eisenhower had ignored Overlord and disregarded Brest, that dramatic change in strategy would have been considered risky, even foolhardy, by many of his superiors on the Anglo-American Combined Chiefs of Staff. Ike's boss, Chief of Staff of the U.S. Army Gen. George C. Marshall, strongly supported the idea of taking Brest because it would eventually become useful as one of the main arrival points in France for U.S. Army divisions en route from the United States. Marshall later noted in his 1945 report to Secretary of War Henry Stimson, "By September 5 (D+90) 2,086,000 Allied troops and 3,446,000 tons of stores had been put ashore in France. This was an outstanding logistical achievement, but nevertheless we were still in urgent need of additional ports if we were to support adequately the fast-moving offensive across France that was operating on a dangerously thin supply basis. Many divisions had a very limited supply on hand."

Eisenhower's chief SHAEF deputy, Sir Arthur Tedder of the RAF, later corroborated that view in his 1966 memoir *With Prejudice*.

> Eisenhower was confirmed in his conviction that the early capture of deep-water ports and improved facilities for maintenance were prerequisites for a final assault on Germany proper. Our situation was that any stretch of seven or ten days of bad weather in the Channel, a condition which grew increasingly likely as winter drew near, would paralyze our activities and make the maintenance of our forces, even in defensive roles, extremely difficult. From the very beginning of the Overlord plan, we had thought it essential to gain deep-water ports.

Brest was certainly a major deep-water port; but Eisenhower's postwar detractors pointed out that several other ports in the European theater could have more than made up for Brest. In Eisenhower's defense, however, at the moment Bradley dispatched the 29th Division to Brittany, it was much too early for Ike to predict definitively when those ports would fall into Allied hands. It was true that Marseille, one of the largest ports in France, would fall to Free French troops on August 28, thirteen days after the Allies' invasion of the Riviera, but Marseille was not ready to receive supplies until September 18, and even then it did not offer Eisenhower a viable alternative to Brest because it was situated an even greater distance from the front in northern France than Brest. Another of France's foremost ports, Le Havre, did not fall to a British assault until September 12, just days before the 29th Division surged into Brest with the rest of VIII Corps, and its docks were not operational until October 9. Le Havre was indeed a highly beneficial acquisition for the Allies, but Eisenhower certainly believed at the time that it was not large enough for him to abandon his plans for Brest altogether.

And then there was Antwerp. The seizure of that enormous Belgian port by the British 11th Armored Division on September 4, nearly two weeks after the 29th Division commenced its attack on Brest, was a decisive success that in itself could have solved Eisenhower's logistical predicament had the Allies' been able to open it up rapidly, but Antwerp's liberation occurred so much earlier than anyone had foreseen that Ike, in late August 1944, can hardly be blamed for failing to anticipate its imminent capture as he remained focused on Brest and other Brittany ports.

Furthermore, two ominous and irrefutable details emerged after the fall of Antwerp that effectively prevented Eisenhower from basing his immediate logistical plans entirely on that great port. First, although the Allies held Antwerp itself, the enemy still controlled the lengthy river approaches to the city and therefore no Allied shipping could move up the estuary to unload supplies. That lamentable situation endured for two months, until November 4, and during that period, Antwerp was, in the words of the Royal Navy's First Sea Lord, Sir Andrew Cunningham, "of no more use to us than an oasis in the Sahara desert." Eisenhower correctly predicted how difficult it would be to use Antwerp when he noted in a September 9 report to the Combined Chiefs of Staff, the same report in which one of his highest priorities was to "capture Brest": "The hostile occupation in force of the Dutch islands at the mouth of the Scheldt is certain to delay the utilization of Antwerp as a port and thus will vitally influence the full development of our strategy."

The second factor concerning Antwerp constraining Eisenhower's logistical plans would be profoundly influenced by the enemy. The Americans had learned at Cherbourg that the Germans would, if forced to yield a port to the Allies, employ ingenious and brutal methods to prevent, or at least disrupt, Allied vessels from docking and offloading cargoes. Those methods included demolishing harbor facilities, setting booby traps, and sinking hulks in the harbor. Happily for Eisenhower, the port of Antwerp fell into Allied hands comparatively intact; but since Antwerp was an inland port, with an estuary almost completely under the enemy's control stretching nearly fifty miles to the North Sea, Ike had to assume that the Germans would do everything in their power to make that estuary impassable to Allied shipping. The more time the Germans had to execute that mission—and ultimately they had more than two months—the tougher the Allies' clean-up operation would be.

When Eisenhower's senior naval officer, Adm. Sir Bertram Ramsay of the Royal Navy, observed, "Antwerp [is] highly vulnerable to mining and blocking [and] if the enemy succeeds in these operations, the time it will take to open [it] cannot be estimated," an anxious Ike had to ponder whether clearing the estuary of naval mines and sunken hulks would actually take longer than restoring heavily damaged ports such as Brest. Even worse, the Germans were sure to saturate Antwerp with their sinister new V-1 flying bombs and even more deadly V-2 rockets. In contrast,

Brest would be immune from those weapons because it was not within their range.

In summary, the Allies' logistical circumstances in August and September 1944 were so volatile that no one, including Eisenhower, could predict with any confidence how the Allies' design for pushing over the Rhine and on to Berlin by late 1944 or early 1945 could be sustained by an adequate flow of supplies. On a daily basis, and under intense pressure, Ike had to make weighty judgments on logistical matters in a strategic situation so fluid that an entirely logical decision one day could appear illogical the next; and when reality diverged from expectations, forcing Ike to change strategic course, it was mandatory that he have viable options on which he could fall back. In that kind of highly uncertain environment, controversy was bound to erupt over momentous strategic choices with which not everyone agreed, and whose outcomes no one could possibly foresee. Rather than reflecting a slavish commitment to an "outdated" Overlord plan, Eisenhower's judgment on the matter of Brest certainly reflected the shifting strategic situation and demonstrated a realistic and flexible plan of action that any far-sighted commander would have followed.

That Eisenhower ultimately decided not to use Brest provided critics with limitless ammunition to label his decision to capture it as foolish. But the fact that Brest was never used as an entry point for American supplies due to the rapidly changing strategic situation is not the point. In truth, the crux of the debate is whether Brest *could* have been vital to the Allies had the strategic situation developed slightly differently, and the answer to that question is unequivocally yes. Ike's supporters could argue credibly that much of the criticism directed at the supreme commander was unwarranted because it was based primarily on conclusions drawn after the proverbial dust kicked up by the campaign had settled rather than on the facts as Eisenhower learned of them day by day. Eisenhower himself observed somewhat caustically after the war that those not in possession of the facts as he knew them could not comment accurately on his decision-making process: "Some of these writers forget that grand tactics and strategy must be decided upon by people who are in possession of the overall situation in such matters as relative strength, mobility, and logistic possibilities."

If Eisenhower erred at Brest, his most manifest lapse was not his decision to order Bradley to capture it, nor his perseverance to sustain the Brest assault as the strategic situation on the main battle front changed, but his significant underestimation of the time and effort required to seize it. Ultimately, the American endeavor at Brest lasted seven weeks and cost more than 10,000 casualties. By fighting so resolutely in such a hopeless situation, therefore, Ramcke's enemy garrison very nearly fulfilled the duty Hitler had demanded of it and thereby delayed the Americans' seizure of the port for so long that by the time it was finally in Allied hands, Eisenhower's rationale for its capture had dwindled by a sizeable factor. Indeed, had the Americans been able to force Ramcke's capitulation more quickly, Brest could have been in Allied hands before Le Havre, and perhaps even Antwerp; and in that event Eisenhower would have had much greater incentive to restore and eventually use it as an Allied port of entry into northwest Europe. Such an occurrence would of course have wholly altered the postwar perception of the value of the Americans' endeavor at Brest.

Eisenhower's state of mind at the time he contemplated his strategy for what he hoped would be the war's final campaign was neatly summed up by Prime Minister Winston Churchill in a cable to his senior military staff on September 8, 1944—just ten days before Brest's capture. "Unless the situation changes remarkably the Allies will still be short of port accommodation when the equinoctial [early autumn] gales are due," Churchill observed. "One can already foresee the probability of a lull in the magnificent advances we have made. . . . No one can tell what the future may bring forth."

Had Ike indeed been able to tell what the future would bring forth, his outlook on Brest would obviously have been much different. But no military leader in history, not even Caesar or Napoleon, had that kind of prophetic power.

4. IN HUMBLE TRIBUTE

The 29ers, along with their comrades from the 2nd and 8th Divisions, as well as the rangers and other corps-level troops, had taken Brest; but now it mattered little to them how Eisenhower would use it. All that mattered was that they had fulfilled the mission Ike had assigned them. They had met the enemy head-on on a battlefield, and they had attacked, day after day, and at dreadful cost in lives, until that enemy was utterly destroyed.

General Middleton tersely summarized the battle for Brest as "a savage fight," and he was right. In truth the struggle had been an unadulterated slugfest, one in which the resolution and fortitude of the common rifleman was almost entirely responsible for the 29th Division's success. In the vicious, close-range melee at Brest, the art of generalship had been entirely outweighed by the skill of senior NCOs and junior officers, who had led their depleted rifle squads and platoons successfully through unremitting rigors of unspeakable intensity for nearly a month. Ultimately the enemy had been overwhelmed; but that accomplishment was accompanied by an exceptionally lengthy list of American casualties—so many that those 29th Division infantrymen who still answered roll call by the enemy's surrender on September 18 faced the stark realization that they were fortunate to still be among the living.

The taciturn General Simpson of Ninth Army observed that Brest "constituted a very unusual chapter in the history of the U.S. Army," without noting whether or not that chapter was worthy of emulation. Whether future historians would view Brest as a model of U.S. Army combat efficiency or a total waste of time and lives was immaterial to the 29ers. According to the uncomplicated outlook of the ordinary fighting man, there could be only one historical verdict. At Brest, the Americans had killed or wounded thousands of Germans and had captured nearly 40,000. The significance of that accomplishment was summarized by a September 24, 1944, *New York Times* article: "Beaming with satisfaction, General Middleton said that three German divisions, the 266th, 343rd, and 2nd Parachute, had been 'entirely erased from the troop list of the German Army' in 26 days of the bitterest fighting." In a congratulatory message to his troops on September 19, Middleton declared, "In the 2nd Parachute Division of the German Army, you have met the best. You will meet no better troops in your future battles." Furthermore, its former commander, the legendary Nazi general Hermann-Bernhard Ramcke, had begun his long journey from Brittany to a POW camp in the United States. How could a military victory marked by such noteworthy achievements possibly be considered a waste?

After the perils the 29th Division had endured in Normandy and Brittany, no outfit in the U.S. Army deserved a break from combat more. The top brass would indeed provide that break, but it would last a mere five days, an interval that could hardly be expected to restore the 29ers' weary bodies and souls to their customary vigor. General Bradley had called the 29th Division back to the main battlefront with all possible speed, and it was probable that it would reenter combat soon.

As the 29ers prepared to board the trucks and trains that would convey them to Holland, two somewhat disquieting details emerged that shed light on what combat operations in the immediate future would be like. First, all reports from the front indicated that the Germans had recovered from their disastrous defeat in the summer. Evidently the enemy was preparing to make a stand on the German frontier, and when the 29th Division eventually entered that battle, just beyond the Dutch-German border, fighting promised to be even more intense than usual because it would be on the enemy's home turf. Winston Churchill articulated this supposition best when he noted to one of his senior generals in early September 1944: "The fortifying and consolidating effect of a stand on the frontier of the [Germans'] native soil should not be underrated."

And then there was the weather. So far in World War II, the 29th Division had experienced combat only in late spring and summer, when the comparatively gentle climate of northern Europe allowed the men to live in reasonable comfort, even given Gerhardt's infamous order that no 29er could sleep or perform administrative duties inside a civilian building. Since the division had entered Brittany, however, the hours of daylight had decreased markedly; and by mid-September morning and evening hours were downright frigid, cold enough on occasion for a soldier to see the vapor of his breath.

That the 29th Division was about to experience something completely new was demonstrated by the new clothing issued to the men by supply officers just prior to the journey to Holland. The most notable of the new items was an olive-drab woolen overcoat, so heavy and bulky that it certainly would keep a soldier warm, but it was also an obvious hint that the 29ers would soon be living outdoors in highly uncomfortable weather. An even more ominous hint was the rubber galoshes supplied to each man. If Holland was anything like what the men had read about as children, those boots would definitely be needed since inundated ground and mud could be expected. How combat would shape up under those conditions, as cold weather and autumn rains set in, was anybody's guess, but it surely would not be pleasant.

The time had finally come for the 29ers to say goodbye to Brittany. They had only occupied that little corner of the world for a month, but its picturesque countryside and agreeable populace had grown on them to such a degree that they were sorry to have to depart. The Brittany campaign was now an integral facet of 29th Division history, and presently, the Bretons would add the 29th Division to a prominent place in the glorious and ancient annals of their homeland. The Americans had flattened Brest to a state that was noteworthy even by the pitiless standards of the current war; and yet somehow the locals had understood why that tragedy had unfolded. Liberation by the Americans from the despicable German occupation was an exhilarating event, one that U.S. Army soldiers could hardly understand since they had never endured the mortification of Nazi tyranny in their young lives. But the Bretons' exhibitions of joy upon liberation served to reinforce to the American troops just how precious was freedom and alleviate in some small way the pain of their recent sacrifices on the battlefield. The battered 29th Division was of course a mere speck amid the vast madness that had engulfed the world, and in little more than three months that cataclysm had slaughtered thousands of good 29ers. If there was a purpose to it all, the Bretons—along with all the other recently liberated peoples of the world—had perhaps just revealed it.

Nearly 700 29ers had been killed in action or died of wounds at Brest, and in the last week of September 1944, as the 29th Division prepared to set out for Holland, the realization that those comrades-in-arms must be left behind, buried deep in the soil of Brittany, was painful beyond measure. Two months in the past, on July 20, 1944, Gerhardt had tried to ease such spiritual pain by conducting a memorial service near the little Norman village of La Cambe in honor of those men of the division who had died in Normandy. It had been an incredibly moving episode that no attendee would ever forget, but unhappily there was no time for a repeat performance at Brest. Gerhardt had departed for England shortly after the enemy's surrender, and in his absence, Colonel McDaniel was far too busy planning the exceptionally complex movement of the 29th Division to Holland to contemplate a memorial service. The farewell to the 29ers' departed comrades must therefore be unspoken.

They had American melting-pot names like Fettinger, Glidewell, Addomio, Martinez, O'Leary, and Jazwienski. Some had been fixtures in their National Guard outfits going back to the 29th Division's mobilization in February 1941 and the early training days at Fort Meade. Many more had been replacements who died a lonely, friendless death after only a few days in the line in a faraway place they had never heard of. One, S/Sgt. Sherwood Hallman, would gain immortality by gaining the division's first Medal of Honor since 1918 and come to symbolize both the pride and sorrow of the 29th Division's harrowing eleven-month combat experience in World War II.

All of them, regardless of how they died, had countless relatives and friends back in the States who would grieve, a spiritual ache that in truth would endure for years—or more likely a lifetime. The bodies of many of those 29ers would eventually return home when, after the war, the U.S. government would give next of kin the choice of disinterring their loved ones from the soil of Brittany for reburial in the United States or allowing them to rest permanently in Brittany under the perpetual and tender care of the American Battle Monuments Commission, created by Congress in 1923 to honor the sacrifices of American servicemen in World War I. Those 29ers whose families wished them to remain buried near where they fell in battle would eventually be moved from the division's spartan wartime cemetery near Brest and reinterred just outside the quaint French village of St. James, 140 miles to the east, in a permanent American cemetery dedicated in 1956. Nearly 350 29ers who died at Brest, including Sherwood Hallman, are buried there, a hushed and beautiful place that invariably triggers among visitors solemn contemplation about human life and war's terrible impact upon it—thoughts that for the most part can hardly be spoken. The number of Americans still living who knew and loved those 29ers in the flesh is of course dwindling, but the simple words inscribed on a wall in the antechamber of the cemetery's chapel gently remind American visitors of their responsibility to cherish those soldiers' memories: "In proud remembrance of the achievements of her sons and in humble tribute to their sacrifices, this memorial has been erected by the United States of America."

America's formal memorialization of its war dead could not have begun until World War II finally ended, but in late September 1944, as the 29ers prepared to move on from Brittany to Holland, no one knew when that momentous event would occur. That the Allies would sooner or later bring down Hitler was a detail that all 29ers took for granted, but when exactly that laudable goal would be fulfilled was anybody's guess. Most assumed that victory would come after one more big offensive, an operation any sensible 29er would gladly have passed up had he been given a choice, but in reality, Ike and Bradley badly needed the 29th Division to be a part of what was about to occur. However, what the 29ers—and all American soldiers in Europe for that matter—did not fully grasp was that the enemy was far from dead, and regrettably, much more than one big offensive would be required to finish it all.

The 29th Division had to play its part in that grand finale. There would be more battles, more triumphs and tragedies, more controversies, more cemeteries, and above all more longing among the 29ers to get it all over with and finally head home.

But those are stories for another time.

Appendix I
29th Infantry Division Organization
August 25, 1944

DIVISION HEADQUARTERS
Commanding General   Maj. Gen. Charles Hunter Gerhardt, Jr.

Assistant Division Commander   Col. Leroy Watson

DIVISION STAFF
Chief of Staff	Col. Edward McDaniel
G-1 (Personnel)	Lt. Col. Cooper Rhodes
G-2 (Intelligence)	Lt. Col. Paul Krznarich ("Murphy")
G-3 (Operations)	Lt. Col. William Witte
G-4 (Supply)	Lt. Col. Louis Gosorn

SPECIAL STAFF
Adjutant General	Lt. Col. Robert Archer
Antitank Officer	Maj. Sewell Watts
Civil Affairs	Maj. Asa Gardiner
Chaplain	Lt. Col. Harold Donovan
Chemical Officer	Maj. Newton Cole
Engineer Officer	Lt. Col. Robert Ploger
Finance Officer	Lt. Col. Louis Lucas
HQ Commandant	Maj. Lloyd Marr
Inspector General	Lt. Col. José Castillo
Judge Advocate	Lt. Col. Joseph Howard

Ordnance Officer	Lt. Col. Philip Root
Provost Marshal	Maj. Vern Johnson
Quartermaster	Lt. Col. William Putnam
Signal Officer	Maj. Murray Little
Special Services	Maj. Thomas Dukeheart
Surgeon	Lt. Col. Edward Beacham

DIVISION ARTILLERY

Commanding General	Brig. Gen. William Sands
Executive Officer	Col. H. Ridgely Warfield
110th Field Artillery Battalion	Lt. Col. John P. Cooper
111th Field Artillery Battalion	Lt. Col. David McIntosh
224th Field Artillery Battalion	Lt. Col. Clinton Thurston
227th Field Artillery Battalion	Lt. Col. Neal Harper

DIVISION TROOPS

121st Engineer Combat Battalion	Lt. Col. Robert Ploger
104th Medical Battalion	Lt. Col. Arthur Eriksen

DIVISION SPECIAL TROOPS

Commanding Officer	Maj. Lloyd Marr
29th Cavalry Reconnaissance Troop	Capt. Edward Jones
29th Military Police Platoon	Maj. Vern Johnson
29th Quartermaster Company	Capt. Frank Hines
729th Ordnance Company	Capt. Harold Price
29th Signal Company	Capt. Arba Williamson
29th Division Band	CWO William Fisher

115TH INFANTRY

Commanding Officer	Lt. Col. Louis Smith
Executive Officer	Maj. Harold Perkins
S-3 (Operations)	Maj. William Bruning
1st Battalion	Maj. Glover Johns
2nd Battalion	Lt. Col. Anthony Miller
3rd Battalion	Maj. Randolph Millholland

116TH INFANTRY
Commanding Officer — Col. Philip Dwyer
Executive Officer — Lt. Col. Harold Cassell
S-3 (Operations) — Maj. Maurice Clift
1st Battalion — Maj. James Morris
2nd Battalion — Maj. Charles Cawthon
3rd Battalion — Maj. William Puntenney

175TH INFANTRY
Commanding Officer — Lt. Col. William Purnell
Executive Officer — Lt. Col. Arthur Sheppe
S-3 (Operations) — Capt. Henry Reed
1st Battalion — Lt. Col. Roger Whiteford
2nd Battalion — Maj. Claude Melancon
3rd Battalion — Lt. Col. William Blandford

Appendix II
29th Infantry Division Casualties
August 24–September 19, 1944

AUGUST 24–31, 1944

Unit	Killed	Wounded	Missing
115th Infantry	70	263	0
116th Infantry	63	192	7
175th Infantry	62	274	5
29th Division HQ	0	3	0
29th Division Artillery	0	0	0
110th FA Bn	0	0	0
111th FA Bn	5	2	0
224th FA Bn	4	10	0
227th FA Bn	2	0	1
104th Medical Bn	5	6	0
121st Engineer Bn	1	4	1
29th Signal Co	0	1	0
29th Recon Trp	0	0	0
821st TD Bn	2	5	0
TOTAL	**214**	**760**	**14**

SEPTEMBER 1–19, 1944

Unit	Killed	Wounded	Missing
115th Infantry	120	392	4
116th Infantry	135	588	1
175th Infantry	174	578	11
29th Division HQ	0	0	0
29th Division Artillery	0	2	0
110th FA Bn	1	6	0
111th FA Bn	2	2	0
224th FA Bn	2	3	0
227th FA Bn	0	0	0
104th Medical Bn	0	0	0
121st Engineer Bn	3	7	3
29th Signal Co	0	1	0
29th Recon Trp	1	4	0
141st Regt RAC	3	7	0
709th Tank Bn	24*	63*	5*
821st TD Bn	0	4	0
2nd Ranger Bn	16*	c.80*	0
5th Ranger Bn	24*	113*	0
TOTAL	**505**	**1,850**	**24**
Aug. 24–Sept. 19	719	2,610	38

GRAND TOTAL: 3,367 Casualties

* Aug. 24–Sept. 19, 1944, totals; Ranger and 709th Tank Battalion casualties include those suffered while attached to non–29th Division units.

Appendix III

Medal of Honor Citation
*Staff Sergeant Sherwood H. Hallman
Company F, 175th Infantry, 29th Infantry Division
General Orders No. 31, April 17, 1945*

For conspicuous gallantry and intrepidity at the risk of his life above and beyond the call of duty. On 13 September 1944 [the actual date was September 11], in Brittany, France, the Second Battalion in its attack on the fortified city of Brest was held up by a strongly defended enemy position which had prevented its advance despite repeated attacks extending over a three-day period. Finally, Company F advanced to within several hundred yards of the enemy position but was again halted by intense fire. Realizing that the position must be neutralized without delay, Staff Sergeant Hallman ordered his squad to cover his movements with fire while he advanced alone to a point from which he could make the assault. Without hesitating, Staff Sergeant Hallman leaped over a hedgerow into a sunken road, the central point of the German defenses, which was known to contain an enemy machine-gun position and at least thirty enemy riflemen. Firing his carbine and hurling grenades, Staff Sergeant Hallman, unassisted, killed or wounded four of the enemy, then ordered the remainder to surrender. Immediately twelve of the enemy surrendered and the position was shortly secured by the remainder of his company. Seeing the surrender of this position, about seventy-five of the enemy in the vicinity surrendered, yielding a defensive organization which the battalion, with heavy supporting fires, had been unable to take. This single heroic act on the part of Staff Sergeant Hallman resulted in the immediate advance of the entire battalion for a distance of 2,000 yards to a position from which Fort Keranroux was captured later the same day. Staff Sergeant Hallman's fighting determination and intrepidity in battle exemplify the highest tradition of the armed forces of the United States.

Appendix IV

29, Let's Go

SPECIAL EDITION
Tuesday, September 19, 1944
by Corporal Jean Lowenthal, HQ Company,
29th Division

Brest, France—Systematically and methodically, mile by mile, fort after fort, the gallant men of the 29th Division, commanded by Maj. Gen. Charles H. Gerhardt, have closed in on the fortress of Brest. It has been a violent, severely contested battle. The Blue and Gray has broken through the most heavily defended citadel in Europe. Today we are victorious. Nothing under the sun—the concrete, the steel, all the gigantic four years of bastion-building, nothing has been able to hold us. The forts are smashed. The Germans, in their thousands, are captured. Brest, the greatest harbor in all France, is ours.

The siege has lasted 25 days. Our magnificent artillery has been heaving shells into the enemy every inch of the going; it and the Air Corps have cleared the way for the doughboys, who, in the ultimate end, have gone in to clinch the day.

First to go down in our great series of victories which led to the final liberation of Fortress Brest was Le Conquet Peninsula. And then came Fort Keranroux—the crux of the defense system around the city. The 175th Infantry Regiment mauled that strongpoint mercilessly until it collapsed. It was a terrific undertaking. When Keranroux had been laid to waste, the road suddenly opened. The Nazis had been struck a mortal blow which sent them reeling backwards.

Back to Fort Montbarey, where the 116th Infantry Regiment took over the reins—the men who had led the Allied spearhead onto the beaches and into Normandy. Their gallant actions have multiplied two-fold since that momentous campaign. The 116th surrounded Montbarey and then went past it—and in the end took the fort right down to the last defender. They pushed forward without swerving, without once faltering, and they leaped up in this final battle of Brittany with the same magnificent brilliance as in Normandy.

The final decisive battle was fought by the 115th Infantry Regiment at Recouvrance, the heart and key to the whole defense system at Brest. Ramcke, commander of Fortress Brest, had declared his intentions to fight here until the last man. The 115th was committed to go in and "keep on poopin'" until the Kraut should be driven from his last mammoth ditch, right down to the edge of the water. And this they did. The men of the 115th surmounted the last gigantic obstacle. They took the Hun down in his deep subterranean citadel—down in his submarine pen, the hard core of an underwater fleet that has been the scourge of the ships that sail the seven seas of the world. The culmination of this great day was the end of German resistance in the entire Blue and Gray battle zone. Down in the pens the 115th Infantry bagged 6,000 Germans.

Meanwhile, over in the city proper, the 2nd Battalion, 175th Infantry, led by Maj. Claude C. Melancon, scaled the city wall and cleared the path for the final liberation of Brest itself. This wall was a tremendous barrier. Other U.S. Army troops had been bogged down behind it for almost a week. After Keranroux, the 2nd Battalion, 175th, went down there and jumped the wall—opened the way for the U.S. troops to enter the city.

The final pressure ended at 0745 hours yesterday morning when the commander of the German bulwarks at the *Ecole Navale* (the location of the submarine pens) hoisted his white flag and asked for conditions for surrender. General Gerhardt sent word to the Nazis to "come on out of there and make no bones about it." The enemy accepted these terms.

Your correspondent went in with Maj. Tony Miller and his party when they occupied the fort. It was Major Miller's battalion that had squeezed the last life-breath from the die-hard Nazis at Brest. The terms were settled in a battered house on the main street in St. Pierre. Lt. Col. Louis G. Smith, commander of the 115th Infantry Regiment, presided. The Germans were all spit-and-polish to the end. It was decided that they would form before

Appendix IV

their own pillboxes and march out of the naval fortress into St. Pierre. They were given time to break up their rifles before surrendering.

The place was a shambles when I got there. The fortifications are beyond human comprehension—the majority of them, in spite of the years of constant air bombardment, still stand. Down deep in their lair the Nazis have been living like kings. They have had every conceivable luxury. The submarine pen itself is perhaps the strongest thing of its kind that has ever been constructed by man. I saw General von der Mosel, Admiral Kähler, and Colonel Kroh surrender. General Ramcke has escaped. I saw the cream of the German Navy, Marines, Paratroopers, and Air Corps go down—smashed forever. The 29th Division has scored another historic victory.

Appendix V
Attached Units, 29th Infantry Division
August 25–September 19, 1944

The following VIII Corps, Ninth U.S. Army, and British units were attached to the 29th Infantry Division during all or part of the siege of Brest:

- Company A, 709th Tank Battalion (M4 Sherman)
- B Squadron, 141st Regiment, Royal Armoured Corps, "The Buffs" (Crocodiles)
- Troop A, 86th Cavalry Reconnaissance Squadron (M8 armored car)
- Troop E, 86th Cavalry Reconnaissance Squadron (M8 SP howitzer)
- Companies A and B, 86th Chemical Mortar Battalion (4.2-inch mortar)
- 333rd Field Artillery Battalion (155mm howitzer)
- 557th Field Artillery Battalion (155mm SP gun)
- 771st Field Artillery Battalion (4.5-inch gun)
- 2nd Ranger Battalion
- 5th Ranger Battalion
- 821st Tank Destroyer Battalion (3-inch, towed)
- Company A, 644th Tank Destroyer Battalion (3-inch, SP)

The following U.S. Army field and evacuation hospitals treated wounded from the 29th Infantry Division:

- 53rd Field Hospital
- 100th Evacuation Hospital
- 102nd Evacuation Hospital
- 107th Evacuation Hospital
- 108th Evacuation Hospital

References

The following citations provide the sources from which the firsthand accounts and factual details included in this book were derived. The following examples demonstrate how citations are read:

Eisenhower, *described by Dante,* Eisenhower, *Crusade in Europe,* p. 279.

Thus, in the part of the book in which General Eisenhower is quoted as stating that Normandy "could only be described by Dante," the source for that quote is Eisenhower's book *Crusade in Europe*, page 279. For more details on the book *Crusade in Europe*, consult the bibliography. Here is another example:

Observer, *This job at Brest,* 29ID, WRJ, Aug. 23.

Thus, in the part of the book in which an unnamed observer states, "This job at Brest should not be too hard for all the troops we are getting here," the source for that quote is the 29th Infantry Division Archives, specifically the division's War Room Journal (WRJ) for August 23, 1944. See below for a full list of abbreviations.

Most of the historical information provided in this book was derived from the 29th Infantry Division Archives, managed by the Military Department, State of Maryland, and housed in the Fifth Regiment Armory, 29th Division St., Baltimore, MD, 21201. The abbreviation "29ID" is used in citations to indicate historical details drawn from this source, followed by more specific information detailing the precise location in the archives where those details can be found. For example, "Brest" indicates that the information can be located in the archival boxes pertaining to the siege of Brest; "Personnel" means that the information can be found in the archival boxes containing files on individual 29th Division soldiers.

Original 29th Division maps of the Brest area, many still showing the marks made by soldiers during the battle, were indispensable during the preparation of this book. These maps are also preserved at the 29th Infantry Division Archives.

Please note that whenever a number of 29th Division casualties are referred to in the text, details on those casualties were obtained from the annual histories prepared by all 29th Division units at the end of 1944, all of which provide comprehensive daily lists of killed, wounded, and missing 29th Division personnel. These histories are held at the 29th Infantry Division Archives as well.

Unless noted otherwise, all dates are assumed to be in 1944.

The following abbreviations are used in the citations:

29ID: 29th Infantry Division Archives, Fifth Regiment Armory, Baltimore, MD, 21201; **AAR:** After-action report; **AF:** Air Force; **AG:** Army Group; **AOR:** Army Operational Records (part of NA RG 407); **CI:** Combat Interview files (part of NA RG 407); **CMH:** Center of Military History, Historical Manuscripts Collection, Ft. McNair, Washington D.C.; **DEP:** Dwight Eisenhower Papers, Johns Hopkins University Press; **FA:** Field Artillery; **FFI:** Forces Françaises de l'Intérieur (French Resistance); **FM:** Field Manual; **FRA:** Fifth Regiment Armory, Baltimore, MD; **GO:** General Orders; **G3J:** 29th Division G-3 Journal; **HQ:** Headquarters; **HMSO:** Her Majesty's Stationary Office; **MANG:** Massachusetts National Guard; **MHI:** Military History Institute, Carlisle Barracks, PA; **MDNG:** Maryland National Guard; **NA:** National Archives and Records Administration, College Park, MD; **NAUK:** National Archives, United Kingdom (Kew, Surrey); **n.d.:** No date; **NG:** National Guard; **RAC:** Royal Armoured Corps; **RG:** NA Record Group; **SGGC:** Statements of German Generals in Captivity (from NAUK); **SHAEF:** Supreme Headquarters Allied Expeditionary Force; **TF:** Task force; **USMA:** U.S. Military Academy, West Point, NY; **WO:** War Office; **WRJ:** 29th Division War Room Journal.

ONE: BRITTANY

1. Next Stop: Berlin? (pages 1–3)
Intelligence summary, *The enemy has lost the war,* SHAEF, *Intelligence Summary No. 21,* Aug. 19, 1944, quoted in Hinsley, *British Intelligence in the Second World War,* Vol. 3, Part 2, p. 368. **Eisenhower,** *described by Dante,* Eisenhower, *Crusade in Europe,* p. 279.

2. Take Brest! (pages 3–6)
Brest, Allied control by Aug. 1, 1944, CMH Historical Manuscripts Collection, *Outline of Operation Overlord,* 8-3.4 AA Vol. 7, p. 10. **Brittany,** German strength, Blumenson, *Breakout and Pursuit,* p. 380. **Patton,** *Take Brest,* Grow, "An Epic of Brittany," *Military Review,* Feb. 1947, p. 5. Grow stated the orders were worded "Capture Brest"; Blumenson, who interviewed Grow in 1952, said the phrase was "Take Brest." **Patton,** Montgomery bet, Blumenson, *Breakout and Pursuit,* p. 370. **Grow,** surrender demand, Blumenson, *Breakout and Pursuit,* p. 387. In his article "An Epic of Brittany," Grow stated the German commander was Ramcke, not von der Mosel. **Third Army,** *Brest is ours,* NA, Aug. 6 Third Army Information Services message; quoted in Blumenson, *Breakout and Pursuit,* p. 378.

3. A Question of Strategy (pages 6–8)
29 Let's Go!, *Yanks in Brest!,* 29ID, Aug. 6 *29 Let's Go!* newsletter. **Historian,** *huge military embarrassment,* D'Este, *Patton: A Genius for War,* p. 633. **Eisenhower,** *secure Brittany ports,* DEP, War Years, vol. IV, p. 2,059. **Marshall,** *seizure of Brest,* DEP, War Years, vol. IV, p. 2,063. **Eisenhower,** *greatly accelerated shipments* and *destruction of remaining enemy,* DEP, War Years, vol. IV, p. 2,078.

4. Get Started Now (pages 8–15)
29th Division, addition of quartermaster truck companies, 29ID, 29th Infantry Division AAR, Aug. 1944. **Truck Companies,** details, *FM 101-10 Staff Officers' Field Manual,* p. 163. **29th Recon Troop,** 29ID, 29th Recon Troop AAR, Aug. 1944. **Jones,** quotes, 29ID, Personnel, Jones, *Memoir,* p. 30. **29th Division MPs,** details, 29ID, 29th MP Platoon AAR, Aug. 1944. **Truck Convoys,** details, 29ID, WRJ, Aug. 20–21; *FM 101-10,* Chap. 2, contains details on troop movements by truck. **First Army,** *no troop movements at night,* 29ID, WRJ, Aug. 21. **Gerhardt,** *get started now,* 29ID, WRJ, Aug. 21. **Cooper,** *Almost bumper to bumper,* Cooper, *History of the 110th Field Artillery,* p. 156. **St. James Cemetery,** history,

American Battle Monuments Commission booklet *Brittany American Military Cemetery,* ABMC website, www.abmc.gov/cemeteries/cemeteries/br_base.pdf. **Yeuell,** *The roads were lined,* 29ID, July 8, 1946 letter to Cooper. **Cooper,** *Everyone enjoyed,* Cooper, *110th Field Artillery,* p. 157. **115th Infantry,** *most glorious day,* Binkoski/Plaut, *115th Infantry Regiment in WWII,* p. 119.

5. Summer Soldiers (pages 15–20)
Smith, Purnell, Millholland, careers, Balkoski, *The Maryland National Guard,* pp. 79–80; and FRA, MDNG personnel records. **Watson,** relief and assignment to 29th Division, Bradley, *A General's Life,* p. 281; and Collins, *Lightning Joe,* p. 246. **Eisenhower,** *keep his mouth shut,* DEP, War Years, vol. III, p. 1,838. **Middleton,** *don't like a horse* and career, Price, *Troy H. Middleton: A Biography,* p. 37.

6. A Lousy Place for War (pages 20–25)
2/115, entry into line, 29ID, 115th Infantry Journal, Aug. 23, 1930 hours. **Observer,** *This job at Brest,* 29ID, WRJ, Aug. 23. **German officer,** *wanted to surrender,* 29ID, WRJ, Aug. 26. **St. Malo,** *German soldier does not surrender,* Blumenson, *Breakout and Pursuit,* p. 407. Gen. von Aulock was the German commander.

7. A Pile of Ruins (pages 26–31)
Propaganda leaflet, *Brest is lost,* original copy reproduced in Gawne, *Americans in Brittany: The Battle for Brest,* p. 70. **Ramcke,** *Faithful to the oath,* Gawne, *Americans in Brittany,* p. 73. **Ramcke,** career, POW website, www.powcamp.fsnet.co.uk. **von Thoma,** *fervent Nazi,* NAUK, SGGC, WO 208/4364, CSDIC (UK), GRGG 203, Sept. 26–27. **Ramcke,** *However bad things looked,* NAUK, SGGC, WO 208/4364, CSDIC (UK), GRGG 203, Sept. 26–27. **June 15, 1944,** FFI attack on Ramcke, Le Berre, "L'embuscade du 15 Juin 1944 à Pluméliau," *39/45 Magazine,* Aug. 2003, pp. 8–15; and Whiting, *Hunters from the Sky,* p. 129. **Ramcke,** *three death sentences* and speech, NAUK, SGGC, WO 208/4364, CSDIC (UK), GRGG 228, Nov. 24–26. **Gerhardt,** *They take few prisoners,* 29ID, 29th Division AAR, Aug. 1944, "Highlights of Division Operations and Battle Lessons." **Middleton,** *ruthless,* quoted in Gawne, *Americans in Brittany,* p. 74. **Intelligence report,** *estimate of 16,500,* 29ID, Brest, Folder 9, "Aug. 21 Estimate of the Enemy Situation, Brittany Peninsula." **FFI intelligence,** *40,000 to 50,000,* Cooper, *110th Field Artillery,* p. 167. **Cooper,** *unexpectedly large number of Germans,* 29ID, Brest, Folder 47, Jan. 14, 1947, Cooper letter to Ewing. **Custer,** *He was taken to,* 29ID, WRJ, Aug. 23.

TWO: FORTRESS BREST
1. Tough Going (pages 33–37)
Gerhardt, *good progress,* 29ID, WRJ, Aug. 25. **RAF,** Aug. 25 attack by 334 bombers, Twelfth AG, *Effect of Air Power on Military Operations in Western Europe,* pp. 129–30. **AAF History,** *no material damage,* Craven and Cate, *The Army Air Forces in World War II,* Vol. II, *Torch to Pointblank,* p. 264.

2. Nothing Short of Sensational (pages 37–41)
116th observer, *exceptional fortifications,* NA, RG 407, 29th Division CI, "Fort Keriolet," Box 24035. **115th Infantry,** Aug. 26 attack, 29ID, 115th Infantry AAR, Aug. 1944. **Bohars,** steeple, Cooper, *110th Field Artillery,* p. 158. **Company L,** *Sergeant Snyder,* Binkoski/Plaut, *115th Infantry,* p. 130. **Gentry,** Silver Star citation, 29ID, *115th Infantry 1944 Unit History,* p. 166. **Hedlund,** *Outstanding Incident,* 29ID, 115th Infantry AAR, Aug. 1944; interview with Hedlund, Aug. 2007. **Smith,** *Sorry I can't report,* 29ID, WRJ, Aug. 26. **1/115,** *forward elements,* Binkoski/Plaut, *115th Infantry,* p. 130.

3. Suicide Attack (pages 41–49)
Morris, *routine assignment* and details of 116th Keriolet attack, NA, RG 407, 29th Division CI, "Fort Keriolet," Box 24035. **Witness,** Sgt. Baker and *bleeding from his legs,* 29ID, Personnel, Sgt. Fred Danzig, "Remembering a Day in Brittany: Aug. 27, 1944." **Morris,** career, 29ID, Stapleton, "The Life of Col. James Morris"; and FRA, MDNG personnel records. **Mulligan,** Silver Star, 29ID, Brest, Folder 27, Oct. 9 GO No. 123. **Air Force liaison officer,** *that's very close* and *didn't do us much good,* 29ID, WRJ, Aug. 27. Details on Aug. 27 air strike: 29ID, Brest, Folder 5, "Air Support in Operations Against Brest," list of close support missions. **Müller,** *The position changed hands,* 29ID, Brest, Folder 27, Oct. 30, 1971, Müller letter to German war cemeteries administration.

4. Rubbed Right Off the Map (pages 50–52)
Whiteford, career, Balkoski, *Maryland National Guard,* p. 79; and FRA, MDNG personnel records. **Hill 103,** details, NA, RG 407, 29th Division CI, "Capture of Hill 103," Box 24035; Créac'h, *Plouzané 1944.* **Purnell,** *very important place,* 29ID, WRJ, Aug. 27. **Montrose,** *at the blink of an eye,* 29ID, Personnel, Nov. 23, 1996, Montrose letter to Ewing. **McKee,** *a rather high hill,* "The Story of an Infantry Medic," Mar. 2005, *The Twenty-Niner,* p. 12. **Purnell,** *right off the map,* 29ID, WRJ, Aug. 27.

5. Enter Task Force Sugar (pages 52–58)
Special task force, details, 29ID, Brest, Folder 30, TF Sugar Journal Troop List, p. 1. **Sheppe,** career, *NG Register 1939,* p. 1,339. **Cavalry,** *little opposition was met,* 29 ID, Brest, Folder 30, TF Sugar AAR. **Graf Spee Battery,** *like a rushing wind,* Binkoski/Plaut, *115th Infantry,* p. 129. **Walker,** *made the earth tremble,* 29ID, Walker, *From Vierville to Victory,* p. 85. **Warspite,** Aug. 25 bombardment, Roskill, *The War at Sea: The Offensive,* Part II, p. 132. **Ninth AF,** Aug. 25 bombardment, 29ID, Brest, Folder 5, "Air Support in Operations Against Brest." **Pointe de Corsen,** *50 in number* and *interrupted by their own artillery,* 29 ID, Brest, Folder 30, TF Sugar AAR. **Rudder,** *I am attempting* and *56 Germans have surrendered,* 29ID, Brest, Folder 30, TF Sugar Journal, 0830 and 1000 hours. **Rudder,** *Patrols indicated,* 29 ID, Brest, Folder 30, TF Sugar AAR. **Russians,** *Joseph 351,* 29 ID, Brest, Folder 30, TF Sugar AAR.

6. Marcelle (pages 58–62)
Cooper, *When we first got to Brest* and *dressed in their pathetic best,* 29ID, Brest, Jan. 14, 1947 Cooper letter to Ewing; and Cooper, *110th Field Artillery,* p. 158. **Gerhardt,** *Regiments will maintain,* 29ID, Brest, Folder 4, "Organization and Employment of FFI." **Krznarich,** *our first encounter,* 29ID, Brest, Folder 4, "Estimate of the Enemy Situation." **Bradley,** *array of equipment,* "Bradley Visits HQ Unit of FFI in Brittany," *Baltimore Sun,* byline Sept. 7. **Gerhardt,** *well commanded and quite efficient,* 29ID, Brest, Folder 4, "Organization and Employment of FFI," p. 2. **Faucher,** career, "Bradley Visits FFI," *Baltimore Sun,* byline Sept. 7. **Marcelle Bouyer,** details, Binkoski/Plaut, *115th Infantry,* p. 127; "Marcelle Bouyer," July 1995, *The Twenty-Niner,* p. 4; interview with Raymond Moon, Aug. 2007; 29ID, Personnel, Henry Green.

THREE: THE KEY TO THE WHOLE THING
1. La Trinité (pages 63–69)
Intelligence officer, *Fortress Brest,* 29ID, 29th Division AAR, Aug. 1944, G-2 Summary, p. 5. **Gerhardt,** *Pull out and go around* and *Take over the full front,* 29ID, WRJ, Aug. 27. **115th Infantry,** *The tremendous frontage,* Binkoski/Plaut, *115th Infantry,* p. 132. **Dwyer,** career, Univ. of St. Thomas, St. Paul, MN, Special Collections. **Dwyer,** *portly, taciturn, and stern,* Walker, *From Vierville to Victory,* p. 51. **116th Infantry,** *strange territory,* 29ID, 116th Infantry AAR, Aug. 1944. **Dwyer,** *estimate the situation,* 1947 Dwyer biography, Univ. of St. Thomas, Special Collections. **116th Infantry,** maneuver details, 29ID, 116th Infantry AAR, Aug. 1944.

Walker, *The shifting of the whole regiment,* NA, RG 407, AOR 116th Infantry, "Disengagement in Vicinity of Guilers." **Cawthon,** *The 2nd Battalion had the lead,* Cawthon, *Other Clay,* p. 139. **116th Infantry,** *The resistance put up,* 29ID, 116th Infantry AAR, Aug. 1944. **Puntenney,** *The German paratroopers,* 29ID, Personnel, Puntenney Memoir, p. 85. **Sproul,** career, *General Officers of the Army and Air NG,* Aug. 1966, p. 597. **Puntenney,** *Shortly after Sproul arrived,* 29ID, Personnel, Puntenney Memoir, p. 85. **Gerhardt,** *I think you better fold up,* 29ID, WRJ, Aug. 29. **Cawthon,** *impervious to our guns,* Cawthon, *Other Clay,* p. 139.

2. Hill 103 (pages 69–76)

Hill 103, German defenses, 29ID, *Defenses of Brest: Forts, Strongpoints, Gun Positions,* G-2 section, p. 18. **Purnell,** *key to the whole thing,* 29ID, WRJ, Aug. 28. **175th intelligence officer,** *Enemy positions were well dug in,* 29ID, WRJ, Aug. 28. **175th report,** *much hand-to-hand combat,* NA, RG 407, 29th Division CI, "Capture of Hill 103," Box 24035. **Gerhardt,** *take that hill* and *drive this thing,* 29ID, WRJ, Aug. 28 and 29. **Purnell,** *good deal of organized troops* and *talked it over with Collins,* 29ID, WRJ, Aug. 29. **Bradley,** *Our men hung on,* "Week's Battle to Capture Brest," *Baltimore Sun,* byline Sept. 3. **Purnell,** *doing any good,* 29ID, WRJ, Aug. 29. **Gerhardt,** *got to get somewhere,* 29ID, WRJ, Aug. 29. **175th report,** *Fields of fire were cleared,* NA, RG 407, 29th Division CI, *Hill 103,* Box 24035. **Bradley,** *smell the sour odor,* "Week's Battle to Capture Brest," *Baltimore Sun,* byline Sept. 3. **Purnell,** *rifle company total,* 29ID, WRJ, Aug. 30. **Krznarich,** *We're on it,* 29ID, WRJ, Aug. 30. **Gerhardt,** prohibition against word "counterattack," 29ID, Personnel, Demond, Jan. 2006 interview. **Melnikoff,** German prisoners, 29ID, Personnel, Melnikoff, Mar. 2006 interview; Purnell also mentioned the incident in WRJ. **Ehlert,** *toughest enemy unit,* NA, RG 407, 29th Division CI, "Operations of the 29th Division at Brest," p. 5, Box 24035. **Purnell,** *We fought hard for the hill,* 29ID, WRJ, Aug. 31. **175th report,** *Supply of food,* NA, RG 407, 29th Division CI, "Hill 103," Box 24035. **Bradley,** *hand grenade duel* and *heaviest battleground,* "Week's Battle to Capture Brest," *Baltimore Sun,* byline Sept. 3. **Darby,** Silver Star, 29ID, Brest, Folder 13, Oct. 11 GO No. 125. **86th Chemical Mortar Battalion,** *whispering death,* Medina, "86th Chemical Mortar Battalion: Devotion to Duty," *Army Chemical Review,* July–Dec. 2005, p. 39. **Witte,** *superb job,* NA, RG 407, 29th Division CI, "Reduction of Brest," p. 2, Box 24035. **Purnell,** *Those 4.2 mortars,* 29ID, WRJ, Aug. 31.

3. Feast or Famine (pages 76–89)
VIII Corps, supply, Ruppenthal, *Logistical Support of the Armies,* Vol. I, pp. 529–37; Blumenson, *Breakout and Pursuit,* pp. 635–37; Morison, *The Invasion of France and Germany,* pp. 301–03. **U.S. Army,** classes of supply, *FM 101-10 Staff Officers' Field Manual,* p. 308. **Ruppenthal,** *evidenced the overextension,* Ruppenthal, *Logistical Support,* Vol. I, p. 536. **Hines,** *During this period,* 29ID, 29th Quartermaster Company AAR, Sept. 1944. **VIII Corps,** *supply problem,* 29ID, Brest, Folder 14, "Operations of VIII Corps in the Brittany Peninsula," p. 7. **Supply vessels,** 25 percent capacity, Ruppenthal, *Logistical Support,* Vol. I, p. 532. **LSTs,** unloading of supplies, *Conquer: The Story of Ninth Army,* p. 29. **Middleton,** *Our ammunition situation,* Ruppenthal, *Logistical Support,* Vol. I, p. 532. **Eisenhower,** *increased intensity,* DEP, War Years, vol. IV, p. 2,155. Eisenhower used this phrase in a Sept. 16 cable to Gen. Vandenberg, commander of Ninth AF. **Gerhardt,** *restriction on artillery ammunition,* 29ID, WRJ, Aug. 31. **U.S. Army,** units of fire, *FM 101-10,* p. 318. **Witte,** *upped our artillery ammunition,* 29ID, WRJ, Aug. 31. **Cooper,** *For our service battery,* 29ID, Personnel, Jan. 14, 1947, Cooper letter to Ewing. **Ninth AF,** fighter-bomber support, 29ID, Brest, Folder 14, "Operations of VIII Corps," p. 12. **Eisenhower,** *utilize maximum number,* Blumenson, *Breakout and Pursuit,* p. 644. **Mortar Battalions,** details, Gawne, *Spearheading D-Day,* p. 175. **Witte,** *leaned heavily on heavy mortars,* NA, RG 407, 29th Division CI, "Reduction of Brest," p. 2, Box 24035. **Tank destroyers,** details, *FM 101-10,* pp. 155–56; 29ID, "821st Tank Destroyer Battalion 1944 Unit History." **Cooper,** *Linesmen installed,* Cooper, *110th Field Artillery,* p. 160. **M3 howitzer,** details, 29ID, Personnel, Cooper, 1984 interview. **VIII Corps,** *Ammunition reached such low levels,* 29ID, Brest, Folder 14, "Operations of VIII Corps," p. 12. **SHAEF,** *Getting ammunition,* Ruppenthal, *Logistical Support,* Vol. I, p. 534. **Custer,** *Our Brest operation,* 29ID, WRJ, Sept. 6. **Patton,** *not sanguine,* Patton, *War As I Knew It,* p. 121. **Simpson,** career, USMA, *Roster of Graduates,* Class of 1909. **Simpson,** *What I did,* MHI, 1972 Simpson oral history interview. **VIII Corps,** 25,000 tons, Ruppenthal, *Logistical Support,* Vol. I, p. 535.

4. Schnitzelwerfer Battery (pages 89–98)
Gerhardt, *Our first replacements,* 29ID, "Memoirs of C. H. Gerhardt," p. 49. **Gerhardt,** *get-acquainted period,* 29ID, 29th Division AAR, "Highlights of Division Operations," Aug. 1944. **Gerhardt,** *We needn't send men,* 29ID, WRJ, Aug. 29. **Gerhardt,** *NCOs and officers,* 29ID, 3/115 Journal, Aug. 31, 2045 hours. **Gerhardt,** 29th Division Training Center,

29ID, Training Center AARs, Oct.–Dec. 1944. **115th Infantry,** *G Company rifleman,* Binkoski/Plaut, *115th Infantry,* p. 133. **115th Infantry,** *23-6 in our favor,* 29ID, 115th Infantry Journal, Sept. 2. **Miller,** career, FRA, MDNG personnel records; and 29ID, Sept. 14 *29 Let's Go* newsletter. **Schnitzelwerfer Battery,** details, Binkoski/Plaut, *115th Infantry,* p. 134. This book used the term "Wienerschnitzel Battery"; S. L. A. Marshall, in NA, RG 407, 29th Division CI, "Capture of Kergonant Fort," Box 24035, used "Schnitzelwerfer Battery." A Sept. 9 *29 Let's Go* article used "Wienerschnitzel Patrol." **Rockets,** details; and Root, *The rocket launcher,* 29ID, 29th Division AAR, *29th Division 4.5-inch Rocket Battery,* Sept. 1944; and 29ID, Personnel, Zingelman, Mar. 2006 interview. **Slingshot,** details, Binkoski/Plaut, *115th Infantry,* p. 134. **Bradley,** *well dug in* and *living on iron rations,* "Allied Bombers Pound Brest Defenses," *Baltimore Sun,* byline Sept. 5. **2nd Battalion,** *combat reconnaissance;* and Miller, *cautioned all companies,* 29ID, 2/115 Journal, Aug. 1944. **Historical officer,** *frequently too close,* NA, RG 407, 29th Division CI, "Kergonant Fort," Box 24035. **115th history,** *The original one-man foxhole,* Binkoski/Plaut, *115th Infantry,* p. 133. **Sweeney,** *The low point,* NA, RG 407, 29th Division CI, "Kergonant Fort," Box 24035.

FOUR: HOLDING NOTHING BACK
1. A Fine Day for the Division (pages 99–108)
Bradley, *desolate waste,* "Week's Battle to Capture Brest," *Baltimore Sun,* byline Sept. 3. **175th officer,** *hear German conversation,* 29ID, Brest, Folder 1, Aug. 18, 1980 Carl Hobbs letter to Sherwood Hallman Jr. **224th Field Artillery,** ammunition, 29ID, WRJ, Aug. 30–31. **G-3 Journal,** *very stubborn,* 29ID, G3J, Sept. 1. **Gerhardt,** *wouldn't be too serious,* 29ID, WRJ, Sept. 2. **Purnell,** *got bogged down* and *pretty stiff resistance,* 29ID, WRJ, Sept. 2. **Middleton,** *get around that thing,* 29ID, WRJ, Sept. 2. **3/115,** *speed of the attack,* Binkoski/Plaut, *115th Infantry,* p. 137. **Purnell,** *clear of Jerries,* 29ID, WRJ, Sept. 3. **Gerhardt,** *did swell today* and *marvelous job,* 29ID, WRJ, Sept. 3. **29 Let's Go,** *From here the general,* 29ID, Sept. 4 *29 Let's Go* newsletter. **Gerhardt,** *just contain them,* 29ID, WRJ, Sept. 4. **Middleton,** *mark time again,* 29ID, WRJ, Sept. 4. **Purnell,** *I don't believe,* 29ID, WRJ, Sept. 4. **Gerhardt,** *a night attack,* 29ID, WRJ, Sept. 4. **I/115 and L/115,** *became confused,* Binkoski/Plaut, *115th Infantry,* p. 137. **Reed,** career, FRA, MDNG personnel records. **Reed,** *some small stuff,* 29ID, WRJ, Sept. 5. **Gerhardt,** *We did it,* 29ID, WRJ, Sept. 5. **Sgt. Blechle,** patrols, Binkoski/Plaut, *115th Infantry,* p. 139; and medal citations, *115th 1944 Unit History.* **Millholland,** *an entire platoon,*

29ID, WRJ, Sept. 6. **Sgt. Graves,** patrols, Binkoski/Plaut, *115th Infantry,* p. 139; and 29ID, Sept. 18 *29 Let's Go* newsletter. **3/115,** *marvelous work,* 29ID, 3/115 Journal, Sept. 9. **Bowen,** career, FRA, MDNG personnel records.

2. Victories Monitored by Death (pages 108–27)

Dwyer, *fire from all directions* and *lower in strength,* 29ID, WRJ, Sept. 1-2. **116th Infantry,** *doggedly pushed,* 29ID, 116th Infantry AAR, Sept. 1944. **5th Rangers,** attachment to 29th Division, 29ID, Brest, Folder 29, 5th Ranger Battalion AAR, Sept. 1944. **Sullivan,** career, MANG personnel records, Worcester, MA. **Raaen,** *stickler for discipline,* 29ID, Brest, Folder 29, Feb. 2006 interview with Raaen. **Sullivan,** *morale poor,* 29ID, WRJ, Sept. 2. **5th Rangers,** Ft. Toulbroch attack, 29ID, Brest, Folder 29, 5th Ranger AAR, Sept. 1944; Glassman, *Lead the Way, Rangers,* p. 33; 29ID, WRJ, Sept. 2. **Cooper,** *perfect example,* 29ID, Personnel, Jan. 14, 1947, Cooper letter to Ewing. **Raaen,** *Sully didn't stay,* 29ID, Brest, Folder 29, Feb. 2006 interview with Raaen. **Sullivan,** *having a little trouble,* 29ID, WRJ, Sept. 3. **Gerhardt,** *some FFI* and *POW report,* 29ID, WRJ, Sept. 3–4. **5th Rangers,** Ft. Minou attack and release of Companies A, C, E, 29ID, Brest, Folder 29, 5th Ranger AAR, Sept. 1944. **Gerhardt,** comments on Sullivan, 29ID, WRJ, Sept. 4–5. **Gerhardt,** *experience in command,* 29ID, Brest, Folder 29, Feb. 2006 interview with Raaen. **Gerhardt,** *successful by 10 AM* and *button up,* 29ID, WRJ, Sept. 3. **29th Division,** *artillery concentrations,* 29ID, 29th Division AAR, Sept. 1944. **Arendt,** *dozen or more prisoners,* Arendt, *Midnight of the Soul,* p. 78. **Cawthon,** *microcosm of war,* Cawthon, *Other Clay,* p. 141. **Garcia,** *devastating shell burst,* 29ID, Personnel, Garcia, "Our Company Medic." **Witte,** *What do you think,* 29ID, WRJ, Sept. 4. **Arendt,** *I can still see,* Arendt, *Midnight of the Soul,* p. 95. **1/116,** *The attack was made,* 29ID, *Defenses of Brest,* p. 7. **Carr,** career, 29ID, D-Day, G/116 D-Day roster. **Cawthon,** *picking them off,* Cawthon, *Other Clay,* p. 140. **Clift,** *took care of it,* 29ID, WRJ, Sept. 5. **Faircloth,** death, Cawthon, *Other Clay,* p. 142. **116th Infantry,** casualties and replacements, 29ID, 116th Infantry AAR, Sept. 1944, p. 6. **Operations Journal,** *evidence of enemy withdrawal,* 29ID, G3J, Sept. 7. **Sullivan,** *greatly aided,* 29ID, Brest, Folder 29, 5th Ranger AAR, Sept. 1944. **5th Rangers,** Fts. Mengant and Dellec, 29ID, Brest, Folder 29, 5th Ranger AAR, Sept. 1944, p. 5. **Sullivan,** *These planes are bombing,* 29ID, WRJ, Sept. 5. **Gerhardt,** *I desire to commend,* Glassman, *Lead the Way, Rangers,* p. 39. **Ryle,** *proud of his trim moustache,* Bailey, *Playboys: History of B Squadron, 141st RAC,* p. 2. **Ryle,** *We* *have fifteen tanks,* 29ID, WRJ, Sept. 6. **B Squadron,** history, Bailey, *Playboys;* and 29ID, Brest, Folder 12, Nov. 14, 2005, Snashall letter. **British officer,** *The "Let's Go" boys,* Bailey, *Playboys,* pp. 49–50. **Cobden,** *Crocodiles were unknown,* 29ID, Brest, Folder 12, Cobden, *The Liberation of Brest.* **Marshall,** career, and *cocky,* Pogue, *Pogue's War,* pp. 185–86; Williams, *SLAM: The Influence of SLA Marshall on the U.S. Army,* pp. 5–35. **Marshall,** *never a maelstrom,* Williams, *SLAM,* June 26 Marshall document *Company Interview After Combat,* pp. 99–108. **Marshall,** *He thought my mission,* and *too much time,* Marshall, *Battle at Best,* pp. 45–47. **Marshall,** *What you did,* Williams, *SLAM,* pp. 99–108. **Marshall,** *If fate had eliminated,* Marshall, "First Wave at Omaha Beach," *Atlantic Monthly,* Nov. 1960. **Bingham,** *Everything that was done,* 29ID, Personnel, Jan. 11, 1947, Bingham letter. **Aide,** *intuitive thinker,* Williams, *SLAM,* p. 30. **Fettinger,** career, 29ID, Personnel, Fettinger. **Fettinger,** *best platoon sergeant,* 29ID, Personnel, fall 1944 Keyes letter. **Marshall,** *D-Day hero,* Marshall, "The Forgotten GIs Who Saved D-Day," *Saga Magazine,* June 1964, p. 78. **Fettinger,** *no claims for bravery,* 29ID, Personnel, July 2 Fettinger letter to parents.

3. Bring on the Planes (pages 127–38)
Ramcke, *I assume you will need,* Price, *Middleton,* p. 194. **Middleton,** *the hospital installations,* Price, *Middleton,* p. 195. **Markle,** *no water to speak of,* 29ID, WRJ, Aug. 28. **Paratrooper NCO,** *not overly impressed,* 29ID, Brest, Folder 28, July 28, 2005, DeWiel letter. **Cooper,** *at an observation post,* 29ID, Personnel, Jan. 14, 1947, Cooper letter to Ewing. **Study,** *For months before,* Twelfth AG, *Effect of Air Power,* p. 131. **Prisoner,** *no damage to us,* NA, RG 407, 29th Division CI, Box 24035, "Air Support in Operations Against Brest," p. 6. **Survey,** *The protection afforded* and *beyond their capabilities,* Twelfth AG, *Effect of Air Power,* pp. 131–32. **Paratrooper,** *always something gurgling,* 29ID, Brest, Folder 28, July 28, 2005, DeWiel letter. **Gerhardt,** *insupportable,* 29ID, Personnel, "Memoirs of C. H. Gerhardt," p. 46. **Gerhardt,** *due to changes,* NA, RG 407, 29th Division CI, Box 24035, "Air Support in Operations Against Brest," p. 4. **Ninth AF,** air alert system and *mutual exchange,* Twelfth AG, *Effect of Air Power,* pp. 66–68. **Gerhardt,** quotes on tactical air support, NA, RG 407, 29th Division CI, Box 24035, "Air Support in Operations Against Brest." **Battalion CO,** *Jerry's boots,* NA, RG 407, 29th Division CI, Box 24035, "Air Support in Operations Against Brest," p. 4. **Observer,** *no immediate effect,* NA, RG 407, 29th Division CI, Box 24035, Sept. 18 Robertson letter to Middleton. **Middleton,** *Effective 4 September,* 29ID,

WRJ, Sept. 3. **Air Support Officer,** *We plot the target,* 29ID, Sept. 10 *29 Let's Go* newsletter. **Cooper,** *Within the 29th Division,* 29ID, Personnel, Jan. 14, 1947, Cooper letter to Ewing. **German AA,** details, Cooper, *110th Field Artillery,* p. 161. **Whitman,** details, Cooper, *110th Field Artillery,* p. 162; 29ID, 29th Division Guestbook; H. Bradley, "Maryland Pilot Bails Out," *Baltimore Sun,* byline Sept. 9. **U.S. Army report,** *worked so closely,* Twelfth AG, *Effect of Air Power,* p. 130. **Witte,** *It can be said,* NA, RG 407, 29th Division CI, Box 24035, Sept. 26 XIX Corps G-2 conference. **Wetherell,** *fabulous network,* 29ID, Sept. 10 *29 Let's Go* newsletter. **Johns,** *without the planes,* 29ID, Brest, Folder 5, 1946, Johns letter to Witte. **Gerhardt,** *We have gotten to a point,* 29ID, WRJ, Sept. 1944.

FIVE: SERGEANT HALLMAN
1. Kerrognant (pages 139–55)
2/115, *Battalion notified,* 29ID, 2/115 Journal, Sept. 5, 1152 hours. **Plaut,** *In groups of four,* Binkoski/Plaut, *115th Infantry,* pp. 139–40. **2/115,** *bombing the hell,* 29ID, 2/115 Journal, Sept. 5, 1712 hours. **Ramcke,** *air attacks were appalling,* NAUK, SGGC, WO 208/4364, CSDIC (UK), GRGG 209, Oct. 7–10. **2/115,** *Company E opened fire* and Wimmer patrol, 29ID, 2/115 Journal, Sept. 6. **Warning,** *Treat all civilians,* 29ID, 2/115 Journal, Sept. 6. **Witte,** *Nothing for you to do,* 29ID, WRJ, Sept. 6. **Johns,** *Brest was clearly visible,* 29ID, Brest, Folder 7, 1946, Johns letter to Witte. **Finder,** patrol, Binkoski/Plaut, *115th Infantry,* pp. 141–42. **Miller,** *I'm going to take it,* 29ID, 115th Infantry Journal, Sept. 7, 1055 hours. **2/115,** *captured Beuzic,* 29ID, 2/115 Journal, Sept. 7, 1330 hours. **Carson,** patrol, 29ID, 2/115 Journal, Sept. 7. **Kerrognant,** *cleverly constructed,* NA, RG 407, 29th Division CI, "Capture of Kergonant Fort," Box 24035. **Smith,** *pretty strongly held,* 29ID, WRJ, Sept. 7. **Gerhardt,** *Give them the works,* 29ID, WRJ, Sept. 8. **Company G,** *Beyond the cleared ground* and Kerrognant details, NA, RG 407, 29th Division CI, "Kergonant Fort," Box 24035; and Binkoski/Plaut, *115th Infantry,* pp. 143–44. **Green,** *I was so scared,* 29ID, Personnel, Mar. 2007 interview with Green. **709th Tank Battalion,** *Greater casualties,* Hughes, *331 Days: The Story of the Men of the 709th Tank Battalion,* p. 15. **Company G Witnesses,** *The tank put 75mm shell* and *stunned and helpless,* 29ID, Brest, Folder 10, "Battalion and Small Unit Study No. 3: 2/115 Infantry and the capture of Fort Kergonant," p. 25. **Rideout,** *perfect radio contact,* NA, RG 407, 29th Division CI, "Kergonant Fort," Box 24035. **Company E Witnesses,** *The bazooka man,* NA, RG 407, 29th Division CI, "Kergonant Strongpoint—Company E at Kergonant," Box 24035. **Observer,** *only by*

the German dead, 29ID, "Study No. 3: Fort Kergonant," p. 26. **Miller,** *Have taken Kergonant,* 29ID, 115th Infantry Journal, Sept. 8, 1805 hours. **Gerhardt,** *You sure did fine,* 29ID, WRJ, Sept. 8. **Johns,** *better fields of fire* and *two hours of sharp fighting,* 29ID, Brest, Folder 7, 1946, Johns letter to Witte. **Company C,** German ambulance, Binkoski/Plaut, *115th Infantry,* p. 145. **Pittinger,** career, FRA, MDNG personnel records and *1940 MDNG Yearbook.* **Pittinger,** Silver Star citation, 29ID, Brest, Folder 7. **Smith,** *We are pushing,* 29ID, WRJ, Sept. 8. **Kerguillo,** details, 29ID, *Defenses of Brest,* p. 2. **Company E,** *No one in chateau,* 29ID, 2/115 Journal, Sept. 9. **Miller,** *mission is complete,* 29ID, 115th Infantry Journal, Sept. 9. **Gerhardt,** *best regiment,* 29ID, WRJ, Sept. 11. **Regimental History,** *final stage,* Binkoski/Plaut, *115th Infantry,* p. 145.

2. Kaput! (pages 155–68)
Purnell, quotes, 29ID, WRJ, Sept. 7–10. **Relihan,** deafness, 29ID, Personnel, May 2006 interview with Relihan. **Laninguer,** details, 29ID, *Defenses of Brest,* p. 5. **Hobbs,** *seeing comrades fall,* 29ID, Brest, Folder 1, Aug. 18, 1980, Hobbs letter to Hallman. **Sandner,** *Wiley,* 29ID, Brest, Folder 1, Sept. 13, 1944, letter to Sherman. **Gerhardt,** quotes, 29ID, WRJ, Sept. 10–12. **2/115 staff officer (Lt. Hill),** *quite a few casualties,* 29ID, WRJ, 1740 hours, Sept. 11. **Gerhardt-Smith,** conversations, 29ID, WRJ, 0300 and 0400 hours, Sept. 12. **Rideout-McNulty,** conversation, Binkoski/Plaut, *115th Infantry,* pp. 149–50. **Gerhardt,** *throw the book at them,* 29ID, WRJ, Sept. 11. **Hobbs,** *It was a warm day,* 29ID, Brest, Folder 1, Aug. 18, 1980, Hobbs letter. **Miller,** *a determined man,* "Sherwood Hallman: Medal of Honor," Mar. 1992, *The Twenty-Niner,* p. 18. **Hallman,** life, 29ID, Brest, Folder 1, details from widow, Virginia, and son, Sherwood, Jr. **Hobbs,** *I heard a hand grenade explode,* 29ID, Brest, Folder 1, Aug. 18, 1980, Hobbs letter. **Relihan,** German POW, 29ID, Personnel, May 2006 interview with Relihan. **Hallman,** Medal of Honor citation, U.S. Congress, *Medal of Honor Recipients, 1863–1963,* pp. 863–64. **Purnell,** *busted through,* 29ID, WRJ, Sept. 11. **1st and 29th Divisions,** D-Day awards for valor, Balkoski, *Omaha Beach,* pp. 359–61.

3. From Sugarloaf to Montbarey (pages 168–78)
175th Action Report, *2nd Battalion's position,* 29ID, 175th Infantry AAR, Sept. 1944, p. 2. **Gerhardt,** *wade right through it,* 29ID, WRJ, Sept. 12. **Hobbs,** *no knowledge* and *three of his buddies,* 29ID, Brest, Folder 1, Aug. 18, 1980, Hobbs letter. **Keranroux,** attack details, NA, RG 407, 29th Division CI, "Capture of Fort Keranroux," Box 24035. **Purnell,**

stuck and *veritable fortress,* 29ID, WRJ, Sept. 12–13. **Sugarloaf Hill,** details, 29ID, *Defenses of Brest,* p. 27. **175th Action Report,** *key point,* 29ID, 175th Infantry AAR, Sept. 1944, p. 2. **Gerhardt,** *fine day,* 29ID, WRJ, Sept. 13. **175th Command Post,** *Our Red Battalion,* 29ID, WRJ, Sept. 12. **Gerhardt,** *fold up,* 29ID, WRJ, Sept. 12. **Montbarey,** details, 29ID, *Defenses of Brest,* p. 8. **Azrael,** Pvt. Kahn, "State Men Lead Attack on Brest," *Baltimore News-Post,* byline Sept. 13. **Bruning,** *Company L is in the fort,* 29ID, 115th Journal, Sept. 12, p. 8. **Dallas,** *When we finally blew,* 29ID, Brest, Folder 32, Feb. 24, 1947, Dallas letter to Ewing. **115th History,** *pushed on into the fort,* Binkoski/Plaut, *115th Infantry,* p. 150. **Morrison,** *Everything went smoothly,* Binkoski/Plaut, *115th Infantry,* pp. 150–51. **115th Journal,** *control the situation,* 29ID, 115th Infantry Journal, Sept. 12. **Van Roosen,** *We went around the end,* "Attack on Ft. Montbarey, Brest," Mar. 2000, *The Twenty-Niner,* pp. 32–37. **Bradley,** *continuous rustle,* "Yanks Plow Into Brest," *Baltimore Sun,* byline Sept. 11. **VIII Corps,** messages from Middleton to Ramcke, 29ID, Brest, Folder 2. **Reeves,** truce mission, 29ID, WRJ, 2015 hours, Sept. 13.

4. Tear Them Apart (pages 178–85)
Middleton, *given an opportunity,* Price, *Middleton,* p. 198. **Middleton,** *tear them apart,* 29ID, WRJ, Sept. 13. **Middleton,** *none too good,* Blumenson, *Breakout and Pursuit,* p. 644. **Middleton,** *I told Smith,* 29ID, WRJ, Sept. 11. **Middleton,** *get back into the siege line,* Price, *Middleton,* p. 192. **Hobbs,** *foolish attempt,* 29ID, Brest, Folder 1, Aug. 18, 1980, Hobbs letter. **Bradley,** Keranroux attack, "Bradley Watches Rout of Nazis From Pillbox," *Baltimore Sun,* byline Sept. 14. **Keranroux,** attack details, NA, RG 407, 29th Division CI, "Capture of Fort Keranroux," Box 24035. **Azrael,** *Through the smoke,* "State Men Lead Attack on Brest," *Baltimore News-Post,* byline Sept. 13. **Purnell,** *nothing but a mass,* NA, RG 407, 29th Division CI, "Air Support in Operations Against Brest," Box 24035. **Gerhardt,** *I've asked G-1,* 29ID, WRJ, Sept. 13. **Gerhardt,** 1964 Simpson letter, 29ID, Personnel, "Memoirs of C. H. Gerhardt." **Hobbs,** *We spent the night,* 29ID, Brest, Folder 1, Aug. 18, 1980, Hobbs letter. **Keranroux,** *The action clearly demonstrated,* NA, RG 407, 29th Division CI, "Fort Keranroux," Box 24035. **Liaison officer,** *a little activity,* 29ID, WRJ, Sept. 13. **115th History,** *Effective regrouping,* Binkoski/Plaut, *115th Infantry,* p. 151. **Perkins,** career, *NG Register 1939,* p. 540. **Perkins,** *a lot of air,* 29ID, WRJ, Sept. 13. **Dallas,** *did not compose a line,* 29ID, Brest, Folder 32, "Attack on Montbarey Fort."

SIX: THEY ALSO SERVED
1. Le Conquet Interlude (pages 187–97)
McDaniel, career, *USMA Roster of Graduates, 1982,* p. 359. **Task Force Sugar,** details, NA, RG 407, 29th Division CI, "Operations of TF Sugar," Box 24035. **Gerhardt,** comments to McDaniel, 29ID, WRJ, Aug. 28–29. **29th Division major,** *more trouble,* 29ID, Personnel, Puntenney, *Memoirs,* p. 85. **C/480th AA,** details, 29ID, WRJ, 1118 hours, Sept. 1. **C/480th AA,** *leave its forwardmost guns,* 29ID, Brest, Folder 30, TF Sugar AAR, p. 3. **TF Sugar Journal,** *very much displeased,* 29ID, Brest, Folder 30, TF Sugar Journal, 2015 hours, Sept. 1. **Hill 63,** details, 29ID, Brest, Folder 30, TF Sugar AAR, pp. 3–4. **McDaniel,** *large amount of artillery,* 29ID, Brest, Folder 30, TF Sugar AAR, p. 2. **Baer,** *Hill 63 was a bitch,* Baer, *D For Dog: The Story of a Ranger Company,* p. 55. **Minor,** *captured 29th Division field order,* 29ID, Brest, Folder 30, Oct. 20, 1945, Witte memo. **DeMoss,** *vendetta* and *concussion,* letter, Mar. 1997, *The Twenty-Niner,* p. 46. **Harvey,** *I fired at the German gun,* 29ID, Personnel, Harvey, *Memoirs,* pp. 24–25. **TF Sugar AAR,** *mop up isolated pockets,* 29ID, Brest, Folder 30, TF Sugar AAR, p. 4. **Rudder,** Sept. 3 attack, 29ID, Brest, Folder 30, TF Sugar AAR, p. 4. **Neal,** *firing point-blank,* 29ID, WRJ, Sept. 3. **Gerhardt,** comments on Rudder, 29ID, WRJ, Sept. 3–4. **Middleton,** *finest combat soldiers,* Price, *Middleton,* p. 191. **McDaniel AAR,** *The troops were tired,* NA, RG 407, 29th Division CI, "Operations of TF Sugar," Box 24035. **Puntenney,** *Well dug-in positions,* NA, RG 407, 29th Division CI, "3rd Battalion on Detached Service with TF Sugar," Box 24035. **Gerhardt,** *too slow,* 29ID, WRJ, 1053 hours, Sept. 6. **Gerhardt,** *another backfield,* 29ID, WRJ, 1055 hours, Sept. 7. **Puntenney,** *fine gentleman,* 29ID, Personnel, Puntenney, *Memoirs,* p. 85. **Sept. 8 attack,** details, NA, RG 407, 29th Division CI, "3rd Battalion with TF Sugar," Box 24035. **Snipas,** *careful search* and l'Hotel des Bains, 29ID, Personnel, Snipas, *Memoirs.* **McGrath,** *the town itself,* 29ID, Brest, Folder 30, TF Sugar AAR, p. 7.

2. Rangers Led the Way (pages 197–204)
Gerhardt, comments on Rudder, 29ID, WRJ, 0807 hours, Sept. 9. **Harvey,** *When TF Sugar advanced,* 29ID, Personnel, June 11, 2007, Harvey letter. **Report,** *heavy concrete structure,* 29ID, *Defenses of Brest,* p. 20. **Bradley,** *heavily constructed* and *bespectacled Nazi,* "48 Hours of Artillery Fire Leaves Port of Brest Ablaze," *Baltimore Sun,* byline Sept. 10. **Edlin,** capture of Fürst, Moen, *The Fool Lieutenant,* pp. 160–67.

Ramcke, *old regular soldier,* NAUK, SGGC, WO 208/4363, CSDIC (UK), GRGG 198, p. 7. **Fürst,** *most difficult moment,* NA, RG 319, "266th Infantry Division, June–Aug. 1944," MS P-176, p. 47. **Evans,** *white flag,* 29ID, WRJ, Sept. 9. **5th Rangers Report,** *The enemy surrendered,* 29ID, *Defenses of Brest,* p. 24. **5th Rangers Report,** *The grimness of war,* Glassman, *Lead the Way Rangers,* p. 36. **Maison Blanche, Old Fort,** Sept. 10 attacks, 29ID, Brest, Folder 30, TF Sugar AAR, pp. 7–8. **Gerhardt,** *paratrooper knives,* 29ID, WRJ, Sept. 10. **Gerhardt-Fürst,** meeting, 29ID, Sept. 10 *29 Let's Go* "Extra" newsletter. **Fürst,** signature, 29ID, 29th Division Guestbook.

3. Rommel, Count Your Men (pages 204–11)
Sands, career, *NG Register 1939,* p. 1,340. **Cooper,** *absolute perfection,* Balkoski, *Beyond the Beachhead,* p. 54. **Cooper,** *ground observation* and *"sniping with artillery,"* Cooper, *110th Field Artillery,* p. 159. **Yeuell,** *Every place was an observation post* and *book solution,* 29ID, Personnel, July 8, 1946, Yeuell letter to Cooper. **Cooper,** *battalion operations sergeant,* 29ID, Brest, Folder 47, Jan. 14, 1947, Cooper letter to Ewing. **Montrose,** *Suddenly the entire hillside,* 29ID, Personnel, Nov. 23, 1996, Montrose letter to Ewing. **333rd FA Battalion,** details, Cooper, *110th Field Artillery,* p. 161; and Binkoski/Plaut, *115th Infantry,* p. 131. **771st FA Battalion,** details, Cooper, *110th Field Artillery,* p. 161. **Sewell,** career, FRA, MDNG personnel records.

4. Blue and Gray Sappers (pages 211–15)
Ploger, details, 29ID, Personnel, Sept. 6, 1998, interview with Ploger. **Ploger,** entry, 29ID, 29th Division Guestbook. **121st Action Report,** *important operation* and *prepare pack and pole charges,* 29ID, 121st Engineer AAR, Aug.–Sept. 1944. **British tanker,** *drive and enthusiasm,* Bailey, *Playboys,* p. 50. **Bailey Bridges,** details, *FM 101-10 Staff Officers' Field Manual,* Chap. 7, "Field Engineering Data." **121st Action Report,** *Schu mines,* 29ID, 121st Engineer AAR, Sept. 1944.

SEVEN: BRESTGRAD
1. Crocodiles (pages 217–35)
Leaflets, *cowardly escape,* 29ID, Brest, Folder 2. **von der Mosel,** *bound to stick,* NAUK, SGGC, WO 208/4364, CSDIC (UK), GRGG 202, p. 5, Sept. 23–25. **German Leaflet,** *Soldaten der Festung Brest,* NA, RG 407, 29th Division CI, "G-2 Periodic Report No. 95," Box 24035. **Ramcke,** Iron Cross, NAUK, SGGC, WO 208/4364, CSDIC (UK), GRGG 211, p. 7, Oct.

14–17. **Dallas,** career, *NG Register 1939,* p. 1,338. **Cawthon,** *muted effort,* Cawthon, *Other Clay,* p. 143. **British tanker,** *one of the few,* Bailey, *Playboys,* p. 50. **Dallas,** *best soldier,* 29ID, Brest, Folder 32, "Attack on Montbarey Fort." **Walker,** *cheerful and charming,* 29ID, Walker, *From Vierville to Victory,* p. 88. **Dallas,** *Supporting my battalion,* 29ID, Brest, Folder 32, Feb. 24, 1947, Dallas letter to Ewing. **Intelligence report,** *300-pound naval shells* and *quite dark,* 29ID, Brest, Folder 32, "121-B at Fort Montbarey." **Action report,** *two 8-yard-wide paths* and *detecting was done in three-man teams,* NA, RG 407, 29th Division CI, "Night Clearance of Minefield," Box 24035. **Dwyer,** *too close to the ground,* 29ID, WRJ, 1840 hours, Sept. 13. **Action report,** *The aerial bombardment,* NA, RG 407, 29th Division CI, "Minefield," Box 24035. **121st Engineer account,** *put up a few flares, four-pronged impaling devices,* and *Clemmer was so certain,* 29ID, Brest, Folder 32, "121-B at Fort Montbarey." **Nelson,** Silver Star, 29ID, Brest, Folder 32, Oct. 7 GO No. 121. **Berkowitz,** Silver Star, 29ID, Brest, Folder 32. **British observer,** *Americans had little experience* and Sgt. Humphrey, Bailey, *Playboys,* p. 50. **Dallas,** *opening of the attack,* 29ID, Brest, Folder 32, Feb. 24, 1947, Dallas letter to Ewing. **29er,** *Everything's quiet,* 29ID, WRJ, Sept. 14. **Dallas,** *Company C was engaged,* 29ID, Brest, Folder 32, Feb. 24, 1947, Dallas letter to Ewing. **Adams,** Silver Star, 29ID, Brest, Folder 32, Oct. 31 GO No. 144. **Gerhardt and Watson,** *slow stuff* and *moving very well,* 29ID, WRJ, Sept. 14. **Dallas,** *smoke screen,* 29ID, Brest, Folder 32, Feb. 24, 1947, Dallas letter to Ewing. **German medic,** note, 29ID, WRJ, 1428 hours, Sept. 15. **Crocodiles,** details, 29ID, Brest, Folder 12, "Infantry-Flamethrower Tank Coordination." **Squadron history,** *colossal explosion,* Bailey, *Playboys,* p. 52. **Cobden,** *Morley's tank blew up,* 29ID, Brest, Folder 12, "The Liberation of Brest: A personal account by Maj. Cobden," p. 51. **British tanker,** *superb courage,* Bailey, *Playboys,* p. 51. **121st report,** *buried too deeply,* 29ID, Brest, Folder 32, "121-B at Fort Montbarey." **116th narrative,** *completely terrified,* 29ID, Brest, Folder 32, "Montbarey Fort." **Squadron history,** *through the minefield,* Bailey, *Playboys,* p. 52. **Squadron history,** *tilt of the tank* and *fearsome abandon,* Bailey, *Playboys,* p. 53. **Cobden,** *I found it necessary* and *Things became confused,* 29ID, Brest, Folder 12, "The Liberation of Brest," p. 51. **British observer,** *cool as a cucumber,* Bailey, *Playboys,* p. 59. **Walker,** tankers distraught, Sept. 1997 interview with Walker. **Dallas,** *as bold an act,* 29ID, Brest, Folder 32, "Montbarey Fort." **Squadron history,** *probably a record,* Bailey, *Playboys,* p. 54. **Gerhardt,** *most enthusiastic,* Bailey, *Playboys,* p. 46. **Ward,** Silver Star, 29ID, Brest, Folder 12, Oct. 26 GO No. 139.

2. A Dangerous Place to Be Caught (pages 235–40)
Gerhardt, *carry the division,* Ewing, *29 Let's Go!,* p. 285. **115th Journal,** *very well entrenched,* 29ID, 115th Infantry Journal, Sept. 14. **29er,** *billiard table,* 29ID, Van Roosen, "Attack on Ft. Montbarey, Brest," Mar. 2000, *The Twenty-Niner,* p. 33. **2/115,** *bad spot* and *retake pillbox,* 29ID, 2/115 Journal, Sept. 14-15. **Van Roosen,** *Around the pillbox* and *200 yards from where we were,* 29ID, "Attack on Ft. Montbarey, Brest," Mar. 2000, *The Twenty-Niner,* p. 34. **Rockman,** German behavior towards, 29ID, Van Roosen, "Attack on Ft. Montbarey, Brest," Mar. 2000, *The Twenty-Niner,* p. 34. **Johns,** Sept. 15 attack, 29ID, Brest, Folder 33, 1946, Johns letter to Witte. **Barnum,** *ran out of grenades,* 29ID, Sept. 22 *29 Let's Go* newsletter. **Darby,** Silver Star, 29ID, Brest, Folder 31, Oct. 15 GO No. 128. **Gerhardt,** *can't count on Meeks,* 29ID, WRJ, Sept. 14.

3. I'll Blow You to Hell (pages 241–49)
Dallas, *bit of engineer work,* 29ID, Brest, Folder 32, Feb. 24, 1947, Dallas letter to Ewing. **Smith,** Silver Star, 29ID, Brest, Folder 32, GO Oct. 25. **Squadron history,** *glorious conflagration,* Bailey, *Playboys,* p. 59. **Ewing,** *moat and walls,* Ewing, *29 Let's Go!,* p. 139. **Dallas,** *heavily barricaded,* 29ID, Brest, Folder 32, Dallas letter to Ewing. **Squadron history,** *mad outburst,* Bailey, *Playboys,* p. 60. **Dwyer,** *This gun fired,* 29ID, Brest, Folder 32, Dwyer letter to Ewing. **Gerhardt,** *blow the thing in,* 29ID, WRJ, Sept. 16. **Dallas,** *large enough for a man,* 29ID, Brest, Folder 32, Feb. 24, 1947, Dallas letter to Ewing. **Marshall,** *If you don't stop,* NA, RG 407, 29th Division CI, "Attack on Montbarey Fort," Box 24035. **Dallas,** "Herman the German," 29ID, Brest, Folder 32, Feb. 24, 1947, Dallas letter to Ewing. **Dallas,** surrender message, NA, RG 407, 29th Division CI, "Montbarey Fort," Box 24035. **Watson,** *2,000 pounds,* 29ID, WRJ, Sept. 16. **Ploger,** *personally directed,* 29ID, Brest, Folder 32. **Marshall,** *the three men dropped,* NA, RG 407, 29th Division CI, "121-B at Fort Montbarey," Box 24035. **Marshall,** *Settles' body,* NA, RG 407, 29th Division CI, "Montbarey Fort," Box 24035. **British observer,** *crescendo of flame,* Bailey, *Playboys,* p. 60. **Smith,** *a few bursts,* 29ID, Brest, Folder 32, Oct. 11 Smith letter to father. **Dallas,** German POW, NA, RG 407, 29th Division CI, "Montbarey Fort" and "121-B at Fort Montbarey," Box 24035. **German NCO,** *gangsters,* 29ID, Brest, Folder 32, "Memoirs of Sgt. Ekehard Priller," pp. 41, 44.

EIGHT: GIVING THEM THE WORKS
1. Front and Homeland (pages 251–54)
Lowenthal, Bronze Star, 29ID, 29th Infantry Division AAR, Sept. 1944, "Awards and Decorations." **Lowenthal,** *full-fledged soldier,* 29ID, Sept. 11 *29 Let's Go* newsletter. **Lowenthal,** *hell of a time,* 29ID, Sept. 12 *29 Let's Go* newsletter. **Lowenthal,** *American First Army,* 29ID, Sept. 14 *29 Let's Go* newsletter. **Lowenthal,** *Our American paper,* 29ID, Sept. 11 *29 Let's Go* newsletter.

2. It Seems to Be a Habit (pages 254–64)
Millholland, *stopped by heavy fire,* 29ID, 3/115 Infantry Journal, Sept. 15. **Gerhardt,** *didn't take advantage,* 29ID, WRJ, Sept. 16. **121st Engineer report,** *Each turret was made,* 29ID, *121st Engineers 1944 Unit History,* p. 8. **5th Ranger report,** *Company D advanced,* 29ID, Brest, Folder 29, 5th Rangers AAR, Sept. 1944, p. 10. **Raaen,** *strong as hell,* 29ID, WRJ, 0732 hours, Sept. 16. **Gerhardt,** *snooty* and *spoiled,* 29ID, WRJ, 1022 hours, Sept. 15. **5th Ranger report,** *heavy concentration,* 29ID, Brest, Folder 29, 5th Rangers AAR, Sept. 1944, p. 10. **Sullivan,** *Is there a possibility,* 29ID, WRJ, 2056 and 2126 hours, Sept. 15. **Middleton,** *finish it up tomorrow,* 29ID, WRJ, 1811 hours, Sept. 15. **Johns,** *like a set in Hollywood,* 29ID, Brest, Folder 33, Johns letter to Witte. **G-3 Summary,** *heavy small-arms,* 29ID, G3J, Sept. 16. **115th history,** *front was extremely narrow,* Binkoski/Plaut, *115th Infantry,* pp. 156–57. **Laborde,** pillboxes, 29ID, Personnel, Jan. 2007 interview with Laborde. **Johns,** *did not hurt* and *ripples,* 29ID, Brest, Folder 33, Johns letter to Witte. **Cooper,** *When the first round,* Cooper, *110th Field Artillery,* p. 166. **Johns,** *pretty good shooting,* 29ID, Brest, Folder 33, Johns letter to Witte. **Plaut,** *blasted by shells,* Binkoski/Plaut, *115th Infantry,* p. 162. **2nd Battalion,** *Planes over again,* 29ID, 2/115 Journal, Sept. 17. **Watson,** *Red Cross buildings,* 29ID, WRJ, 1127 hours, Sept. 17. **5th Ranger report,** *At 1506 hours* and *quite nervous,* 29ID, Brest, Folder 29, 5th Rangers AAR, Sept. 1944, p. 12. **Witness,** *explosion came at 2210,* 29ID, Brest, Folder 29, Testimony of 1st Lt. James Greene, "The 5th Ranger Battalion at Ft. Portzic."

3. Good Going (pages 264–77)
2/175, Croix de Guerre, *Army Lineage Book,* Vol. II, p. 503. **Purnell,** decorations, *NG Register 1953,* p. 904. **Watson,** *south of Laninguer,* 29ID, WRJ. **Purnell,** *no dope on the wall* and *quite a few prisoners,* 29ID, WRJ, Sept. 15. **Reed,** *They could see the wall,* 29ID, WRJ, 0700 hours, Sept. 16. **Gerhardt,** *I want to get down,* 29ID, WRJ, Sept. 16. **Azrael,** *Purnell*

seemed to know and *"I had a feeling," "*Purnell Leaves Rich Memories*," Baltimore News American,* June 25, 1971. **Bradley,** *a rifle in one hand* and *heavily fortified passageways,* "The Beginning of the End for Foe," *Baltimore Sun,* byline Sept. 17. **Gerhardt,** *call off the artillery,* 29ID, WRJ, 1945 hours, Sept. 16. **Purnell,** *old medieval walls,* 29ID, WRJ, 2037 hours, Sept. 16. **Gerhardt,** *Hang on!,* 29ID, WRJ, 2145 hours, Sept. 16. **Bradley,** *Far from the tough,* "The Beginning of the End for Foe," *Baltimore Sun,* byline Sept. 17. **Action report,** *necessarily slow,* 29ID, 29th Division AAR, Sept. 1944, p. 7. **Trethewey,** *started forward,* 29ID, Brest, Folder 39, Trethewey letter to Ewing. **Cawthon,** *cordite, dust, and charred wood,* Cawthon, *Other Clay,* p. 144. **Gerhardt,** *It's a nice day,* 29ID, WRJ, 0837 hours, Sept. 17. **Observer,** *There are few buildings,* "40-Foot Walls Shield Stubborn Nazis," Bradley, *Baltimore Sun,* byline Sept. 16. **Puntenney,** *I saw a soldier,* 29ID, Brest, Folder 39, Puntenney memoir. **Witte,** *move the clock back,* 29ID, WRJ, 2333 hours, Sept. 16. **Gerhardt,** *Give them the works!,* 29ID, WRJ, 0837 hours, Sept. 17. **116th Journal,** *heartbreakingly slow,* 29ID, 116th Infantry AAR, Sept. 1944. **Puntenney,** *lifeless stretch,* 29ID, Brest, Folder 39, Puntenney memoir. **Cawthon,** *dwindled by the hour* and *In their presence,* Cawthon, *Other Clay,* p. 144. **Trethewey,** *A German soldier appeared* and *Someone inside the church,* 29ID, Brest, Folder 39, Trethewey letter to Ewing. **Pelchuck,** *looked after his men,* 29ID, Brest, Folder 39, 1994, Pelchuck letter. **Keyes,** *My tour of duty,* 29ID, Brest, Folder 39, Oct. 1944 Keyes letter. **Gerhardt,** *Commit your whole regiment,* 29ID, WRJ, Sept. 17. **Company E comrade,** *Mexican-American,* 29ID, Personnel, John Smith. **Jimenez,** *Germans formed a column,* 29ID, Personnel, Jimenez, Feb. 23, 2000, interview. **Purnell,** *raking in prisoners,* 29ID, WRJ, 1425 hours, Sept. 17. **Intelligence officer,** *administrative troops,* 29ID, 175th Infantry AAR, Sept. 1944, "Enemy Forces Engaged." **Azrael,** *This is to report,* "2 Nazis Give Up To Louis Azrael," *Baltimore News-Post,* byline Sept. 17. **Bradley,** *shabbiest processions,* "The Beginning of the End for Foe," *Baltimore Sun,* byline Sept. 17.

CHAPTER 9: THE TRAGEDY IS COMPLETE
1. Heinies to the End (pages 279–89)
Gerhardt, *no terms,* 29ID, WRJ, 0905 hours, Sept. 18. **Medical officer,** *liquor supplies,* 29ID, Brest, Folder 42, "Operations of the 29th Division at Brest," p. 42. **Plaut,** surrender negotiations, Binkoski/Plaut, *115th Infantry,* pp. 161–63. **Johns,** *I reported this fact,* 29ID, Brest, Folder 33, Johns letter to Witte. **Azrael,** *We saw German soldiers,* "Louis Azrael

Says," *Baltimore News-Post,* Aug. 20, 1945. **Journal,** *Companies E and G,* 29ID, 2/115 Journal, Sept. 18. **Plaut,** *200 or 300 prisoners,* Binkoski/Plaut, *115th Infantry,* p. 162. **Bradley,** *tenser moments* and *stare a moment,* "Baltimoreans See Surrender of Brest," *Baltimore Sun,* byline Sept. 18. **Bradley,** *Who's surrendering here?,* 29ID, Personnel, Bradley, June 17, 2005, interview. **Azrael,** surrender details, "Azrael Sees Surrender At Brest," *Baltimore News-Post,* n.d. **Ramcke,** *poor, deaf, dull-witted,* NAUK, SGGC, WO 208/4364, CSDIC (UK), GRGG 211, Oct. 14–17. **Journal,** *groups of hundreds,* 29ID, 2/115 Journal, Sept. 18. **Johnson,** *generally of a higher type,* 29ID, 29th MP Platoon AAR, Sept. 1944. **Azrael,** *no note of regret,* "Azrael Sees Surrender At Brest," *Baltimore News-Post,* n.d. **Cawthon,** *No Stalingrad,* Cawthon, *Other Clay,* p. 145. **Ramcke,** *sat in a shelter,* NAUK, SGGC, WO 208/4364, CSDIC (UK), GRGG 211, Oct. 14–17. **Ewing,** *It was a rebuff,* Ewing, *29 Let's Go!,* p. 283. **Gerhardt,** *We asked those fellas,* 29ID, WRJ, 1725 hours, Sept. 18. **von der Mosel and Kähler,** *Just wait and see,* NAUK, SGGC, WO 208/4364, CSDIC (UK), GRGG 205, Sept. 29–Oct. 1.

2. The Fruits of Victory (pages 289–96)
Plaut, *discarded everything,* Ewing, *29 Let's Go!,* p. 147. **Henne,** *stunned,* 29ID, Henne letter, Mar. 2000, *The Twenty-Niner,* p. 39. **Trethewey,** *Looking around,* 29ID, Brest, Folder 39, Trethewey letter to Ewing. **Walker,** *big and portly,* 29ID, Walker, *From Vierville to Victory,* pp. 90–91. **Lowenthal,** *not a human emotion,* 29ID, Sept. 21 *29 Let's Go* newsletter. **Eisenhower,** *I am happy to report,* DDE, *War Years,* Vol. IV, p. 2,131. **Krznarich,** *The Germans reported,* 29ID, Brest, Folder 14, Sept. 8 Krznarich letter. **Ramcke,** *I had the houses,* NAUK, SGGC, WO 208/4363, CSDIC (UK), GRGG 198. **Plaut,** *When word reached the rear* and *any but their own,* Binkoski/Plaut, *115th Infantry,* p. 164. **Steele,** visit to sub pens, 29ID, Personnel, interview with Steele, Oct. 2000. **Liaison officer (Custer),** *Two car loads of liquor,* 29ID, WRJ, 2015 hours, Sept. 17. **Lowenthal,** *perhaps the strongest thing,* 29ID, Sept. 19 *29 Let's Go-Extra* newsletter. **Azrael,** *Over 600 wounded,* "Azrael Sees Surrender At Brest," *Baltimore News-Post,* n.d. **Report,** *5,500 prisoners,* 29ID, Brest, Folder 14, "VIII Corps in Brittany."

3. Limestone Cove (pages 296–305)
Morris, *just finished a tough job,* 29ID, Stapleton, *The Life of Col. James Morris,* p. 58. **Gerhardt,** *locked up since May,* 29ID, WRJ, 0920 hours, Sept. 19. **Gerhardt,** *Have you read the PWI report,* 29ID, WRJ, Sept. 18.

Gerhardt, *The reason we were beaten,* Marshall, "Souvenirs: An Incident After Battle," *Infantry,* Mar.–Apr. 1970, pp. 50–51. **Division headquarters,** *Recaptured Americans,* 29ID, 115th Infantry S-2 Journal, Sept. 17, Lt. Col. Rhodes message. **Van Roosen,** *We were deposited* and *maintained our position,* "Attack on Ft. Montbarey, Brest," Mar. 2000, *The Twenty-Niner,* p. 36. **Witness,** *several tried to arise,* Marshall, "Souvenirs: An Incident After Battle," *Infantry,* Mar.–Apr. 1970, p. 50. **Lowenthal,** *Doggedly,* 29ID, Sept. 23 *29 Let's Go* newsletter. **Staff officer,** *well satisfied with the work,* 29ID, Brest, Folder 42, "Operations of the 29th Division at Brest," pp. 28–29. **Plaut,** *The night of September 18–19,* Binkoski/Plaut, *115th Infantry,* pp. 164–65. **Cooper,** *Everyone expected* and *the cannoneers passed,* Cooper, *110th Field Artillery,* p. 168. **Plaut,** *previous rest periods,* Binkoski/Plaut, *115th Infantry,* p. 167. **29 Let's Go,** Limestone Cove, 29ID, Sept. 21 *29 Let's Go* newsletter. **Cooper,** *first social affair,* Cooper, *110th Field Artillery,* p. 168. **Cawthon,** *The French girls,* Cawthon, *Other Clay,* p. 147.

4. Blue and Gray Riding Academy (pages 305–11)
Cooper, *standards and guidons flying,* Cooper, *110th Field Artillery,* p. 169. **Shelley,** *Some jackass,* 29ID, Personnel, Johnson. **B/104,** details on personnel, 29ID, Personnel, Shelley. **Gerhardt,** *Riding Academy,* 29ID, WRJ, Sept. 18. **McMullen,** *shuttling GIs,* 29ID, Personnel, June 13, 2005, interview with McMullen. **Gerhardt,** *take a bath,* 29ID, WRJ, 1018 hours, Sept. 16.

TEN: HERE ARE OUR CREDENTIALS
1. You'll End Up in Hollywood (pages 313–17)
General (von Thoma), *look after number one,* NAUK, SGGC, WO 208/4364, CSDIC (UK), GRGG 203, Sept. 26–27. **Ramcke,** *the Führer wanted* and *no embrasures,* NAUK, SGGC, WO 208/4363, CSDIC (UK), GRGG 198, p. 2. **War Room Journal,** *Unidentified seaplane,* 29ID, WRJ, 1119 hours, Sept. 18. **Canham,** *These are my credentials, The Story of the 8th Infantry Division,* p. 1. **Ramcke,** *played a big trick,* NAUK, SGGC, WO 208/4363, CSDIC (UK), GRGG 198, pp. 3–4. **Officer,** *conceited Nazi,* NAUK, SGGC, WO 208/4363, CSDIC (UK), GRGG 198, p. 2. **Custer,** Ramcke-Middleton meeting, 29ID, WRJ, 1135 hours, Sept. 20. **Ramcke,** *go down with honor,* NAUK, SGGC, WO 208/4364, CSDIC (UK), GRGG 201, Sept. 24–27, p. 7.

2. Enthusiasm versus Judgment (pages 317–30)
Gerhardt, *furloughs,* 29ID, WRJ, 0920 hours, Sept. 19. **Gerhardt,** *the leave business,* 29ID, WRJ, Sept. 19. **Cooper,** *worked feverishly,* Cooper, *110th Field Artillery,* p. 169. **Cawthon,** *depended on the riflemen,* Cawthon, *Other Clay,* p. 146. **Gerhardt,** *my artillery commander,* 29ID, WRJ, 1806 hours, Sept. 19. **McDaniel,** *Ninth Army informed me,* 29ID, WRJ, Sept. 20. **Simpson,** meeting in Paris, MHI, *Simpson Diary,* Sept. 20. **Rhodes,** *The chief of staff,* 29ID, WRJ, 1146 hours, Sept. 20. **Moore,** *talked to the big boss,* 29ID, WRJ, Sept. 22. **McDaniel,** *return at once,* 29ID, WRJ, 1225 hours, Sept. 22. **Thrasher,** *So far unable,* 29ID, WRJ, Sept. 24. **Witte,** *combination rail and motor,* 29ID, WRJ, Sept. 20. **Gosorn,** *get us moving,* 29ID, WRJ, 0845 hours, Sept. 21. **Gerow,** *war with Germany,* 29ID, "V Corps Operations in the ETO," p. 256. **MacDonald,** *From the British front,* MacDonald, *The Siegfried Line Campaign,* p. 115. **Orders,** *Move 29th Division,* 29ID, WRJ, Sept. 22. **Gosorn,** *The truck movement,* 29ID, WRJ, 1936 hours, Sept. 21. **Moore,** *wanted recommendations,* 29ID, WRJ, 2400 hours, Sept. 21. **Thrasher,** *has received the info,* 29ID, WRJ, 1415 hours, Sept. 24. **Bradley,** *exceeded his judgment,* Bradley, *A Soldier's Story,* p. 236.

3. What the Future May Bring Forth (pages 330–43)
Eisenhower, *When at last,* Eisenhower, *Report by the Supreme Commander to the Combined Chiefs of Staff,* p. 46. **U.S. Navy,** Brest survey, Ruppenthal, *Logistical Support of the Armies,* Vol. II, p. 52. **D'Este,** *Brittany became a monument,* D'Este, *Eisenhower: A Soldier's Life,* p. 565. **Bradley,** *This costly siege,* Bradley, *A Soldier's Story,* p. 366. **Eisenhower,** Sept. 9 report, DEP, War Years, vol. IV, p. 2,126. **Eisenhower,** September 13 cable, DEP, War Years, vol. IV, p. 2,137. **Bradley,** *might well have been advised,* Bradley, *A General's Life,* p. 305. **Patton,** *quite a conversation,* Patton, *War As I Knew It,* p. 128. **Bradley,** *We must take Brest,* Blumenson, *The Patton Papers: 1940–1945,* p. 532. **Ruppenthal,** *not yet ready to abandon Brest* and *given the lowest priority,* Ruppenthal, *Logistical Support of the Armies,* Vol. II, pp. 51–52. **Weigley,** *excessively cautious,* Weigley, *Eisenhower's Lieutenants,* p. 286. **D'Este,** *military embarrassment,* D'Este, *Patton: A Genius for War,* p. 633. **Blumenson,** *problem of port capacity,* Blumenson, *Breakout and Pursuit,* p. 656. **Montgomery,** *thrust toward Berlin,* DEP, War Years, vol. IV, p. 2,120. **Marshall,** *By September 5,* Marshall, *Biennial Reports of the Chief of Staff,* p. 139. **Tedder,** *Eisen-*

hower was confirmed, Tedder, *With Prejudice,* p. 591. **Cunningham,** *an oasis in the Sahara,* Cunningham, *A Sailor's Odyssey,* p. 609. **Eisenhower,** *hostile occupation in force,* DEP, War Years, vol. IV, p. 2,126. **Ramsay,** *Antwerp is highly vulnerable,* Ellis, *Victory in the West,* Vol. II, p. 5. **Eisenhower,** *Some of these writers,* DEP, War Years, vol. IV, p. 2,060. **Churchill,** *Unless the situation changes,* Churchill, *Triumph and Tragedy,* pp. 195–96.

4. In Humble Tribute (pages 343–47)
Middleton, *savage fight,* 29ID, Brest, Folder 14, "Fortress Brest." **Simpson,** *very unusual chapter,* 29ID, Brest, Folder 14, "Fortress Brest." **NY Times,** *Beaming,* "36,389 Prisoners Captured in Brest," *New York Times,* Sept. 24. **Middleton,** *2nd Parachute Division,* 29ID, Brest, Folder 14, Sept. 19 message. **Churchill,** *consolidating effect,* Churchill, *Triumph and Tragedy,* p. 196.

Bibliography

Anonymous. *These Are My Credentials: The Story of the 8th Infantry Division.* Paris: Stars and Stripes, 1944.
Arendt, William. *Midnight of the Soul.* Omaha: PRA, Inc, 2000.
Baer, Alfred. *D for Dog: The Story of a Ranger Company.* Memphis: Private Publication, 1946.
Bailey, Harry. *Playboys: A History of B Squadron, 141st Regiment Royal Armoured Corps (The Buffs).* UK: Private Publication, n.d.
Balkoski, Joseph. *Beyond the Beachhead: The 29th Infantry Division in Normandy.* Harrisburg, PA: Stackpole, 1989.
———. *The Maryland National Guard: A History of Maryland's Military Forces.* Baltimore: Maryland Military Historical Society, 1991.
———. *Omaha Beach: D-Day, June 6, 1944.* Mechanicsburg, PA: Stackpole, 2004.
Barnes, John. *Fragments of My Life with Company A, 116th Infantry.* New York: JAM, 2000.
Binkoski, Joseph, and Arthur Plaut. *The 115th Infantry Regiment in World War II.* Nashville: Battery Press, 1988.
Black, Col. Robert. *The Battalion: The Dramatic Story of the 2nd Ranger Battalion in World War II.* Mechanicsburg, PA: Stackpole, 2006.
Bland, Larry, ed. *The Papers of George Catlett Marshall,* vols. 3 and 4. Baltimore: Johns Hopkins, 1991.
Blumenson, Martin. *Breakout and Pursuit.* Washington: Office of the Chief of Military History, 1961.
———. *The Patton Papers, 1940–1945.* Boston: Houghton Mifflin, 1974.
Bradley, Omar. *A Soldier's Story.* New York: Henry Holt, 1951.

Bradley, Omar, and Clay Blair. *A General's Life.* New York: Simon and Schuster, 1983.
Brewer, James. *History of the 175th Infantry (Fifth Maryland).* Baltimore: Maryland Historical Society, 1955.
Cawthon, Charles. *Other Clay.* Niwot: University Press of Colorado, 1990.
Chandler, Alfred, ed. *The Papers of Dwight David Eisenhower: The War Years.* Baltimore: Johns Hopkins, 1970.
Churchill, Winston. *Triumph and Tragedy.* Boston: Houghton Mifflin, 1953.
Collins, J. Lawton. *Lightning Joe: An Autobiography.* Baton Rouge: LSU Press, 1979.
Cooper, John. *History of the 110th Field Artillery.* Baltimore: Maryland Historical Society, 1953.
Craven, Wesley, and James Cate. *The Army Air Forces in WWII,* vol. 3, Europe: Argument to V-E Day. Chicago: University of Chicago, 1951.
Créac'h, Yannick, and Francoise Floury. *Plouzané 1944.* Plouzané: Private publication, n.d.
Cunningham, Andrew. *A Sailor's Odyssey.* New York: Dutton, 1951.
D'Este, Carlo. *Decision in Normandy.* London: William Collins, 1983.
———. *Eisenhower: A Soldier's Life.* New York: Henry Holt, 2002.
———. *Patton: A Genius for War.* New York: HarperCollins, 1995.
Eisenhower, Dwight. *Crusade in Europe.* New York: Doubleday, 1948.
———. *Report by the Supreme Commander to the Combined Chiefs of Staff on the Operations in Europe of the Allied Expeditionary Force, 6 June 1944 to 8 May 1945.* Washington: CMH, 1994.
Ellis, L. F. *Victory in the West,* Vol. II. London: HMSO, 1968.
Ewing, Joseph. *29 Let's Go!* Washington: Infantry Journal Press, 1948.
Gawne, Jonathan. *1944: Americans in Brittany, The Battle for Brest.* Paris: Histoire & Collections, 2002.
———. *Spearheading D-Day.* Paris: Histoire & Collections, 1998.
Glassman, Henry. *"Lead the Way, Rangers": A History of the 5th Ranger Battalion.* Munich, Germany: 5th Ranger Battalion, 1945.
Grow, Robert. "An Epic of Brittany," *Military Review,* Feb. 1947.
Hinsley, F. H. *British Intelligence in the Second World War,* vol. III, pt. 2. London: HMSO, 1984.
Hughes, Dale. *331 Days: The Story of the Men of the 709th Tank Battalion.* Tucson: Private publication, 1980.
Le Berre, Alain. "L'embuscade du 15 Juin 1944 à Pluméliau ou les Malheurs du Général Ramcke," *39/45 Magazine,* Aug. 2003.

MacDonald, Charles. *The Siegfried Line Campaign.* Washington: Office of the Chief of Military History, 1963.
Mahon, John. *The Army Lineage Book, Vol. II: Infantry.* Washington: Office of the Chief of Military History, 1953.
Marshall, George. *Biennial Reports of the Chief of Staff of the U.S. Army to the Secretary of War, 1 July 1939–30 June 1945.* Washington: CMH, 2001.
Marshall, S. L. A. *Battle at Best.* New York: William Morrow, 1964.
Maryland National Guard. *Historical and Pictorial Review of the National Guard and Naval Militia of the U.S., State of Maryland, 1940.* Baton Rouge: Army and Navy, 1940.
Moen, Marcia, and Margo Heinen. *The Fool Lieutenant.* Elk River, Minnesota: Meadowlark, 2002.
Morison, Samuel E. *The Invasion of France and Germany, 1944–1945.* Boston: Little Brown, 1962.
Parker, Theodore, and William Thompson. *Conquer: The Story of Ninth Army.* Nashville: Battery Press, 1993.
Patton, George. *War As I Knew It.* New York: Pyramid, 1966.
Pogue, Forrest. *Pogue's War: Diaries of a WWII Combat Historian.* Lexington: University Press of Kentucky, 2001.
———. *The Supreme Command.* Washington: Office of the Chief of Military History, 1954.
Price, Frank. *Troy H. Middleton: A Biography.* Baton Rouge: LSU Press, 1974.
Roskill, S. W. *The War at Sea: The Offensive,* Vol. III, Part 2. London: HMSO, 1961.
Ruppenthal, Roland. *Logistical Support of the Armies,* Vols. I and II. Washington: Office of the Chief of Military History, 1959.
Stanton, Shelby. *WWII Order of Battle.* New York: Galahad, 1984.
Stapleton, Gregory. *Out in Front All the Way: Lt. Col. James S. Morris.* Kentucky: Private publication, 2006.
Tedder, Arthur. *With Prejudice.* Boston: Little, Brown, 1966.
Twelfth U.S. Army Group. *Effect of Air Power on Military Operations in Western Europe.* Wiesbaden, Germany: Twelfth Army Group, 1945.
U.S. Congress. *Medal of Honor Recipients, 1863–1963.* Washington: Government Printing Office, 1964.
U.S. Military Academy. *Roster of Graduates and Former Cadets, 1982.* West Point: Association of Graduates, 1982.

Walker, Robert. *From Vierville to Victory: With the Stonewallers of the 116th Infantry.* Los Angeles: Private publication, 1998.

Weigley, Russell. *Eisenhower's Lieutenants.* Bloomington: Indiana University Press, 1981.

Whiting, Charles. *Hunters from the Sky: The German Parachute Corps.* London: Leo Cooper, 1974.

Wilkerson, Edgar. *V Corps Operations in the ETO.* Germany: V Corps, 1945.

Williams, F. D. G. *SLAM: The Influence of S. L. A. Marshall on the U.S. Army.* Washington: CMH, 1999.

Wilmot, Chester. *The Struggle for Europe.* London: Collins, 1952.

Index

Page numbers in italics indicate maps

Abramson, Sorrel, 261
Adams, Joseph, 228
Addomio, Nick, 144
aircraft, 131
American Battle Monuments
 Commission, 346
ammunition
 shortages, 76–89, 107–8
 unit of fire, 83
Antwerp, 340–41
Arbury, Howard, 85
Arendt, William, 114, 116
Arnold, Edgar, 57–58
artillery tactics, 205
Ashlock, Willard, 115
Aust, Richard, 263
Azrael, Lou, 172, 181, 266, 277, 283, 284, 287
 on German wounded, 295–96

Baer, Al, 191
Bailey bridge, 213–14
Baker, Samuel, 44
Baltimore News-Post, 172, 181, 266, 277

Baltimore Sun, 60, 136, 174, 266
Barnes, Hubert, 209
Barnum, Bruce, 239
Becker, William, 307
Berkowitz, William, 226
Beuzit, village of, 146
Bingham, Sidney, 125–26
Blandford, William, 71, 100, 265
 at Keriolet, 157–58
Blechle, Francis, 106
Blumenson, Martin, on Brest
 campaign, 338
Bohars church, destruction of, 38–39
Bouyer, Marcelle, 61–62
Bowen, Millard, 107, 158, 160, 164
Boyd, Robert, 93, 284
Bradford, Paul, 208
Bradley, Holbrook, 60, 99, 136, 181, 199, 266–67, 283
 on German spiritual collapse, 174–76
 on Hill 103 attack, 72, 73
 on march of German troops into captivity, 277
Bradley, Omar, 2, 18–19, 79, 205, 319, 320, 328

on Brest campaign, 334, 335
Brest campaign strategy, 6–8
view of Gerhardt, 328
Breher, William, 200
Brest
air bombardment of, 129–38
civilians, 58–59
destruction of, 291, 292
environs, 20–25
population of, 22
terrain, 25
Brest campaign, 3–6, 22
air support, 127–38
analysis of, 331–43
casualties, 128, 185, 346
enemy's defenses during, 37–41
German surrender, 280–89
opening day of, 33–37
second day of attack, 37–41
strategy, 6–8
suicide attack, 41–49
see also individual battles
Brittany
geography of, 11
inhabitants of, 11
route from Normandy to, *10*
see also Brest campaign
Bruning, William, 146, 173
Burke, Edward, 86
Butler, Edmund, 113

Canham, Charles, 125
phrase coined by, 315
Ramcke capture, 314–16
Carr, Wilson, 116–18
Carson, Delmar, 146–47
Cassel, Harold, 319
Cawthon, Charles, 65, 114, 222, 268, 287, 304, 319
at Recouvrance, 270–73
Chadwick, Arthur, 237

Churchill, Winston, 343, 345
Clare, George, 232
Clayton, George (Tommy), 39
Clemmer, Shelton, mine clearing, 224–27
Clift, Maurice, 118
Coatuélen, 163
Cobden, Harry, 227, 233–34
Collins, Joseph Lawton, 18, 329
Collins, Sherwood, 71
COM-Z, 79
Cooper, John, 31, 129, 206–8, 261, 301, 319
on Brest civilians, 58–59
Corlett, Charles, 326–27
Cota, "Dutch," 15
Courtney, William, 200
Cowe, Albert, 234
Cox, Robert, 173
Cuff, Robert, 319
Custer, Charles, 31, 87, 316

Dallas, Thomas, 173, 185, 268, 274
at Fort Montbarey, 222–35, 241–49
Darby, Grant, 75, 239
DeMoss, Herman, 193
Dennis, Sheldon W., 303
D'Este, Carlo, 337–38
Donovan, Harold, 207, 310-11
Dwyer, Philip, 42, 225, 244, 290
at Fort Montbarey, 268
at La Trinité, 64–69, 108, 114–16

École Navale, *see* French Naval Academy
Edlin, Robert, capture of Fürst, 199–200
Ehlert, Siegfried, 74
Eighth Air Force, Kerrognant air attacks, 140–43
VIII Corps, Third Army affiliation, 79

Index

8th Infantry Division, 6
  Ramcke capture at Pointe des Capucins, 313
86th Cavalry Reconnaissance Squadron, Troop F, 194
86th Chemical Mortar Battalion, 228
  Company A, at Fort Keranroux, 181
  Company A, at Hill 103, 75–76
821st Tank Destroyer Battalion, 85–86
Eisenhower, Dwight, 8
  Antwerp and, 340–41
  decision not to use Brest as port, 331–43
  Operation Overlord and, 330–31
Europe, Northwest, *4*
Evans, John, 201
Ewing, Joseph, 223, 242, 288

Faircloth, Elmer, 118
Faucher, Baptiste, *see* Louis, Commandant
Felty, Carlton, 151
Fettinger, Theodore, 126–27
  at Recouvrance, 273–74
FFI, *see* French Resistance
5th Ranger Battalion, 109–13, 221
  destroying pillboxes, 263
  at Fort du Dellec, 120
  at Fort du Mengant, 119–20
  at Fort du Portzic, 120, 255–64
  at Fort La Maison Blanche, 202–3
  La Trinité and Coastal Forts positions, *117*
  at Le Conquet, 202
  September 14, 1944 positions, *219*
  September 15–17, 1944 positions, *259*
Finder, Sergeant, 146
Flöter, First Lieutenant, 241
Floyd, Dudley, 148, 149
Fogelsanger, John, 226

Fort du Dellec, 120
Fort du Mengant, 119–20
Fort du Portzic, 120, 221, 255–64, 263
Fort Keranroux, 180–83, 264
Fort La Maison Blanche, 202–3
Fort Minou, 112–13
Fort Montbarey, 171–78, 184–85, 221–35, 268
  assault on, *229*
  capture of, 241–49
  destruction of, 247–48
Fort Penfeld, 152–53
Fort Toulbroch, 111–12
480th Anti-Aircraft Artillery Battalion, Company C, at Le Conquet, 190–91
French Naval Academy, 262
  surrender of Germans at, 281–89
French Resistance, 28, 29–30, 59–62
friendly fire, 257–58
Frudd, A., 234
Fuller, J. F. C., 123
furloughs, 318–19
Fürst, Martin, 187, 288
  capture and surrender of, 199–202
  formal surrender ceremony of, 203
  Gerhardt meeting, 203–4

Garcia, Robert, 115
Garner, Harry, 307
Gawler, John, 202
Gentry, Dwight, 39–40
Gerhardt, Charles Hunter, Jr., 19, 241, 258
  advancing 29th Infantry Division to Brest, 8–15
  August 26th scheme of attack, 38
  Bradley's view of, 328
  captured men incident, 236–37, 297–99
  commenting on his troops, 299

favorite regiments of, 264
on 5th Ranger Battalion, 120–21
Fort Montbarey and, 168–78
on French Resistance, 61
furlough incident, 319–21, 327–30
Fürst meeting, 203–4
Germans refusal to sign guest book of, 288
Graf Spee Battery and, 52–58
guest book, 204
Hill 103 and, 69–76, 99–102
Ilioc and, 104–6, 159–60
issuing furloughs, 318–19
Le Conquet peninsula and, 187–97
Lowenthal relationship, 251–52
Middleton relationship, 178–83
opening day plan, 34
postwar career of, 328–29
replacement policy, 90–92
returns to headquarters, 327
"Riding Academy," 309–11, 317–18
on Rudder, 197–98
strategy on fourth day, 64
Sugarloaf Hill and, 168–78
surrender terms of, 279–80
29th Division Training Center, 91–92
on 29th's leaders, 15–17
Gerow, Leonard, 323
Glidewell, Ambers, 173, 174
Goebbels, Josef, 127
Gombosi, Louis, 111
Gondek, Joseph, 309
Gosiewski, Mack, 242
Gosorn, Louis, 322
Graf Spee Battery, 52–58, 188
Graves, Edd, 106
Green, Henry, 62, 149
Grow, Robert, 5–6
Guy, E., 234

Hallman, Sherwood, 164–68, 240, 264, 346, 347
death of, 167
Medal of Honor citation, 167
Hare, Neal, 234
Harris, Austin, 173
Hart, Basil Liddell, 123
Harvey, Cecil, 193, 198
Hazlitt, Guy, 151
Hecht, Louis, at Recouvrance, 266–67
Hedlund, Walter, 40–41
Heffner, William, caring for German wounded, 295–96
Henne, Robert, 289
Herrick, George, 116
Hill 103, 42, 50–52, 69–76, 99–102
casualties, 73
counterattack on, 73–76
night attack on, 72–73
Hill 48, 202
Hill 53, 195
Hill 54, 195
Hill 63, 191
Hines, Frank, 80
Hobbs, Carl, 158, 165, 169, 181, 183
Hoopes, John, 161
Howie, Tom, 125
Humphrey, Edward, 227

Ilioc, 156–68
Irving, Frederick Augustus, 329

Jimenez, Pete, 276
Johns, Glover, 41, 138, 143, 145–46, 155, 173, 237–38, 260, 282
cracking pillboxes, 261–62
at Fort Montbarey, 254–55
at Fort Penfeld, 152–53
Johnson, Bobby, 308
Johnson, Vern, 283, 284
Jones, Edward, 9
Jones, John C., 161

Kähler, Otto, 288
Kahn, Herman, 172
Keranroux, 168–69
Kerarbélec, 163
Kerguillo
  chateau, 154
  village of, 146–47
Keriel, 160–61
Keriolet, 42–49, 157–58
  German version of battle at, 49
Kerrognant, 139–55
Kervillou, 203
Keyes, Daniel, 274
Kimbrough, Orman, 48
Kohler, Hans, 288
Kramer, Gerald, 151
Kroh, Hans, 288
Krznarich, Paul "Murphy," 60, 73, 104, 230, 291, 298

La Trinité, 63–69, 108–9, 114–16
Laborde, Lucien, 260–61
Lamour, Bénoni, 28
Le Conquet peninsula, 187–97, 202
  rest areas, 301–5
Le Cosquer, 256–57
Le Trez Hir, 196
leaflets, 218–20
Lee, John C. H., 79, 320, 336
Lee, William, at Recouvrance, 266–67
Levin, Arnold, 307
Limestone Cove, 303
Little, Murray, 320
Louis, Commandant, 60–61
Low, Morris, 151
Lowenthal, Jean, 251–54
  on destruction of Brest, 291
Lucas, Louis, 253

McCormack, Wilbur, at Keriolet, 44–49
McDaniel, Edward, 328

  in Le Conquet, 188–97
  moving 29th to Holland, 322–27
  trying to locate Gerhardt, 319–22
MacDonald, Charles, 325
McGrath, Maurice, 195
  at Recouvrance, 270–73
McKee, Donald, 52
McMullen, Conley, 310
McNulty, Warren, 163
Maddox, Lawrence, 181
  at Recouvrance, 266–67
Mahaney, Edward, 272
Mair, John, 173, 174
Marcelle, 58–62
Markle, Captain, observations of enemy, 128–29
Marshall, George C., 8, 65, 189, 339–40
Marshall, Samuel Lyman Atwood, 123–27, 244, 245, 246, 273
Masny, Otto, 191
Mauldin, Bill, 158
Meeks, Lawrence, 240
Melancon, Claude, 70, 100, 107, 180, 209
  at Hill 103, 51–52
Melnikoff, Steven, 74
Middleton, Troy, 20, 87, 101, 155, 176, 205, 258, 318, 343
  appeal for Ramcke's surrender, 177–78
  Gerhardt relationship, 178–83
  Patton on, 87–88
  plan of attack, 24–25
  Ramcke meeting, 316–17
  on Rudder, 194
  supply issues and, 78–79
  under command of Simpson, 88
Milholland, Randolph, 155
Miller, Anthony, 22, 38, 93, 142, 145–46, 147, 154, 155, 260, 281, 282, 284, 295

at Coatuélen, 163–64
at Fort Montbarey, 222
south of Fort Montbarey, 235–38
Miller, Robert, on Hallman, 165
Millholland, Randolph, 18, 38, 90, 255, 260
  at Fort Montbarey, 172
  at Hill 103, 101–2
mine clearance, 214–15, 224–27
Minor, Robert, 112, 191
Montgomery, Field Marshal, Market-Garden operation, 326–27
Montrose, Jack, 209
Moon, Ray, 61, 62
Moore, James, 320–21
Moore, John, 148, 149
Morley, Leslie, 231
Morris, James, 44–45, 114, 296
  at Keriolet, 42–49
Morrison, Angus, 173
Mosel, Hans von der, 5, 204, 218
  surrender of, 284–89
Moss, Roy, 242
Müller, Rudolf, 49
Mulligan, Daniel, 47–48
Myers, James, 197

Neal, Thomas, 194
Nelson, John, 226
Newton, Alva, 115
Ninth Air Force, 84
  fighter bombers, 108
  Kerrognant air attacks, 140–43
Normandy, Hill 108 battle, 50

O'Grady, Pat, 59
104th Air Observation Squadron, 136
104th Medical Battalion
  care for German wounded, 295
  Company B, at Le Conquet, 307–9
110th Field Artillery Battalion, 208
  ceremony in Le Conquet, 307

115th Infantry Regiment, 89–98, 260
  August 28 through September 5, 1944 positions, 94
  cognac cache incident, 98
  Company E, 280–81
  Company H, captured men incident, 236–37, 297–99
  cracking pillboxes, 261–62
  at Fort Montbarey, 172–78, 184–85, 254–55
  at Kerrognant, 139–55
  Kerrognant positions, *150*
  Schnitzelwerfer Battery, 93–95
  2nd Battalion, at Coatuélen, 163–64
  2nd Battalion, at Fort Montbarey, 222
  2nd Battalion, south of Fort Montbarey, 235–38
  September 6–9, 1944 positions, *141*
  September 12–13, 1944 positions, *175*
  September 15–16, 1944 positions, *243*
  September 15–17, 1944 positions, *259*
  snipers, 92–93
  3rd Battalion, at Hill 103, 101–2
116th Infantry Regiment
  capture of Fort Montbarey, 241–49
  1st Battalion, at Fort Montbarey, 222–35
  1st Battalion, at Keriolet, 42–49, *46*
  at Fort Montbarey, 268
  at La Trinité, 66–69, 108–9, 114–16
  La Trinité and Coastal Forts positions, *117*
  patrolling, 119
  at Recouvrance, 270–74, 273–74
  at St. Pierre Quilbignon, 268–69
  September 15–16, 1944 positions, *243*

September 15–17, 1944 positions, *271*
3rd Battalion, at Le Conquet, 194–97
visitors to, 121–27
121st Engineer Combat Battalion, 211–15
Company B, 242
Company C, 158
at Fort Keranroux, 182
mine clearing operation, 224–27
141st Regiment, Royal Armoured Corps, B Squadron, at Fort Montbarey, 222–35
175th Infantry Regiment, 99–108
1st Battalion, at Sugarloaf Hill, 170–71, 183–84
at Hill 103, 42, 50–52, 69–76, 99–102
Hill 103 positions, *103*
at Ilioc, 104–6, 156–68
at Keranroux, 168–69
at Recouvrance, 265–67, 275–77
2nd Battalion, at Fort Keranroux, 180–83, 264
September 12–13, 1944 positions, *175*
September 15–17, 1944 positions, *271*
at Sugarloaf Hill, 238–40
Operation Market Garden, 326–27
Operation Overlord, 8, 330–31

Padian, Luke, 238
paratroopers, German, 129
Parsch, Roderick, 146–47, 151, 236, 280–81
patrolling, 97, 119, 139–40
Patton, George S., 5, 19, 79
on Brest campaign, 335
on Middleton, 87–88
Pearce, Graham, 115
Pelchuck, John, 274

Penfeld River, 143
Peregory, Frank, 167
Perkins, Harold, 91, 145, 184, 297
Perry, Thomas, 101
pillboxes, 261–62, 263
Pittinger, Lennis, 153
Plaut, Art, 142, 262, 281
Ploger, Robert, 211–15, 242, 263
Plougonvelin, 197
Pogue, Forrest, 123, 127
Poliakoff, Manuel, 310–11
Porter, James, 137
Price, Harold, 253
Puntenney, William, 66–67, 268
and capture of Fort Montbarey, 241–49
at Le Conquet, 194–97
Purnell, William, 17, 42, 99–108, 180, 264
at Fort Montbarey, 168–78
at Hill 103, 69–76
at Ilioc, 156–68
at Recouvrance, 265–67, 275–77
at Sugarloaf Hill, 168–78, 238–40

Raaen, John, 110, 112, 257
RAF Bomber Command, Kerrognant air attacks, 142–43
Ramcke, Hermann-Bernhard, 26–31, 176, 344
awards of, 220
capture and surrender of, 313–17
leaflets of, 218–20
Middleton meeting, 316–17
Middleton's appeal for surrender of, 177–78
portrayal of Fürst, 200
Ramsay, Bertram, Sir, 341
Rayman, Jack, 234
Reagor, Elmer, 196
Recouvrance, 265–67, 270–77
Reed, Henry, 105, 266

Reed, Ollie, 17
Reeves, Andrew, 176, 177–78
Relihan, Dan, 157, 166
Rhodes, Cooper, 182, 320
Rideout, Robert, 62, 97, 144, 146, 148, 149, 152, 163, 236
Ridgway, Matthew, 329
"Riding Academy," 309–11, 317–18
Roc Trévezal, 11
Rockman, Joe, 237
Root, Philip, 96
Rowan, Walter, 51
Rudder, James Earl, 53, 57–58
  at Le Conquet, 188–97
  Middleton on, 194
  2nd Ranger Battalion, 197–204
Ruppenthal, Roland, 80, 336
Ryle, Nigel, 121–23, 223
  capture of Fort Montbarey, 241–49

St. Pierre Quilbignon, 268–69
Sandner, Fritz, 158–59
Sands, William, 19, 206, 261, 329
Schmidt, Herbert, 28
Schnitzelwerfer Battery, 93–95
2nd Infantry Division, journey to Brittany, 6
2nd Ranger Battalion, 197–204
  at Le Conquet, 188–97
Settles, Durwood, 247
709th Tank Battalion, 149–51
  Company A, 194
771st Field Artillery Battalion, 210–11
Sewell, Joseph, 210–11
Shelley, Joseph, on Company B experiences at Le Conquet, 308–9
Sheppe, Arthur, 53–54, 56, 188
Sherman, Abe, 159, 253
Simpson, William H., 88, 183, 235, 318, 320, 344
6th Armored Division, 6

Slater, Harold, 191
Slowik, Stanely, 308
Smith, Louis, 17, 38, 102, 154, 164, 178, 235–38, 255, 257, 281, 282
  August 27th line of attack, 41
  at Fort Montbarey, 172–78, 184–85
  at Kerrognant, 139–55
  at La Trinité, 64–69
  115th Infantry Regiment, 89–98
Smith, Sidney, 242, 248
  mine clearing, 224–27
Smith, Sidney, 246
Snipas, Benjamin, 196
Snyder, Ralph, 39
Spizzirri, Louis, 308
Sproul, Archibald, 67
Steele, Frank, 236, 281
  entering submarine pens, 293–94
Steinberg, Herbert, 303
Stroh, Donald, 6
  Ramcke capture, 313
submarine pens, 130, 292–95
Sugarloaf Hill, 170–71, 183–84, 221, 238–40
Sullivan, Richard, 110–13, 134, 221, 263
  at Fort du Dellec, 120
  at Fort du Mengant, 119–20
  at Fort du Portzic, 120, 255–64
  at Fort La Maison Blanche, 202–3
  at Le Conquet, 202
supplies
  Class III, 78
  Class V, 78
  issues concerning, 76–89
surrender, German, 280–89
  at Recouvrance, 290
  on September 18, 1944, *285*
  terms of, 279–80
Sweeney, Edwin, 98, 151
Sypek, Thomas, 308–9

Index

Talley, Benjamin, 321
Tanks
  Crocodile, 121–23, 222–35
  Sherman, 149–51
Tarko, Pete, 308
Task Force Sugar
  August 25–30, 1944 positions, *55*
  August 30–September 10, 1944 positions, *192*
  Graf Spee Battery and, 52–58
  in Le Conquet, 188–97
Tedder, Arthur, Sir, on Brest campaign, 340
Thoma, Wilhelm Ritter von, 27
Thrasher, Charles, 321, 328
333rd Field Artillery Battalion, 209–10
334 RAF, air attack on Brest, 35–37
Thull, Walter, 151
Thurston, Clinton, 100
Todd, William, 185, 237
Trémeur, 197
trenches, 97
Trethewey, James, 272, 290
  at St. Pierre Quilbignon, 268–69
Trovern, 199
Tweed, Earl, 39, 172
29 Let's Go newsletter, 2, 7, 93, 95, 102, 136, 137, 239, 251–54, 290, 294
29th Division Training Center, 91–92
29th Infantry Division
  advance to Brest, 8–15
  air-ground coordination, 131–38
  August 25–27, 1944 positions, *36*
  band, 304–5
  Brest campaign and, 7
  casualties, 128, 185, 346
  entering battle near Dutch-German border, 344–45
  evolution of, 305–6
  5th Ranger Battalion reinforcements, 109–13
  Hill 103 and La Trinité positions, *68*
  journey to Brittany, 2–3
  leaders, 15–20
  memorials, 346–47
  move to Holland, 322–27
  in Normandy, 1–2
  officially entering Brest campaign, 22
  opening day accomplishments of, 35
  Reconnaissance Troop, advance to Brest, 9–12
  rest areas, *300*, 301–5
  rest period experiences, 301–11, 344
  returned to XIX Corps, 326
  "Riding Academy," 309–11, 317–18
  September 8–12, 1944 positions, *162*
  September 14, 1944 positions, *219*
  supply issues, 76–89
  Task Force Sugar, 188–97
  tribute to, 343–47
  U.S. Army artillery battalions supporting, 204–11
  see also individual battalions; individual regiments
224th Field Artillery Battalion, 239
227th Field Artillery Battalion, Battery C, 193

U.S. Army
  close-order drill, 306–7
  infantry-artillery techniques, 204–11
  responsible for care of German wounded, 295
U.S. Navy, memorial tower, destruction of, 291–92

Van Roosen, Donald, 174, 237, 298
Vandenberg, Hoyt, 84

Walker, Robert, 56, 66, 223, 290
Wallis, Bob, 288
war, American way of, 76–77

Ward, Charles, 193
Ward, Hubert Anthony
  award, 235
  at Fort Montbarey, 230–35
Warfield, Al, 261, 282
Warspite, HMS, 23, 56
Watson, Leroy, 18–19, 195–96, 228, 245, 262
weapons, 84–85
  Nebelwerfer, 95
  rocket launchers, 95–96
  see also ammunition
Weigley, Russell, on Brest campaign, 337
Wetherell, Horace "Hank," 137–38
Whiteford, Roger, 69, 221, 238
  at Hill 103, 50–52
  at Keriel, 160–61
  at Sugarloaf Hill, 170–71, 183–84
  wounding of, 239–40
Whitman, Edward, 136–37
Wickland, Captain, at Le Conquet, 190–91
Wiley, Louis Richard, 159
Williams, Herbert, 158
Williams, Shirley, 242
Wimmer, William, 144
Witte, William, 51, 137

Yeuell, Donovan, on Bretons reaction to 29th's arrival in Brittany, 14–15

Ziegler, Robert, 244